Web Application Development

Using Microsoft®
Visual InterDev® 6.0

Microsoft®

Mastering

PUBLISHED BY
Microsoft Press
A Division of Microsoft Corporation
One Microsoft Way
Redmond, Washington 98052-6399

Library of Congress Cataloging-in-Publication Data
Microsoft Mastering : Web Application Development Using Microsoft
     Visual InterDev 6.0 / Microsoft Corporation.
        p. cm.
     ISBN 0-7356-0902-0
     1. Microsoft Visual InterDev.   2. Web sites--Design.
   I. Microsoft Corporation.
   TK5105.8885.M55M52   1999
   005.7'2--dc21   99-39053
                                                              CIP

Printed and bound in the United States of America.

4 5 6 7 8 9   WCWC   4 3 2 1 0

Distributed in Canada by Penguin Books Canada Limited.

A CIP catalogue record for this book is available from the British Library.

Microsoft Press books are available through booksellers and distributors worldwide. For further information about international editions, contact your local Microsoft Corporation office or contact Microsoft Press International directly at fax (425) 936-7329. Visit our Web site at mspress.microsoft.com.

Acquisitions Editor: Eric Stroo
Project Editor: Wendy Zucker

Acknowledgements

Authors:
Tony Jamieson
Jeff Brown
Steve Merrill

Program Manager: Juan Fernando Rivera

Lead Instructional Designer: Tony Jamieson

Subject Matter Expert: Jeff Brown

Instructional Designer: Steve Merrill

Production Manager: Miracle Davis

Production Coordinator: Susie Bayers (Online Training Solutions, Inc.)

Media Production: Geoff Harrison (Modern Digital)

Build and Testing Manager: Julie Challenger

Book Production Coordinator: Katharine Ford (ArtSource)

Book Design: Mary Rasmussen (Online Training Solutions, Inc.)

Book Layout:
R.J. Cadranell (Online Training Solutions, Inc.)
Jennifer Murphy (S&T Onsite)

Companion CD-ROM Design and Development: Jeff Brown

Companion CD-ROM Production: Eric Wagoner (Write Stuff)

About This Course

This course is designed to teach experienced developers how to create custom solutions and enterprise-level Web sites using Microsoft Visual InterDev 6.

Course Content

The course content is organized into the following nine chapters:

Chapter 1: Planning a Web Site

Chapter 1 teaches you about Web technologies and Microsoft's recommended strategies for Web site development, including architecture, Web life cycle, tools and technologies, and approach to security planning. This chapter also introduces you to the class Web application, the State University Web site.

Chapter 2: Introducing Visual InterDev

Chapter 2 demonstrates the tools in Microsoft Visual InterDev 6 that you can use to build a Web application. This chapter also introduces the Site Diagram tool, new to Visual InterDev 6, for Web site design. You will learn how to create Web projects, use the different views in the tool, and how the tool supports source code control.

Chapter 3: Using Dynamic HTML

Chapter 3 teaches you about advanced features of Dynamic HTML and scriptlets. This chapter extends the introduction to these topics located in the Mastering Web Site Fundamentals course.

Chapter 4: Using Active Server Pages

Chapter 4 shows you how to create a Web application using Active Server Pages (ASP) and server-based COM components. You will learn about the HTTP protocol. You will also learn the properties and methods of the ASP intrinsic objects. You will then use these objects to customize responses. This chapter also covers how to set security access at the file, directory, and server level and how to provide user authentication.

Chapter 5: Accessing Databases

Chapter 5 teaches you how to add database functionality in a Web project. You will learn how to retrieve and update information in a database using Visual InterDev data tools and wizards. You will also learn how to set up security for an SQL database.

Chapter 6: Understanding Data Access Technologies

Chapter 6 demonstrates how to create Web pages that retrieve and update information in a database using ActiveX Data Objects (ADO) and Remote Data Services (RDS). You will learn how OLE-DB technology provides the foundation for ADO and RDS.

Chapter 7: Creating COM Components

Chapter 7 discusses how to create a middle tier (using Microsoft Visual Basic) consisting of COM components to implement business rules. You will learn how to test these components and call them from ASP.

Chapter 8: Using Microsoft Transaction Server

Chapter 8 describes the Microsoft Transaction Server (MTS) and why it is important in an Internet or intranet solution. You will also learn how to create a COM component that participates in transactions as a business object with MTS. This chapter will teach you how to add support for transactional ASP. Furthermore, this chapter will solidify why a three-tier solution with MTS is better than a two-tier solution without MTS. Additionally, you will learn about security considerations with MTS, and the use of roles in MTS to implement security for business components.

Chapter 9: Integrating Other Server-Side Technologies

Chapter 9 discusses using services from Microsoft BackOffice and other server technologies. This chapter will show you how to integrate the following Microsoft Server technologies: Microsoft mail servers and Microsoft Index Server.

Labs

Most chapters in this course include a lab that gives you hands-on experience with the skills you learn in the chapter. A lab consists of one or more exercises that focus on how to use the information contained in the chapter. At any time, you can review the solution code to learn more about the approach taken by the authors. Lab hints, which provide code or other information that will help you complete an exercise, are included in Appendix B. You will see the following icon in the margin, indicating that a lab hint is given.

Lab Hint Icon

To complete the exercises and view the accompanying solution code, you will need to install the lab files that are found on the accompanying CD-ROM as well as the following software and resources:

◆ Microsoft Windows NT Server version 4.0 or later. (Microsoft Windows NT Workstation can be used with the Developer Edition of Microsoft SQL Server.)

◆ Microsoft Windows NT 4.0 Service Pack 3 or later.

◆ Microsoft Internet Explorer version 4.01 or later

Internet Explorer is included with many Microsoft products, including *Mastering Web Application Development Using Visual InterDev 6*.

◆ Microsoft Windows NT 4.0 Option Pack. At a minimum, install the following components:

- FrontPage98 Server Extensions
- Microsoft Internet Information Server version 4.0, including:
  - Internet Service Manager
  - Documentation
  - Microsoft SMTP Service
  - World Wide Web Server
- Microsoft Management Console
- Microsoft Transaction Server version 2.0
- Microsoft Index Server version 2.0
- Windows NT Option Pack common files

- Microsoft Visual InterDev RAD Remote Deployment Support
- Optionally, Microsoft Data Access Components (MDAC) version 1.5 or later. (Installation of Visual InterDev will upgrade these components to version 2.0.)

◆ Microsoft Visual InterDev 6, Professional or Enterprise Edition

◆ Microsoft Visual Basic 6, Professional or Enterprise Edition

◆ Microsoft SQL Server version 6.5 or later with Service Pack 3

◆ State University lab database

This SQL database is located in the <Install Folder>\Labs\Lab05.1\New folder. You will be directed on how to install this database in Lab 5.1.

Note The Microsoft developer tools, the Microsoft Windows NT 4.0 Option Pack, Windows NT Service Pack 3, Internet Explorer 4.01, and the Developer Edition of Microsoft SQL Server are included in Visual Studio Enterprise Edition.

Lab Scenario

The scenario used for all labs is a Web site for a fictional university called State University (StateU). On this Web site, university students can retrieve information about classes, enroll in classes, and receive customized transcripts of their grades.

In Lab 2, "Developing a Web Project," you create a Web project with a home page. In Lab 5.1, "Accessing Data," you build the database used by the Web site. In subsequent labs, you add and modify Web pages to refine the Web site.

The following table lists the tasks that you perform with the State University Web site, and provides a description of the lab in which you accomplish each task.

Task	Lab Description
Browse the prototype of the State University Web site	In Lab 1, "Browsing the State University Web Site," you install and examine a prototype of the final StateU Web site.
Create the StateU Web project	In Lab 2, "Developing a Web Project," you create the Visual InterDev StateU Web project. Additionally, you create and modify several project files.

table continued on next page

Task	Lab Description
Redirect the user based on the browser	In Lab 3.1, "Detecting the Browser Version," you add client-side script to detect Internet Explorer 4.0 (or later), and load the correct version of the main navigation file, Links.htm, accordingly.
Create a dynamic navigational tree-type outline	In Lab 3.2, "Creating a Dynamic Outline," you use Dynamic HTML to create a dynamic outline for navigating the State University Web site.
Create a reusable scriptlet for dynamic navigation	In Lab 3.3, "Creating an Outline Scriptlet," you use the script developed in Lab 3.2 to create a dynamic outline scriptlet.
Track the current user profile as persistent information	In Lab 4, "Using Active Server Pages," you store the information that the user fills out in a profile page as ASP session state, and store it in a client-side cookie.
Set up and connect to the State University database to display current course offerings	In Lab 5.1, "Accessing Data," you create a data connection to the StateU SQL database. You also create a data command that queries for a list of current classes, and place design-time controls to display this information in a Web page.
Create the State University registration form page	In Lab 5.2, "Creating an Event-Driven Form," you modify the Registration page of the StateU Web site to make it an interactive form by using the **FormManager** control.
Display student transcript information and store student feedback	In Lab 6, "Using ActiveX Data Objects," you read transcript information from and update feedback information to the StateU database by using ADO code in ASP pages.
Implement business rules as middle-tier COM objects	In Lab 7, "Creating COM Components," you create the **Enrollment** business object in Microsoft Visual Basic, and implement the Add, Drop, and Transfer business services within it.

table continued on next page

Task	Lab Description
Add transactional support to enrollment processing	In Lab 8, "Using Microsoft Transaction Server," you add transactional support to the enrollment processing by creating MTS packages and components. You also add transactional support to the calling ASP page.
Sending e-mail confirmation	In Lab 9.1, "Sending E-mail," you extend the State University Web application so that when a student registers for a new course, the student receives an e-mail confirmation.
Implement content-indexing and search services	In Lab 9.2: Adding Search Services, you examine the default search service and replace it with a page that accesses Microsoft Index Server through server-side script.

Self-Check Questions

This course includes a number of self-check questions at the end of each chapter. You can use these multiple-choice questions to test your understanding of the information that has been covered in the course. Answers to self-check questions are provided in Appendix A. Each answer includes a reference to the associated chapter topic, so that you can easily review the content.

CD-ROM Contents

The *Mastering Web Application Development Using Visual InterDev 6* CD-ROM that is included with this book contains multimedia, lab files, sample applications, and sample code that you may wish to view or install on your computer's hard drive. The content on the CD-ROM must be viewed by using an HTML browser that supports frames. A copy of Microsoft Internet Explorer has been included with this CD-ROM in case you do not have a browser or do not have one that supports frames, installed on your computer. Please refer to the ReadMe file on the CD-ROM for further instructions on installing Internet Explorer.

To begin browsing the content that is included on the CD-ROM, open the file, default.htm.

Lab Files

The starting point and solution for each lab is included in *Mastering Web Application Development Using Visual InterDev 6* CD-ROM. If you installed the labs from the CD, these files are in the folder *<install Folder>*\Labs\Lab*xx* on your hard disk. If you did not install the labs, you can find them in the folder \Labs\Lab*xx* on the *Mastering Web Application Development Using Visual InterDev 6* CD-ROM. To install the lab files, go to the "Installing Course Files" page on the CD.

Note 2.01 MB of hard disk space is required to install the labs.

Lab Folder Structure

The supplied code for each lab can be found in a folder with the same name as the lab, for example MWD6\Labs\Lab05.1. Most lab folders have the following three subfolders:

Subfolder	Contents
Starter	Contains the set of folders and files representing the progress of StateU Web site at the beginning of the current lab. This subfolder contains the full solution for the previous lab.
New	Contains pre-supplied StateU Web files required for the current lab.
Solution	Contains completed versions of all new and modified files for the current lab. Does not contain the entire Web site.

In addition, the lab's root folder may contain miscellaneous files.

Note If you use lab solution files in your project, you may need to modify them in order for them to work correctly within your existing project. Any modifications needed are discussed in the README.txt file in the Solution subfolder for the lab.

Multimedia

This course provides numerous audio/video demonstrations and animations that illustrate the concepts and techniques that are discussed in this course. The following icon will appear in the margin, indicating that a multimedia title can be found on the accompanying CD-ROM.

Multimedia Icon

In addition, at the beginning of each chapter is a list of the multimedia titles that are found in the chapter.

Note You can toggle the display of the text of a demonstration or animation on and off by choosing **Closed Caption** from the **View** menu.

Sample Code

This course contains numerous code samples.

Sample code has been provided on the accompanying CD-ROM for you to copy and paste into your own projects. The following icon appears in the margin, indicating that this piece of sample code is included on the CD-ROM.

Sample Code Icon

Internet Links

The following icon appears in the margin next to an Internet link, indicating that this link is included on the accompanying CD-ROM.

Internet Link Icon

Sample Applications

The following paragraphs provide short introductions to three sample applications that are included with the *Mastering Web Application Using Microsoft Visual InterDev 6* CD-ROM.

◆ Tutorial.exe

Use this tutorial to gain experience with Visual InterDev in building a simple Web application based on a fictitious insurance company.

◆ Adomts.exe

Adomts.exe is a sample application that demonstrates using ActiveX Data Objects (ADO) to pass a disconnected recordset from a Microsoft Transaction Server (MTS) hosted DLL to a remote client via Distributed Component Object Model (DCOM).

◆ Using Rdsvb.exe with Visual Basic

The Rdsvb.exe sample application demonstrates how use Remote Data Service (RDS) within Visual Basic to build, debug, and test a custom business object.

Conventions Used In This Course

The following table explains some of the typographic conventions used in this course.

Example of convention	Description
Sub, If, Case Else, Print, True, BackColor, Click, Debug, Long	In text, language-specific keywords appear in bold, with the initial letter capitalized.
File menu, **Add Project** dialog box	Most interface elements appear in bold, with the initial letter capitalized.
Setup	Words that you're instructed to type appear in bold.
Event-driven	In text, italic letters can indicate defined terms, usually the first time that they occur. Italic formatting is also used occasionally for emphasis.
Variable	In syntax and text, italic letters can indicate placeholders for information that you supply.

table continued on next page

Example of convention	Description
[expressionlist]	In syntax, items inside square brackets are optional.
{While | Until}	In syntax, braces and a vertical bar indicate a choice between two or more items. You must choose one of the items, unless all of the items are enclosed in square brackets.

`Sub HelloButton_Click()`
`Readout.Text = _`
`"Hello, world!"`
`End Sub`
	This font is used for code.

ENTER	Capital letters are used for the names of keys and key sequences, such as ENTER and CTRL+R.
ALT+F1	A plus sign (+) between key names indicates a combination of keys. For example, ALT+F1 means to hold down the ALT key while pressing the F1 key.
DOWN ARROW	Individual direction keys are referred to by the direction of the arrow on the key top (LEFT, RIGHT, UP, or DOWN). The phrase "arrow keys" is used when describing these keys collectively.
BACKSPACE, HOME	Other navigational keys are referred to by their specific names.
C:\Vb\Samples\Calldlls.vbp	Paths and file names are given in mixed case.

The following guidelines are used in writing code in this course:

◆ Keywords appear with initial letters capitalized:

```
' Sub, If, ChDir, Print, and True are keywords.
Print "Title Page"
```

◆ Line labels are used to mark position in code (instead of line numbers):

```
ErrorHandler:
Power = conFailure
End Function
```

◆ An apostrophe (') introduces comments:

```
' This is a comment; these two lines
' are ignored when the program is running.
```

◆ Control-flow blocks and statements in **Sub, Function,** and **Property** procedures are indented from the enclosing code:

```
Private Sub cmdRemove_Click ()
    Dim Ind As Integer
    ' Get index
    Ind = lstClient.ListIndex
    ' Make sure list item is selected
    If Ind >= 0 Then
        ' Remove it from list box
        lstClient.RemoveItem Ind
        ' Display number
        lblDisplay.Caption = lstClient.ListCount
    Else
        ' If nothing selected, beep
        Beep
    End If
End Sub
```

◆ Intrinsic constant names appear in a mixed-case format, with a two-character prefix indicating the object library that defines the constant. Constants from the Visual Basic and Visual Basic for Applications object libraries are prefaced with "vb"; constants from the ActiveX Data Objects (ADO) Library are prefaced with "ad"; constants from the Excel Object Library are prefaced with "xl". Examples are as follows:

```
vbTileHorizontal
adAddNew
xlDialogBorder
```

For more information about coding conventions, see "Programming Fundamentals" in the MSDN Visual Basic documentation.

Table of Contents

Chapter 1:
Planning a Web Site

Web sites have become servers for client/server applications that are widely distributed over an intranet or the entire Internet (World Wide Web).

In this chapter, you will learn how to plan a Web site that uses a service-based application model. You will also learn about architectural concepts, various development models and resources, and available technologies and their implications. In addition, you will learn about the importance of security in developing Web-based solutions and how to effectively address security issues. Finally, you will be introduced to the members of a Web site development team and the development tools available to them.

Objectives

After completing this chapter, you will be able to:

- ◆ Explain the relationships between Microsoft Web tools and technologies, especially Active Server Pages (ASP), database access technologies, and Microsoft Transaction Server (MTS).

- ◆ Discuss the recommended process for developing a Web-based solution.

- ◆ Explain the function of the Web Life Cycle in creating a Web-based solution.

- ◆ Summarize the responsibilities of Web site development team members.

- ◆ Describe how different Microsoft server and client products address security issues such as authentication, authorization, and privacy.

- ◆ Describe the general architecture of the State University Web application.

Overview of Web-Related Technologies

When planning a Web-based solution, you should base the Web site's design on the architectural implementation as well as the tools and technologies you will be using.

In this section, you will learn about the architecture of a generic client/server Web-based solution and the supporting Microsoft tools and technologies. In addition, you will learn which programming tasks, concepts, tools, and technologies specific to Web site development are covered in this course.

Web Site Architecture

Client/server applications that are deployed from a Web site require an architecture that is robust, secure, and scalable, and that can accommodate rapidly changing technologies.

The following illustration shows the structure of a modern Web-based solution.

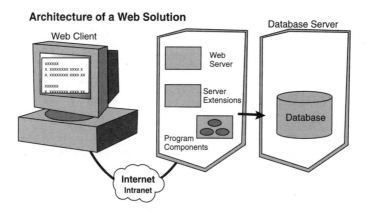

Using the Microsoft Distributed Component Object Model (DCOM), program components can be easily deployed on remote servers.

Evolution of Web Servers

Internet protocols and technologies have advanced rapidly since the World Wide Web's inception in 1993. There have been three distinct generations of Web servers during this time period:

◆ First-generation Web servers delivered mostly static content — HTML pages with embedded graphics, sound files, and other basic features.

♦ Second-generation servers supported dynamic content through server-side extensions, such as CGI and binary server APIs, and database integration.

♦ Third-generation servers support Web-based applications that integrate with other enterprise services, such as transaction support. Optimally, these Web-based applications can be developed in popular programming languages and can make use of the existing object technologies and services for the platform.

Evolution of Web Browsers

Web browsers have also evolved to support new technologies and capabilities. There are three general phases that comprise the evolution of Web browsers:

♦ Static content, which primarily consisted of static HTML and embedded media.

♦ Dynamic content, which included scripting and client-side active components such as Java applets, ActiveX controls, and plug-ins.

♦ Integration, which includes XML, Dynamic HTML, and scriptlets. Better integration also occurs between the host user interface and the operating system.

For information about newer versions of the HTML specification and the new XML meta-language specification, go to the W3C Organization Web site at www.w3.org.

Note In this chapter, the term "Web-based solution" describes a generic solution that employs the Web to solve a particular business need. Subsequent chapters focus on the actual Web site and the applications that run on it.

Microsoft Web Technologies and Products

Microsoft has a full range of products and technologies for enabling solutions that range from publishing simple Web sites to integrating the Web into a comprehensive business solution platform. Almost all Microsoft products and technologies now contain some Internet capability, and can be grouped according to their specific functionality or purpose. Internet functionality spans client and server products, development tools, and content authoring tools.

The following tables list some of the main Microsoft Internet-related products and technologies, and provide links to the appropriate Web site for more information.

Client Products

Product	Description	Web Site
Microsoft Internet Explorer 4.0	Web, ftp, and gopher browser with desktop integration features. Add-ons give NetMeeting, NetShow, VRML, and other capabilities.	www.microsoft.com/ windows/ie/default.htm
Microsoft Outlook Express	E-mail and Internet news client.	www.microsoft.com/ ie/ie40/oe
Microsoft Outlook 98	The client for Microsoft Exchange Server.	www.microsoft.com/ office/outlook/default.htm

Server Products

Product	Description	Web Site
Microsoft Internet Information Server	Web server integrated into Windows NT Server.	www.microsoft.com/ ntserver/web/default.asp
Microsoft BackOffice	Windows NT Server and integrated products: Exchange Server (mail), SQL Server (database), Proxy Server (Internet access and firewall), and others.	www.microsoft.com/ backoffice/
Microsoft Windows NT Option Pack	Update to Windows NT Server components, as well as additional components such as Index Server, Certificate Server, Microsoft Transaction Server, and Microsoft Message Queue Server (MSMQ).	www.microsoft.com/ NTServer/nts/exec/ overview/WhatNew.asp

table continued on next page

Product	Description	Web Site
Microsoft Site Server	Products to help enhance, deploy, and manage Microsoft Web servers. Includes Commerce Server, Content Replication System, Site and Usage Analysis, and more.	www.microsoft.com/ siteserver

Development Tools

Product	Description	Web Site
Microsoft Visual Studio 6.0	Integrated development products including Visual Basic, Visual C++, Visual J++, and Visual InterDev™.	msdn.microsoft.com/ default.asp
Microsoft Developer Network Library (MSDN)	Developer CD-ROM reference, newsletter, and online resources.	msdn.microsoft.com/msdn

Content Authoring Tools

Product	Description	Web Site
Microsoft FrontPage 98	HTML authoring and Web construction product. Includes Image Composer for graphic composition.	www.microsoft.com/ frontpage
Microsoft Office	Integrated package including Microsoft Word, Excel, PowerPoint, and Access. All include HTML export or authoring capabilities.	www.microsoft.com/office

Note This course focuses on the Microsoft development tools and technologies necessary to build and deploy Web solutions. Because *Mastering Web Application Development Using Microsoft Visual InterDev 6* is primarily a course for developers, it focuses on the programming aspects of the various products and technologies, especially Microsoft Visual InterDev.

What This Course Covers

This course is not intended to provide detailed information about the entire range of Internet-related products and technologies. Rather, most chapters cover a set of programming tasks, concepts, or the use of specific technologies related to Web site development.

Chapter 2, "Introducing Visual InterDev" shows how to create a Web project and explores the Visual InterDev environment.

Chapter 3, "Using Dynamic HTML" discusses client-side scripting in Internet Explorer using Visual Basic, Scripting Edition (VBScript) and Dynamic HTML.

Chapter 4, "Using Active Server Pages" examines server-side scripting using VBScript and the Active Server Page object model.

Chapter 5, "Accessing Databases" and Chapter 6, "Understanding Data Access Technologies" explain how to access ActiveX Data Object sources, such as Microsoft SQL Server, through Visual InterDev and direct ADO programming.

Chapter 7, "Creating COM Components" explains how to build COM middle-tier business components in Visual Basic 6.0.

Chapter 8, "Using Microsoft Transaction Server" describes how to install COM business objects into Microsoft Transaction Server to gain transaction support, security, and scalability.

Chapter 9, "Integrating Other Server-Side Technologies" shows how to integrate the following additional Microsoft server technologies into your Web site:

◆ The SMTP mail server component of IIS

◆ Index Server search services

Models for Web Site Development

In this section, you will learn about various models for developing a Web-based solution. Models provide proven methodologies that can save you time and effort.

To plan an effective Web-based solution, you must first understand several Web-related concepts and processes. You should also be familiar with the application models used in client/server architecture. In addition, you should be aware of the roles of the development team members.

The Services Model

When designing your Web site, you can use a service-based application model. The term service-based means that the functionality of an application is specified as collections of services that meet specific user needs.

A service-based application is typically comprised of three categories: user services, business services, and data services. To see the animation "Web Site Architecture," see the accompanying CD-ROM.

> **Note** The term ActiveX server component that was used in the media clip is no longer current, and is now referred to as COM component, or server-based COM component.

User services provide an application with its user interface. The user of a service can be a person or another service. Therefore, the interface for a service can provide a graphical user interface or a programmatic interface.

Business services enforce business rules and handle transactions. These services may impose constraints or apply transformations to change user input or raw database information into usable business information.

Data services provide storage and low-level manipulation of data in a database. Examples of data services include create, read, update, and delete, which are used by business services to modify a database. A business service does not need to know where data is located, how it is implemented, or how it is accessed. These tasks are handled by data services.

The following illustration shows the services model:

Benefits of Using the Services Model

After determining what capabilities you need for your Web site, you can then decide how to implement the site. Using services to define the division of functionality in your Web site provides the following benefits:

◆ Clear and consistent development goals

By dividing your Web site into services, you enable a Web development team to easily envision the direction of development. The functionality of each service, implemented as a component, is clearly defined.

◆ Better manageability

Because services divide the functionality of your Web site into distinct tasks, any changes in the implementation of one service will not introduce changes to another service component.

◆ Isolation of functionality

The functionality of a specific service is encapsulated, so any error in the implementation of a service can be easily traced to the corresponding component.

◆ Division of labor

Identifying services enables you to determine which member of the Web development team is best suited to build and complete the corresponding component.

Application Models

Over the past few decades, the architecture of applications, especially large enterprise, mission-critical ones, have evolved from single-tier to n-tier designs. The driving force for this change has been the following general goals: scalability, separation and encapsulation of functionality, maintainability, multi-user support, and the ability to be distributed.

Understanding Service Tiers

Tiers are a *logical* concept that provide a way to describe how applications can be segmented into services, specifically the three types of services discussed in "The Services Model"—user, business, and data.

The three types of tiers are generally described as user (first), business (second or middle), and data (third) service tiers. The concept of tiers emphasizes the logical segmentation of the services, and is not about implementing the services nor about the number of physical computers involved in deploying the solution.

Single-Tier Applications

A single-tier application is simply a monolithic, stand-alone program that runs on the user's computer. It may communicate with a database, but that database resides on the same computer (or perhaps on a mapped network drive). The key point about a single-tier application is that all three services—user, business, and data—are architecturally combined into a single program.

Typically, each installation of a single-tier application is used only by a single person.

The following illustration shows a single-tier application.

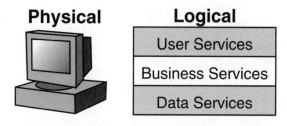

Two-Tier Client/Server Applications

The simplest type of distributed computing is the two-tier client/server application. In this type of application, the database (and perhaps a portion of the data services) is separated from the user interface and business logic. Typically, the database is placed on a dedicated server.

Two-tier client/server applications are the most common type of client/server applications built today. They offer significant benefits over single-tier applications because data processing is centralized and becomes a shared resource among potentially many users.

Note There is not necessarily a perfect mapping between the corresponding physical and logical tiers. For example, while business logic is generally placed on a separate application server, some business services such as validation code may map to a client computer, or be partially implemented in stored SQL procedures on the database server. Likewise, data services may be distributed on either the application server or the database server.

The following illustration shows how services map generally to physical components in a two-tier client/server application.

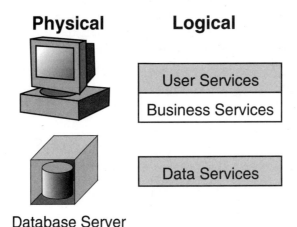

Three-Tier Client/Server Applications

Over time it has become apparent that the two-tier client/server model is simply not flexible or powerful (scalable) enough to handle many larger applications. Maintaining a dialog between each client workstation and the central database server can result in high network traffic and poor performance, for example when many users try to do simultaneous access to a database.

Three-tier client server applications help address these issues by putting another layer between the users and the database—the application server. This type of central application service can manage network traffic and database server loads more efficiently.

Typically, the application layer handles most of the business services, and may be implemented on its own server computer, separate from the database. One of the main advantages of a three-tier architecture is the ability to extract the business logic from the user and data tiers and into the middle tier, where it is easier to maintain.

The following illustration shows how services map generally to physical components in a three-tier client/server application.

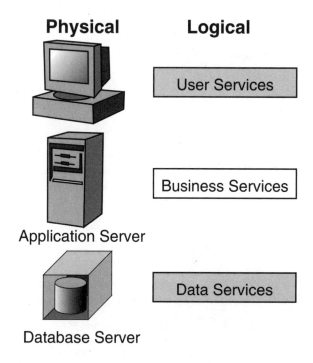

Web-Based Applications

Web-based applications, by their browser/server nature, follow the two- or n-tier model.

The application models discussed so far leave a substantial part of the application on the client workstation. Conversely, applications designed for the World Wide

Web place as little of the application as possible on the client, and keep all the processing centralized on one or more servers.

The following illustration shows how services map generally to physical components in a Web-based application.

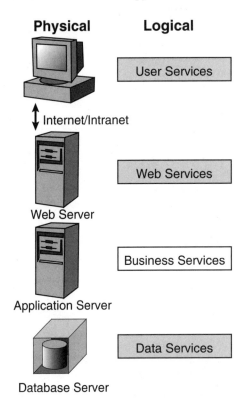

Web Site Development Team

In the early days of the Web, all code writing, authoring, publishing, and administration were often performed by a single person—the Webmaster. However, modern Web development is typically performed by a specialized Web site development team, which consists of a minimum of three people: a Web developer, a programmer, and an HTML author.

To see the animation "Web Site Development Team," see the accompanying CD-ROM.

The following table summarizes each team member's responsibilities and lists Microsoft-specific development tools.

Team member	Responsibilities	Primary tools used
Web developer	Analyzes and designs Web site architecture; creates the code for client-side and server-side scripts necessary for tying together the logic of the Web site.	Visual InterDev Script Wizard
Programmer	Creates and maintains the applications and components used for a Web site: COM and MTS server components, ActiveX controls, Java programs, stored SQL procedures, and others.	Visual Studio language tools: primarily Visual Basic, Visual C++, and Visual J++ MTS
HTML author	Authors Web site content; creates HTML files; gathers appropriate graphics and other media.	FrontPage 98, Office 98, Image Composer, Liquid Motion

Several supporting team members may also play roles in Web site development, such as those described in the following table:

Supporting team member	Responsibilities	Primary tools used
Graphic artist	Designs and creates the graphic and multimedia elements.	Image Composer, Liquid Motion Third-party drawing and graphics editing packages
Test/documentation specialist	Documents the Web site for maintenance; tests the content, navigation, and active content.	Visual InterDev Internet Explorer
Web administrator	Installs the content and maintains server processes.	Windows NT administration tools Internet Service Manager Microsoft Site Server

table continued on following page

Supporting team member	Responsibilities	Primary tools used
Database administrator	Installs and maintains the database management system (DBMS) and data sources used by the Web solution.	Microsoft SQL Server Windows NT administration tools

Microsoft Visual InterDev contains the tools most team members will use for Web site development, enabling team members to collaborate on the development of a Web site.

Web Life Cycle

For most businesses, the return on investment (ROI) is a key factor for determining a Web site's success. To help manage the total cost of ownership and increase the value of both internal and external Web sites, many businesses are implementing Web Life Cycle solutions.

Defining the Web Life Cycle

The Web Life Cycle represents the cycle of events involved in creating, managing, and maintaining a typical business Web site. These events include:

◆ Analyzing customer requirements and available technologies.

◆ Designing the site architecture and content areas.

◆ Developing content including:

- Static HTML, media elements, Active Documents, and links to outside resources.
- Dynamic elements such as client-side and server-side script and server components.
- Integrated database information.

◆ Staging and deploying new and updated content quickly and securely.

◆ Applying and managing site security.

◆ Managing and troubleshooting the site environment.

◆ Measuring and analyzing site usage.

◆ Incorporating site enhancements that drive business value.

The following illustration represents the Web Life Cycle:

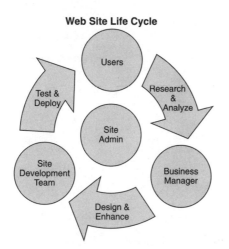

Importance of the Web Life Cycle for Developers

Like other Microsoft Mastering Series titles, *Mastering Web Application Development* is primarily a developer's course that focuses mainly on developing active content and database services. However, this course also addresses topics such as Web site security and maintenance, issues that are becoming increasingly integrated with this level of development.

Developers should understand the Web Life Cycle because Web site development team members are playing increasingly important roles in creating, maintaining, and improving sites.

Microsoft Solutions Framework

To help customers design and develop enterprise applications, Microsoft developed the Microsoft Solutions Framework (MSF). MSF is a collection of resources that includes enterprise architecture planning guidelines and an approach for designing complex, distributed applications. This framework helps organizations realize the benefits of new technology by applying a series of models that addresses different aspects of distributed computing. Each model provides reusable guidelines for a specific area of technology decisions.

MSF includes the following models:

- Team
- Process
- Solutions Design Architecture
- Infrastructure
- Total Cost of Ownership

MSF also introduces an application model that uses a services paradigm to describe an application. The model includes standards and guidelines for designing distributed, multi-tier client/server applications. For more information about a services-based application model, see "The Services Model" on page 7 in this chapter.

For information about MSF, go to the Microsoft Enterprise Services Web site at http://www.microsoft.com/Enterprise/.

Security Issues

Because the Web presents specific security challenges, there are many factors to consider before designing and maintaining a Web site. In this section, you will learn about types of security considerations that apply to any computer system and how the Web magnifies the potential for security problems.

You will also learn about Microsoft solutions that help you plan for an effective security implementation.

Security in Networked Systems

Ever since the first computers were connected with networks, security has been a major concern of network operating system vendors, developers, and administrators. Implementing a security plan can help protect a computer system and its data from loss, corruption, and unauthorized use.

The Internet has made addressing security concerns even more critical. Now all computers connected to the Internet directly (termed *hosts*) or indirectly though a proxy server are potential victims of security attacks.

Categories of Security Threats

Security threats can be divided into four broad categories based on the consequences of the attack. The following table describes each type of security threat (listed in decreasing order of seriousness).

Security threat	Description
System modification attacks	Unauthorized or malicious actions that alter computer files or settings. For example, a program that surreptitiously deletes important operating system files.
Invasion of privacy attacks	Unauthorized access to private computer data or monitoring of the computer user's actions. For example, a program that surreptitiously reads the contents of the user's file-system and reports this information back to a software vendor.
Denial of service attacks	Overuse or hoarding of a computer's resources, which effectively blocks the user from using that aspect of the computer. For example, Java applets can be created that lock up browsers, forcing the user to close the browser.
Misdirection attacks	Any purposely misleading information presented to the user. For example, a program can mimic system dialogs to try to mislead the user into performing unnecessary actions.
Antagonistic attacks	Any purposefully annoying but essentially harmless action. For example, changing the user's desktop color settings in an unauthorized manner.

Often a security penetration will consist of a combination of the categories described in the previous table. A complete security strategy will include deterrence, protection, detection, and response measures. This course will concentrate on protection measures implemented programmatically or through administrative tools.

Web Security

Because of the ubiquitous nature of the Web, security issues can be much more complex than those of a typical file server environment. When planning a Web site, you must consider various aspects of Web technology and develop a security plan based on specific scenarios. For example, consider the following aspects of a Web site and the resulting security implications:

◆ Client issues

Generally, the client's main concern is that the browser or the downloaded dynamic content does not endanger the user.

Client compatibility is an important security concern, especially in a heterogeneous client environment such as the Web. For example, although basic (plain text) authentication is not as secure as the Windows NT Server Challenge-Response (NT/CR) mechanism, the former is supported by all commercial Internet browsers, whereas NT/CR is currently supported only by Internet Explorer.

◆ Server issues

For the server, the most important security concerns are to determine who can access your Web site, what files a user can access, and what type of access rights — read, write, or execute — the user has to each.

◆ Shared issues

Secure communications and user identity are critically important for both client and server. Certain security issues and technologies apply differently to internal (trusted) users versus external (inherently non-trusted). In fact, a whole class of products — Internet proxies and firewalls — was created to bridge the different concerns of these two types of access.

The following illustration shows the architecture of a Web site and highlights important security issues.

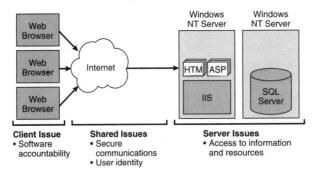

Microsoft Security Solutions

When designing a Web-based solution using Microsoft tools, you can implement security using existing security features of both server and client products. Microsoft client and server security technologies comprise an extensible security model upon which you can build your solution.

To see the expert point-of-view "Internet Security," see the accompanying CD-ROM.

> **Note** The term Microsoft Information Security Framework (MISF) that was used in the media clip is no longer current.

Microsoft Client Solutions

Microsoft Internet Explorer relies on a number of security technologies to protect the client from malicious attacks.

- The **Internet Options** dialog box in Internet Explorer allows the user to set the security level for Java applets, ActiveX controls, cookies, scripts, Certificate Authorities (CAs), and other entities. With the Internet Explorer Administrator's Kit (IEAK), these options can be set during installation.

  Using Internet Security Zones, security restrictions can be specified for the following Internet zones: Local, Trusted, Internet, Restricted.

- Microsoft Java Virtual Machine (JVM) protects the user against non-trusted applets by running them in a secure process space called a sandbox.

- The ActiveX Scripting architecture of Internet Explorer allows only safe embedded scripts to be executed from within a Web page.

- Authenticode allows trusted code to be downloaded, optionally installed, and run on the client's computer. Authenticode uses digital signatures and certificate authorities to identify the author and assure the authenticity of a component.

Microsoft Server Solutions

Every Microsoft server product has built-in access security that is integrated with Windows NT Server's Access Control Security. This model satisfies the following two requirements:

♦ Verification of user identity (authentication)

All users must have a Windows NT account to log on to the network. An account consists of a unique account name and password. This is called the NT Challenge/Response logon protocol. The User Manager tool is used to set users, groups, and rights.

♦ Controlled access to resources (authorization)

Each user or group of users is given access rights to the computer's resources. The Windows NT Explorer is used to set access rights to files and folders.

Shared Solutions

Both the client and server can utilize Windows NT Server's Access Control Security to provide secure communications and user authentication.

In addition, Microsoft Internet products support the Windows NT security model and extend it in the following ways:

♦ Internet Information Server (IIS) also allows anonymous and basic text log on of Internet users. The Internet Service Manager tool can be used to set security options for this Web server.

♦ Microsoft Certificate Server enables the creation of certificates that can be used for identifying Internet users, establishing private communications, and signing code components.

♦ IIS and Internet Explorer support the Secure Sockets (SSL) 3.0, Private Communications Technology (PCT) 1.0, and Secure Electronic Transaction (SET) protocols for private point-to-point communication.

To see the animation "Using Digital Certificates to Authenticate a User," see the accompanying CD-ROM.

For more information about authentication and authorization, see "Security Issues in ASP" on page 213 in Chapter 4, "Using Active Server Pages."

For more information about Microsoft security solutions, initiatives, and news, go to the Microsoft Security Advisor Web site at http://www.microsoft.com/security/default.asp.

Overview of the State University Web Application

In this section, you will learn about the general purpose and requirements of the State University Web site, and about security outcomes for the site.

This section presents an overview of the site architecture and the services used in the application. The section also identifies development team member roles and the tools used by each member.

Description of the State University Web Site

In the labs for this course, you will create a Web site for the fictitious State University. This topic describes the purpose, capabilities, and user needs for the State University Web site.

The State University Web site application provides an electronic means for students to view different types of information and perform various university-related activities.

Information

In the State University Web site, students can view the following types of information:

- State University information—includes the home page and related pages with general information about the university and guidance to subtopics.

- Course information—a course catalog with descriptions for each class and the number of seats available. Descriptions include a class title and identification number, an associated major, and a general subject classification. Students need to be able to look at this information in different ways; for example, they need to be able to find out which classes are offered for each major.

- Student information—students view their individual transcripts, showing classes completed and grades. Security considerations require a valid logon password to prevent unauthorized access to private information.

Additionally, the Web site tracks site usage through a hit counter.

Student Activities

Students can register for classes if seats are available. In addition, they can add, drop, and transfer classes. These capabilities are implemented as business rules and are transaction-based.

Students can submit feedback electronically, and will receive immediate acknowledgement. Feedback is stored in a database for future use.

All visitors to the State University Web site must first log on. A student profile form is provided to gather information from students, such as name, valid student ID number, and preferred major. The information is validated and then submitted to a database. The profile form is reentrant and directs new students to the home page.

State University Site Map

A site map is a document that shows graphically how a user will navigate within a Web site and how files are connected.

The following illustration shows the State University site map.

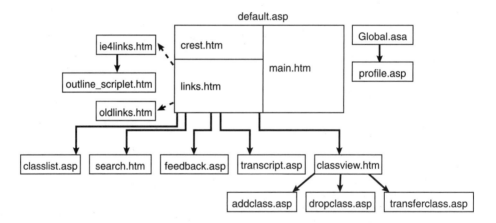

Services in the State University Web Site

This topic describes some of the user, business, and data services of the State University Web site and explains how they are implemented.

State University Services

The user services for the State University Web site enable a student to enroll in a class, view grades, and enter feedback.

The business services for the State University Web site implement business logic when adding and deleting students. An example of this business logic would be a business service that verifies class availability before adding a new student.

The data services for the State University Web site perform the actual update of the State University database, as determined by the business services.

The following illustration shows all the services used for the State University Web site.

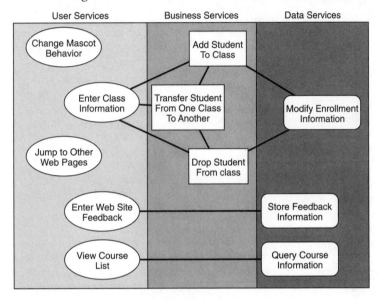

State University Application Design

The user services for the Web site are implemented by the user's Web browser with Hypertext Markup Language (HTML) files and Active Server Page (ASP) files. These files commonly contain inline scripts that execute on the client or server, respectively.

The business services for the State University Web site are provided by server-based COM components installed on the Web server.

The data services are provided by Microsoft SQL Server. The database is installed on the State University Web server, but could have easily been installed on a separate server computer.

Listing of Files by Service

The following table lists the files used to implement some of the services for the State University Web site:

Files	User service
classview.htm	Enters class information
classlist.asp	Displays a current course list
links.htm (ie4links.htm, oldlinks.htm)	Jumps to other Web pages

Files	Business service
addclass.asp, enroll.dll (Add component)	Adds a student to a class
dropclass.asp, enroll.dll (Drop component)	Drops a student from a class
transferclass.asp, enroll.dll (Transfer component)	Transfers a student from one class to another

Files	Data service
SQL Server 6.5 Enrollment table	Modifies enrollment information
SQL Server 6.5 Feedback table	Stores feedback information

The following illustration shows the physical implementation for some of the State University Web site services.

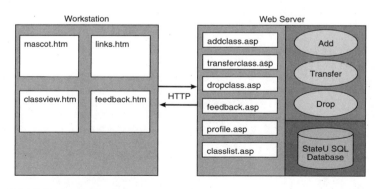

Responsibilities of the Development Team

A Web team is commonly composed of a number of specialists, including Web developers, programmers, and HTML authors, among others.

The following table lists the files for which each development team member is primarily responsible, and includes a short functional description of each file.

Web Developer

As the Web developer of the State University Web site, you will use Visual InterDev 6 to create the following files.

File	Description
links.htm	A page containing client-side script that detects the type of browser being used and loads the appropriate contents page (oldlinks.htm or ie4links.htm).
outline_scriptlet.htm	A page containing the contents scriptlet.
feedback.asp	Uses server-side script to store feedback submitted by a student into the Feedback table in the StateU database.
profile.asp	Uses client-side script to validate user input. Uses server-side script to save the user input so other Web pages can access it.
addclass.asp	Uses server-side script to call an Add component that adds a student to a class.
dropclass.asp	Uses server-side script to call a Drop component that drops a student from a class.
transferclass.asp	Uses server-side script to call a Transfer component that transfers a student from one class to another.
transcript.asp	Uses server-side script to retrieve a student's transcript.
classlist.asp	Uses server-side script to display a table of current classes.
classview.htm	Uses controls to display class information in a list box.

Web Programmer

As the Web programmer of the State University Web site, you will use Microsoft Visual Basic 6 to create COM components and ActiveX controls. You will also use MTS to provide transaction and resource management for server-based COM components. You will create the following files:

File	Description
stateu.dll	Performs the enrollment functions **Add, Drop**, and **Transfer**. You will create stateu.dll first, and then later split it into add.dll, drop.dll, and transfer.dll.
add.dll	Adds a student to a class.
drop.dll	Drops a student from a class.
transfer.dll	Transfers a student from one class to another class.

HTML Author

As the HTML author of the State University Web site, you will use Visual InterDev to create the following HTML files:

File	Description
default.htm	The State University home page. This page contains three frames that reference home.htm, crest.htm, and links.htm.
main.htm	The main informational page for State University.
ie4links.htm, oldlinks.htm	Navigation pages containing hyperlinks to most of the pages in the State University Web site.
crest.htm	A page that contains the State University logo.
feedback.asp	A page that gathers feedback from a student and submits it.

As the student of this course, you will be playing the role of the Web developer, programmer, and HTML author.

Lab 1: Browsing the State University Web Site

In this lab, you will examine a prototype of the State University (StateU) Web site and familiarize yourself with the site's overall design, architecture, navigational structure, user services, and additional capabilities.

To see the demonstration "Lab 1 Solution," see the accompanying CD-ROM.

The following diagram shows the site structure of this StateU Web site prototype.

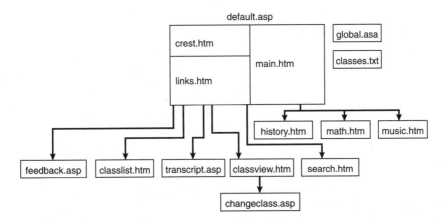

Note This prototype uses a more basic implementation than that of the site version you will be developing in subsequent labs. Some of the functionalities, such as database lookup, have been emulated through scripting. Some of the more advanced features have been omitted. Therefore, the previous site diagram only approximates the final production version of the StateU Web site.

Estimated time to complete this lab: **20 minutes**

To complete the exercises in this lab, you must have the following required software: Microsoft Windows NT Server, version 4.0 (or later); Microsoft Internet Information Server (IIS), version 4.0 (or later); and Microsoft Internet Explorer, version 4.01 (or later). For detailed information about the labs and the setup for the labs, see "Labs" in "About This Course."

Objectives

After completing this lab, you will be able to:

◆ Install a simple Web site onto a Web server, such as IIS.

◆ Test the installation to verify that the Web server is functioning properly.

◆ Describe the general architecture and navigational structure of the StateU Web site.

◆ List the services that the StateU Web site provides to a student at State University.

Prerequisites

Before working on this lab, you should be familiar with the following:

◆ Advanced user experience with and beginner-level administration of Windows NT Server.

◆ Browsing Internet sites with Microsoft Internet Explorer.

◆ The basics of Web site construction as explained in the course *Mastering Web Site Fundamentals*.

Exercises

The following exercises provide practice working with the concepts and techniques covered in this chapter:

◆ Exercise 1: Installing the Prototype

In this exercise, you will install the prototype State University Web site onto your Web server. To do this you will copy a folder containing the Web site to your computer's Web publishing folder. You will then test that the site was installed correctly.

◆ Exercise 2: Browsing the State University Web Site

In this exercise, you will use Internet Explorer to browse and examine various pages in the StateU Web site. You will investigate the Web site's architectural and navigational structure, and familiarize yourself with the site's look and feel.

◆ Exercise 3: Registering for Classes

In this exercise, you will use the class registration services of the StateU Web site to add and drop classes. You will then view the results of your choices by retrieving your transcript.

Exercise 1: Installing the Prototype

In this exercise, you will install the prototype State University Web site onto your Web server. To do this you will copy a folder containing the Web site to your computer's Web publishing folder. You will then test that the site was installed correctly by browsing to the home page.

▶ **Verify that the Web publishing service is running**

This procedure and subsequent labs assume that Microsoft Internet Information Service (IIS) 4.0 and its Web publishing service are running.

1. From the desktop's **Start** menu, click **Settings,** and then click **Control Panel.**

2. In the Control Panel, start the Services applet.

3. In the **Service** list box, locate and select the World Wide Web Publishing Service entry.

4. Verify that its status is Started and its start-up mode is Automatic. If this service is stopped, click the **Start** button. If the start-up mode is not Automatic, click the **Startup** button and change it to this value.

Note If you do not see the World Wide Web Publishing Service listed in the Service applet, then IIS is probably not installed. IIS 4.0 can be installed from the NT Option Pack CD-ROM.

Tip This course does not use the FTP Publishing Service. If you are not depending on this service in other applications, you can shut it down and set its startup mode to Disabled.

▶ **Copy the prototype StateU Web site files to the Web publishing directory**

Because the prototype contains only HTML files and Active Server Page (ASP) files, and does not contain COM components or use databases, installing it is a relatively straightforward operation. Simply copy the folder containing the prototype site to your computer's Web publishing folder.

1. Start a copy of Windows Explorer or Internet Explorer. If you have done a full installation of *Mastering Web Application Development Using Visual InterDev 6,* navigate to the *<root-folder>*\MWD6\Labs\Lab01 folder.

If you have not fully installed *Mastering Web Application Development*, then this folder can be located on the CD-ROM in the \Labs\Lab01 folder.

2. Select the Prototype subfolder and press the CTRL+C key combination to copy it.

3. Navigate to the machine's Web publishing folder. This is the default virtual root folder from which IIS services HTTP requests. By default, this is C:\InetPub\wwwroot.

4. Press the CTRL+V key combination to copy the Prototype directory to the Web publishing directory.

▶ **Mark the Protoype folder as a Web application**

Sub-folders (subdirectories) under the WWWRoot folder are, by default, treated as simple Web sites by Internet Information Server (IIS). If Active Server pages are to be supported, the site folder must be specially marked. (Note that Visual InterDev automatically does this for you when creating a new site or publishing an existing one through Visual InterDev.)

1. Open the Internet Service Manger. From the Start button of Windows, choose Programs, Windows NT 4.0 Option Pack, Microsoft Internet Information Server, then the Internet Service Manager command (shortcut).

2. In the left-hand pane, expand the node under Internet Information Server, then under your computer, then Default Web Site, then locate the Prototype node. It should have a folder icon associated with it indicating that it is a simple Web site.

   If you do not see the Prototype folder listed, try right clicking on the Default Web Sites node and selecting the Refresh command from the context menu.

3. Right-click the Prototype node and choose the Properties command. The Prototype Properties dialog box should be displayed.

4. In the Directories tab, in the **Application Setting** group box, click the **Create** button.

   In the same group box, verify the **Permissions** are set to **Script,** which is the default.

5. Click OK to close the dialog box. You can also close the Internet Service Manager if you wish.

▶ **Test that the Web site has been properly installed (published)**

1. Open Internet Explorer.

2. In the Address text box, type the following URL and press **Enter**:

    `<computer-name>/prototype`

    For *<computer-name>*, enter the name of your computer. The home page of the prototype StateU Web site should be displayed.

    To find your computer's name, do the following:

    a. From the Control Panel, open the Network applet.

    b. Click the **Identification** tab.

    c. Copy the string in the Computer Name read-only text box

Note that the Microsoft Web server's default publishing directory name is the same as the computer name.

Exercise 2: Browsing the State University Web Site

In this exercise, you will use Internet Explorer to browse and examine various pages in the StateU Web site. You will investigate the Web site's architectural and navigational structure, and familiarize yourself with the site's look and feel.

▶ **Examine the home page**

1. If you do not have the prototype StateU home page open from the last exercise, type the URL *<computer-name>*/**protoype** to display it in Internet Explorer.

2. On the **View** menu, click **Source**.

    Notepad should display the contents of the page Default.htm. Notice that it established a frameset containing the following three pages:

    • Crest.htm — the upper left frame simply contains the StateU graphic.

    • Links.htm — the lower left frame contains a navigational list similar to a table of contents.

    • Main.htm — the right frame contains the home page's main contents. This frame will be changed when you navigate the StateU Web site.

3. Close Notepad.

▶ **Test the hyperlinks on the home page**

1. In the right frame, click the graphics of the three majors. Each is linked to the home page for that department. These department sites are under construction.

2. In the left frame, click the two links in the University Information section of the navigational list.

   - The **General Information** hyperlink navigates back to the home page.

   - The **Provide Feedback** hyperlink displays a user feedback form. Enter some information and submit the form. This page uses client-side script to validate that all the options have been chosen before form submission.

3. In the navigational list, click the single link in the Course Information section.

   - The Course Catalog page displays the list of currently available classes, with additional information on each class, such as major, number of open seats, class start date, and so on.

4. In the navigational list, click the two links in the Student Information section.

   - **Get Transcript** retrieves a student transcript for the current user (assumed to be student number 1).

   - **Register For Courses** allows the user to add or drop courses.

   In the final version of the StateU Web site, these pages will connect to an SQL database to get course and student information. This prototype has limited functionality, which you will be testing in the next exercise.

5. In the navigational list, click the two links in the Site Services section.

   - **Search the Site** will let users search the StateU Web site, although in this prototype it is not operational.

   - **E-mail the Webmaster** will launch a client-side e-mail message to the fictitious address webmaster@stateu.edu. This capability assumes that users have e-mail clients installed on their machines.

Exercise 3: Registering for Classes

In this exercise, you will use the class registration services of the StateU Web site to add and drop classes. You will then view the results of your choices by retrieving your transcript.

▶ **Register for several classes**

1. Click the **Register for Courses** link to go to the Class Registration page.

2. Click a class from the list box. Note that class details are automatically entered for you.

3. Click the **Add** button to register for this class. An enrollment confirmation page is returned to let you know that you were successful.

4. Try adding the same class again. The returned confirmation page will indicate that your redundant request has been rejected.

5. Repeat this for several more, different classes.

6. In the left-hand frame, click the **Get Transcripts** link to view your student transcript. This page is simplified and only shows the course numbers of the classes you are registered for.

▶ **Drop a class**

1. Navigate back to the Class Registration page.

2. Pick a class that you added in the last procedure and then click the **Drop** button.

3. Navigate again to the transcript page and note that the dropped course has been deleted from your transcript.

4. Repeat this process, but try dropping a class you have not registered for. You will get a returned page indicating this mistake.

Note The class register information for this prototype is stored in temporary Web session variables. If you shut down Internet Explorer and return to the Transcript page, all the information on previously registered courses will be lost.

Self-Check Questions

To see the answers to the Self-Check Questions, see Appendix A.

1. Which of the following is an example of a business service?

A. An ActiveX control that displays a calendar on the screen.

B. A stored procedure in an SQL Server.

C. A database table that stores payroll information.

D. A COM component that can place an order in a database.

2. Which service provides the application with its graphical interface?

A. User services

B. Business services

C. Data services

3. Which member of a Web development team is responsible for creating code that invokes COM components?

A. Web developer

B. Programmer

C. HTML author

D. Graphic artist

4. Which member of a Web development team is responsible for defining the architecture of a Web site?

A. Web developer

B. Programmer

C. HTML author

D. Graphic artist

5. Which programming tool enables the programmer to create COM components and ActiveX controls?

A. Visual InterDev

B. Visual Basic

C. Microsoft Transaction Server

D. Microsoft SQL Server

6. Which tool provides transaction and resource management for COM components?

A. Visual InterDev

B. Visual Basic

C. Microsoft Transaction Server

D. Microsoft SQL Server

Student Notes:

Chapter 2:
Introducing Visual InterDev

In this chapter, you will learn how to use Microsoft Visual InterDev to build and manage Web sites. You will also learn how to author static HTML pages.

Objectives

After completing this chapter, you will be able to:

◆ Create a Web site using Microsoft Visual InterDev.

◆ Author a static HTML page.

◆ Create a site diagram.

◆ Use Visual InterDev version-control tools.

Assumed Skills

Before beginning this chapter, you should be able to:

◆ Hand-code a simple Web page.

Note This chapter assumes no prior experience with Visual InterDev.

What is Visual InterDev?

Microsoft Visual InterDev 6 is for developers who are designing, building, testing, debugging, deploying, and managing component-based, data-intensive Web applications.

Visual InterDev is used to create:

◆ Data-driven Web applications using data sources supported by ODBC or OLE DB.

◆ Broad-reaching Web pages using HTML and script in Web applications that take advantage of the latest advances in browser technology.

◆ Integrated solutions that can include applets or COM components created in Microsoft Visual Basic, Microsoft Visual C++, Microsoft Visual J++, and Microsoft Visual FoxPro.

Visual InterDev provides a robust development environment with a scripting object model, design-time controls, and an extensible toolbox for rapid design, testing, and debugging.

Creating a Simple Web Project

This section introduces you to the first step in Web application development—creating a Web project.

Types of Projects

The first step in developing a Web application is to create a new Web project.

Starting a Web Project

The Web Project Wizard walks you through five steps that create a new project for you and set default properties for the project.

The following illustration shows the opening screen for the Web Project Wizard.

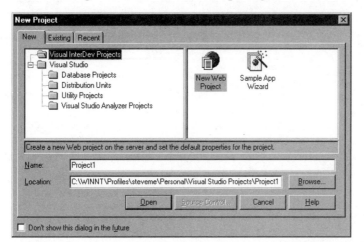

The Web Project Wizard helps you complete the tasks listed in the following table.

Task	Description
Start a new project	Creates the project and sets its default values.
Open an existing project	Takes you directly to the list of Visual Studio projects that exist on the developer's workstation.
Open one of the most recently used existing projects.	Takes you directly to the Visual InterDev solutions that exist on the developer's workstation.

Starting Other Types of Projects

The wizard can also be used to start other types of related Visual Studio projects, as described in the following table.

Task	Description
Start a database project	Lets you create a new database project and allows direct manipulation of the database objects and data. For more information on creating a database project from within Visual InterDev, see "Accessing Data" on page 232 in Chapter 5, "Accessing Databases."

table continued on next page

Task	Description
Create a distribution unit	Automates the process of creating any one of three ways of distributing software. Here you can create cabinet files, self-extracting setup files, and ZIP files.
Create a utility project	Creates a project to be used as a container for files that you want to build, such as a master project for several sub-projects, or a list of custom build rules.
Create a Visual Studio Analyzer project	Creates a project that contains performance data from all the components and systems. For more information on the Visual Studio Analyzer, see "Analyzing Performance" and "Understanding Visual Studio Analyzer View" in Visual InterDev Help.

Web Server and Site Structure

When a team builds a Web site, there are three different locations where files can be hosted. These locations are shown in the following illustration.

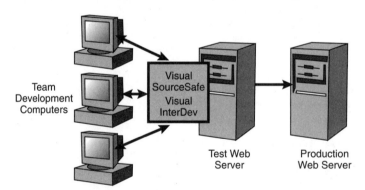

Project site location	Description
Test Web server	When a Web development process begins, a team member creates a project in Visual InterDev on a test Web server. This is where the master files for a site are hosted until the site is fully developed and tested.

table continued on next page

Project site location	Description
Team development computers	Team members edit files on their local development computers and save them to the Web site test server. When a master file is available on the test server (no one has a working copy of the master), any team member can retrieve and edit a copy of the master file.
Production Web server	Once the files for the Web site are finished, the Web team publishes the files to a secure Web server. This ensures that files are not arbitrarily changed. The team can also provide the appropriate security on the production Web server so that any malicious tampering cannot occur.

Web Application File Types

Web applications are composed of a number of different files. The following table lists those that are commonly used. Each file type is described in further detail later in this chapter.

File type	Description
Global.asa	Each project may contain a single Global.asa file. This Active Server Application file contains global data and scripts for the Web application — global variables, database connections, and initialization and cleanup code.
.asp	Active Server Page files, which contain static text as well as data-bound controls that display data from a database.
.css	Cascading style sheet files, which contain information on customizing page element appearance.
.gif, .jpg, .jpeg, .bmp	Graphics files of various types that can be displayed in a Web application.
.htm or .html	HTML pages, which can contain forms and controls, static text, images, and links to other pages.
.sln	Solution files, which contain references to project, page, and other files that compose a Web application.
.vip	Project definition files, which contain Visual InterDev-specific information about the project.

Project Directory Structure

The Web Project Wizard creates the following folders for a new Web project.

Folder name	Description
<root>	Named after the project; contains the default home page and the top-level pages for the site.
_Layouts	Contains the template HTML files for your selected layout, if you chose to apply a layout to the project.
_private	Contains miscellaneous internal project files.
_ScriptLibrary	Contains the source for script objects used by Visual InterDev controls.
_Themes	Contains the bitmaps and the cascading style sheets for a selected theme, if you chose to apply a layout to the project.
Images	Created empty, this folder contains bitmaps added to the site's HTML pages.

By default, the Web Project Wizard creates two pages in the root directory: Search.htm (the Web site search page) and Global.asa (the ASP application-wide script file).

Editing Modes

The files for your Web application reside in two places: in the project directory on your computer and in the virtual directory on the master Web server. When you are working in your project, you are working on the local files. The way in which your changes are made to the version on the master Web server depends on one of two project modes—local mode or master mode.

In local mode, changes made to the files are not immediately saved to the master Web server. The new versions are sent to the master Web server when you explicitly request that the master Web server be updated. In master mode, changes are saved to the local version and the master version at the same time.

Note When you import an existing page into your project, Visual InterDev adds the page to the master Web server and locks it. In order to edit the page, you must first request a working copy.

Web Project Wizard

To create a new project, you typically use the **New Project** dialog box to specify a new project and then launch the Web Project Wizard to generate a set of starter Web directories and pages.

The **Web Project** Wizard features four steps, each having its own dialog box. The following list outlines the choices that you have in each of these dialog boxes.

- Create a new project
  - Enter a project name.
  - Enter a project location.
- Specify a server and development mode
  - Enter the name of the server that you will be using.
  - Select if you want to connect to that server using Secure Socket Layer.
  - Select the mode that you want to work in. Master mode updates the master Web application automatically. Local mode lets you control when updates are made.
- Specify the name for your Web application
  - Create a new application with the same name as that of the project.
  - Connect to an existing Web application on the server to which you connected in the first step.
  - Enable or disable site searching.
- Apply navigation control layout to your project
  - Specify the location for navigation bars on the pages you will create. For more information on layouts and themes, see the practice exercise later in this chapter.
- Apply a visual look and feel to your project
  - Specify default backgrounds, headings, and list styles to the pages that will be created in this project.

Practice: Creating a Simple Web Project

The following practice exercise shows you how to create a simple Web project. Later practices will show you how to add a site diagram, pages, page navigation, themes, and layouts.

Note To complete the practices in this course, you must have the following required software: Microsoft Windows NT Server, version 4.0 or later; Microsoft Internet Information Server (IIS), version 4.0 or later; and Microsoft Internet Explorer, version 4.01 or later.

▶ **Create a simple Web project**

1. From the **Start** button, start Visual InterDev.

2. From the **File** menu, click **New Project**.

3. On the **New** tab, click the **New Web Project** icon.

4. Note the name and the physical location for the new project that you are creating and click **Open**.

5. In the drop-down list box, set the name of the server to the name of the computer you are using. If you do not know the computer name, start **Control Panel**, click the Network icon, and inspect the Computer Name field on the **Identification** tab.

6. Leave the working mode check box set to **Master mode,** and click **Next**.

7. Leave the default value for the name of the Web project that you are creating, but notice that you can connect to an existing Web application on this server. Click **Next**.

8. Select several of the layouts that are offered, inspect them for their content, and note the differences between them. Notice that you can browse for other layouts on other computers. Click **Next**.

9. Select several of the themes that are offered, inspect them for their content, note and the differences between them. Click **Finish**.

Note If you know the name of other servers that you want to connect to, you can add their names to the list of servers. Visual InterDev uses FrontPage extensions to communicate with servers using Hypertext Transfer Protocol (HTTP).

Creating a Web Site

Once you've created a new project, you can begin designing the site. You do this by creating a site diagram, and then adding and organizing the pages that will make up the site. You can also create or add cascading style sheets to customize the look and feel of individual pages.

Adding a Site Diagram

The easiest way to design a Web site is to create a site diagram. A site diagram is a graphical tool that lets you design the hierarchical relationships among pages in a site.

How a Site Diagram Works

In a site diagram, you create hierarchical relationships among pages by grouping them into trees. A tree contains one or more parent pages and one or more child pages. Each Web application can have multiple site diagrams, and each site diagram can have multiple trees.

To create parent, child, and sibling relationships, you drop pages beside or beneath one another in a site diagram. Use the dashed link lines to aid you in creating relationships.

Site diagrams use layouts to create and maintain the links between pages.

▶ **To add a site diagram to a project**

1. From the **Project** menu, click **Add Web Item**.

2. Click **Site Diagram**.

3. Assign a name to the diagram in the **Name** text box and click **Open**.

When you create a site diagram, a home page with a file name of default.htm for the site is automatically created for you and placed at the top of the diagram.

The following illustration shows you what a new site diagram looks like.

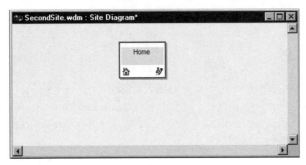

To create the rest of the site, you add either HTML or ASP pages to the site diagram. The following table explains when to use each type of page.

Scenario	Page type
All of the content of the Web page is static	HTML pages
Some or all of the content of the Web page is dynamic	ASP pages

▶ **To add a Web page to a site**

1. Place the cursor anywhere on the site diagram and right-click.

2. From the pop-up menu, select the type of page that you want to add: a new HTML page, a new ASP page, an existing page, or another home page.

3. Use the drag-and-drop feature to create the hierarchical relationship among the pages in the site.

4. Apply the appropriate layouts for the pages at the various levels of the site.

Note You can convert an ASP page to an HTML page by changing the extension, but you cannot convert an HTML page to an ASP page.

Practice: Creating a Site Diagram

In the following practice, you learn how to add a site diagram, and add pages, page navigation, themes, and layouts to the project that you started in an earlier practice.

In this practice exercise you will add two HTML pages and three ASP pages. One HTML page will contain the company's mission statement. The other will contain links to three ASP pages that will list information about authors and titles in a database.

▶ **Add a site diagram**

1. Open the sample project.

2. Right-click the project file in the Project Explorer window.

3. Click **Add** from the pop-up menu and click **Site Diagram**.

4. Give the diagram a usable name and click **Open**. Note that a .wdm file has been added to your project.

▶ **Add HTML and ASP pages to your site diagram**

1. Right-click anywhere on the site diagram.

2. On the pop-up menu, select **New HTML Page** and name the page **Mission**.

3. Right-click the site diagram again, select **New HTML Page** and name the page **Products**.

4. Right-click the site diagram again, select **New ASP Page** and name the page **Authors**.

5. Create two more ASP pages using the same technique and name one page **Titles** and the other page **Publishers**.

▶ **Create the hierarchical relationships among the pages**

1. Drag the mission statement page so that it becomes a child page of the home page.

2. Drag the **Authors, Titles,** and **Publishers** pages so that they become child pages of the **Products** page.

3. Drag the products tree so that it becomes a child page of **Home**. This will also make it a sibling of the **Mission** page.

4. Drag search.htm from the Project Explorer window and make it a child page of the home page.

5. From the **File** menu, click **Save All** to save the site diagram and create all of the page files in **Project Explorer**.

▶ **Add site navigation**

1. Right click **Products** and click **Open** from the popup menu.

2. Click the **Design Time Controls** tab on the **Toolbox**.

3. Drag a **PageNavbar** control and drop it on the **Products** page.

4. Right click the **PageNavbar** control and select **Properties**.

5. Make sure that the **PageNavbar** control has **Children Pages** selected in the **Type** option group.

▶ **Save and view the site navigation on the Products page**

1. On the **File** menu, click **Save Products.htm**.

2. On the **View** menu, click **View in Browser**.

3. You should see the products page with three links at the top — one to **Authors**, one to **Titles**, and one to **Publishers**.

4. Close the browser.

▶ **Add a layout and theme to your Web project**

1. Select several of the layouts that are offered, inspect them for their content, and note the differences between them. Notice that you can browse for other layouts on other computers.

2. Click **Next**. You will learn more about layouts in "Understanding Layouts."

3. Select several of the themes that are offered. Inspect them for their content, and note the differences between them.

4. Click **Finish**. You will learn more about themes in "Understanding Themes."

Understanding Layouts

Before you begin using site diagrams, you should understand what layouts are and how they are related to site diagrams.

Using Layouts

Layouts define how the navigation controls of a site are arranged on a page. Layouts depend upon setting parent, children, and sibling relationships among pages on a site. Layouts make use of different combinations of regions on a page.

The following illustration shows you the five possible regions of the page that can be controlled by a layout.

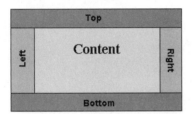

For the most part, layouts make use of the top, left, and bottom portions of a page. Visual InterDev creates these regions by using HTML tables, and each layout is based on a unique HTML template. The template contains the source text for the layout. When the layout is applied to the page, Visual InterDev inserts header and footer information into the page.

Changing Layouts

You can specify a layout for a site when you create the project. You can also change layouts for individual pages while you are creating the site diagram. In addition, you can change the layout and theme for a page at any time during the development process. To change the theme and/or the layout for a page, select the page then from the **Edit** menu (or the context menu), choose the **Apply Theme and Layout** command.

Note You can use the layout templates available in Visual InterDev, but you can also create a custom layout template by modifying an existing template and saving it with a new name to the _Layouts directory.

Understanding Cascading Style Sheets

Cascading style sheets (CSS) let you define a set of styles that override the browser's standard HTML styles. For example, you can use a cascading style sheet to set a specific font style, face, and color attribute for all H1 tags. Cascading style sheets also let you adjust layout and formatting—for example line spacing, justification, and border properties—for HTML elements and the entire document. This lets you give your pages a unique and consistent design.

Implementing Style Sheets

You can implement style sheets in three ways.

♦ Linked

Style definitions are stored in a document that is separate from the HTML pages to which it applies. A single style sheet can be linked to many different HTML pages. To copy this code for use in your own project, see "Linked CSS Sample" on the accompanying CD-ROM.

The following lines would represent the contents of a cascading style sheet file, for example, Color0.css:

```
H1      {font: 17pt "Arial";
        font-weight: bold;
        color: teal}
H2      {font: 13pt "Arial";
        font-weight: bold;
        color: purple}
P       {font: 10pt "Arial";
        color: white}
TABLE {
        table-border-color-light:  rgb(102,102,102);
        table-border-color-dark:  rgb(51,51,51);
}
```

◆ Embedded

Style definitions are stored in the header section within an HTML document. The style definition applies to all instances of that style within that HTML page. To copy this code for use in your own project, see "Embedded CSS Example" on the accompanying CD-ROM.

```
<HEAD>
<STYLE TYPE="text/css">
    H1    {font: 17pt "Arial";
           font-weight: bold;
           color: teal}
    H2    {font: 13pt "Arial";
           font-weight: bold;
           color: purple}
    P     {font: 10pt "Arial";
           color: white}
    TABLE {
           table-border-color-light:  rgb(102,102,102);
           table-border-color-dark:  rgb(51,51,51);
           }
</STYLE>
</HEAD>
```

◆ Inline

Style definitions, created for individual elements within an HTML page, are added as properties to the elements to which they apply. To copy this code for use in your own project, see "Inline CSS Example" on the accompanying CD-ROM.

```
<P STYLE="margin-left: 1.0in; color: teal">
This text appears indented and in the color teal.
<P>
```

Of these, linked CSS allow for the highest degree of reuse and site consistency. If you use all three methods listed, the inline styles take precedence over the embedded <STYLE> block, which overrides the linked styles.

▶ **To link a style sheet to a page**

1. Create a new CSS file for the style (or use an existing one).

   Typically, these files have an extension of .css. Visual InterDev contains a CSS Editor that allows you to create and modify CSS files. The following illustration shows an example of a CSS file loaded in the CSS Editor:

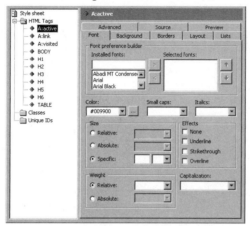

2. Apply the style sheet to a page by adding a <LINK> tag in the HTML document heading section (between <HEAD> and </HEAD> tags).

   You can do this by manually inserting a statement such as the following into your page.

   ```
   <LINK REL="stylesheet" TYPE="text/css" HREF="YourStyles/COLOR0.CSS">
   ```

   In Visual InterDev you can also simply drag the name of the style sheet from Project Explorer and drop it in within the head tags of the HTML or ASP page whose styles you want to set.

Note You will see how to create a cascading style sheet in the practice at the end of this section.

Understanding Themes

Themes are comprised of sets of graphics and one or more cascading style sheets that control styles, font, and graphics. Themes provide your pages with a consistent look and feel.

You can set a default theme for an entire project so that each page you create in that project will have the same theme applied. Even with a default theme for a project, you can override the default on particular files where you might want to apply a different theme or no theme at all.

There are two advantages to using themes:

◆ They provide your pages with a consistent look and feel.

◆ You can change themes without changing content.

The following two illustrations contain the same content rendered with two different themes.

 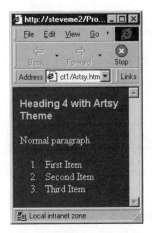

Practice: Adding a Theme to a Site

In this practice, you learn apply a theme to an existing project.

▶ **Add a theme to the site**

1. Open the site diagram, right-click **Products** and click **Apply Theme and Layout**.

2. Click **Apply Theme** on the **Theme** tab, and then select one of the themes — such as **Raygun** — from the list box and click **OK**.

3. Watch as all of the cascading style sheets and related .gif files are added to the project in the Project Explorer window.

4. On the **File** menu, click **Save All** to save your changes to the files and the site diagram.

5. Select the **Products** page in your site diagram.

6. On the **View** menu, click **View in Browser** to see a more professional version of the page.

7. Save the project. You will be using these files in the final practice exercise for this chapter.

Optional Practice: Advanced Features of Themes

If you have the time and interest, extend the practice by:

◆ Completing the design for all pages.

◆ Adding the same theme to all pages.

◆ Adding a **PageNavBar** control to the home page and make it a global navigation bar. Determine how to add the Search and Publishers pages to it. (Hint: Look for a **Diagram** menu.)

◆ Viewing the results.

Introducing Visual InterDev Tools

Now that you have created a Visual InterDev project, you are ready to use the tools that it contains. This section focuses on the individual windows that make up the Visual InterDev interface.

Project Explorer Window

The Project Explorer window displays a hierarchical list of all the projects within a solution, and all of the items contained within each project.

Typically, you use the Project Explorer window to:

◆ View the contents of a project.

◆ Open files within a project.

◆ Synchronize local files with files on the master Web server.

◆ Remove files from a project.

◆ Copy files.

◆ Display the Properties window for a given file.

To fully understand the architecture of Visual InterDev and the Project Explorer window, it is important to understand the key concepts defined in the following table.

Term	Definition
Solution	A collection of Web projects and dependent projects that makes up a Web application.
Local Web application	The collection of Web pages that resides on the developer's workstation. These pages are used for creating, developing, and testing prior to propagation to the master Web server.
Master Web application	The collection of Web files that is saved and stored on the Web server. The master Web application is accessible to multiple developers and authors. It can also be made available to intranet or Internet users.
Web application	A collection of elements that makes up a Web site or a distinct portion of a Web site. Web applications are built from Web projects.
Web project	A collection of files that specifies elements of a Web application.

To see the demonstration "Using the Project Explorer Window," see the accompanying CD-ROM.

For more information on version control in Visual InterDev, see "Tools Supporting Team Development" later on page 80 in this chapter.

The following illustration shows a sample solution within the Project Explorer window.

For more information about the elements on the **Project Explorer** toolbar, see "Project Explorer Window" in Visual InterDev Help.

Toolboxes

The Toolbox contains groups of similar tools that you will use to build Web pages.

The names and purposes for each of the tool groups in the default Toolbox are described in the following table.

Tool group	Purpose	Examples
Server objects	Objects available from a Web server	Dictionary, Filesystem, My Info
ActiveX controls	Reusable components that provide added functionality to your Web page	Calendar, Toolbar, Treeview, Slider
Design-time controls	Reusable, primarily data-bound components that provide a graphical user interface for run-time activities such as connecting to a database	Label, Textbox, Checkbox, Grid
HTML	Standard graphical controls that are available within HTML	Form, Textbox, Listbox, the **Submit** button
General	A place to collect objects to which you want easy access	Fragments of HTML code

The following illustration shows the default Toolbox.

Typically you use the mouse to select and drag a toolbox item onto pages and designers. Double-clicking an item will have the same result, but the item will be placed in the center of the active designer.

Adding Tabs to the Toolbox

When you write code or create your own set of tools, you will want to make them readily available. You can add more tabs to the Toolbox and add items to them.

▶ **To add a tab to the Toolbox**

1. Right-click anywhere on the Toolbox and click **Add Tab**.

2. Enter a name for the tab at the blinking insertion point.

Adding Items to a Tab

There are two methods for adding items to a tab. The method that you use depends upon the item that you want to add.

▶ **To add either a design-time control or an ActiveX control**

1. Right-click on any blank part of the Toolbox.

2. From the context menu, click the **Customize Toolbox** command.

3. Click the appropriate tab and locate the control that you want to add.

4. Select it by clicking the check box.

5. Click **OK**.

Note You can also browse to other sites to locate controls that you want to add to the project.

▶ **To add fragments of HTML code or script to a tab**

1. Select the fragment of code to save.

2. Drag it onto the appropriate tab.

Properties Window

The Properties window lists the design-time properties for the selected object or objects and their current settings.

The elements of the Properties window show you what object currently has focus in the editor, and let you list those properties either alphabetically or by category.

The following illustration shows you a sample Properties window.

Note To display the Properties window for an HTML element, you must be in Design view to see a list of the element's properties.

HTML Editor Window

The HTML Editor offers three separate views of files: Design view, Source view, and Quick View. The following illustration shows a sample HTML file in Source view.

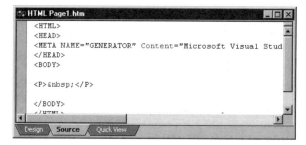

To see the demonstration "Using the HTML Editor," see the accompanying CD-ROM.

The following three lists present the key functionalities of each view.

Using Source View

Source view allows you to work directly with the underlying HTML and scripting code on a page. Source view enables you to:

◆ View and edit text and HTML tags.

◆ View and edit scripts in the page.

- Work with design-time controls, Java applets, and most other objects using the visual representation they will have in the browser.
- Use the Properties window and custom properties dialog boxes to edit the appearance and behavior of HTML text and controls on the page.
- Use the HTML Outline window to jump to any element on the page.
- Use the Script Outline window to view and create scripts for elements on the page.
- Perform debugging functions, such as setting breakpoints and viewing the current line indicator.

Using Design View

Design view allows you to view and edit a page in a WYSIWYG environment. Design view enables you to:

- Work with HTML controls such as buttons and text boxes, Java applets, and most ActiveX controls, using the visual representation they will have in the browser.
- Use menu and toolbar commands to apply certain types of formatting, such as paragraph alignment, that are not available in Source view.
- Use menu and toolbar commands to add and edit certain elements, such as tables and lists, that you must edit as HTML text in Source view.
- Use the drag-and-drop operation to reposition absolutely positioned elements.
- Use the Properties window and custom properties dialog boxes to edit the appearance and behavior of HTML text and controls on the page.
- Use the HTML Outline window to jump to any element in the page.

Using Quick View

Quick view allows you to quickly test the look and feel of a page as it will be displayed in Internet Explorer 4. Quick view enables you to:

- View .htm files in a manner similar to how they will look in your browser.
- View the client elements in an .asp page, such as HTML intrinsic controls.
- See the results of your most recent changes instantly, without saving the document.

◆ Test client run-time elements of your page such as links, bookmarks, marquees, and client scripts.

Note Server-side script, such as in ASP files, will not execute within the Quick View window because there is no Web server supporting this window. To fully preview a page, including running ASP files, right-click on the file in the Explorer window and select the **View In Browser** command.

Getting Help

Online help is always available while you are designing and developing Web sites. Help is available in HTML-style format with Previous, Next, Back, and Forward buttons for easy navigation.

Online help contains a wide variety of materials:

◆ Individual product documentation   ◆ Knowledge Base articles

◆ Platform SDKs   ◆ Resource Kits

◆ White papers   ◆ Backgrounders

The following illustration shows the initial screen for online help.

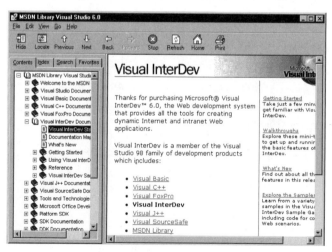

Online help offers you four separate views of the documentation. The following table outlines those views.

View	Description
Contents	A table of contents of the entire Visual Studio library.
Index	An alphabetical index of the library. Enter a word in the text box and the tool displays a listing of related topics.
Search	A ranked listing of all topics related to a query.
Favorites	A location for pointers to commonly used resources.

▶ **To start MSDN Library Visual Studio 6.0**

1. Click **Help**.
2. Select the appropriate view command: **Contents, Index,** or **Search**.

Task List Window

The Task List window helps you customize, categorize, and manage work associated with your project. The Task List window contains:

♦ Specially marked comments and tasks.

♦ Named short cuts in files.

♦ Warning errors detected while you type in the Text Editor window.

♦ Errors detected while you are compiling a project.

The following illustration contains a sample task list.

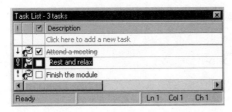

▶ **To display the Task List window**

1. From the **View** menu, click **Other Windows**.

2. Click **Task List.**

Creating an HTML Page

The section shows you how to author a simple, static HTML page. You will learn how to set global attributes for individual pages such as background color. You will also learn how to add text, graphics, and hyperlinks to a page as well as how to use tables and frames to arrange items on a page.

Note The goal for this section is to show you how to hand code some of the typical HTML tags. Larger sites will use style sheets, themes, and layouts to handle layout and formatting issues.

For more information about creating dynamic pages using ASP, see Chapter 4, "Using Active Server Pages" on page 220.

Setting Page Properties

Each HTML page has properties that you can set in the HTML Editor.

These properties affect the appearance of the page and provide information about the scripting language and model to use with the page.

▶ **To display the property page for an HTML page**

1. Double-click the file name in the Project Explorer window.

2. Click the **Source** tab at the bottom of the HTML Editor window.

3. Place the cursor on the page and right-click.

4. Select **Properties** from the pop-up menu.

The **Property Pages** dialog box contains two tabs — **General** and **Color and Margins**. The following illustration shows the **Color and Margins** tab of this dialog box.

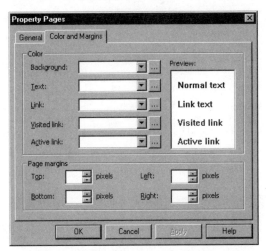

The following table lists and describes some of the common visual properties you can set.

Property	Description	Tab location
Background color	The color that appears behind the contents of the page	Color and margins
Background image	The image that appears on a page behind the contents of the HTML page	General
Link text color	Default color for link text	Color and margins
Page margins	Default settings for the top, bottom, left, and right margins for the page	Color and margins
Page title	A descriptive word or phrase that appears in a browser's title bar when the page is displayed	General
Text font color	Default color of the text font used on the page	Color and margins
Default Scripting Language	Default client and server scripting language used if not specifically overridden by the code author.	General

The General tab also has advanced settings to determine the behavior of ASP script and Design-Time Controls (DTCs).

Adding Text and Images

The HTML editor makes it easy for you to add text and graphics to an HTML page.

To format text portions for a page, you use the **HTML** toolbar. To design the look and feel of the individual page, you use the **Design** toolbar.

The following two illustrations show the **Design** and the **HTML** toolbars.

Note These two toolbars are only enabled for Design view.

Adding Text to a Single Static Page

You use the HTML editor to apply formatting to an HTML page in the same way that you apply formatting to a Microsoft Office document. For example, you can cut and paste text or use the drag-and-drop feature to move text to a new location.

To change font and paragraph properties, you use the **HTML** toolbar or the **HTML** menu.

Some of the available formatting options include:

- ◆ Centering the style of a paragraph to make it centered or aligned right.
- ◆ Changing the text font to make it bold, italic, or underlined.
- ◆ Changing text to a bulleted or numbered list.

Adding Images to a Single Static Page

Images make a Web site look interesting, but many users turn off image display to download Web pages faster. Therefore, you should always provide alternate text for images on your Web pages.

The HTML Editor includes a library of clip art for commonly used buttons, icons, and backgrounds.

▶ **To insert an image**

1. Add the image to the images folder.

2. Open the page where you want to insert the image.

3. Drag the image file from Project Explorer onto the page.

4. To set properties for the image, such as alternate text, or alignment and size, right-click the image, and then click **Properties** to display the **Property Pages** dialog box.

Types of Graphics Formats Allowed on Web Pages

There are two different graphics formats commonly used in Web pages:

◆ **Graphics Interchange Format (.gif)**

A .gif file is an encoded and compressed file for images of up to 8 bits of color.

◆ **Joint Photographic Expert Group (.jpeg)**

A .jpeg file is an encoded and compressed file for images of up to 24 bits of color.

Note Web pages can also embed other graphic format files, such as Windows .bmp files, but such formats are not supported on all platforms.

Creating Tables

In an HTML file, tables can contain any valid HTML text, images, forms, or controls. With the HTML Editor, you can create a table with the **Insert Table** dialog box.

▶ **To create a table**

1. Click the location where you want the table to appear on the page.

2. On the **Table** menu, click **Insert Table**.

3. In the **Insert Table** dialog box:

    a. Select the number of rows and columns.

    b. Select an alignment.

    c. Select a border size.

    d. If you want the table to use a specific percentage of the page, or if you want it to be a fixed pixel size, modify the Width setting in the Table Attributes option group.

The following illustration shows the properties you can set in the **Insert Table** dialog box.

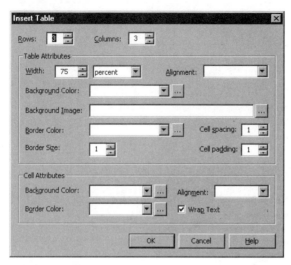

After you have inserted a table, you can customize it using the **Table** menu.

To change the properties for individual table cells, right-click the cell, and then click **Properties**. The following illustration shows the properties you can set in the **Properties** dialog box for cells.

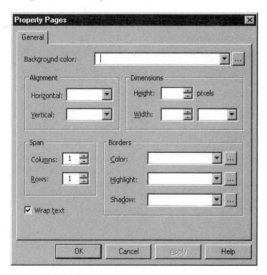

The following table lists and describes some of the cell properties you can set.

Property	Description
Background color	Sets the background color of the cell.
Cell alignment	Sets vertical and horizontal alignment of cell content.
Rows spanned	Sets the cell to span down more than one row.
Columns spanned	Sets the cell to span across more than one column.

Note Understanding how Visual InterDev builds and uses tables is important because tables are the primary tool for constructing multi-column layouts on Web pages.

Adding Hyperlinks

HTML lets you link text or images to another document. The browser highlights these elements to indicate that they are hyperlinks.

You add hyperlinks from pages in your current project to a page either on an intranet or on the Web.

▶ **To create a hyperlink with the HTML Editor**

1. Select the text that will identify the hyperlink.

2. On the **HTML** menu, click **Link**, or click the **Hyperlink** button on the toolbar.

3. In the **Hyperlink** dialog box, specify the relative or absolute URL to which you want to link and click **OK**.

   For example, to create a hyperlink to the page Classview.asp in your current Web project, select the content on the page that will be the link text, click the **Link** button, and then type **classview.asp** in the URL box.

The following illustration shows the **Hyperlink** dialog box.

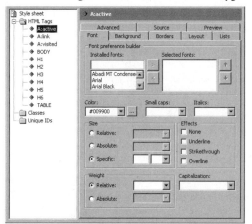

HTML Syntax for Hyperlinks

The single hyperlink-related tag for HTML is <A>, which stands for anchor.

The following example code shows the HTML that the HTML Editor adds to a Web page when you create a hyperlink.

```
<A HREF="finance.htm">ABC Co. Financial Statement</A>
```

In this example, the syntax makes the text "ABC Co. Financial Statement" a relative hyperlink to the page Finance.htm, which is located in the same folder.

Using Frames

Web pages that use frames include two main elements:

◆ **Main frame HTML file**

This file contains the tags necessary to implement each frame on a page, along with references to the HTML files for each frame. The file does not contain a <BODY> tag.

◆ **Source HTML files**

Each frame on a page contains its own source HTML file.

Creating Frames

▶ **To create an HTML page with frames**

1. Create one source HTML file for each frame on a Web page.

   The source files can contain any HTML tags.

2. Create a new HTML file that contains <HTML> and <HEAD> tags, but not a <BODY> tag.

   This is the main frame file that users open with a Web browser.

3. In the area of the document that typically contains the <BODY> tag, add a <FRAMESET> tag for each group of frames.

4. For each frame on a page, add a <FRAME> tag, and set the SRC (source) attribute to the name of the HTML file that you want to appear in the frame.

The following example code creates two vertical frames:

```
<FRAMESET COLS="*, 2*">
  <FRAME SRC="Cell_1.htm">
  <FRAME SRC="Cell_2.htm">
</FRAMESET>
```

The left frame will be half as wide as the right frame because of the relative size attributes given in the FRAMESET tag.

The following illustration shows what you will see in the browser if you use these <FRAMESET> tags.

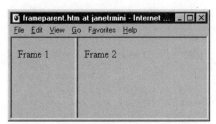

The <FRAMESET> Tag

The <FRAMESET> tag defines the location, size, and orientation of frames on an HTML page. This tag has two attributes: ROWS and COLS. You can create a frameset with either rows or columns.

The ROWS attribute defines horizontal frames. It is followed by a comma-delimited list of the sizes for each frame on the page. The following example code defines a page with two horizontal frames:

```
<HTML>
<FRAMESET ROWS="100, *">

</FRAMESET>
</HTML>
```

You can specify actual pixel sizes, percentages, or relative sizes. In the following example code, the first frame is 120 pixels, the third frame is 20 percent of the total height, and the second frame occupies the remainder of the height:

```
<FRAMESET ROWS="120, *, 20%">
```

You can create vertical frames by using the COLS attribute. You specify the frame in the same way as the ROWS attribute.

The following example code creates two vertical frames:

```
<FRAMESET COLS="2*, *">
```

The left frame will be twice as wide as the right frame.

Browsers That Do Not Support Frames

Not all browsers support the frames feature in HTML 3.0. As a consideration to users of these browsers, you can supply alternate HTML by placing it in the <NOFRAMES> tag of the main frame HTML file.

The <NOFRAMES> tag appears after the <FRAMESET> tag, as shown in the following example code:

```
<HTML>
<FRAMESET COLS="*, 2*">
  <FRAME SRC="Cell_1.htm">
  <FRAME SRC="Cell_2.htm">
</FRAMESET>
```

code continued on following page

code continued from previous page

```
<NOFRAMES>
<BODY>
. .
</BODY>
</NOFRAMES>
</HTML>
```

Creating Hyperlinks in Frames

When a user clicks a hyperlink in a frame, the link loads in the target frame.

When you create a hyperlink, you can change the default target frame where a link should be loaded by using the TARGET attribute of the <A> tag.

The following table lists and describes the values of the TARGET attribute.

Attribute	Description	Example
"frame_name"	Sets the link to load the specified page into a named frame. In the <FRAMES> tag, this is the NAME attribute of the frame you want to load. In the sample code, the sample.htm will be loaded into the target frame named "frame1."	<A TARGET="frame1" HREF="sample.htm">.
"_blank"	Sets the link to load into a new blank window. The window is not named.	<A TARGET="_blank" HREF="sample.htm">
"_parent"	Sets the link to load into the parent window of the window in which the link is located.	<A TARGET="_parent" HREF= "sample.htm">
"_self"	Sets the link to load into the same window in which the link was clicked. This is the default.	<A TARGET="_self" HREF="sample.htm">
"_top"	Sets the link to load into the entire window.	<A TARGET="_top" HREF="sample.htm">

You can also specify that the target frame for loading all hyperlinks on a page should be in the same location. To set this location, you use the <BASE> tag with the TARGET attribute.

In the following example code, the <BASE> tag specifies that all links should be loaded in the body of a window:

```
<BASE TARGET="_top">
```

Note With the HTML editor, you set the target frame in which a link should be loaded by using the **Hyperlink** dialog box. To set the base target frame for all hyperlinks on a page, you use the **Property Pages** dialog box.

Practice: Building an HTML Page

The following practice exercise continues the work that you began in the previous exercise. Here, you will add text and a cascading style sheet to the practice sample.

This practice brings together a number of topics that have been covered in this section and earlier sections in this chapter.

▶ **Add text to a page**

1. In Project Explorer, right-click the mission page and click **Open** from the pop-up menu.

2. If the page does not open in Source view, select the Source view tab.

3. Add a mission statement at the top of the page. Then add a second short paragraph that gives more detail.

4. Format the first paragraph so that it is centered and is a Heading 1 <H1></H1>.

5. Format the second paragraph so that it is centered and is a Heading 2 <H2></H2>.

6. From the View menu, click **View in Browser** to see the results.

▶ **Customize the formatting of content using cascading style sheets**

1. From the **Project** menu, click **Add Web Item**, and click **Style Sheet**.

2. Click **Open** to save the stylesheet with an appropriate name.

3. Create a customized H1 tag, by right-clicking **HTML Tags**, clicking **Insert HTML Tag**, adding H1 to the list box, and clicking **OK**.

4. Create a customized font for this style sheet in the **H1**properties pages dialog box by adding the Lucida Console font from the **Installed fonts** dropdown listbox and adding them to the **Selected fonts** list box using the right arrow button.

5. Set the specific font size to 18 points

6. Set the font color to gray or to the color of your choice.

7. Follow the same process to create an <H2> tag with a font size of 14 points.

8. On the **File** menu, click **Save All** and then close the window that contains the style sheet.

▶ **Add a cascading style sheet to a page**

1. Open the mission page in Source view.

2. Single-click the style sheet file in Project Explorer, and drag it to the header section of the mission page to link the style sheet to the file.

4. From the **File** menu, save the mission page.

5. From the **View** menu, click **View in Browser** to see the changes to the page.

▶ **Add a theme to a page**

1. Open the site diagram, and right-click the mission page.

2. Select **Apply Theme and Layout** from the pop-up menu.

3. Click **Apply Theme**, select **Raygun** from the list box, and click **OK**.

4. Save the site diagram and mission page.

5. From the **View** menu, click **View in Browser** to see the effects of the changes that you've made.

Using DIVs and SPANs

DIV (short for Division) and SPAN are HTML tags that group elements of an HTML page when you want to perform an action on all of them. You use these tools to apply style or absolute positioning information.

To view a sample Web page that uses DIV and SPAN, see sampapps/webcode/divspan.htm on the accompanying CD-ROM.

Using DIVs and SPANs

Both DIVs and SPANs are used to group HTML elements together, typically so that an action can be uniformly applied, for example, a cascading style sheet or dynamic HTML operation. In other words, both DIVs and SPANs act as containers for other elements.

The difference between these two tags is that an implicit line break is inserted after the closing DIV tag.

▶ **To create a DIV**

1. Switch to Design view.

2. Select the portion of the HTML document that you want to include in the DIV.

3. From the **HTML** menu, choose **DIV**.

4. In the **Insert DIV** dialog box, choose a positioning option, either **Absolute** or **Inline**.

▶ **To create a SPAN**

1. Switch to Design view.

2. Select the portion of the HTML document that you want to include in the SPAN.

3. From the **HTML** menu, choose **SPAN**.

To see more on how DIVs are used in Dynamic HTML, see Lab 3.2, "Creating a Dynamic Outline" on page 145 in Chapter 3, "Using Dynamic HTML."

Creating HTML Forms

One way to obtain information from a user and send it to a Web server is to use an HTML form.

An HTML form contains standard HTML controls, which are also referred to as intrinsic controls. These controls are supported by all Web browsers. Standard controls include text boxes, command buttons, radio buttons, and drop-down list boxes.

In this section, you will learn how to add standard HTML controls and forms to an HTML page.

Note If you want to place the data that you get from the user into a database, use the data-bound design-time controls located on the Toolbox. HTML forms are included here for completeness and backward compatibility.

Adding Standard HTML Controls

Standard HTML controls reside within forms on an HTML page. On a form, controls are also known as form fields.

The following illustration shows an HTML form that contains standard HTML controls.

Note Microsoft Internet Explorer does not require standard HTML controls to be contained on forms, but other browsers do. Therefore, you should always place standard HTML controls on forms.

▶ **To add an intrinsic control**

• From the HTML tab of the Toolbox, drag the control to its desired position on the page.

To set properties for each control, click the control and edit its properties in the Properties window.

The following list contains the name of each of the controls that are available on the HTML toolbox.

- ◆ Button
- ◆ File field
- ◆ Password
- ◆ **Submit** button

- ◆ Check box
- ◆ Form
- ◆ **Option** button
- ◆ Text area

- ◆ Drop-down down list box
- ◆ List box
- ◆ **Reset** button
- ◆ Text box

Note This tab also contains entries for the following HTML elements: horizontal rule, line break, paragraph break, and space.

For information about the HTML syntax for standard controls, see Visual InterDev Help.

Handling Control Data Using HTML Forms

When you use the HTML editor to add standard controls to an HTML document, you must also add a form control.

The following example code shows how to create a form that contains a text box, two check boxes, and two buttons.

```
<FORM METHOD=POST>
  Email name: <INPUT NAME="txtEditBox" VALUE="My Name"><P>
  Check all that apply:
  <INPUT TYPE="CHECKBOX" NAME="chkBusinessUse"> Business use
  <INPUT TYPE="CHECKBOX" NAME="chkHomeUse"> Home use<P>
  <INPUT TYPE=SUBMIT VALUE="Submit">
  <INPUT TYPE=RESET VALUE="Reset">
</FORM>
```

Forms can contain any HTML elements except other forms. You can add more than one HTML form to a document; however, forms cannot be nested.

HTML forms package the names and values of each control, and then send them to the location specified by the ACTION attribute. The location can be a CGI application, an ISAPI application, or an ASP.

In the following example code, the form will send information to the file Events.asp.

```
<FORM ACTION=events.asp METHOD=POST>
```

In HTML, the ACTION attribute is referred to as a form handler. To set a handler for a form, right-click in the form to see the **Properties** dialog box.

Sending Control Values to a Server

To send values of a control to the Web server, place a **Submit** button on the form. Only controls with the NAME attribute will be sent to the server.

> **Note** Microsoft Internet Explorer does not require that all standard controls be placed on forms. However, if you want to send the information from controls to the server, you must use a form.

Only standard HTML controls are submitted with a form. To submit the value of an ActiveX control or Java applet with a form, set the VALUE attribute of a standard HTML control to an appropriate property of the ActiveX control or Java applet.

Typically, you use hidden controls to submit values of ActiveX controls or Java applets with a form. You create a hidden control in the form, and then add client-side script to the **OnSubmit** event procedure for the form.

In the **OnSubmit** event procedure of the form, you set the VALUE attribute of the hidden control to an appropriate property of the ActiveX control or Java applet. A hidden control is a standard HTML control, so the value of the control will be submitted with the other HTML controls on the form.

For more information about adding client-side script for controls, see Chapter 3, "Using Dynamic HTML" on page 101.

Deploying a Web Project

You can choose from a variety of methods for making your Web application available to your users. Your choice may depend on the software available on the production server. The following table describes each of the three methods for deploying your Web application.

Type of deployment	Description
Using Copy Project	This is the easiest method and it is found on the **Project** menu of Microsoft Visual InterDev. This method requires the Microsoft FrontPage Server Extensions on the production Web server.
Using Posting Acceptor	This method does not require the FrontPage Server Extensions.
Manual Deployment	This method is possible through the Windows Explorer and your Web server administration software. However, if you have all your files included in your Web project, Visual InterDev can set up everything for you.

For any method you use, you need to provide some basic information so that the application is copied to the correct Web server with the correct application name.

Copying a Project to a Production Server

If your production server has FrontPage Server Extensions installed, you can quickly deploy your application by copying the project. The extensions are provided with Microsoft Internet Information Server (IIS).

▶ **To deploy through FrontPage Server Extensions**

1. In Project Explorer, select the project that points to the Web application you want to deploy.

2. From the **Project** menu, choose **Web Project**, and then **Copy Web Application**.

3. In the **Copy Project** dialog box, choose the copy of the application you want to deploy. Typically, you deploy the master version.

4. In the **Server name** box, enter the name of the destination Web server.

5. In the **Web project** box, enter the name you want the users to type for the URL.

6. Clear the **Copy changed files only** check box.

The following illustration shows you the choices that you have in the **Copy Project** dialog box.

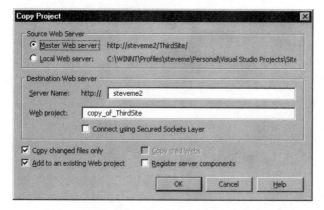

For information on the other two approaches to deployment, see Visual InterDev Help.

Tools Supporting Team Development

Version control is an issue for any kind of team development environment. Visual InterDev offers two levels of support here. For smaller teams there is Visual InterDev Professional Edition. For larger teams, Visual InterDev Enterprise Edition provides SourceSafe.

Working with Files

In a Visual InterDev project, the pages of a Web application are stored in two places: a copy is stored locally in the Visual InterDev project folder, and the master copy is stored in a folder on the test server.

Using Local Working Copies

Members of the development team create their own Visual InterDev projects. Each project contains local copies of the Web application's files. Visual InterDev allows team members to modify project files through its developer isolation feature.

Tip For information about setting up Visual InterDev team projects, see the topic "Working with Multiple Developers" in Visual InterDev online help.

To work with an existing file in a team setting, you use the following four basic steps:

1. Retrieve a working copy of the file from the Web server to your local development computer.
2. Edit the local copy of the file.
3. Preview and confirm the changes in a Web browser. If the page has dynamic content such as script code, test and debug this content as well.
4. Submit the files back to the Web server (release the working copy).

You can perform all of these steps in Microsoft Visual InterDev.

Note This same process can be used by an individual developer working in master mode. However, it is not strictly necessary to release working copies after each edit since the server files are updated automatically when the local version is saved.

▶ To get the latest version of a file from the server

1. Right-click on the file node in Project Explorer.
2. Click **Get Latest Version** on the pop-up menu.

Note that the icon next to the file node in Project Explorer changes from a lock to a pencil to indicate you have an editable, working copy of the file. If other team members subsequently try to get working copies of the same file, they will receive a warning that it is already in checked out. Note that they can choose to ignore this warning and still get their own working copies.

▶ To release the working copy of a file on your computer

1. Right-click your local copy of the file.
2. Click **Release Working Copy**.

Only when you release the file does Visual InterDev update the master copy of the file located on the Web server. If a team member has also changed the master copy during this period, Visual InterDev automatically displays the Merge Local Version window. This window allows you to integrate the changes to the file made concurrently by both team members.

Updating Your View of the Project

The procedures for getting and releasing working copies allow a developer to update the master project with changes. However, because there can be multiple developers concurrently updating the project files on the master Web server, it is also important that a developer's local project also maintains up-to-date information. Visual InterDev provides two mechanisms to update local machines.

Button	Name	Description
	Refresh Project View	Refreshing Project Explorer causes the file list in the local project to be synchronized with the master list. Files added or deleted from the master project by other developers will now appear in your local Project Explorer.
	Synchronize Files	Synchronizing the project will refresh the file list with the master Web project and update the contents of existing files that have been changed by other developers.

The pictured buttons are located on the **Project Explorer** toolbar. They can also be found under the **Web Project** submenu of the **Project** menu.

Using Visual SourceSafe

Visual InterDev's management of local and master copies works well for small teams. If two developers have the same file checked out, Visual InterDev gives them the option of merging, overwriting, or discarding differences. However, with larger teams, a more robust version control, such as that provided by Microsoft Visual SourceSafe (VSS), is preferable.

Features of Visual SourceSafe

Visual SourceSafe, like most modern version control management systems, enhances file-based development projects through the following features and capabilities:

◆ Version archiving of text-based and binary files (version control) enables developers to recall any past versions of a file. If desired, changes to a file can be rolled back by restoring a previous version of the file.

◆ File access management allows the project administrator to determine team member access to files and folders within the SourceSafe project. In addition, by default, only one member of a team may check out an individual file at a time.

◆ Flexible interface to user and administrative functions is provided through the GUI Visual SourceSafe Explorer, through command-line arguments and utilities, or programmatically through COM interfaces.

◆ Integration with Visual Studio lets developers access the main version control functionality from within their main development environment.

Visual SourceSafe can be purchased as a separate product or as part of Microsoft Visual Studio Enterprise Edition.

How Visual SourceSafe Works

After you install Visual SourceSafe on the master Web server for a project and enable the source control system for a Web site, you can open files just as you did without Visual SourceSafe. When you want to check out a working copy of a file, and the file has not been checked out by someone else, Visual SourceSafe provides you with a local, write-enabled copy of the file.

After you have a write-enabled copy of the file, Visual SourceSafe marks the file as checked out so no one else can edit it. When you check in the working copy, Visual SourceSafe marks the file as checked in so someone else can check out and edit the file.

If you request a working copy of a file that another user has already checked out, Visual SourceSafe will display a warning message. If you still want the file, it provides you with a read-only version. Multiple users can have read-only copies of the file, but only one user can have a write-enabled copy. (Because Visual InterDev supplies all team members with local versions of Web project files, there is little reason to request read-only versions of Web project files.)

For more information about using Visual SourceSafe with Visual InterDev, search for "Source Control" in Visual InterDev Help.

Additional Visual InterDev Tools

This chapter has discussed some of the tools available in Visual InterDev 6.

The following table outlines other tools and functionalities that are available in Visual InterDev and lists the chapter in which they are discussed.

Tool	Chapter
Writing client-side script	Chapter 3: Using Dynamic HTML
Writing server-side script	Chapter 4: Using Active Server Pages
Creating scriptlets	Chapter 3: Using Dynamic HTML
Debugging script	Chapter 3: Using Dynamic HTML
Creating pages with dynamic content	Chapter 5: Accessing Databases
Creating databases in Visual InterDev	Chapter 5: Accessing Databases
Building components to enhance performance	Chapter 7: Creating COM Components
Adding transaction processing to dynamic pages	Chapter 8: Using Microsoft Transaction Server

Lab 2: Developing a Web Project

In this lab, you will create the State University Web site. You will start by copying an existing starter project, and will continue to develop the site by editing existing files as well as adding new files. You will use the results of this lab in subsequent exercises.

To see the demonstration "Lab 2 Solution," see the accompanying CD-ROM.

The following diagram shows how the files you edit in this lab will fit into the State University Web site.

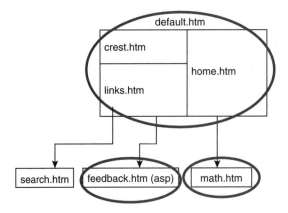

Estimated time to complete this lab: **75 minutes**

To complete the exercises in this lab, you must have the required software. For detailed information about the labs and setup for the labs, see "Labs" in "About This Course."

Objectives

After completing this lab, you will be able to:

◆ Create a new Visual InterDev project and add existing files to it.

◆ Crete new files in the project, such as HTML and ASP files.

◆ Add static elements, such as graphics and hyperlinks, to existing pages.

◆ Alter the appearance of a set of pages by creating and applying a cascading style sheet (CSS).

◆ Add dynamic content, such as HTML forms and simple scripts, to Web pages.

Prerequisites

Before working on this lab, you should be familiar with the following:

◆ Using the Windows Explorer or Internet Explorer to manipulate local files and folders.

◆ Browsing files with Internet Explorer 4.0 (or later).

◆ Syntax of basic HTML tags.

Exercises

The following exercises provide practice working with the concepts and techniques covered in this chapter:

◆ Exercise 1: Creating a New Project

In this exercise, you will create a new project for the State University Web site. You will then add a set of existing starter files to the site.

◆ Exercise 2: Creating a Static HTML Page

In this exercise, you will create a static HTML page, Links.htm, which contains a table, hyperlinks, and images. This page is the navigation frame for the home page of the StateU Web site.

◆ Exercise 3: Creating Dynamic Content

In this exercise, you will alter an HTML page, Feedback.htm, to produce an ASP file, Feedback.asp. In the process, you will add dynamic elements such as an HTML form, and simple client- and server-side scripts. You will test this page by viewing it with Internet Explorer.

◆ Exercise 4: Creating and Applying a Style

In this exercise, you will apply a CSS to the feedback page, Feedback.htm, and note its effects. You will then edit the style sheet using the CSS Editor in Visual InterDev to alter its effects on several HTML elements.

Exercise 1: Creating a New Project

In this exercise, you will create a new project for the State University Web site. You will then add a set of existing starter files to the site.

▶ **Create a new Visual InterDev web project**

1. If you have not already done so, start Microsoft Visual InterDev 6.0.

2. If the New Project dialog box does not automatically appear, In the **File** menu click **New Project.**

3. Change the following options in the New Project dialog box:

   a. In the left pane, select **Visual InterDev Projects** node.

   b. In the right pane, select the **New Web Project** icon.

   c. Change the name of the project to "StateU".

   d. Optionally, specify a non-default location for the project files. Since you will be using these same files in future labs, you may want to place the project in a central location, for example by creating a new folder, such as *<root-directory>*\MWD6\Labs\Projects\StateU. Do *not* create the project folder in the Internet publishing directory, typically C:\InetPub\WWWRoot.

   Click **Open** when you are done with your changes. The Web Project Wizard should appear.

4. The Web Project Wizard has four steps.

   a. In the first step, supply the name of the server that will be hosting the Web site. Since it is assumed you are hosting the site on your current, virtual root, so the local machine name should be supplied here. If VI does not automatically display the name of the local Web server, then enter its name manually.

Tip To find the name of the local Web server on a Windows machine, perform the following:

   1. Open the Control Panel's Network applet.

   2. Click on the Identification tab.

   3. Copy the string in the Computer Name read-only text box.

Note that Microsoft Web server's default publishing (virtual) directory name is the same as the computer name.

   Since you are working on this site locally and single-handedly, select **Master Mode**.

   It is *not* recommended that you connect using secure sockets layer.

   b. In the second step, the default options **Create a new Web application** and **Create search.htm to enable full text searching** should remain checked.

c. In step three, keep the desired layout at none.

d. In step four, keep the desired theme at none.

Click **Finish** and both the base Web site and a set of project files will be created.

Tip After the Web Project Wizard successfully runs, the Project Explorer window displays the new set of project files and folders created for StateU. By default, it shows the _ScriptLibrary folder expanded. Since you will not be working in this folder, you can contract this node.

5. Click **Save All** on the toolbar to save the project files.

▶ **Inspect the Web site and project files**

Visual InterDev creates both a Web site containing the files that will appear in the final published site, and a project directory that contains control files as well as a copy of the Web site. Visual InterDev changes these copies whenever you perform an editing or design operation.

1. Using one copy of the Windows Explorer or Internet Explorer, view the StateU subdirectory under the Web server root directory (typically C:\InetPub\wwwroot). The files comprise the StateU Web site.

2. Using another copy of the explorer, view the Visual InterDev project for this site. (The project will be located at the directory you supplied in step 3d of the previous procedure.) Note that it should contain four project files — StateU.vic, StateU.suo, StateU.vip, and StateU.sln — and a subdirectory, StateU_Local.

Tip If you do not see any file extensions, then you need to change the viewing options in the Windows Explorer (or Internet Explorer if you have integrated Web browsing with the desktop).

1. Start the Windows Explorer (Internet Explorer).

2. In the Explorer, from the View menu, choose the Options (Folder Options) command.

3. In the Option (Folder Options) dialog box, click on the View tab.

4. Deselect the option Hide MS-DOS File Extensions For File Types That Are Registered. (Hide File Extension For Known File Types).

5. Click the OK button to save your changes.

3. Expand the StateU_Local subdirectory (the local files directory). Now horizontally tile both copies of the explorer and compare the contents of their right panes. Both contain two files — Global.asa and Search.htm — and similar subdirectories. Expand a few subdirectories and compare their contents also.

You should find that most corresponding directories contain an equivalent set of files and subdirectories.

Note If you have enabled the explorer to view hidden directories, you will note differences in the local and project versions of these directories. Different subdirectories are used by VI and FrontPage to maintain and administer the project and site.

4. Minimize both explorer copies. You will be using them later in this lab.

▶ Add existing files to the project

1. In Visual InterDev, highlight the *<server-name>*/StateU node in the Project Explorer window. From the **Project** menu, click **Add Item**. The Add Item dialog box should appear.

Warning Visual InterDev will add new items under the currently highlighted node in the Project Explorer window, so make sure that the *<server-name>*/ StateU node is highlighted. However, if you make a mistake, you can easily relocate a file by simply dragging and dropping it in the Project Explorer window.

2. Click on the **Existing** tab, then navigate to the \MWD6\Labs\Labs02\New directory. Change the file mask to All Files (*.*). Select the four files found there — Crest.htm, Default.htm, Feedback.htm, and Main.htm—and then click **Open**.

Tip If you do not see any file extensions, then you need to change the viewing options in the Windows Explorer (or Internet Explorer if you have integrated Web browsing with the desktop).

1. Start the Windows Explorer (Internet Explorer).

2. In the Explorer, from the View menu, choose the Options (Folder Options) command.

3. In the Option (Folder Options) dialog box, click on the View tab.

4. Deselect the option Hide MS-DOS File Extensions For File Types That Are Registered. (Hide File Extension For Known File Types).

5. Click the OK button to save your changes.

Note that, after a pause, these files are added to the list of project files in the Project Explorer window (expand the StateU project node if necessary).

3. Expand both previously minimized copies of the explorer. Press the F5 key to update the listings. Note that these four new files have been added to both the StateU Web server and project subdirectories.

4. Again, use the Add Item command to navigate to the \MWD6\Labs\Labs02\New directory. highlight the \images, \stylesheets, and \math subdirectories then click **Add Folder** . Click **Yes** in response to any confirmation messages.

Tip Visual InterDev's Project Explorer window is drag and drop enabled. Therefore, another method of adding directories and files to your Web project is to drag them from a source, like the Windows Explorer, and drop them on the project node where you want to add them.

▶ **View the StateU home page**

1. In the Project Explorer window, right-click the node **Default.htm,** and from the context menu, chose **View In Browser.**

The draft home page should be displayed. The illustration on the following page shows how this page should look.

2. On Internet Explorer's **View** menu, click **Source**. Note that page contains three frames.

In the next exercise, you will be creating the Links.htm page and substituting it in for the second, lower left-hand frame.

Exercise 2: Creating a Static HTML Page

In this exercise, you will create the page for the links frame of the State University Web site. You will update the home page (default.htm) to include this page as the second frame. The following illustration depicts the home page after this exercise.

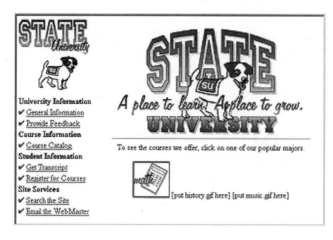

▶ Create and edit the links.htm page

1. In the StateU Web project, create a new HTML page named links.htm.

   a. On the Project Explorer window, right-click the *<server-name>/StateU* node. In the context menu, chose the **Add** submenu, then **HTML Page**. The Add Item dialog box should appear, with most of the proper entries already highlighted.

   b. Change the name of the HTML page to "links.htm". Click **Open**. The new file should be added to your project in the StateU parent directory.

   Note that in the Project Explorer window, the small icon associated with this file is a pencil, indicating that it is a working copy.

2. Links.htm should automatically be brought up in Visual InterDev's HTML Editor. (If it does not, in the **Project Explorer** window, double-click the **links.htm** node to open it.) Click the **Design** tab to view the page in design mode.

3. If the Properties Window is not displayed, click the **Properties Window** toolbar button or press F4 to display it. In the drop-down list box in the **Properties Window**, select the **DOCUMENT** object. Change the following properties:

   - Set the background color, **bgColor**, to white

   - Set the title property to "StateU Links".

   For information about setting the background color and image, see "Setting Page Properties" on page 63 in this chapter.

4. Insert an eleven-row, two-column table in the HTML page.

   The following illustration shows how the table will look when finished:

a. On the **Table** menu, click **Insert Table**. The Insert Table dialog box appears.

b. Set the Rows to a value of 11 and the Columns to 2.

c. Set the Width to 100 Percent.

d. Set the alignment to left.

e. Set the border size of the table to zero.

f. Turn off text wrapping.

g. Click **OK** to insert that empty table. (If you do not see the table cells in the editor, click the **Visible Borders** toolbar button or press CTRL+Q.)

For information about creating tables, see "Creating Tables" on page 66 in this chapter.

5. Edit the cells to look like the previous illustration.

a. Enter the appropriate text for the cells.

b. Change the Cell Properties for the four categories—University Information, Course Information, Student Information, and Site Services—as follows:

- Merge the two cells in the row to form one cell. With the cursor, highlight both cells in the row. On the **Table** menu, click **Merge Cells**.

- Change their font to bold and set horizontal alignment to left. (Alternately, change these cells to header cells by editing the HTML source.)

6. Add the checkmark image to the left of each non-header selection.

a. Place the cursor in the cell to the left of the cell containing "General Information".

b. On the **HTML** menu, click **Image**. The Insert Image dialog box should appear.

c. For the picture source, enter or browse to the file images\bullet.gif.

d. Click **OK** to insert the first image.

e. For the other duplicate images, simply copy and paste the first one.

7. Create hyperlinks from the table to other pages in the State University Web site, as shown in the following table.

Text	Hyperlink (relative link unless otherwise noted)
General Information	main.htm
Provide Feedback	feedback.htm
Course	Catalog classlist.asp
Get Transcript	transcript.asp
Register for Courses	classview.htm
Search the Site	search.htm
Email the WebMaster	mailto:webmaster@stateu.edu

   a. Select the string you whish to make a hyperlink with the mouse cursor.

   b. Click the **Link** toolbar button to display the Hyperlink dialog box.

   c. For all except the last link, select a hyperlink type of other, and then enter the target filename in the URL box. This creates a relative hyperlink. (For the last link, Email The WebMaster, choose a hyperlink type of **mailto**.)

8. Change the hyperlinks to target the main frame.

   a. Click the **Source** tab of the editor window.

   b. Insert the following line after the ending header tag, </HEAD>.

```
<base target="main">
```

9. Click the **Quick View** tab of the editor to preview this page.

10. On the **View** menu, click **View Links**. A link view window will appear for this page. Note that three of the links are broken (the red, bisected links). This is appropriate because these pages do not exist yet.

11. Save your changes to links.htm and close the open link view and editor windows.

▶ **Add Links.htm to the StateU home page**

1. View the StateU home page, Default.htm, in Internet Explorer. In the Project Explorer, right-click this file and choose **View in Browser**.

Notice that in the left-hand frame, that under the State University logo, there is a small HTML file bitmap. This was used as a place marker.

2. Get a working copy of Default.htm. In the Project Explorer, right-click this file node and on the context menu, click **Get Working Copy**.

Warning You should always obtain a working copy of a file before making permanent changes to it. Otherwise, synchronization or other file management problems might result.

3. Make the following change in the Source view of the HTML Editor. Locate the frame element that includes the file Htmlfile.gif. Delete this line and then uncomment the subsequent line, which includes Links.htm.

4. Save the changes and view the home page again in the browser. The contents of Links.htm should be shown in the lower left-hand frame when viewing Default.htm.

Exercise 3: Creating Dynamic Content

In this exercise, you will alter an HTML page, Feedback.htm, to produce an Active Server Page (ASP) file, Feedback.asp. In the process, you will add dynamic elements such as an HTML form, and simple client- and server-side scripts. You will then run (view) the file with Internet Explorer and then debug it with Visual InterDev's integrated debugger. The following illustration shows how the page should look.

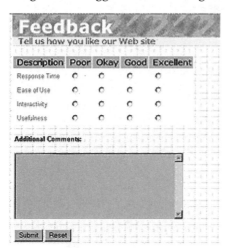

▶ **View the base HTML page**

1. Get a Working copy of Feedback.htm.

    a. In the Project Explorer window, right-click the **feedback.htm** node.

    b. On the context menu, click **Get Working Copy**.

       Note that in the Project Explorer, the small icon to the left of the feedback.htm node changes from a lock to a pencil to indicate that you have a local, working copy of this file.

2. Double-click the **feedback.htm** node to open this file in the editor.

3. View the file in Quick View and Source mode. Note that it contains header lines and a form containing a table of radio buttons and a submit button (or more correctly, a standard button with a value of Submit).

▶ **Edit feedback.htm to add dynamic elements**

In this section, you will first be adding an intrinsic text area and reset button HTML controls to the feedback.htm page.

1. Edit Feedback.htm in Design mode. If not already selected, click the **Show Details** toolbar button.

2. If it is not already visible, display the Toolbox window by clicking the **Toolbox** toolbar button or pressing CTRL+ALT+X. Click the **Toolbox** tab, then click the HTML divider.

3. Click on the **Text Area** control in the ToolBox, and drag it to the page, positioning it just above the Submit button. Set the following properties of the text area control:

    • Visually resize it to allow the user to enter several sentences.

    • Set the **name** to taFeedBack.

    • Set the **.backGroundColor** to lightblue.

4. After the Submit Button, but horizontally inline with it, add a Reset Button.

5. Next, add a provided client- and server-side script to the feedback.htm page:

    a. Open the file \MWD6\Labs\Lab02\Scripts.txt in Notepad or VI's editor. This file contains prepared client- and server-side VBScript code.

    b. In VI, switch to Source mode view of Feedback.htm. Locate the HTML comment that identifies the location for the client-side script.

    c. Copy the client-side script code from Scripts.txt to Feedback.htm.

    d. Repeat these last two steps for the server-side script code.

Note that Visual InterDev's HTML editor adds color coding to help you maintain and debug HTML and script code.

6. Save your changes to Feedback.htm.

7. Change the name of the page to Feedback.asp to reflect the fact that it now must execute server-side code.

   a. In the **Project Explorer** window, right-click **Feedback.htm** and click **Release Working Copy**.

   b. Again, right-click this node, but this time click **Rename**.

   c. Change the file extension from **htm** to **asp**. VI should prompt you to update all links to this page. Click **Yes**.

▶ **Viewing and testing the Active Server Page.**

1. View Feedback.asp in Internet Explorer.

2. Test the client-side validation code by not making a Response Time selection and trying to submit the form. You should get an error message indicating you need to make all selections. (Note that validation code has only been provided for the first radio button group, Response Time.)

3. Test this page again by providing all the required feedback and clicking the Submit button. You should receive a page with a summary of the information you supplied.

Note Feedback.asp is a *reentrant* page, meaning the response is the same page. This page contains a self-targeting form and server-side code that allows it to both collect information and display summary information.

Exercise 4: Creating and Applying a Style

Since most modern browsers can read Cascading Style Sheets (CSS) files, they provide an excellent, cross-platform way of providing a consistent look and feel to a Web site.

In this exercise, you will apply a CSS to a file (Feedback.asp) and note its effects. You will then edit the style sheet using the CSS Editor in Visual InterDev to alter its effects.

▶ **Apply the style sheet to Feedback.asp**

1. Get a working copy of Feedback.asp and open it in the HMTL Source Editor.

2. Locate the HTML to-do comment about applying a style sheet, located near the top of the page.

3. Remove the comment begin and end tags to apply the StateU1.css style to the page.

4. Save your changes to this file.

5. View the effects of this style sheet by viewing Feedback.asp in the Internet Explorer.

▶ **Edit the style sheet**

1. Get a working copy of the file \stylesheets\StateU1.css. Then in the Project Explorer, double-click on this file to open it in the CSS Editor.

2. Edit the Body tag.

   a. Expand the HTML Tags node in the left pane of the CSS Editor and select the Body element.

   b. Click the **Font** tab. Make the following changes:

   - In the Installed Fonts list box, select the font Verdana (if you do not have Verdana installed, select another similar font, such as Tahoma or Century Gothic).

   - Click on the selection button, denoted with a >, to add this font to the list of selected fonts.

   - In the Selected Fonts list box, move Verdana above the previous default font, Arial.

   Now when this page is browsed, body text will preferentially be displayed using Verdana font. If that font is not available on the client, then Arial will be used instead.

   Also note that under the Background tab, the image ../images/back2.jpg is specified as the background image.

 Tip Note that the relative URL supplied denotes the relationship between the CSS file and the background image file, *not* the relationship between the HTML (here ASP) file and the image file.

3. Repeat this process to specify Verdana as the default font for the H1 and H3 elements.

4. For the H1 element only, make the following change:

- Click the **Background** tab.

- In the Use Background Image text box, enter **../images/nav1.jpg**.

5. Briefly look at the other tabs and their options that are available in the CSS editor.

6. Save your changes to the file StateU1.css.

▶ **View the changes**

1. In the **CSS Editor**, click the **Preview** tab to preview your style on a hypothetical page.

2. Optionally, open \stylesheets\StateU1.css in Notepad to see the format and contents of this cascading style sheet file.

3. View the page Feedback.asp in Internet Explorer. If you still have this page loaded in the browser from the previous exercise, you must click the **Refresh** button to view the changes to StateU1.css.

▶ **Release all working copies of files (Optional)**

In a multi-developer environment, it is important to update the server with changes and allow other developers to have access to new project files as soon as possible. Therefore, typically after you have finished an editing pass on one or more files, and you are satisfied with the changes, you release your project's local, working copy of files back to the master Web server.

1. In the **Project Explorer** window, right click the **<server-name>/StateU** project node.

2. On the context menu, click **Release Working Copy**. This will release all local, working copies of the project's files back to the server.

   Note that in the Project Explorer window, the icon for all the project files have changed to locks to indicate these are *not* working copies.

Note In this lab, you opened the StateU Web project in master mode, which automatically updates local and server copies at the same time when you save file changes in VI. The previous procedure applies more to team projects where each developer is working in local mode.

Since this course is directed at the individual developer, this check-in process will *not* be repeated in future labs.

Self-Check Questions

To see the answers to the Self-Check Questions, see Appendix A.

1. What is a Visual InterDev Web project?

A. An autonomous Web site.

B. A container of files that create a Web site.

C. A container for .gif and .jpg files used in a Web site.

D. A container for .asp files used in a Web site.

2. How are Active Server Pages different from HTML pages?

A. Active Server Pages contain only server-side script; HTML pages contain only client-side script.

B. HTML pages can contain <SCRIPT> sections; Active Server Pages can only contain in-line script.

C. Active Server Pages are processed by the server before being returned to the client; HTML pages are sent to the client without being processed.

D. Active Server Pages can be edited with the Visual InterDev Source Editor; HTML pages can be edited with the FrontPage Editor.

3. Which view lets you work with design-time controls, Java applets, and most other objects using the visual representation they will have in the browser?

A. Data view.

B. Design view.

C. Source view.

D. Quick view.

4. Which HTML tag would you use to create a nested frame?

A. <FRAMESET>

B. <FRAME>

C. <IFRAME>

D. None of the above

5. What is the purpose of using forms?

    A. To contain license information about controls on a Web page.

    B. To group standard HTML controls visually on a Web page.

    C. To place controls in a file so they can be included with the same layout in other Web pages.

    D. To send information to a Web server.

6. Which of the following is not a standard HTML control?

    A. Multi-select list box

    B. Frame

    C. Check box

    D. Command button

7. Which type of file can you edit with the source editor?

    A. .gif file

    B. .sln file

    C. .ocx file

    D. .htm file

8. Which of the following is the correct syntax for a hyperlink?

    A. <ANCHOR="finance.htm">ABC Co. Financial Statement</A>

    B. <A="finance.htm">ABC Co. Financial Statement</A>

    C. <A HREF="finance.htm">ABC Co. Financial Statement<A>

    D. <A HREF="finance.htm">ABC Co. Financial Statement</A>

Chapter 3:
Using Dynamic HTML

Dynamic HTML (DHTML) is a technology that offers Web developers and designers a whole new array of tools to make the Web interactive.

To take advantage of these new capabilities, however, you must understand a new programming model, one that is built on traditional HTML tags, but that makes use of event-driven programming as well as object-oriented programming techniques.

In this chapter, you will learn about the different scripting languages available to you. You will also learn how to use objects exposed by the Document Object Model (DOM), and how to handle errors and debug scripts and scriptlets.

The following illustration highlights the technologies you will learn about in this chapter.

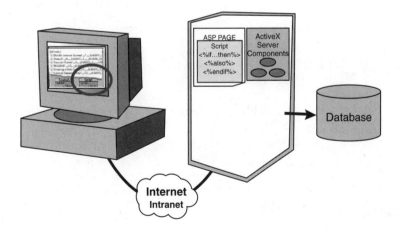

Objectives

After completing this chapter, you will be able to:

◆ Describe the purposes of Microsoft Visual Basic Scripting Edition (VBScript), JavaScript, and JScript.

◆ Explain the purpose and structure of the Browser Object Model and the DOM as implemented by Microsoft Internet Explorer 4.0.

◆ Explain the advantages of using DHTML in Web applications.

◆ Bind an element's events to a script.

◆ Explain different approaches to event handling within the DOM.

◆ Use dynamic styles to modify the look of a page element.

◆ Use dynamic positioning to modify the arrangement of page elements.

◆ Develop and run scriptlets.

Assumed Skills

Before starting this chapter, you should be able to:

◆ Create a static Web page using HTML tags.

◆ Create and use cascading style sheets to customize the look of text items on a Web page.

◆ Explain the purpose of methods, properties, objects, and events in general.

◆ Use frames and framesets to create static Web sites.

What is Dynamic HTML?

Dynamic HTML is built on top of HTML. That is, DHTML includes all the elements that make up a traditional Web page. However, with DHTML all of those elements are now programmable objects. You can assign each element an ID and then use scripting to alter them after the page has been downloaded.

To see the expert point-of-view "Dynamic HTML," see the accompanying CD-ROM.

Dynamic HTML allows you to dynamically control the look and content of a Web page. The following table describes the four Web page features that you can set dynamically. To view these pages, see the accompanying CD-ROM.

Web page feature	Example	Description
Dynamic styles	dynamicstyles.htm	Changes element styles on a page.
Dynamic positioning	dynamicpositioning.htm	Changes the position of an element on the page.
Dynamic content	dynamiccontent.htm	Adds new text or HTML content to a page.
Data binding	databinding.htm	Binds elements to records in a database.

For example, adding two functions—an ID for the H1 tag and calls to the two functions—lets you dynamically change the color of the text in the following example whenever the user moves the cursor over that text.

Note When you add the ID attribute to the H1 tag and assign it the value "header," you are creating a programmable object whose properties can then be manipulated in script.

```
<HTML>
<SCRIPT LANGUAGE="VBScript">
<!-
Sub ChangeColor()
     header.style.color = "red"
End Sub

Sub ChangeBack()
     header.style.color = "black"
End Sub
->
</SCRIPT>
<BODY>
<H1 ID="header" onmouseover="ChangeColor()"
onmouseout="ChangeBack()">Hello, world!
</BODY>
</HTML>
```

Both Microsoft and Netscape have worked closely with the W3C to create a standard for DHTML. Both models propose the following items: a Document Object Model (DOM); a way to control elements on the page using scripting; multimedia controls for animations and other effects; and a way to bind data to an HTML page. The primary differences are in the extent of the object model and the scripting language to be used.

Note The Internet Explorer 4.0 implementation of DHTML is platform independent. This means that it will run on any platform that supports Internet Explorer 4.0, including Macintosh and UNIX.

The DOM proposed by Microsoft is both browser and language independent.

The following illustration shows you the structure of the Microsoft DOM.

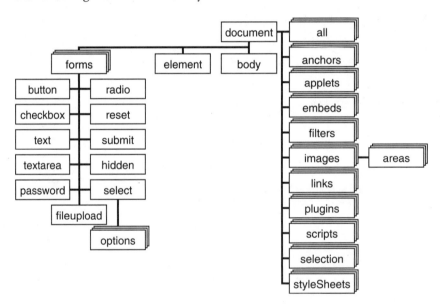

For more information about the W3C specification for Dynamic, go to the W3 web site at www.w3.org/dom/.

DHTML enables data binding and multimedia effects. Data binding is discussed in later chapters. Multimedia effects are beyond the scope of this course.

Creating Client Script

Scripting is the primary tool that enables dynamic pages. However scripting is more than a language because it combines:

- A language
- An object model
- Event handling

Scripting Languages

Most major Web browsers currently support one or more of the three scripting languages: VBScript, JScript, and JavaScript.

Choosing a Scripting Language

When choosing a scripting language, consider the following two issues:

- Browser compatibility

    Web browsers must include a scripting interpreter for the language you choose. Internet Explorer 4.0 and later has interpreters for VBScript, JScript, and JavaScript. Netscape Navigator provides an interpreter for JavaScript.

- Programmer familiarity

    Choose a scripting language that is similar to a language you know. If you have Visual Basic experience, you can quickly learn VBScript. If you have Java or C experience, JScript and JavaScript will be more familiar to you.

The following table describes the key features of each language and provides links to language tutorials.

Language	Description	Links
VBScript	A subset of Microsoft Visual Basic for Applications, VBScript lets you create variables and constants, use conditional logic, and create procedures.	http://msdn.microsoft.com/ scripting/default.htm?/scripting/ vbscript/default.htm

table continued on next page

Language	Description	Links
JScript and JavaScript	JScript is the Microsoft implementation of the ECMAScript standard. It is fully compliant with the standard, and based on JavaScript.	http://msdn.microsoft.com/ scripting/default.htm?/scripting/ jscript/default.htm

Note Netscape Navigator does not natively support VBScript, but you can acquire a plug-in from Netscape at http://www.ncompasslabs.com/.

For more information on VBScript, see "VBScript" in Visual InterDev Help.

Differences Between VBScript and JScript

The following table shows VBScript and JScript code that defines a procedure for displaying a message box.

VBScript	JScript

<pre><SCRIPT LANGUAGE=VBScript>
<!–
Sub SayHello()
      MsgBox "Hello, world!"
End Sub
–>
</SCRIPT></pre>
	<pre><SCRIPT LANGUAGE=JScript>
	<!–
	function SayHello()
	{
	            alert ("Hello, world!");
	}
	//–>
	</SCRIPT></pre>

Note Browsers that do not support scripting code will display the code as text in a Web page. To prevent browsers from displaying code, add comment tags (<!— and —>) around the script code.

You can place script code anywhere on a Web page, but to simplify code maintenance, place all of your code within the same <SCRIPT> section. You can insert the <SCRIPT> tag in either the <BODY> or <HEAD> sections of the HTML page.

JavaScript

JavaScript was created by Netscape Communications Corporation. Netscape Navigator 4.0 and later provides a JavaScript interpreter.

JavaScript differs from VBScript in a number of important ways:

◆ All procedures are declared as functions.

◆ Statements are semi-colon terminated.

◆ Var statements are used to declare variables.

◆ Braces are used to group statements together.

ActiveX Scripting Architecture

Microsoft ActiveX Scripting introduces a new way for an application to add scripting and OLE Automation capabilities. With ActiveX Scripting, hosts can call upon disparate scripting engines from multiple sources and vendors to perform scripting between components. The implementation of the script itself—language, syntax, persistent format, execution model, and so on—is left to the script vendor.

Using the Script Outline for Client Script

Script Outline displays the objects that are available to your document and the scripts on the page when you are working in Source view. In Script Outline, you can:

◆ Display a tree view of all elements on your page that have their ID or NAME attributes set.

◆ Display events for each element.

◆ Navigate quickly to any script in the page.

◆ Quickly create new handlers for events on the page.

To see the demonstration "Using the Script Outline for Client Script," see the accompanying CD-ROM.

In its initial state, the tree view of Script Outline displays the nodes described in the following table.

Node	Description
Client objects and events	The elements that support client script or have client script attached to them with a list of events for the element.
Client scripts	The client script for the page with each function or subroutine defined within the script block.
Server objects and events	The elements that support server script or have server script attached to them with a list of events for the element.
Server scripts	The server script for the page with each function or subroutine defined within the script block.

Note This topic discusses client objects, events, and scripts. For information on server objects, events, and scripts, see "Using the Script Outline for Server Script" on page 175 in Chapter 4, "Using Active Server Pages."

The following illustration shows Script Outline for a sample page in Source view.

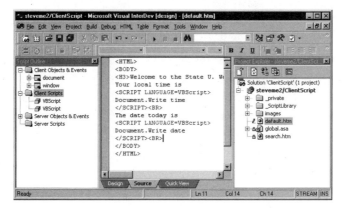

Using Script Outline

Script Outline generates either VBScript or JavaScript, depending on the default scripting language settings you have made.

▶ **To set the default language for a project**

1. Right-click the project file in Project Explorer and click **Properties**.

2. Click the **Editor Defaults** tab.

3. Select the default language from the **Client** drop-down list box in the **Default script language** option group.

If Script Outline is not open when you open a window, you can open it manually.

▶ **To open the Script Outline window for a page**

1. On the **View** menu, click **Other Windows**.

2. Select **Script Outline** from the pop-up menu.

Instead of creating a script block manually, you can let Script Outline create a script template for you.

▶ **To add a client script block to a page**

1. Place the cursor at the location for the script block.

2. Right-click and select **Script Block** from the pop-up menu.

3. Select **Client** from the second pop-up menu.

Adding Objects and Writing Script for Them

When you add HTML, design-time, and ActiveX controls to a page in your project, the HTML Editor adds the ID for the object and all the events associated with the object to Script Outline.

▶ **To add a Textbox control and an event procedure to a project**

1. Click the **HTML** tab in the Toolbox.

2. Drag the **Textbox** control to an appropriate location on the page. The HTML Editor will add the ID for the control to Script Outline under Client Objects and Events.

3. Open the text1 node to display the events associated with the control.

4. Double-click the event procedure that you want to implement. The HTML Editor adds a template for the event procedure to the top of the page. It also adds an item for the script under the Client Scripts node.

Note Targeting design-time controls for client or server script determines the node in which they will appear. For more information, see "How Data-Bound Controls Work" on page 245 in Chapter 5, "Accessing Databases."

Debugging Client Script

Script debugging is integrated into Microsoft Visual InterDev 6 and Internet Explorer 4.0. This debugging functionality allows Web developers to browse, debug, and edit .htm and .asp files.

The debugger works with JScript, VBScript, and other scripting languages. All scripting languages can reference the Internet Explorer scripting object model to interact with Web documents, the browser, and the current window.

Enabling Client Scripting

If you are writing client script in a .htm page, debugging is enabled automatically. For information on enabling debugging in Active Server Pages (ASP), see "Debugging Server Script" on page 177 in Chapter 4, "Using Active Server Pages."

Starting Script Debugging

The following table describes four different techniques for starting script debugging.

Situation	Technique
In response to an error on a page	If the browser or server encounters a syntax or run-time error in a script, it displays a message that offers you the opportunity to start the debugger at the line where the error occurred.
From Microsoft Internet Explorer	Choose **Script Debugger** from the **View** menu in Internet Explorer, and then **Open** or **Break at Next Statement**. Script Debugger starts, and then opens the current HTML source file. This starts the Visual InterDev debugger.

table continued on following page

Situation	Technique
From Visual InterDev	From the **Debug** menu, click **Start**.
In a script	When writing a script, include a **Stop** statement (VBScript) or a **Debugger** statement (JScript) in a script. When script execution reaches that line, the Visual InterDev debugger will start.

The following illustration shows the debugger in Break mode.

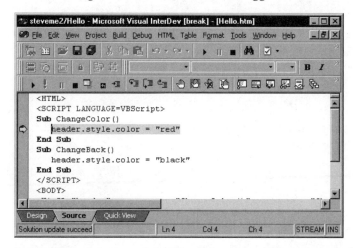

Some of the features of the Visual InterDev debugger include:

◆ Breakpoints

You can set breakpoints anywhere in your code. In Break mode, you can single-step through the code. An Immediate window will display the value of variables.

◆ Call Stack

A Call Stack window displays which procedures have been invoked.

◆ Syntax coloring

The HTML and script syntax is displayed with different colors to help you read and debug your script.

Note The debugger opens a copy of a Web page in a temporary Internet cache. Any edits you make while running the debugger will apply only to the cached Web page. To correct an error permanently, you must edit the source file on the Web server.

For more information about debugging, see "The Script Debugging Process" in Visual InterDev Help.

Handling Run-Time Errors in Client Script

To create a robust Web application, you should anticipate possible script errors and include error-handling code in your Web pages. The error-handling code should attempt to resolve the error or return an appropriate message to the user.

On Error Statement

The **On Error** statement enables an error-handling routine and specifies the location of the routine within a procedure.

The **On Error** statement syntax can have any of the forms described in the following table.

Statement	Description
On Error Resume Next	Specifies that when a run-time error occurs, control will go to the statement immediately following the statement where the error occurred, and execution will continue. Use this form rather than **On Error Go To** when accessing objects.
On Error GoTo 0	Disables any enabled error handler in the current procedure.
On Error GoTo *line*	Enables the error-handling routine that starts at the line specified in the required line argument. The specified line must be in the same procedure as the **On Error** statement; otherwise, a compile-time error occurs.

Note VBScript does not support the **On Error GoTo** *<label>* statement, and you cannot write an error handler that is called automatically when an error occurs. Therefore, you must implement inline error handling to check for an error after each statement that can cause an error.

Handling Errors with the Err Object

When an error does occur, Internet Explorer stores the error information in the **Err** object.

To detect run-time errors, check the **Number** property of the **Err** object after each statement that might cause an error. If **Number** is zero, an error has not occurred. If it is not zero, an error has occurred.

To retrieve information about the error, check the **Description** property of the **Err** object.

When an error occurs, the **Err** object will contain the error information until another error occurs. If a statement runs successfully, the **Err** object will not be cleared. Therefore, after an error occurs, you should clear the error by invoking the **Clear** method of the **Err** object.

The following sample code shows the general syntax for handling errors. To copy this code for use in your own project, see "Error Handling" on the accompanying CD-ROM.

```
'Error Handling Code Sample
Sub cmdSubmit_OnClick
  On Error Resume Next
  'Statement that might cause an error
  If Err <> 0 Then
      Msgbox "An error occurred. " & Err.Description
      Err.Clear
  End if
  'Statement that might cause an error
  If Err <> 0 Then
      Msgbox "An error occurred. " & Err.Description
      Err.Clear
  End if
End Sub
```

To test your own error-handling code, you can purposely cause an error by using the **Raise** method of the **Err** object.

VBScript does not use all available numbers for its errors. If you want to generate your own errors, begin a numbering scheme with 65535 and work your way down. For example:

```
Err.Raise 65000
```

Using Objects

To use objects, you must first create the object, and then identify it by setting its **ID** or **NAME** attributes. You can set an **ID** attribute for any object, but the **NAME** attribute only applies to standard HTML controls and Java applets. You use the **ID** or **NAME** attribute to create event procedures and to access an object's properties and methods. The syntax for assigning names varies slightly for different types of objects.

The following table lists the standard objects that you can use on a Web page and describes how you identify each in code.

Object type	ID	Name	Example
Standard HTML objects	Y		`<H1 ID="myH1">`
Standard HTML	Y	Y	`<INPUT TYPE="BUTTON" NAME="btnMyButton">`
ActiveX controls	Y		`<OBJECT classid="clsid:99B42120-6EC7-11CF-A6C7-00AA00A47DD2" id=lblOccupation>`
Java applets	Y	Y	`<APPLET CODE=Outline.class NAME=outline HEIGHT=150 WIDTH=200> </APPLET>`

Note If an element has both an **ID** and **NAME** attribute set, then VBScript event handlers must use the **NAME** attribute. Also, you must use the **Name** attribute for standard HTML controls to implement forms.

Accessing Properties

To access the value of a property, you use the following syntax:

Object.Property = Value

To retrieve the values of properties, you use this syntax:

Value = Object.Property

The following example sets the value of shiptime equal to the value property of the **ShipDate** object.

```
shiptime = ShipDate.Value
```

Invoking Methods

You invoke methods in script by using the following syntax:

[Call] Object.Method

The following example calls the **Today** method of the **ShipDate** object.

```
Call ShipDate.Today()
```

In VBScript you are not required to use the **Call** keyword when calling a procedure. However, if you use the **Call** keyword to call a procedure that requires arguments, the argument list must be enclosed in parentheses. If you omit the **Call** keyword, you also must omit the parentheses around the argument list.

Using Object Collections

Object models are composed of two different types of entities—objects and collections of objects.

For example, a window can contain one or more frames. A document can contain one or more images or forms. A collection is a feature of DHTML and object-oriented programming in general that makes it easy to organize and access similar objects.

The **Document** object contains a number of collections, including anchors, frames, forms, links, and scripts. For a complete list, see Visual InterDev Help.

There are two methods for accessing members of a collection—you can use either the index of the collection member, or its name.

For example, in the following example code, the first line accesses the second member of the images collection using the index 1. The second line accesses the member of the images collection that is named myimage.

```
document.images(1)
document.images("myimage")
```

Note Collections in Dynamic HTML are zero-based.

Every collection in Dynamic HTML has two properties, which are explained in the following table.

Property	Definition
Length	The **Length** property contains the number of elements in the collection.
Item	Using the **Item** property, you can retrieve an element or a collection of elements from the current collection.

Using Browser Objects

The DOM exposes several important browser objects and collections that you will access on a regular basis. In this section, you will learn how to use four commonly used browser objects.

The following illustration depicts the browser object hierarchy.

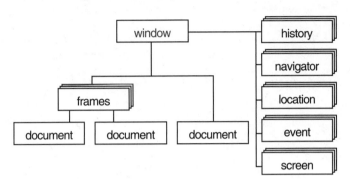

Window Object

The **Window** object represents the browser window that contains the HTML document the user is viewing. It is the top-level object in the object model hierarchy. You can use methods and properties of the **Window** object to modify the appearance of a window and retrieve information about the browser. The **Window** object has several sub-objects and collections as properties, including the **Navigator** object, the Frames collection, and the **Location** object.

Initialization and Clean-Up

The **Window** object has an **OnLoad** event that is called to initialize a page when the browser has finished loading the page. The object also has an **OnUnLoad** event that is called when the page has been unloaded.

Using the Onload Event

When an HTML page loads, the **OnLoad** event of the **Window** object will run. To use this event, you can either create a subprocedure named **Window_OnLoad** or add the **OnLoad** attribute to the <BODY> tag.

In the following example code, the **Window_OnLoad** event procedure initializes a form by calling the **Initialize_ShipForm** procedure:

```
Sub Window_OnLoad
  Initialize_ShipForm
End Sub
```

The following example code sets the **OnLoad** attribute of the <BODY> tag to call the **Initialize_ShipForm** procedure when the page loads:

```
<BODY LANGUAGE=VBScript Onload = Initialize_ShipForm()>
```

Displaying and Retrieving Information

To display and retrieve information from a user, you use the **Alert** and **Prompt** methods of the **Window** object. The **Alert** method displays a message. The **Prompt** method prompts a user for input.

The following example code prompts the user for a name with the **Prompt** method, and displays the name to the user with the **Alert** method:

```
<SCRIPT Language=VBSCRIPT>
Sub Window_OnLoad
  strName = Window.Prompt ( "Enter your name")
  Window.Alert "Hello " & strName
End Sub
</SCRIPT>
```

Navigator Object

The **Navigator** object contains information about the browser application being used to view the HTML document. It includes the browser name and version number.

You can use the **Navigator** object to detect the browser and use other objects in the object model to load an alternate document that was specifically authored for the browser. Different browsers have different capabilities, so by using this object you can ensure that the user gets the appropriate content.

The following table describes the properties of the **Navigator** object that expose the browser name and version.

Property	Description
appCodeName	Mozilla, for both Internet Explorer and Netscape Navigator.
appName	Either Internet Explorer or Netscape Navigator.
appVersion	Version number for the browser.

table continued on following page

Property	Description
userAgent	Contains the HTTP user-agent string that was specified in the HTTP request. It is a concatenation of the **appCodeName** and **appVersion** properties.

The following example code illustrates using the **Navigator** object to display the name and version of the browser:

```
<HTML>
<HEAD><TITLE>Displaying the all collection</TITLE>
<SCRIPT LANGUAGE="VBScript">
Sub DisplayBrowserVer()
    Dim strName, strVersion

    strName = window.navigator.appName
    strVersion = window.navigator.appVersion

    Alert("The browser is " & strName & _
            ", version " & strVersion)
End Sub
</SCRIPT>
</HEAD>
<BODY onload="DisplayBrowserVer()">
</BODY>
</HTML>
```

Frames Collection

The **Frames** object represents a collection of frames in a window. Each frame is also a **Window** object with its own properties, including a **Document** property that returns a **Document** object.

Scope of Script in Frames

The scope of scripting code is at the frame level of a document. If you want to write script in one frame to access an object in another frame, you must navigate the object model to retrieve the parent window, and then use the Frames collection to retrieve the frame you want to access.

To access a different frame with script, refer to the Frames collection of the parent window of the current frame by using one of these syntax methods:

Parent.Frames("FrameName")

*Parent.*FrameName

Location Object

The **Location** object represents the URL of the current document. To load another document, you change properties of the **Location** object.

Navigating Programmatically

To load another document, you set the **HRef** property of the **Location** object.

The following example code would load the default document from the Microsoft Web site:

```
Location.HRef = "http://www.microsoft.com/"
```

Running Script from a Hyperlink

You can define a hyperlink as an object, and then create an event procedure for the hyperlink that performs some logic and, depending on the result, loads another document.

To define a hyperlink as an object with events, you set the **HREF** and **ID** attributes of the hyperlink. If you set the **HREF** attribute to a URL, the script will run and then display the new document. If you set **HREF** to "", the script will run, but will not display a new document.

The following example code assigns the identifier JumpNext to the hyperlinked text:

```
<A HREF="" ID="JumpNext">Next Page</A>

<SCRIPT LANGUAGE=VBSCRIPT>
Sub JumpNext_OnClick()
  If Navigator.appName = "Microsoft Internet Explorer" Then
      Location.HRef = "IEPage1.htm"
  Else
      Location.HRef = "OtherPage1.htm"
  End If
End Sub
</SCRIPT>
```

In the **OnClick** event procedure, the script determines which browser is viewing the page, and then goes to the location for another document on a Web site.

The primary reason for creating an event procedure for a hyperlink is to perform more than one action, such as changing a document in multiple frames, in response to one user event.

The following illustration shows a document with three frames. The hyperlink in the links frame has an event procedure that changes the documents contained in all three frames.

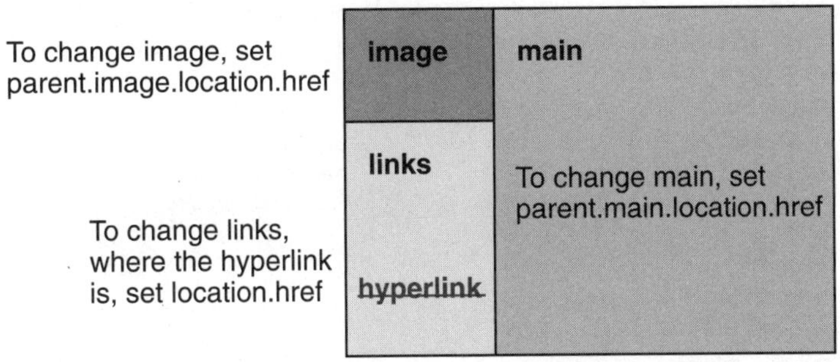

To change image, set
parent.image.location.href

image	**main**
links	To change main, set parent.main.location.href
hyperlink	

To change links,
where the hyperlink
is, set location.href

The following example code shows this hyperlink event procedure discussed in the previous illustration:

```
'Change the source of the frame the hyperlink is in
Location.HRef = "Page1.htm"
'Change the source of the frame named "main"
Parent.main.Location.HRef = "Page2.htm"
'Change the source of the frame named "image"
Parent.image.Location.HRef = "Page3.htm"
```

Lab 3.1: Detecting the Browser Version

In this lab, you will add script to a new Links page for the State University Web site that detects the version of the browser that loaded it. You will add script that loads a new page that uses Dynamic HTML if the browser is Internet Explorer 4.0 or later. If the browser is not that version, your script will load the static HTML version of the Links page created in Lab 2.

To see the demonstration "Lab 3.1 Solution," see the accompanying CD-ROM.

The following diagram shows how the files you edit in this lab will fit into the State University Web site.

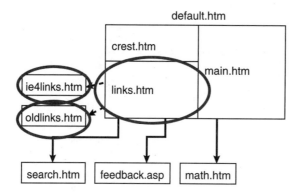

Estimated time to complete this lab: **30 minutes**

To complete the exercises in this lab, you must have the required software. For detailed information about the labs and setups for the labs, see "Labs" in "About This Course."

The solution code for this lab is located in the folder \Labs\Lab03.1\Solution.

Objectives

After completing this lab, you will be able to:

◆ Write script that detects the version of the browser in which a page is loaded using browser objects.

◆ Write script that instructs the browser to load alternate pages.

Prerequisites

Before working on this lab, you should be familiar with the following:

◆ Working with Web projects in Visual InterDev, and adding and removing HTML pages in the project.

◆ Creating and editing HTML pages in Visual InterDev.

◆ Writing and debugging VBScript code in Visual InterDev.

Exercises

The following exercises provide practice working with the concepts and techniques covered in this chapter:

◆ Exercise 1: Detecting the Browser Version

In this exercise, you will add script to a new Links page for the State University Web site to determine the browser that loaded it. You will write a function that returns the version number of the browser if it is Internet Explorer, or zero if it is not.

◆ Exercise 2: Loading a Browser-Specific Page

In this exercise, you will add script that calls the function created in Exercise 1. The script will load an alternate page that uses Dynamic HTML if the return value from the function indicates the browser is Internet Explorer 4.0 or later. If the browser is not that version, your script will load the static HTML version of the Links page created in Lab 2.

Exercise 1: Detecting the Browser Version

In this exercise, you will add script to a new Links page for the State University Web site to determine the browser that loaded it. You will write a function that returns the version number of the browser if it is Internet Explorer, or zero if it is not.

▶ **Create a new Links page**

1. Open the State University Web project in Visual InterDev.

If you have not created the project, see Lab 2, "Developing a Web Project" on page 84.

2. Add the file Oldlinks.htm from the \Labs\Lab03.1\New folder to the project.

This is a copy of the Links.htm file that was created in Lab 2.

3. Delete the current Links.htm file from the project.

4. Add a new HTML file named Links.htm to the project.

▶ **Write the script that detects the browser**

You will use properties of the **Navigator** object to determine if the browser is Internet Explorer, and to get the version number of the browser.

For more information about the **Navigator** object, see "Navigator Object" on page 119 in this chapter.

1. Open the new Links page you created in the previous procedure (Links.htm).

2. Create a VBScript function named **GetIEVersion.**

3. Declare variables named strName and strVersion in the function.

These will be used to store information about the browser. The strName variable will store the name of the browser, and the strVersion variable will store the version number of the browser.

4. Set the value of strName equal to the **appName** property of the **Navigator** object.

5. Set the value of strVersion equal to the first character in the **appVersion** property of the **Navigator** object, using the VBScript function **Left.**

6. Add an **If...Then** statement to check if strName equals "Microsoft Internet Explorer." If it does, return the value of strVersion from the function. If it does not, return 0 from the function.

To see an example of how your code should look, see Lab Hint 3.1 in Appendix B.

▶ **Detect the browser when the page loads**

1. Write an event handler for the **OnLoad** event for the page.

For more information about the **OnLoad** event, see "Window Object" on page 117 in this chapter.

2. Call **GetIEVersion** and display its return value using the VBScript function **MsgBox.**

```
MsgBox("Your Internet Explorer version is " & GetIEVersion())
```

3. Save your changes, and view Links.htm in the browser. The message box should display the version number of your browser.

Exercise 2: Loading a Browser-Specific Page

In this exercise, you will add script that calls the function created in Exercise 1. The script will load an alternate page that uses Dynamic HTML if the return value from the function indicates the browser is Internet Explorer 4.0 or later. If the browser is not that version, your script will load the static HTML version of the Links page created in Lab 2.

▶ **Modify the OnLoad event handler to load alternate Link pages**

1. In Visual InterDev, open the new Links.htm file that you created in Exercise 1.

2. Add an **If...Then** statement to the **OnLoad** event handler in Links.htm that calls **GetIEVersion** and checks if it returns a value >= 4.

3. For the case where the return value is >= 4, set the value of the **href** property for the **Location** object of the current window to "ie4links.htm".

   The Ie4links.htm file is a version of the Links page that uses Dynamic HTML.

   For more information about the **Window** and **Location** objects, see "Using Browser Objects" on page 117 in this chapter.

4. Add an **Else** clause for the case where the return value is not >= 4. In this case, set the value of the **href** property to "oldlinks.htm".

   The Oldlinks.htm file is the static HTML version of the Links page created in Lab 2.

   To see an example of how your code should look, see Lab Hint 3.2 in Appendix B.

▶ **Test your work**

1. Add the file Ie4links.htm in the \Labs\Lab03.1\New folder to the project.

   The Ie4links.htm file is a version of the Links page that uses Dynamic HTML. You will be adding to this page in subsequent labs.

2. Save your changes, and view Links.htm in Internet Explorer 4.0 or later. The browser should load the alternate Links page, Ie4links.htm.

Handling Events

In this section, you will learn about the **Event** object. You will also learn how to write event procedures, and how to use event bubbling to make your scripts more compact and efficient.

Events and event handling form the basis of Dynamic HTML. Events are notifications that an action has taken place. For example, a notification occurs when the user clicks a **Submit** button or rolls the mouse pointer over an element on a Web page.

Dynamic HTML provides the mechanism for capturing and handling these events. With the introduction of Internet Explorer 4.0, the **Window** object now contains an **Event** object, which provides your Web application with detailed information about a user's actions.

The Event Object

In order to create interactive Web applications, you should understand the following terms:

◆ Event binding

The association of a script with a notification from a document, or an element in a document.

◆ **Event** object

Exposes the information related to an event to the script.

◆ Standard user events

Mouse, keyboard, focus, and help events that are available on almost every element in a document.

Properties of the Event Object

The **Event** object is a language-independent mechanism for accessing information related to an event, and for controlling whether the event bubbles and the default action for the event occurs.

The **Event** object is a property of the **Window** object and exposes the properties discussed in the following table.

Property	Description
srcElement	What element originated the event sequence.
cancelBubble	Whether to cancel event bubbling. By setting **cancelBubble** to **False,** you prevent the parent element from receiving the event.
returnValue	The default action for the event. By setting **returnValue** to **False,** you prevent the default action for that event.

The following example code shows you how to use the **srcElement** property to determine where an event occurred:

```
<html>
<body>
<script for="document" event="onmousedown()" language="VBScript">
  msgbox "The click event happened in the " &
window.event.srcElement.tagName & " element."
</script>

</body>
</html>
```

Standard User Mouse Events

Dynamic HTML exposes events for tracking the different states of the mouse, including moving over and off of page elements.

The following table describes three common mouse events.

Event	Description
onclick	The left mouse button or the default button was clicked.
onmouseover	The mouse pointer entered the scope of an element on the page.
onmouseout	The mouse pointer exited the scope of an element on the page.

For a complete list of mouse events, see "Events" in Visual InterDev Help.

To see code that uses the **onclick** event, see "Dynamic Styles" on page 134 in this chapter.

To see sample code that uses the **onmouseover** and **onmouseout** events, see "Dynamic Content" on page 141 in this chapter.

Writing Event Procedures

After creating and naming the objects on a Web page, you create event procedures and bind them to elements on the page.

Binding Events to Scripts

There are four methods for binding an event to a script. Three of them will work in both VBScript and JScript. The method that you choose depends upon which language you use and what you want to accomplish.

There are four different ways to create an event procedure for an object:

◆ Create a separate <SCRIPT> block for the event procedure.

◆ Assign the event procedure in an HTML tag for the object.

◆ Include the script in the HTML tag that defines the object.

◆ Name a procedure **ObjectName_Event**.

To see the demonstration "Binding Events to Elements," see the accompanying CD-ROM.

Create a Separate <SCRIPT> Block

You can create a separate <SCRIPT> block that contains script that runs for a specific event of a control.

The following example code shows script that will run when the **Click** event of the **Calendar1** control occurs:

```
<SCRIPT LANGUAGE="VBScript" FOR="Calendar1" EVENT="Click()">
  ' code goes here.
</SCRIPT>
```

You can use this method in either JavaScript or VBScript to create event procedures for ActiveX controls and standard HTML controls.

Assign the Event Procedure When Creating the Object

In the HTML tag that creates an object, you can specify an event name and the procedure to be invoked when that event occurs. You must include a <SCRIPT> block that includes the procedure declaration before the HTML tag that defines the object.

This method is useful if you want events from different objects to invoke the same procedure. You can use this method to assign event procedures for standard HTML controls.

In the following example code, the **ProcessOrder** procedure is called when the user clicks the option button:

```
<SCRIPT LANGUAGE=VBScript>
Sub ProcessOrder ()
  ' code goes here.
End Sub
</SCRIPT>
<INPUT TYPE=RADIO NAME=RadioGroup onClick="ProcessOrder">
```

This method is supported by both VBScript and JavaScript.

Include Script in the HTML Tag

In the HTML tag that creates the object, you can specify an event name and the script to run when that event occurs. You can use this method to assign event procedures for standard HTML controls.

The following example code displays the message "Hello World" when a user clicks the **Hello** button:

```
<INPUT LANGUAGE="VBScript" TYPE=button VALUE="hello"
onClicK="Msgbox &quot;Hello World&quot;">
```

This method is supported by JavaScript and VBScript.

Name the Procedure ObjectName_Event

If you name a procedure **ObjectName_Event,** the procedure will run automatically when the event for the object occurs. This naming convention is the same as the convention used to define event procedures in Visual Basic. This method is supported by VBScript only.

In the following example code, the procedure runs when the user clicks **Button1**:

```
Sub Button1_OnClick ()
  ' code goes here.
End Sub
```

Event Bubbling

When an event occurs, it fires first on the source element and then on the parent of the source element. It continues to fire on successive parent elements until it has reached the top element, the document.

For example, when the user clicks a button on a Web page, the **onclick** event is first fired on the button itself, then on the form that contains the button, then the document, and so on.

The following illustration shows an event bubbling through the browser object hierarchy.

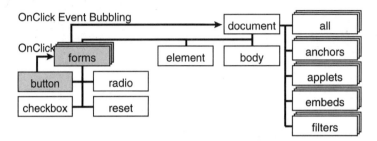

Event bubbling is useful because:

◆ It allows multiple common actions to be handled centrally.

◆ It reduces the amount of overall code in the Web page.

◆ It reduces the number of code changes necessitated by changes in the document.

In the following example code, when the user moves the mouse pointer over the text "This is some text," a dialog box appears with the text "OuterSpan." When the user moves the mouse over the second span, another dialog box appears with the text "InnerSpan."

```
<html>
<body>
<span id=OuterSpan style="background-color: red" language=vbscript
onclick="Alert('You clicked ' &  window.event.srcElement.id)">
This is some text
<span id=InnerSpan style="background-color: blue">
This is some more text
</span>
</span>
</body>
</html>
```

The **onclick** event for the **InnerSpan** element is handled even though it does not have an event handler. The **onclick** event from the **InnerSpan** element bubbles up to its parent element, which is the **OuterSpan** element. **OuterSpan** does have an event handler registered for the **onclick** event, so it fires.

Every time an event is fired, a special property on the **Window** object is created. This special property contains the **Event** object. The **Event** object contains context information about the event that just fired, including mouse location, keyboard status, and most importantly the source element of the event.

Note   Set the **cancelBubble** property of the **Event** object to **True** when you want to prevent an event from bubbling to the element's parent.

Using Document Objects

Objects exposed by the Document Object Model provide all of the functionality that DHTML exploits.

In this section, you will learn about scripting, object models, and event handling. You will focus on two content areas—writing script to handle routine page-level issues, and adding dynamic features to your page.

Using Element Objects

Every HTML tag and its attributes in a document are represented in the object model as an element object. An element object exposes methods and properties that enable you to get information about and change the attributes of the corresponding element.

You do not refer to an element object through the object model directly, but indirectly through document collections. For more information on document collections, see "Using Document Collections" on page 133 in this chapter.

Most element properties have the same name and take the same values as the corresponding attributes. Some properties do not correspond to element attributes. These properties typically give additional information about the element that is not available through attributes.

The following table lists the commonly used properties of element objects.

Property	Purpose
ID	Gets the string identifying the element.
tagName	Gets the name of the HTML tag of the element.
className	Sets and gets the style sheet class name of the element.
style	Sub-object used to set and get styles associated with the element.
children	Gets the collection of child elements in the element hierarchy.
parentElement	Gets the parent element in the element hierarchy.

The following example code illustrates how the **className** property of an element object can be used in a procedure:

```
Sub DoClick()
    If (window.event.srcElement.className = "parent") Or
(window.event.srcElement.className = "image") Then
        ExpandCollapse
    End If
    window.event.cancelBubble = True
End Sub
```

You can use three of these properties to identify elements in code: **tagName, ID,** and **className**. The following table describes the scenario that best suits each property.

Scenario	Solution
When you want your code to apply to a particular element.	Use the **ID** property to reference a single element.
When you want your code to apply to all the elements of the same type.	Use the **tagName** property to reference all elements of a single type.
When you want your code to apply to a set of elements with the same style sheet class name.	Use the **className** property to reference any set that you define.

Using Document Collections

The DOM contains several collections that enable finding and adding different types of elements in an HTML document. Three important document collections are the **all, children,** and **styleSheets** collections.

You can access individual element objects within collections with their index, name, or ID. For information on accessing objects in a collection, see "Using Object Collections" on page 116 in this chapter.

Using the all Collection

The **all** collection represents all of the elements in the document in the order that they appear in the HTML source code. It can also include elements not in the document, comments, and unknown or invalid tags. The reason for including these other elements is to give you accurate information about the document. The **all** collection is automatically updated to reflect any changes in the document such as when elements and their content are added or removed.

The following example code uses the **all** collection to display a list of all the tags in the document:

```
<HTML>
<HEAD><TITLE>Displaying the all collection</TITLE>
<SCRIPT LANGUAGE="VBScript">
Sub ShowElements()
    Dim i, tagNames
    tagNames = ""
    For i = 0 To document.all.length-1
        tagNames = tagNames & document.all(i).tagName & " "
    Next
    Alert("This document contains: " + tagNames)
End Sub
</SCRIPT>
</HEAD>
<BODY onload="ShowElements()">
<!- A comment ->
<P>This document has an <ZZZ>unknown</ZZZ> and an invalid</B> tag.
</BODY>
</HTML>
```

Using the children Collection

The **children** collection contains all the elements directly contained by a parent element. For example, examine the following example code:

```
<DIV ID=parentDiv>
<IMG SRC="images/blue.gif">
<DIV ID=childDiv>
<A HREF="home.htm">General Information</A>
</DIV>
</DIV>
```

The **children** collection for the <DIV> tag with the ID **parentDiv** will contain the image and the <DIV> tag with the ID **childDiv**. The **children** collection for **childDiv** will contain the hyperlink.

Using the styleSheets Collection

The **styleSheets** collection contains all the style sheet objects corresponding to each instance of a <LINK> or <STYLE> element in the document.

The following example code uses the **styleSheets** collection to add a style sheet to a document:

```
Sub AddStyleSheet(strUrl)
    ' pass URL for .css file
    ' containing the style sheet
    document.stylesheets(0).addImport(strUrl)
End Sub
```

Dynamic Styles

DHTML offers Web designers the ability to alter the style for elements dynamically, in response to interaction with the user. For example, you might change the font family or font color of an item when the cursor is over it to show users their immediate choices. This approach is often found in tables of contents.

Using static HTML, you would need to download a new page in order to change the size of the font, which means a trip to the server. With DHTML, you can change font size without having to reload the page.

To see an example of dynamic styles in your Web browser, see dynamicstyles.htm on the accompanying CD-ROM.

Advantages of Dynamically Changing Styles

There are a number of reasons to dynamically change the styles for elements on a page:

◆ To make the page visually interesting.

◆ To provide feedback to users as they interact with the page.

◆ To provide visual customizing to users who might not otherwise be able to use the page.

To create dynamic styles, you need to be familiar with using CSS and defining styles for a Web page. For more information on creating and using cascading style sheets, see "Understanding Cascading Style Sheets" on page 50 in Chapter 2, "Introducing Visual InterDev," or go to http://msdn.microsoft.com/workshop/author/css/css.asp.

Process for Adding Changeable Styles

Changing styles on a Web page entails completing the following three processes.

▶ **To change elements in an HTML document**

• Define two styles with class names and attributes.

▶ **To dynamically change a section of text**

1. Create an object with the **ID=** attribute.

2. Add a style class name to the section using the **CLASS=** attribute.

3. Add a script function name to the event attribute for the section.

▶ **To create a style-changing function**

• Create a separate script function that changes the style to one of those defined in the style tags.

Changing Styles Using the Style Object

You can change styles using the **Style** object for the element. Each CSS style is a property of the **Style** object for the element.

The following example code shows how to change an element's style inline:

```
<H1 id=myStyle onclick="this.style.color=blue">This text will
change to blue when clicked </H1>
```

Dynamic Positioning

Dynamic positioning enables you to change the placement of elements in the document. The **Positioning** attributes set for an element determine how it is affected by changes in the flow of the document, such as when the user resizes the browser window, or when content is added or removed.

The following describes the concepts involved with dynamic positioning.

♦ Absolute positioning

The x- and y- coordinates for the element are relative to the parent element, regardless of the position of any other elements. To copy this code for use in your own project, see "Nesting Absolute and Relative Positioned Elements" on the accompanying CD-ROM.

```
<HTML>
<HEAD><TITLE>Center the DIV</TITLE>
<SCRIPT LANGUAGE="JScript">
<!-
function doPosition() {
document.all.two.style.top = document.all.one.offsetHeight/2 -
document.all.two.offsetHeight/2;
document.all.two.style.left = document.all.one.offsetWidth/2 -
document.all.two.offsetWidth/2;
}
->
</SCRIPT>
<META HTTP-EQUIV="Content-Type" CONTENT="text/html;
CHARSET=iso8859-1">
<META NAME="MS.LOCALE" CONTENT="EN-US">
<META NAME="ROBOTS" CONTENT="all">
</HEAD>
<BODY TOPMARGIN=0 BGPROPERTIES="FIXED" BGCOLOR="#FFFFFF"
LINK="#000000" VLINK="#808080" ALINK="#000000"
onload="doPosition()">
```

code continued on next page

code continued from previous page

```
<!-TOOLBAR_START->
<!-TOOLBAR_EXEMPT->
<!-TOOLBAR_END->
<P>Some text in the beginning.</P>
<DIV ID=one STYLE="position:relative;
top:10;height:200;width:200;background-color:green">
Some text in the outer DIV
<DIV ID=two
STYLE="position:absolute;left:50;width:100;color:red;border:red2px
solid">
text in the inner DIV - color should be red
</DIV>
</DIV>
</BODY>
</HTML>
```

◆ Relative positioning

The x- and y- coordinates for the element are relative to the preceding element in the document. To copy this code for use in your own project, see "Creating Animated Content" on the accompanying CD-ROM.

```
<HTML>
<HEAD><TITLE>Glide the DIV</TITLE>
<SCRIPT LANGUAGE="JScript">
<!-
var action;
function StartGlide() {
  document.all.Banner.style.pixelLeft = document.body.offsetWidth;
  document.all.Banner.style.visibility = "visible";
  action = window.setInterval("Glide()",50);
}
function Glide() {
  document.all.Banner.style.pixelLeft -= 10;
  if (document.all.Banner.style.pixelLeft<=0) {
      document.all.Banner.style.pixelLeft=0;
      window.clearInterval(action);
  }
}
->
</SCRIPT>
```

code continued on next page

code continued from previous page

```
<META HTTP-EQUIV="Content-Type" CONTENT="text/html;
CHARSET=iso8859-1">
<META NAME="MS.LOCALE" CONTENT="EN-US">
<META NAME="ROBOTS" CONTENT="all">
</HEAD>
<BODY TOPMARGIN=0 BGPROPERTIES="FIXED" BGCOLOR="#FFFFFF"
LINK="#000000" VLINK="#808080" ALINK="#000000"
onload="StartGlide()">
<!-TOOLBAR_START->
<!-TOOLBAR_EXEMPT->
<!-TOOLBAR_END->
<BR><P>
<P>With dynamic positioning, you can move elements and their
content anywhere in the document even after the document has
loaded!
<DIV ID="Banner" STYLE="visibility:hidden;position:absolute;top:0;
left:0">Welcome to Dynamic HTML!</DIV>
</BODY>
</HTML>
```

◆ z-index

The z-index affects how elements positioned in the same place in the document are displayed. Positive z-index values are positioned above a negative (or lesser value) z-index value. Two elements with the same z-index value are stacked according to the order in which they appear in the HTML source code. To copy this code for use in your own project, see "Using Z-Order" on the accompanying CD-ROM.

```
<HTML>
<HEAD><TITLE>Stack the Image</TITLE>
<META HTTP-EQUIV="Content-Type" CONTENT="text/html;
CHARSET=iso8859-1">
<META NAME="MS.LOCALE" CONTENT="EN-US">
<META NAME="ROBOTS" CONTENT="all">
</HEAD>
```

code continued on next page

code continued from previous page

```
<BODY TOPMARGIN=0 BGPROPERTIES="FIXED" BGCOLOR="#FFFFFF"
LINK="#000000" VLINK="#808080" ALINK="#000000">
<!-TOOLBAR_START->
<!-TOOLBAR_EXEMPT->
<!-TOOLBAR_END->
<P STYLE="position:absolute; top:0; left:0">Text Over Image</P>
<IMG SRC="/msdn/sdk/inetsdk/samples/dhtml/overview/sample.jpg"
STYLE="position:absolute; top:0; left:0; z-index:-1">
</BODY>
</HTML>
```

◆ Visibility

Setting the **Visibility** property to **hidden** means that an element has a reserved space on the document but its contents are not visible on screen. Setting visibility to **visible** means that an element appears in the document. To copy this code for use in your own project, see "Display and Visibility Properties" on the accompanying CD-ROM.

```
<HTML>
<HEAD><TITLE>Visibility Demo</TITLE>
<STYLE>
P {font-weight:bold}
</STYLE>
<SCRIPT language=jscript>
<!-
function change_visibility() {
if (document.all.MyDiv1.style.visibility == "hidden") {
document.all.MyDiv1.style.visibility = "visible";}
  else{
document.all.MyDiv1.style.visibility = "hidden";
}
}
function change_display() {
if (document.all.MyDiv2.style.display == "") {
document.all.MyDiv2.style.display = "none";}
  else{
document.all.MyDiv2.style.display= "";
}
}
->
</SCRIPT>
```

code continued on next page

code continued from previous page

```
<META HTTP-EQUIV="Content-Type" CONTENT="text/html;
CHARSET=iso8859-1">
<META NAME="MS.LOCALE" CONTENT="EN-US">
<META NAME="ROBOTS" CONTENT="all">
</HEAD>
<BODY TOPMARGIN=0 BGPROPERTIES="FIXED" BGCOLOR="#FFFFFF"
LINK="#000000" VLINK="#808080" ALINK="#000000">
<!-TOOLBAR_START->
<!-TOOLBAR_EXEMPT->
<!-TOOLBAR_END->
<P> Click the Button to change the visibility of the DIV
<DIV ID=MyDiv1
STYLE="position:relative;top:10;left:20;height:100;width:100;
  visibility:hidden;background-color:blue"></DIV>
<P> A paragraph below the DIV element<br>
<BUTTON onclick=change_visibility() style="background-
color:blue;color:white">
Change Visibility
</BUTTON>
<HR>
<P> Click the Button to change the display of the DIV
<DIV ID=MyDiv2
STYLE="position:relative;top:10;left:20;height:100;width:100;
  display:none;background-color:green"></DIV>
<P> A paragraph below the DIV element<br>
<BUTTON onclick=change_display() style="background-
color:green;color:white">
Change Display
</BUTTON>
</BODY>
</HTML>
```

◆ Display

Setting the **Display** attribute to **none** means that an element does not appear in the document, and no space is reserved for it on screen. The element is completely removed from the flow of the document.

The differences among these concepts are based on the following facts about DHTML:

◆ A document has a default flow in which elements are consecutively placed on the page, with the spacing depending on the type of element and the content of the element.

◆ Elements can contain other elements (i.e., be parents of other elements). If an element is not contained by another element, its default parent is the <BODY> tag.

◆ Absolute positioning takes the element out of the default flow, and allows you to specify exact x-, y- coordinates relative to the parent of the element.

◆ Relative positioning leaves the element in the default flow, but allows you to specify exact x-, y- coordinates relative to the previous element in the document flow.

◆ When using absolute positioning and two or more elements occupy the same x-, y- position in the document, their z-order determines which is displayed on top of the other.

Dynamic Content

Dynamic content enables you to add or remove text or HTML content in an HTML document, without having to reload the page from the server. The Web browser will automatically reflow the document when you add or remove content.

To see an example of dynamic content in your Web browser, see dynamiccontent.htm on the accompanying CD-ROM.

Process for Adding Dynamic Content

The process for adding dynamic content is the same as for adding dynamic styles.

▶ **To add content to an element**

1. Add an **ID=** attribute.

2. Add event attributes and assign them function names.

3. Add script for each of the functions and assign the additional content to the **ID=** attribute.

4. Use the appropriate text or HTML property to add the content.

You add content using two different kinds of properties—text properties and HTML properties (described in the following table). Text properties insert text, including HTML tags, as text. For example the browser will read <H3> as the string <H3>, not as the HTML tag to render the following text as an H3. In contrast, the browser will read any tags within the HTML properties with the correct format.

The following tables list dynamic content properties and methods that you can use.

Text properties	HTML properties
innerText	innerHTML
outerText	outerHTML

Text methods	HTML methods
insertAdjacentText	insertAdjacentHTML

The **insertAdjacentText** and **insertAdjacentHTML** methods take two parameters — where and text. The following table describes the values for the parameter where.

Parameter	Description
BeforeBegin	Inserts the text immediately before the element.
AfterBegin	Inserts the text after the start of the element but before all other content in the element.
BeforeEnd	Inserts the text immediately before the end of the element but after all other content in the element.
AfterEnd	Inserts the text immediately after the end of the element.

Note   These parameters are case sensitive.

Creating a Dynamic Outline

You can create a dynamic outline using DHTML. A dynamic outline is a list of items that you add to or remove items from. You can also expand and collapse items in the outline at any time using parent items and child items.

Building an Outline Using Parent and Child Items

A parent item is associated with a graphic and a name and can contain zero or more child items. A parent item consists of a DIV element and contains an IMG element and another DIV element. The inner DIV is a container for all the child items for the parent. This nesting structure makes it easier to insert child items, and control the appearance of all the child items for a parent as a group.

The DIV for the parent item also has an ID. The ID is used to uniquely identify the parent and make it easy to locate it within the document. It also allows you to add new child items to a specific parent at any time. The following example code illustrates the HTML structure of a parent item:

```
<DIV ID=Id CLASS="parent">
<IMG CLASS="image" SRC="images/blue.gif" ALT="*" ALIGN=MIDDLE
BORDER=0 WIDTH=11 HEIGHT=11>Parent Name
<DIV CLASS="child">
</DIV>
</DIV>
```

In this example, a child item is a hyperlink that is inserted within its parent, and has the following HTML structure:

```
<A HREF="Url" CLASS="link">Child Name</A><BR>
```

Making the Outline Expand and Contract

In addition to adding and removing items, the dynamic outline supports expanding and collapsing items. The following example code is a VBScript procedure that expands and collapses all of the child items for a parent:

```
Sub ExpandCollapse()
  Dim objElement
  Dim objTargetDiv
  Dim imgIcon

  Set objElement = window.event.srcElement

  ' Did the user click the image or the parent name?
  If objElement.className = "parent" Then
      Set objTargetDiv = objElement.children(1)
      Set imgIcon = objElement.children(0)
  Else
      Set objTargetDiv = objElement.parentElement.children(1)
      Set imgIcon = objElement
  End If

  ' If the parent has children, expand or collapse them.
  If objTargetDiv.children.length > 0 Then
      If objTargetDiv.style.display = "none" Then
          objTargetDiv.style.display = ""
          imgIcon.src = "images/red.gif"
      Else
          objTargetDiv.style.display = "none"
          imgIcon.src = "images/blue.gif"
      End If
  End If
End Sub
```

This procedure expands or collapses all the child items by checking the class name of the element the user has clicked. It first checks to see if the user clicked the image or name of a parent item. It does this so it can get the element object for the inner DIV of the parent (which contains all its child items) and the element object for the image associated with the parent.

If the parent does have child items, it expands or collapses them and changes the image associated with the parent depending on the current state. If the child items are currently expanded, it sets their style to **display:none** to hide them, and changes the image to a blue triangle. If the child items are currently collapsed, it sets their style to **display:""** to make them visible, and changes the image to a red triangle.

Lab 3.2: Creating a Dynamic Outline

In this lab, you will use Dynamic HTML to create a dynamic outline for navigating the State University Web site. You will write client script that adds new items to the outline. You will write event handlers that change the appearance of the outline based on user input, and use the outline as the new Links page.

To see the demonstration "Lab 3.2 Solution," see the accompanying CD-ROM.

The following diagram shows how the files you edit in this lab will fit into the State University Web site.

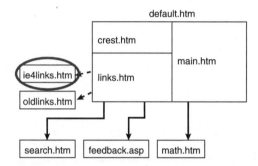

Estimated time to complete this lab: **60 minutes**

To complete the exercises in this lab, you must have the required software. For detailed information about the labs and setups for the labs, see "Labs" in "About This Course."

The solution code for this lab is located in the folder \Labs\Lab03.2\Solution.

Objectives

After completing this lab, you will be able to:

♦ Write script using the dynamic content features of Dynamic HTML to add and remove HTML content on a page.

♦ Write script using the dynamic styles features of Dynamic HTML to change the appearance of HTML elements on a page.

♦ Write script to handle events on a page and determine their source element.

Prerequisites

Before working on this lab, you should be familiar with the following:

◆ Opening Web projects in Visual InterDev, and adding HTML pages to the project.

◆ Creating and editing HTML pages in Visual InterDev.

◆ Writing and debugging VBScript code in Visual InterDev.

Exercises

The following exercises provide practice working with the concepts and techniques covered in this chapter:

◆ Exercise 1: Adding and Removing Items

In this exercise, you will write client script to create a dynamic outline on a page and add new items to the outline.

◆ Exercise 2: Changing the Appearance

In this exercise, you will write client script to change the appearance of the outline so items can be expanded and collapsed when the user clicks on them. You will write client script that changes the appearance of hyperlinks in the outline when the user moves the mouse cursor over them.

Exercise 1: Adding and Removing Items

In this exercise, you will write client script to create the dynamic outline, and write functions to dynamically add new items to the outline.

▶ **View the structure of the dynamic outline page**

Open Ie4links.htm in Visual InterDev and look at the structure of the page.

1. Locate the <STYLE> tag near the top of the page. You will be using the classes listed there with the different elements of the dynamic outline to change their appearance.

2. Locate the <DIV> tag with an ID of outlineDiv. You will be writing script to add HTML content within this tag after the page has already been loaded. You will add event handlers to handle events for all the tags enclosed within this <DIV> tag.

3. Remove the existing text within the <DIV> tag.

▶ **Add image files for the outline**

- Add the files Blue.gif and Red.gif from the \Labs\Lab03.2\New folder to the images subfolder of the project.

▶ **Write the script to add a parent item**

A parent item has a graphic and a name associated with it, and contains zero or more children items that are hyperlinks. For a description of the implementation of a dynamic outline using Dynamic HTML, see "Creating a Dynamic Outline" on page 143 in this chapter.

1. Create a client script block, and declare a global variable named intCount. Set its initial value to 0.

   It will be used to assign a unique ID to each parent.

2. Create a function named **AddParent**. It takes one argument named **strName**.

   This argument is the name that will be displayed in the outline for the parent.

3. Declare two variables in **AddParent** named strID and strTemp.

   These will be used to construct a unique ID for the parent, and to insert HTML for the parent, respectively.

4. Set the value of strID equal to the string "ID" concatenated with intCount.

5. Increment intCount.

   This will create a unique ID for the next parent added.

6. Set the value of strTemp equal to the text from the file Strtemp.txt in the \Labs\Lab03.2 folder. The file contains the new HTML content for the parent that includes its unique ID, its name, and the inner <DIV> tag to contain its child items.

   To insert the text go to Source view, click **Insert File as Text...** on the **Edit** menu, then select Strtemp.txt.

7. Call the **insertAdjacentHTML** method for **outlineDiv**. Use strTemp for the content and pass "BeforeEnd" as the first argument in order to include the new content within **outlineDiv**, before its closing tag.

   For more information about dynamically adding new HTML content to a document, see "Dynamic Content" on page 141 in this chapter.

8. Return strID from the function to identify the parent item that was added.

To see an example of how your code should look, see Lab Hint 3.3 in Appendix B.

▶ **Write the script to add a child item**

Each child item has an associated hyperlink. The script you write will add the following HTML for a child item within the parent you specify:

```
<A HREF="Url" CLASS="link">Child Name</A><BR>
```

1. Create a VBScript procedure named **AddChild**. It takes three arguments named **strParentID**, **strName**, and **strUrl**.

2. **strParentID** is the unique ID for the parent this child is to be added within. **strName** is the text to appear for the child in the outline, and **strUrl** is the URL for the hyperlink for the child.

3. Declare two variables in **AddChild** named strTemp and objTemp.

   strTemp will be used to insert the HTML for the child. objTemp will be used to store the **element** object for the parent once it is found on the page.

4. Set the value of strTemp equal to the following string:

```
"<A HREF=""" & strUrl & """ CLASS=""link"">" & strName & "</A><BR>"
```

   This is the new HTML content that will be added to the document for a child item.

5. Set the value of **objTemp** equal to the item in the **all** collection that has an ID of **strParentID**.

Note To assign an object to an object variable, use the VBScript **Set** statement.

For more information about document collections, see "Using Document Collections" on page 133 in this chapter.

6. Insert the content for the child within its parent. Use the **all** collection and call the **InsertAdjacentHTML** method. Remember that the <DIV> tag for each parent contains an inner <DIV> tag that will contain all the child items for that parent. To get to the inner <DIV> tag, use the **children** collection of the **all** collection. Use strTemp for the content and pass "BeforeEnd" as the first argument in order to include the new content within the inner <DIV> tag, before its closing tag.

To see an example of how your code should look, see Lab Hint 3.4 in Appendix B.

▶ **Test your work**

1. Create a **Window_OnLoad** procedure in Ie4links.htm. The code for the procedure is in the Onload.txt file in the \Labs\Lab03.2 folder.

2. Save your changes, and view Ie4links.htm in the browser. You should see the headings and links added to the page.

Exercise 2: Changing the Appearance

In this exercise, you will write client script to change the appearance of the dynamic outline so items can be expanded and collapsed when the user clicks them. You will write script to change the appearance of hyperlinks on the outline when the user moves the mouse cursor over them.

▶ **Make the child items hidden by default**

- In the **AddParent** function modify the string assigned to **strTemp** so that the last substring looks like the following:

```
"<DIV CLASS=""child""  STYLE=""display:none""></DIV></DIV>"
```

This adds the **display:none** style to the inner <DIV> tag of the parent. This will hide all the child items for the parent, so they are not visible on the outline by default.

For more information about element visibility, see "Dynamic Positioning" on page 136 in this chapter.

▶ **Add the script to expand and collapse items**

- Create a VBScript procedure named **ExpandCollapse** to expand and collapse all the child items for a parent. The code for the procedure is in the file Expandcollapse.txt in the \Labs\Lab03.2 folder.

For a complete description of how this code works, see "Creating a Dynamic Outline" on page 143 in this chapter.

▶ **Expand and collapse items when the user clicks on them**

1. Create a VBScript procedure named **DoClick**.

2. Write an **If...Then** statement to check the **className** property of the element that is the source of the event using the **srcElement** property of the **event** object. If **className** is equal to "parent" or "image" then call **ExpandCollapse**.

These are the class names that were included in the HTML when the parent was added to the page.

For more information about element objects, see "Using Element Objects" on page 131 in this chapter. For more information about event objects, see "Handling Events" on page 125 in this chapter.

3. Prevent the event from being bubbled up to parent elements by setting the **cancelBubble** property of the **event** object equal to **True**.

   To see an example of how your code should look, see Lab Hint 3.5 in Appendix B.

4. Modify the <DIV> tag for **outlineDiv** and add an **OnClick** event handler that calls **DoClick**, like the following code:

```
<DIV ID="outlineDiv" LANGUAGE="VBScript" ONCLICK="DoClick">
```

5. Save your changes, and view Ie4links.htm in the browser. Click on the images and names for parent items in the outline. You should see them expand and collapse their child items.

▶ **Change the color of links to red when the user moves the mouse cursor over them**

1. Declare a global variable named oldColor.

   This will be used to store the color style when changing the color of the link.

2. Create a VBScript procedure named **DoMouseOver**.

   This procedure will change the color of a link to red when the user moves the mouse cursor over it.

3. Add an **If...Then** statement and check the **tagName** property of the element that is the source of the event using the **srcElement** property. If **tagName** is equal to "A", meaning the source element is an anchor (hyperlink), then store the color style of the element in oldColor, and set its new value to "red".

4. Prevent the event from being bubbled up to parent elements by setting the **cancelBubble** property of the **event** object equal to **True**.

   To see an example of how your code should look, see Lab Hint 3.6 in Appendix B.

5. Modify the <DIV> tag for **outlineDiv** and add an **OnMouseOver** event handler that calls **DoMouseOver**, like the following:

```
<DIV ID="outlineDiv" LANGUAGE="VBScript" ONCLICK="DoClick"
ONMOUSEOVER="DoMouseOver">
```

▶ **Restore the old color of links when the user moves the mouse cursor off them**

1. Create a VBScript procedure named **DoMouseOut**.

    This procedure will restore the old color of a link when the user moves the mouse cursor off it.

2. Add an **If...Then** statement and check the **tagName** property of the element that is the source of the event using the **srcElement** property of the **event** object. If **tagName** is equal to "A", meaning the source element is an anchor (link), then restore the color style of the element to oldColor.

3. Prevent the event from being bubbled up to parent elements by setting the **cancelBubble** property of the **event** object equal to **True**.

    To see an example of how your code should look, see Lab Hint 3.7 in Appendix B.

4. Modify the <DIV> tag for **outlineDiv** and add an **OnMouseOut** event handler that calls **DoMouseOut**, like the following:

```
<DIV ID="outlineDiv" LANGUAGE="VBScript" ONCLICK="DoClick"
ONMOUSEOVER="DoMouseOver" ONMOUSEOUT="DoMouseOut">
```

5. Save your changes, and view Ie4links.htm in the browser. Click on the images and names for parent items in the outline to expand them. Then move the mouse cursor over links in the outline. You should see their color change to red when you move mouse cursor over them, and see their old color restored when you move the mouse cursor off them.

Creating DHTML Scriptlets

Scriptlets allow Web page authors to create reusable components with script, without having to harness the full power of C, C++, or other control-building environments.

Introducing Scriptlets

Microsoft Scripting Components (scriptlets) provide you with a way to create reusable controls and components. You create scriptlets using a scripting language such as JavaScript or Visual Basic Scripting Edition (VBScript).

A scriptlet is a complete Web-ready .htm file, but includes information that allows you to work with it as a control—you can get and set its properties, call its methods, and so on.

Advantages of Using Scriptlets

Scriptlets provide the following four advantages. They:

◆ Allow Web page authors to create reusable user interface components without having to harness the full power of C, C++, or other control-building environments.

◆ Allow developers using Visual Basic, Visual InterDev, and other development environments that support controls to make use of features built into Web pages.

◆ Are easy to create and maintain.

◆ Are small and efficient.

For example, with scriptlets you can:

◆ Use the graphical and hypertext capabilities of Web pages as a visually rich interface for an application (such as a calendar control that you can display in a Web page) in Visual Basic or in another environment.

◆ Create components that incorporate business rules that you can call from a Web server, a browser, or any other type of application.

◆ Prototype controls that you intend to write in other environments. Because writing a scriptlet is quick and easy, you can test ideas. When you have completed your design, you can reimplement the control in another environment, such as C++, Visual Basic, or J++, if you want greater performance or a different means of packaging your control.

Type of Scriptlets

There are two kinds of scriptlets—DHTML and server scriptlets. DHTML scriptlets are used in the browser, while server scriptlets are used in external applications or on a Web server. DHTML scriptlets typically display a user interface, while server scriptlets do not.

Exposing Methods and Properties

By default, the browser exposes standard methods and properties to scriptlets. Scriptlets expose standard properties, methods and events to the browser.

Using Standard Methods and Properties

The following table describes some of the methods and properties that the browser exposes.

Properties and methods	Description
Frozen property	Indicates whether the browser window containing the scriptlet is ready to handle events. Syntax *boolean = window.external.frozen*
bubbleEvent method	Sends event notification from the scriptlet to the browser window when a standard event has occurred. Syntax *window.external.bubbleEvent()*
raiseEvent method	Passes a custom event notification from the scriptlet to the browser window. Syntax *window.external.raiseEvent(eventName, eventObject)*
setContextMenu right-clicks	Constructs a context menu that is displayed when a user Method a scriptlet in the browser window. Syntax *window.external.setContextMenu(menuDefinition)*

The following table describes some of the properties that scriptlets expose.

Properties and methods	Description
Event property	Provides state information about a standard DHTML event passed from the scriptlet to the browser window. Syntax *value = ScriptID.event.member*
readyState property	Returns information about the load state of the scriptlet from the browser. Syntax *ScriptID.readyState = integer*

For more information on methods, properties, and events in scriptlets, see "Defining Properties and Methods in DHTML Scriptlets," and "Exposing Events in DHTML Scriptlets," in Visual InterDev Help.

Exposing Custom Methods and Properties

You can expose any number of properties and methods in VBScript by using the keywords described in the following table.

Scenario	Solution
To create a read/write property	Declare a variable scoped at the page level, and assign it the public_ prefix.
To create a readable property function	Define a function with the public_get_ prefix.
To create a writable property function	Define a function with the public_put_ prefix.
To create a method	Define a function with the public_ prefix.

The following example code creates a property function that imports the style sheet from a URL and makes it the style sheet for the current document.

```
Sub Public_Put_StyleSheet(strUrl)
    document.stylesheets(0).addImport(strUrl)
End Sub
```

Exposing Events

When you use a DHTML scriptlet in your Web page, you can be notified about events that occur in the scriptlet. A scriptlet can expose two types of events:

◆ Standard DHTML events such as the **onclick** event and the **onkeypress** event.

◆ Custom events, which are events that you define or DHTML events that are not provided as standard events. For example, a scriptlet can fire an event when a property value changes. You can expose custom events in either DHTML or server events.

Handling Standard Events

A DHTML scriptlet can expose the following standard DHTML events:

- onclick
- onkeypress
- onmousemove
- ondblclick
- onkeyup
- onmouseup
- onkeydown
- onmousedown

Standard events are triggered for the scriptlet container object. Use a custom event to pinpoint which control in the scriptlet triggered the event.

To work with standard events in the host application, you must write handlers in two places: one in the scriptlet to send the event, and another in the host application to capture the event.

The following list outlines the procedures for passing a standard event from a scriptlet to a host application.

▶ **To pass a standard DHTML event from a scriptlet**

1. Attach an event handler script to the event that you want to pass.

2. Within the event handler script, call the **bubbleEvent** method to send the event to the host application.

3. Check the scriptlet's **frozen** property to be sure that the container object is ready to handle events.

The following example code shows how you can pass a text box's **onkeyup** event to the host application:

```
<INPUT TYPE=text ONKEYUP="passKeyUp" NAME="t1" VALUE="">

<SCRIPT LANGUAGE="VBScript">
Sub passKeyUp
   // script statements here if required
    window.external.bubbleEvent
   // further script statements here if required
End Sub
</SCRIPT>
```

Creating and Handling Custom Events

Custom events allow you to:

◆ Notify the hosting page about non-standard changes in the scriptlet, such as when the value of a property changes.

◆ Send more detail about a standard event that occurred—for example, which of several buttons in the scriptlet was clicked.

◆ Notify the host page about DHTML events that are not among the standard events handled by the **bubbleEvent** method.

As with standard DHTML events, you must send the event from the scriptlet and capture the event in the host page.

The following listings show you how to send a custom event in the scriptlet to a host page.

▶ **To send a custom event in the scriptlet to the host page**

1. Check the scriptlet's **frozen** property to make sure that the host page is ready to handle events.

2. Call the scriptlet's **raiseEvent** method.

▶ **To handle a custom event in the host page**

• Create an event handler for the **onscriptletevent** event.

For example, the following example code shows how you can send a custom event called **oncolorchange** whenever the scriptlet's **backgroundColor** property is reset:

```
<SCRIPT LANGUAGE="VBScript">
Sub public_put_backgroundColor(value)

    window.document.bgColor = value
    window.external.raiseEvent
"event_onbgcolorchange",window.document
End Sub
</SCRIPT>
```

The following example code (in Visual Basic) shows how you can determine what control triggered an event:

```
Sub MyScriptlet_onscriptletevent(txtTitle, eventData)
    objName = eventData.srcElement.ID
    MsgBox "The event " & txtTitle & " occurred in " & objName
End Sub
```

Adding a Scriptlet to a Page

After you have created a DHTML scriptlet, you can use it in your applications. Using DHTML scriptlets is similar to using other controls and components.

If you are working with a Web page, you can use the <OBJECT> tag to reference the scriptlet. You can add a scriptlet to the Microsoft Visual InterDev Toolbox.

▶ **To add a DHTML scriptlet to the Toolbox**

- In Project Explorer, right-click the scriptlet's .htm file, and then choose **Mark As Scriptlet**.

An <OBJECT> tag containing a pointer to that scriptlet is added to the **Scriptlet** tab of the Toolbox. (If this is the first scriptlet on the Toolbar, the **Scriptlet** tab is created.) You can then drag the scriptlet from the Toolbox onto another page and automatically create the <OBJECT> tag necessary to implement the scriptlet.

Note When you add a scriptlet to the Toolbox, it includes the scriptlet's absolute URL. After you drag a scriptlet onto your page, you might need to modify the <OBJECT> tag's URL property in the Properties window or in Source view to make the link relative.

Alternatively, you can create an <OBJECT> tag yourself that references the scriptlet.

▶ **To refer to a DHTML scriptlet in an <OBJECT> tag**

- Create an <OBJECT> tag with the following syntax, substituting the scriptlet's URL and name for url/scriptletName:

```
<OBJECT ID="MyScriptlet" TYPE="text/x-scriptlet" WIDTH=300
HEIGHT=200>
    <PARAM NAME="url" VALUE="url/scriptletName">
</OBJECT>
```

After creating an instance of the DHTML scriptlet, you can write scripts for it as you would for any other control. The object you are using to work with properties and methods is the scriptlet host page; the exact properties and methods you can use are defined by the scriptlet identified in the container's URL property.

Before getting a scriptlet's properties or calling its methods, you must be sure that the scriptlet has been fully loaded. For details, see the container object's **onreadystatechange** event and **readyState** property, and the scriptlet's **frozen** property.

Lab 3.3: Creating an Outline Scriptlet

In this lab, you will create a reusable scriptlet that exposes methods, a property, and a custom event. You will use the script developed in Lab 3.2 to create a dynamic outline scriptlet, and will incorporate it into the Links page for the State University Web site.

To see the demonstration "Lab 3.3 Solution," see the accompanying CD-ROM.

The following diagram shows how the files you edit in this lab will fit into the State University Web site.

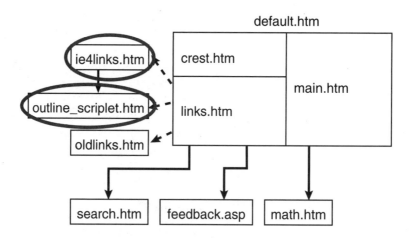

Estimated time to complete this lab: **45 minutes**

To complete the exercises in this lab, you must have the required software. For detailed information about the labs and setups for the labs, see "Labs" in "About This Course."

The solution code for this lab is located in the folder \Labs\Lab03.3\Solution.

Objectives

After completing this lab, you will be able to:

◆ Create a reusable scriptlet that exposes methods, properties, and a custom event.

◆ Incorporate a scriptlet into another page, and set up an event handler for a scriptlet event.

Prerequisites

Before working on this lab, you should be familiar with the following:

◆ Opening Web projects in Visual InterDev, and adding HTML pages to the project.

◆ Creating and editing HTML pages in Visual InterDev.

◆ Writing and debugging VBScript code in Visual InterDev.

Exercises

The following exercises provide practice working with the concepts and techniques covered in this chapter:

◆ Exercise 1: Exposing Methods and Properties

In this exercise, you will use the script developed in Lab 3.2 to create an outline scriptlet that exposes methods to add and remove parent items in the outline, and to add child items. You will also write script to expose a property for the scriptlet.

◆ Exercise 2: Exposing a Custom Event

In this exercise, you will write script to fire a custom event from the outline scriptlet when the user clicks on a child item in the outline that is a link.

◆ Exercise 3: Handling the Custom Event

In this exercise, you will write script to handle the custom event that the outline scriptlet fires when the user clicks on a hyperlink. You will write script to load the page the user selected into the main frame of the State University Web site.

Exercise 1: Exposing Methods and Properties

In this exercise, you will use the script developed in Lab 3.2 to create an outline scriptlet that exposes methods to add and remove parent items in the outline, and to add child items. You will also write script to expose a property for the scriptlet.

▶ **Add the outline scriptlet page to the Web project**

- Add the file Outline_scriptlet.htm from the \Labs\Lab03.3\New folder to the State University Web project in Visual InterDev.

   This file is a copy of Ie4links.htm you worked with in Lab 3.2. You will be modifying this file to convert it to a DHTML scriptlet.

▶ **Modify the procedure names to expose methods**

1. Add a prefix of **Public_** to the **AddParent, DeleteParent** and **AddChild** procedures.

   By adding the **Public_** prefix to the names of these procedures you are exposing them as public methods of the scriptlet.

   For more information about exposing methods and properties from a DHTML scriptlet, see "Exposing Methods and Properties" on page 152 in this chapter.

2. Modify the **AddParent** procedure so the return value is being assigned correctly. The return value should now be assigned to **Public_AddParent** because of the change in the procedure name.

▶ **Write script to expose a write-only property**

1. Create a VBScript procedure in Outline_scriptlet.htm and name it **Public_Put_StyleSheet**. It has one argument named **strUrl**.

   This procedure will expose a write-only public property that can be used to import a style sheet into the outline scriptlet. This enables the user of the scriptlet to specify a URL for any style sheet they want to use with the scriptlet to affect its appearance.

2. Write script to call the **AddImport** method of the **StyleSheet** object using the **stylesheets** collection of the **Document** object. Pass **strUrl** as the argument to **AddImport**.

   For more information about the **stylesheets** collection, see "Using Document Collections" on page 130 in this chapter.

   To see an example of how your code should look, see Lab Hint 3.8 in Appendix B.

▶ **Remove unneeded script and HTML from the page**

- Remove the **OnLoad** event handler from Outline_scriptlet.htm.

  This script is no longer needed for the scriptlet. It will be the responsibility of the pages hosting the scriptlet to add items to the outline.

▶ **Create a new Links page that uses the outline scriptlet**

1. In the Project Explorer window, mark Outline_scriptlet.htm as a scriptlet, so it is added to the Toolbox.

2. Create a new HTML page in Visual InterDev named Ie4links.htm that replaces the existing page in the project.

3. On the **Scriptlet** tab of the Toolbox, drag the outline scriptlet, named "StateU Links", to Ie4links.htm.

4. Select the scriptlet on the page, and in the Properties window set the following properties:

   a. Set (**Id**) equal to "outline".

   b. Set **height** equal to 100%.

   c. Set **width** equal to 100%.

   d. Set **Scrollbar** equal to **True**.

   For more information about including DHTML scriptlets on a page, see "Adding a Scriptlet to a Page" on page 157 in this chapter.

5. Create a **Window_OnLoad** procedure in Ie4links.htm. The code for the procedure is in the file Onload.txt in the \Labs\Lab03.3 folder.

6. Save your changes, and view Ie4links.htm in the browser. The dynamic outline as a scriptlet should behave just as it did in Lab 3.2.

Exercise 2: Exposing a Custom Event

In this exercise, you will write script to fire a custom event from the outline scriptlet when the user clicks on a link in the outline.

▶ **Create the procedure to fire the custom event**

1. Create a VBScript procedure in Outline_scriptlet.htm named **DoLinkEvent**.

2. Declare a variable named strUrl.

   This will store the URL for the link the user clicked.

3. Set strUrl equal to the **href** property of the **link** object that was clicked. Use the **srcElement** property of the **event** object to get the **link** object that was the source of the event.

4. To prevent the browser from doing the default action for a user clicking on a link, set the **returnValue** property of the **event** object equal to **False**

   By default, the browser will load the page that the link's URL points to. Instead of allowing the browser to do this, you will fire a custom event from the scriptlet, so the page that uses the scriptlet can decide how to handle the event.

   For more information on using **event** objects, see "Handling Events" on page 125 in this chapter.

5. Call the **raiseEvent** method to fire the custom event from the scriptlet, like the following:

```
window.external.raiseEvent "linkClick", strUrl
```

   You are passing the name for the custom event as "linkClick", and the URL for the link that was clicked in strUrl.

   For more information about using custom events with scriptlets, see "Exposing Events" on page 154 in this chapter.

   To see an example of how your code should look, see Lab Hint 3.9 in Appendix B.

▶ **Fire the event when the user clicks on a link**

- Add an **If...Then** statement to the **DoClick** procedure in Outline_scriptlet.htm to check if the source of the event was an anchor (hyperlink). Use the **tagName** property of the **element** object. If **tagName** is equal to "A", which indicates the source of the event was a link, then call **DoLinkEvent**, like the following code:

```
If window.event.srcElement.tagName = "A" Then
    DoLinkEvent
End If
```

▶ **Test your work**

1. For testing purposes add a call to the VBScript function **MsgBox** at the end of the **DoLinkEvent** procedure in Outline_scriptlet.htm. Display a message that the link event was fired.

2. Save your changes, and view Ie4links.htm in the browser. Expand items in the outline and click on a link. Verify that the message box is displayed indicating that the scriptlet fired the link event.

3. Remove the call to **MsgBox** in the **DoLinkEvent** procedure.

Exercise 3: Handling the Custom Event

In this exercise, you will write script to handle the custom event that the outline scriptlet fires when the user clicks on a hyperlink. You will write script to load the page the user selected into the main frame of the State University Web site.

▶ Write an event handler for the scriptlet event

1. Create a VBScript procedure in Ie4links.htm named **Outline_OnScriptletEvent**. It takes two arguments named **strEventName** and **varEventData**.

   The custom event the scriptlet fired is named **strEventName**. For the outline scriptlet it is "linkClicked." **varEventData** is any data associated with the event. For the outline scriptlet this is the URL for the link that the user clicked on.

2. Using the **frames** collection, set the **href** property of the **location** object for the frame named "main" to **varEventData**.

   By changing the **href** property to **varEventData** you are instructing the browser to load the page into the frame named "main".

   For more information about the **frames** collection and the **location** object, see "Using Browser Objects" on page 117 in this chapter.

To see an example of how your code should look, see Lab Hint 3.10 in Appendix B.

▶ Test your work

- View Default.htm in the browser. Expand items in the outline in the left frame and click on a link. Verify that the browser loads the page you selected.

Self-Check Questions

To see the answers to the Self-Check Questions, see Appendix A.

1. Assume you have an object defined in your Web page as follows:

```
<INPUT TYPE="BUTTON" NAME="ValidateOrder" VALUE="Order">
```

When a user clicks the button, you want to display a Validating Order message box. What do you need to do?

A. In a <SCRIPT> section of your Web page, create a procedure named **ValidateOrder_OnClick,** and add the appropriate code.

B. In a <SCRIPT> section of your Web page, create a procedure named **Order_OnClick,** and add the appropriate code.

C. Before you close the <INPUT> tag, create a procedure named **OnClick,** and add the appropriate code.

D. In an <EVENTS> section of your Web page, create a procedure named **Button_Click,** and add the appropriate code.

2. Which of the following is NOT a part of the browser object hierarchy?

A. Screen

B. Forms

C. Frames

D. Document

3. The Visual InterDev Debugger can be used for which of the following activities?

A. Debugging server-side script only.

B. Debugging client-side script only.

C. Viewing the relationships of files that comprise frames.

D. Debugging server and client scripts.

4. What types of procedures can you create with JavaScript?

   A. Functions

   B. Sub-procedures

   C. Event procedures

   D. All of the above

5. Why should you enclose client script in HTML comment tags (<!— —>)?

   A. Script-enabled browsers require that you use comment tags to distinguish script code from HTML code.

   B. To hide the script from users.

   C. To prevent browsers that do not support the <SCRIPT> tag from displaying the script in the HTML page.

   D. To help programmers understand the script code.

6. Which kind of scriptlets are normally used as visual controls?

   A. Active scriptlets.

   B. DHTML scriptlets.

   C. Automation scriptlets

   D. COM scriptlets.

7. In order to create a readable property function you need to?

   A. Define a function with the prefix `public_put_`.

   B. Create a **Public_Description** function.

   C. Define a function with the prefix `public_`.

   D. Define a function with the prefix `public_get_`.

8. Which statement about absolute positioning is True?

   A. Takes elements out of the default flow of text.

   B. Specifies the exact x, y position of the element relative to previous elements.

   C. Reflows content on the Web page as necessary.

   D. None of the above.

9. Which of the following steps is not part of the process needed to send a custom event in a scriptlet to a host application?

A. Call the **Scriptlet** event.

B. Call the scriptlet's **raiseEvent** method.

C. Create an event handler for the **onscriptletevent** event.

D. Check the scriptlet's **Frozen** property.

Chapter 4:
Using Active Server Pages

In this chapter, you will learn how to use Active Server Pages (ASP) in your Web application. You will also learn how to add server-side script that manipulates objects on a Web server and how to create a Web application.

ASP provides a server-side scripting environment that enables you to perform the following tasks:

◆ Read information from an HTTP request.

◆ Customize an HTTP response.

◆ Store information about a user.

◆ Extract the capabilities of the user's browser.

The following illustration highlights the technologies you will learn about in this chapter.

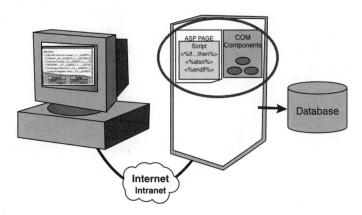

Objectives

After completing this chapter, you will be able to:

◆ List and describe types of ASP objects.

◆ Use the **Request** and **Response** objects to dynamically change an HTTP response.

◆ Create and use cookies.

◆ Process form data with server-side scripting.

◆ Save session-specific information by using the **Session** object.

◆ Save application-specific information by using the **Application** object.

◆ Use a COM component in your Web application.

◆ Set Internet Information Server and NTFS permissions.

◆ Allow and deny anonymous logon.

Assumed Skills

Before starting this chapter, you should be able to:

◆ Write client-side scripts.

Creating ASP Applications

In this section, you will learn how ASP applications are managed by Microsoft Internet Information Server, and about the protocol that they use.

Overview

Under Internet Information Server (IIS) 4.0, an application is any collection of files in a directory whose properties can be set and that can run in a separate process space. ASP applications are just one type of application that can run under IIS 4.0.

This topic explains what ASP applications are and describes two of their main features.

ASP applications are like conventional stand-alone applications. They can retain user information between sessions, or uses, of the application. These types of applications can also retain information while the user moves from one page to another.

ASP applications have two important features:

◆ A starting-point directory

◆ Global data

A Starting-Point Directory

When you create an application, you use Internet Service Manager to designate the application's starting-point directory for your Web site. All files and directories under the starting-point directory in your Web site are considered part of the application until another starting-point directory is found. You thus use directory boundaries to define the scope of an application. You can have more than one application per Web site, but each application must be configured differently. Visual InterDev handles all of these tasks for you when you create a new Web project.

Internet Information Server supports ASP, ISAPI, CGI, IDC, and SSI applications.

Note Under IIS 4.0, Web applications are handled like Visual Basic applications. That is, you can unload them in the same way that you can unload Visual Basic applications. You can also set your application to run in a process space separate from IIS.

Global Data

ASP applications declare global data in a Global.asa file. This optional file is processed by the Web server and can be used to make data available to all pages in the application.

A Global.asa file is processed automatically by the server whenever the following processes occur:

◆ The application starts or ends.

◆ Individual users start and stop browser sessions that access the application's ASP pages.

In a Global.asa file, you can:

◆ Initialize application or session variables.

◆ Declare COM components with application or session scope.

◆ Perform other operations that pertain to the application as a whole.

An application does not start until a user requests an ASP file in the starting-point directory.

Data Connections

One type of global data for any Web application is a data connection. If you intend your Web application to use data in an ODBC database, you connect to the database by adding a data connection to your Web application. Visual InterDev generates script within the Global.asa file to save all of the information for connecting to the database in application variables.

For information about data connections, see Chapter 5, "Accessing Databases" on page 231 and Chapter 6, "Understanding Data Access Technologies" on page 271.

HTTP Protocol

Web applications use Hypertext Transfer Protocol (HTTP) to implement communication between the browser and the server.

When a user requests a page, the browser creates an HTTP request message and sends it to the server. In response, the server creates an HTTP response message that is returned to the Web browser. The response message contains an HTML document.

An HTTP Session

The following illustration shows an HTTP session and the process that occurs when a user opens an HTML document on a Web server.

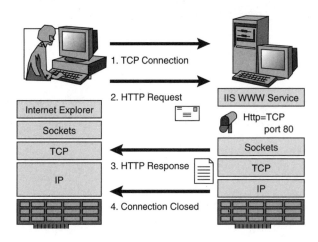

The following steps describe this process:

1. The browser creates a TCP/IP connection to the server.

2. The browser packages a request for an HTML document from the server into an HTTP request message, and then sends the message to the server by using a TCP/IP connection. The first line of the message contains the HTTP request method. For a simple page request, the **GET** method is used.

3. The server receives the HTTP request and processes it based on the request method contained in the request line.

4. The server then sends back an HTTP response message. Part of the response message is a status line that contains code indicating whether the attempt to satisfy the HTTP request was successful.

5. When the Web browser receives the HTTP response message, the TCP/IP connection is closed, and the HTTP session terminates.

If the requested HTML document contains embedded objects, such as graphic images, the browser makes subsequent requests for each embedded object. For example, if a page contains three GIF images, a background sound, and an ActiveX control, six separate HTTP sessions are required to retrieve the entire page—five for the embedded objects and one for the page itself.

Note If both the Web browser and Web server support HTTP Keep-Alive packets and retransmissions, connections are maintained even after a connection's initial request is completed. The connection is active and available for subsequent requests. Keep-Alives avoid the substantial cost of establishing and terminating connections. Keep-Alives are supported by Internet Information Server version 1.0 (and later), Internet Explorer version 2.0 (and later), and Netscape Navigator version 2.0 (and later).

Creating Server Script

In this section, you will learn about Active Server Pages and the objects they contain. You will also learn how to create and debug server scripts.

Introduction to Active Server Pages

Active Server Pages (ASP) are a type of Web application that use .asp files. The .asp extension tells the Web server that the page contains server script that it should process before returning the page to the browser.

The main difference between ASP and HTML pages is the location where the script is run. DHTML, or client script, is run on the client, in the browser, after the page is sent from the server. ASP, or server script, is run on the server before the page is sent to the browser. The Web server processes the script and generates the HTML pages that are returned to the Web browser.

Coding Active Server Pages

Server script and client script look very similar because they both use the same languages. The main difference is in how script blocks are specified. The following table highlights how different kinds of server script are specified.

Server Script Code Sample	Description

`<SCRIPT LANGUAGE=your_choice RUNAT=SERVER>`
`        some_server_script`
`</SCRIPT>`
	Preferred syntax, especially when writing functions. You can specify script language on a per-block basis. This method is easier to read and maintain.

`<% some_server_script %>`	Used for inline scripting. Uses the default script language for the page or project. Can be more difficult to read and maintain.
`<%= some_result %>`	Used for inline scripting to use the value of an expression.

In contrast, the following two snippets of sample code contain server and client script that adds date and time information to a page. The main difference is that the server script tells users the time and date at the server while the client script tells users the time and date at their computers.

Server script	Client script
| ```
<HTML>
<BODY>
<H3>Welcome to State U.</H3>
The time here is <%=Time()%><BR>
The date is <%=Date()%>.
</BODY>
</HTML>
``` | ```
<HTML>
<BODY>
<H3>Welcome to State U.</H3>
The time here is
<SCRIPT LANGUAGE=VBScript>
Document.Write time()
</SCRIPT>.<BR>
<SCRIPT LANGUAGE=VBScript>
Document.Write date()
</SCRIPT>.
</BODY>
</HTML>
``` |

ASP Processing Directives

You can use @ processing directives in your scripts to send information to IIS about how to process .asp files. For example, the following script uses the @LANGUAGE processing directive to set the scripting language to VBScript.

```
<%@Language=VBScript
Dim myvar
Application("myvar") = This is my var
Response.Write(myvar)
%>
```

The following five @ processing directives are supported by ASP in IIS 4.0.

◆ @CODEPAGE

◆ @ENABLESESSIONSTATE

◆ @LANGUAGE

◆ @LCID

◆ @TRANSACTION

ASP Built-In Objects

Because script in ASP pages runs on the server, it has access to a number of objects available on the server. The following table describes these objects:

Object	Description
Request	Retrieves the values that the browser passes to the server during an HTTP request.
Response	Controls what information is sent to a browser in the HTTP response message.
Session	Used to manage and store information about a particular user session.
Application	Used to manage and store information about the Web application.
Server	Provides access to resources that reside on a server.
ObjectContext	Used to commit or abort a transaction managed by Microsoft Transaction Server (MTS) for ASP pages that run in a transaction. For more information about MTS, see "MTS and Active Server Pages" on page 373 in Chapter 8, "Using Microsoft Transaction Server."

With Active Server Pages, you can:

◆ Retrieve information passed from the browser to the server using the **Request** object.

◆ Send output to the browser using the **Response** object.

◆ Store information for a specific user using the **Session** object.

◆ Share information among all users of your application using the **Application** object.

◆ Work with the properties and methods of components on the server using the **Server** object.

Using the Script Outline for Server Script

You use Script Outline to develop server script as you do to develop client script.

To see the demonstration "Using the Script Outline for Server Script," see the accompanying CD-ROM.

In its initial state, the tree view of Script Outline displays the nodes described in the following table.

Node	Description
Client objects and events	The elements that support client script or have client script attached to them with a list of events for the elements.
Client scripts	The client script for the page with each function or subroutine defined within the script block.
Server objects and events	The elements that support server script or have server script attached to them with a list of events for the elements.
Server scripts	The server script for the page with each function or subroutine defined within the script block.

Note This topic discusses server objects, events, and scripts. For information about client objects, events, and scripts, see "Using the Script Outline for Client Script" on page 108 in Chapter 3, "Using Dynamic HTML."

The following illustration shows Script Outline for a sample page in Source view.

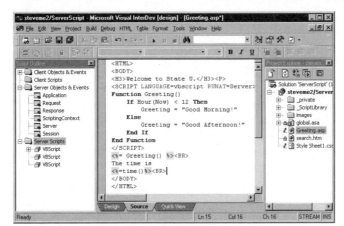

Using the Script Outline Window

Script Outline generates either VBScript or JavaScript, depending on your default scripting language settings.

▶ To set the default language for a project

1. Right-click the project file in the Project Explorer window and click **Properties**.

2. Click the **Editor Defaults** tab.

3. Select the default language from the **Server** drop-down list box in the **Default script language** option group.

If Script Outline is not open when you open a window, you can open it manually.

▶ To open Script Outline for a page

1. On the **View** menu, click **Other Windows**.

2. Select **Script Outline** from the pop-up menu.

Instead of creating a script block manually, you can let Script Outline create a script template for you.

▶ To add a server script block to a page

1. Place the cursor at the location for the script block.

2. Right-click and select **Script Block** from the pop-up menu.

3. Select **Server** from the second pop-up menu.

Adding Objects and Writing Script for Them

When you add design-time and server components to a page in your project, the HTML editor adds the ID for the object and all the events associated with the object to Script Outline.

▶ **To add a Textbox design-time control to a project**

1. Click the **Design-Time Controls** tab in the Toolbox.

2. Move the **Textbox** control to an appropriate location on the page. The HTML editor will add the ID for the textbox to Script Outline under **Server Objects and Events**.

3. The editor will also add header and footer information to the page for handling data from the control.

Note Design-time controls can be targeted for client or server script, which determines the node in which they will appear. For more information, see "How Data-Bound Controls Work" on page 245 in Chapter 5, "Accessing Databases."

Debugging Server Script

Before you can debug script in ASP pages, you must first enable debugging.

To debug scripts in ASP, you must be running Microsoft Internet Information Server (IIS) version 4.0 or later.

▶ **To enable script debugging in ASP pages**

1. In the Project Explorer window, right-click the project and click **Properties** to display the **Property Pages** dialog box.

2. Click the **Launch** tab.

3. Under **Server script**, make sure **Automatically enable ASP server-side debugging on launch** and **Automatically enable ASP client-side debugging on launch** are checked.

When these options are set, Visual InterDev checks to see that the server is correctly configured for debugging. This includes:

♦ Setting the IIS application to run in its own memory space.

♦ Enabling the IIS application's debugging options.

♦ Setting up a Microsoft Transaction Server package to allow you to attach the debugger to the Web application.

When you quit your debugging session, Visual InterDev restores the server debugging settings and out-of-process settings to their previous values.

You can set breakpoints in server script, client script, or both. If you set breakpoints in both, the debugger will stop at the server script breakpoints first. When you continue to run and the page is sent to the browser, the debugger will then stop at breakpoints in the client script.

Handling Run-Time Errors

Handling run-time errors in server script uses many of the same tools that are used for client script. The most important tools are the **On Error Resume Next** statement and the **Err** object.

For more information on both topics, see "Handling Run-Time Errors in Client Script" on page 112 in Chapter 3, "Using Dynamic HTML."

Reading Requests and Sending Responses

A Web application can use information from an HTTP request when a user requests an HTML document.

For example, when a user submits a form by using the **POST** method, the values of the controls on the form will be passed in the body of the HTTP request. A Web application can then read these values and use them to return a customized HTML document to the user.

In this section, you will learn how to read and use the information provided by a user.

HTTP Request and Response Messages

Communication between Web browsers, or clients, and servers via HTTP consists of two actions:

1. A request by a browser for a page.
2. A response by the server with that page.

The request from the browser can come in one of two forms:

1. A request to simply retrieve a page.
2. A request with information to be used on the page before the page is returned to the browser.

To handle this exchange of data, HTTP request and response messages have two parts: a header and a body. The following illustration shows these two parts.

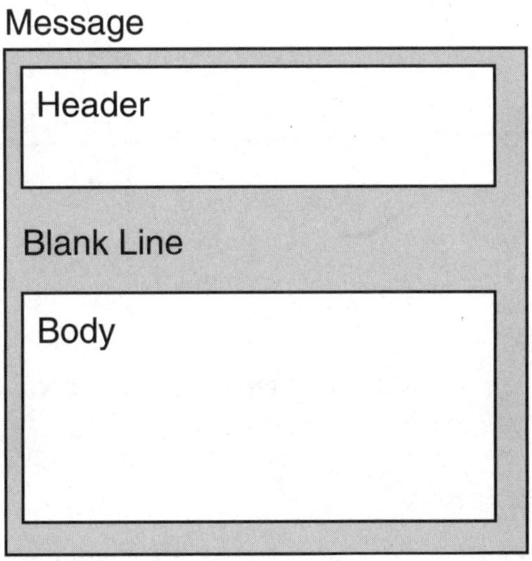

Message

The header contains one or more header fields (described in the following table). The body contains information sent by the browser or the server. For example, when a browser requests a page from a server, only header information is necessary. When a browser requests a page and form data is included in the request, both the header and the body are used. Responses from servers typically use both header and body information.

The following table lists the types of header fields and describes the types of messages they use.

Header field	Message type	Description
Content-Type	Request and Response	The media type contained in the body.
Date	Request and Response	The date and time the message was generated.
Expires	Response	The date and time the content should be considered obsolete.
From	Request	The Internet e-mail address of the user running the browser.
If-Modified-Since	Request	Used with the **GET** request method to return a page only if it has been modified after the specified date.
Location	Response	The absolute URL of the page.
Refer	Request	The URL initiating the request.
User-Agent	Request	Information about the client software initiating the request.

For more information about header fields, go to the HTTP Specification Web site at http://www.w3.org/pub/WWW/Protocols/Specs.html.

HTTP Request Messages

Each HTTP message contains an element that uniquely identifies it. For an HTTP request message, this identifier is the method line (also referred to as the method field).

A request method line has the following basic syntax:

```
HTTP-method    resource-identifier    HTTP/version
```

The method will be either **GET** or **POST**, the resource identifier is the requested file, and the HTTP/version is the version number of the HTTP protocol being used in the request.

For example, a request to view the URL http://www.company.com/default.htm will use this method line:

```
GET default.htm HTTP/1.0
```

Note The domain name for the resource identifier is unnecessary because the HTTP request message created a TCP/IP communication session prior to establishing a connection with the server.

The following table describes two important types of HTTP methods.

HTTP method	Description
GET	Retrieves a specified page. This is the default method of a request.
POST	Sends data to a page.

With the **GET** method, any information will be appended to the HTTP request for a page and sent in the message header. The size of the information sent with the **GET** method is limited to 1024 characters.

With the **POST** method, any data is sent in the body of the HTTP request message.

HTTP Response Messages

The header of a response message is composed of a status line and any additional response header fields.

The body section, if present, is preceded by a blank line.

The Request Object

The **Request** object provides access to any information that is passed to the Web server from the browser.

Request Object Collections

The **Request** object contains five collections that you can use to extract information from an HTTP request.

The following table lists and describes these five collections.

Collection	Description
ClientCertificate	The values of the certification fields in the HTTP request.
Cookies	The values of cookies sent in the HTTP request.
Form	The values of form elements posted to the body of the HTTP request message by the form's **POST** method.
QueryString	The values of variables in the HTTP query string, specifically the values following the question mark (**?**) in an HTTP request.
ServerVariables	The values of predetermined Web server environment variables.

For more information about the **Request** object, search for "Request Object" in Visual InterDev Help. For more information about the **ClientCertificate** object, see "ClientCertificate" in Visual InterDev Help.

Using the Request Object

Each collection of the **Request** object contains variables that you use to retrieve information from an HTTP request.

In the following example code, the SERVER_NAME variable of the ServerVariables collection retrieves the name of the Web server:

```
Request.ServerVariables("SERVER_NAME")
```

You can use the values of these variables to return information to the user.

In the following example code, the name of the Web server is used to create a hyperlink to an HTML document on the same server:

```
<A HREF="http://<%= Request.ServerVariables("SERVER_NAME")%>
/MyPage.asp">Link to MyPage</A>
```

Using the QueryString Collection

You use the **QueryString** collection of the **Request** object to extract information from the header of an HTTP request message. For example, when a user submits a form with the **GET** method, or appends parameters to a URL request, you use the QueryString collection to read the submitted information.

The values you read from the request are the parameters that appear after the question mark (?).

> **Tip** The **QueryString** collection is a parsed version of the QUERY_STRING variable of the **ServerVariables** collection. The **QueryString** collection enables you to retrieve the QUERY_STRING parameters by name.

For example, a user clicks the **Submit** button on the following form:

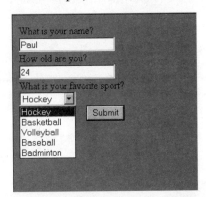

As a result, the following HTTP request is made:

```
http://name_age.asp?name=Paul&age=24&sport=Hockey
```

You can loop through all of the values in a query string to extract information passed by the user.

The following example code loops through all of the values in an HTTP request:

```
<%For Each Item In Request.QueryString
  'Display the Item
Next %>
```

If more than one value is submitted with the same value name (which can occur with a multi-select list box on a form), you can use the index of the QueryString collection variable to access the individual values.

The following example code shows how to access the first and second values of a variable called "sport" in the QueryString collection:

```
Request.QueryString("sport")(0)
Request.QueryString("sport")(1)
```

Using the Form Collection

You use the Form collection of the **Request** object to extract information from the body of an HTTP request message.

Tip If the form method is GET, the **QueryString** collection will contain all information passed in the form.

The Form collection contains the values of each standard HTML control that has a **NAME** attribute. When a user submits a form with the **POST** method, you can read the values of the controls by using the Form collection.

For example, a user completes and submits a form with the following HTML:

```
<FORM ACTION="submit.asp" METHOD=POST>
Name: <INPUT TYPE=TEXT NAME="name"><P>
Favorite Color: <SELECT MULTIPLE NAME="color">
                    <OPTION>Red
                    <OPTION>Green
                    <OPTION>Blue
                </SELECT><P>
<INPUT TYPE=SUBMIT NAME="cmdSubmit" VALUE="Submit">
</FORM>
```

You can read the submitted information by using the following script in the Submit.asp file:

```
Request.Form("name")
Request.Form("color")
```

You can also loop through all of the values on a form to extract information passed by the user.

The following example code loops through all of the standard HTML controls in an HTTP request:

```
<% For Each Item in Request.Form
  'Display Item
Next %>
```

If more than one value is submitted for a control on a form with the same value (which can occur with a multi-select list box), you can use the index of the Form collection variable to access the individual values.

The following example code shows how to access the first and second color values selected in the color list box:

```
Request.Form("color")(0)
Request.Form("color")(1)
```

Posting Values to a Form

With Active Server Pages, you can define a form that posts its input values back to the .asp file that contains the form. To do this, you break the .asp file into two parts —one part that displays the form and a second part that responds to the submitted form.

To determine whether a request for an Active Server Page has resulted from the form being submitted, you test to see if the HTML controls contain values. If the controls do not contain values, the user has not yet submitted the form. Therefore you need to display a blank form that the user can complete and submit.

The following example code displays a blank form:

```
<% If IsEmpty (Request.Form("txtName")) Then
  ' Display form
Else
  ' Form was submitted
End If %>
```

The Response Object

The **Response** object enables you to control the information sent to a user by the HTTP response message.

Properties and Methods of the Response Object

The **Response** object provides properties and methods that you can use when sending information to the user.

The following table describes some properties of the **Response** object.

Property	Description
Buffer	Indicates whether a response is buffered.
Expires	Specifies the length of time before a page cached on a browser expires. If the user returns to the same page before it expires, the cached version is displayed.
ExpiresAbsolute	Specifies the date and time on which a page cached on a browser will expire.
IsClientConnected	Indicates if the client has disconnected from the server since the last **Response.Write**.
Status	Specifies the value of the status line returned by the server. Status values are defined in the HTTP specification.

The following table describes some methods of the **Response** object.

Method	Description
Clear	Clears any buffered response.
End	Stops the processing of a Web page and returns whatever information has been processed thus far.
Flush	Sends buffered output immediately.
Redirect	Sends a redirect message to the user, causing the response message to try to connect to a different URL.
Write	Writes a variable to the current HTTP output as a string.

The **Response** object also contains the Cookies collection, which you can use to specify the values of cookies. For information about cookies, see "Using Cookies" on page 197 in this chapter.

For more information about the **Response** object, search for "Response Object" in Visual InterDev Help.

Response Object Syntax

You use the following syntax for the properties and methods of the **Response** object:

```
Response.property|method
```

In the following example code, the **Expires** property of the **Response** object is set to 0. This indicates that the content of the response message returned to the user will expire immediately.

```
<% Response.Expires = 0 %>
```

If the user refreshes the page, the browser will not read it from its cache, but will need to request it again from the Web server.

The Write Method

You use the **Write** method of the **Response** object to send information to a user from within the server-side script delimiters.

Write Method Syntax

The **Write** method adds text to the HTTP response message, as shown in the following example code:

```
Response.Write variant
```

The variant can be any data type (including characters, strings, and integers) that is supported by your default scripting language.

The variant cannot contain the character combination %>, which is used to denote the end of a script statement. Instead, you can use the escape sequence %\>, which the Web server will translate when it processes the script.

Note If VBScript is your default scripting language, don't use a variable longer than 1022 characters.

Using the Write Method

The following example code uses the **Write** method within a loop to display the values of each standard HTML control on a form that is sent in an HTTP request:

```
<%For Each Item In Request.Form
  Response.Write Item
Next %>
```

In the following example code, an HTML tag is added to a Web page:

```
<% Response.Write "<TABLE WIDTH = 100%\>" %>
```

The string returned by the **Write** method cannot contain the characters %> in an HTML tag, so the escape sequence %\> is used instead.

Buffering Data

To prevent the Web server from sending the HTTP response to the user until all server-side script on the current Active Server Page has been processed, you can buffer the content of the response message.

Note Waiting for the server to finish processing all server-side script may cause a lengthy delay. To send pieces of the response to the user, you can use the **Flush** method of the **Response** object throughout your code.

Setting the Buffer Property

To enable buffering, you set the **Buffer** property to **True**, as shown in the following example code:

```
Response.Buffer = True
```

Note You cannot set the **Buffer** property after the server has sent output to the user. For this reason, you should set the **Buffer** property in the first line of the .asp file.

Handling Errors with Buffering

If an error occurs during processing, you can use the **Redirect** method of the **Response** object, with buffering enabled. First, you clear the buffer with the **Clear** method, and then you use the **Redirect** method.

When an error occurs, the following example code will clear the buffer and redirect the user to an error page:

```
Response.Buffer = True
On Error Resume Next
'code that may cause an unrecoverable error,
'such as failing to open a data connection
If Err.number <> 0 Then
  Response.Clear
  Response.Redirect "error.htm"
End If
```

The Redirect Method

Instead of sending content from the response message to the user, you can use the **Redirect** method to redirect the user to another URL.

Redirect Method Syntax

When you use the **Redirect** method of the **Response** object, you provide the URL as an argument to the method.

```
Response.Redirect URL
```

The URL specifies the absolute or relative location to which the browser is redirected.

Note If you use the **Redirect** method after information has already been sent to the user, an error message will be generated.

Using the Redirect Method

The following example code uses the **Redirect** method to display a page in high or low resolution, depending on the user's screen resolution:

```
<%
If Request.ServerVariables("HTTP_UA_PIXELS") = "640x480" Then
  Response.Redirect "lo_res.htm"
Else
  Response.Redirect "hi_res.htm"
End If
%>
```

Note In addition to doing redirects programmatically with ASP, an IIS 4.0 administrator can also change settings through Internet Service Manager to redirect requests for files in a directory to other files or programs.

Practice: Sending a Response

In this practice exercise, you will create an Active Server Page that displays values in the query string of a request. Remember that the query string is made up of all the named values that appear after the question mark (?) in a URL.

▶ **Display all the values from the query string**

1. Create a new ASP file in Visual InterDev.

2. Insert a server script block in the file.

3. Add some server script that uses the **Write** method to create a response that displays all the values in the **QueryString** collection.

4. View the ASP file in the browser, and test it with different query strings.

▶ **Display a named value from the query string**

1. Add server script that displays the value for a specific item in the query string called "sport".

2. View the ASP file in the browser, and test it using different values for the item called "sport".

Saving State Data

ASP enables you to maintain state in a Web application. State is the ability to retain user information in a Web application. You can maintain two types of state data for a Web application:

◆ Application state

  Information is available to all users of a Web application.

◆ Session state

  Information is available only to a user of a specific session.

You can also maintain state on a user's computer by using cookies.

In this section, you will learn how to maintain state in a Web application.

The Application Object

You can use the **Application** object to share information among all users of a Web application. For example, you might store the total number of visitors to a Web site in an application-level variable.

An **Application** object is created when the user of the application requests an .asp file from the starting-point directory of the ASP application. It is destroyed when the application is unloaded.

Using Application Variables

In the following example code, MyVar is a variable that contains a string. MyObj is a component instance. To assign a component instance to an application variable, you use the VBScript **Set** statement.

```
<% Application("MyVar") = "Hello"
Set Application("MyObj") = Server.CreateObject("MyComponent") %>
```

Locking and Unlocking the Application Object

All users share the same **Application** object, so it is possible that two users might attempt to modify the object simultaneously. The **Lock** and **Unlock** methods of the **Application** object prevent this possibility.

To reduce the inconvenience of a user not being able to access the **Application** object when it is necessary, try to minimize the amount of time you use the **Lock** method.

The following example code shows how to use the **Lock** and **Unlock** methods when changing the value of a hit counter used in a Web application:

```
<%
Application.Lock
Application("NumVisits") = Application("NumVisits") + 1
Application.Unlock
%>
This application has been visited
<%= Application("NumVisits") %> times.
```

Notice that the **Application** object needs to be locked only while it is being modified.

The Session Object

You use the **Session** object to store information that is needed for a particular user session. Variables stored in the **Session** object will not be discarded when the user goes between pages in the Web application. Instead, these variables will persist for the entire user session.

The Web server automatically creates a **Session** object when a session starts. When the session expires or is abandoned, the Web server will destroy the **Session** object.

A session can begin in three ways:

◆ A new user requests a URL that identifies an .asp file in an application, and the Global.asa file for that application includes a **Session_OnStart** procedure.

◆ A user stores a value in the **Session** object.

◆ A user requests an .asp file in an application, and the application's Global.asa file uses the <OBJECT> tag to instantiate an object with session scope. See "Using COM Components" on page 197 in this chapter for more information about using the <OBJECT> tag to instantiate an object.

A session automatically ends if a user has not requested or refreshed a page in an application for a specified period of time. This value is 20 minutes by default. You can change the default for an application by setting the **Session Timeout** property on the **Application Options** tab of the Application Configuration property sheet in Internet Service Manager. Set this value according to the requirements of your Web application and the memory capacity of your server. For example, if you expect that users browsing your Web application will linger on each page for only a few minutes, then you may want to significantly reduce the session time-out value from the default. A long session time-out period can result in too many open sessions, which can strain your server's memory resources.

If, for a specific session, you want to set a time-out interval that is shorter than the default application time-out interval, you can also set the **Timeout** property of the **Session** object. For example, the following script sets a time-out interval of 5 minutes:

```
<% Session.Timeout = 5 %>
```

You can also set the time-out interval to be greater than the default value, the value determined by the **Session Timeout** property.

You can also explicitly end a session with the **Abandon** method of the **Session** object. For example, you can provide a **Quit** button on a form with the ACTION parameter set to the URL of an .asp file that contains the following command:

```
<% Session.Abandon %>
```

A session starts the first time a user requests an .asp file. When the session starts, the Web application generates a session ID. The session ID is stored as a cookie that is sent back to the browser.

Disabling Cookies

If a user selects **Disable all cookie use** on the **Advanced** tab of the **Internet Options** dialog box of Internet Explorer, the session ID cookies cannot be created for that user.

Session state can be disabled through the Internet Service Manager and through the following ASP processing directive:

```
<%@ ENABLESESSIONSSTATE=True|False %>
```

For more information on how ASP creates and manages session IDs, see Visual InterDev Help.

Session Object Syntax

The **Session** object has two properties and one method that use the following syntax:

```
Session.property|method
```

The following table describes the uses for these features.

Feature	Description
SessionID property	Used to determine the session identification of a user.
Timeout property	Used to set the amount of time that needs to elapse before the server can shutdown an unused session.
Abandon method	Used to destroy a **Session** object and release its resources.

Using the Session Object

The **Session** object enables you to create values that store information about a user.

For example, you can create and store the nickname and hometown values of a user with the following code:

```
<% Session("nickname") = "Nancy"
Session("hometown") = "Redmond %>
```

The following example code shows how to use the information stored in the **Session** object:

```
Hello <%= Session("nickname") %>.<BR>
How is the weather in <%= Session("hometown") %>?<BR>
```

Handling Application and Session Events

Application and **Session** objects both have **On_Start** and **On_End** events.

Application Object Events

The **Application** object has the two events **Application_OnStart** and **Application_OnEnd**. You can add script to these events in the Global.asa file.

Any script you add to the **Application_OnStart** event will run when the application starts. Conversely, any script you add to the **Application_OnEnd** event will run when the application ends.

The following example code shows how to add the **Application_OnStart** event to the Global.asa file:

```
<SCRIPT LANGUAGE=VBScript RUNAT=Server>
Sub Application_OnStart
  'Your Code Here
End Sub
</SCRIPT>
```

Session Object Events

Similar to the **Application** object, the **Session** object has the **Session_OnStart** and **Session_OnEnd** events. Any script you add to the **Session_OnStart** event will run when a user without an existing session requests an .asp file from your application. Any script you add to the **Session_OnEnd** event will run when a user session ends.

You can use the **Session_OnStart** event to direct users to a page that logs on to your site, regardless of which ASP file they request from your Web application.

The following sample code directs users to a log-in page. To copy this code for use in your own project, see "Session_OnStart Redirect" on the accompanying CD-ROM.

```
'when a session starts, redirect the user to a logon page
Sub Session_OnStart
  If Session("username") = "" Then
      'save the name of the page the user wanted to visit
      Session("startpage") = Request.ServerVariables("SCRIPT_NAME")
      'redirect them to a logon page
      Response.Redirect "profile.htm"
  End If
End Sub
```

Using Cookies

Cookies are a mechanism by which state can be maintained in a file on the user's computer. For example, user preferences or other personalization information that should be saved between sessions would be stored in cookies. A cookie file is typically stored in a folder named Cookies.

A cookie is like a token for a specific page that a Web server sends to a user. The user sends the cookie back to the server during each subsequent visit to that page or to a number of pages.

Cookies enable information to be associated with a user. You can set and get the values of cookies by using the Cookies collection.

When the Web server returns an HTTP response to a user, the response message may also include a cookie. The cookie includes a description of the saved range of URLs for which that cookie is valid.

A cookie is introduced to the user by including a Set-Cookie header as part of an HTTP response. Any HTTP requests made by the user included in that range will provide a transmittal of the current value of the cookie from the user back to the server.

Creating Cookies

To set the value of cookies that your Web server sends to a user, you use the Cookies collection of the **Response** object. If the cookie does not already exist, Response.Cookies collection will create a new cookie on the user's computer.

The following example code creates a cookie with the city set to Redmond:

```
<% Response.Cookies("city")="Redmond" %>
```

If you want the cookie to apply to all of the pages in your Web application, you set the **Path** attribute of the cookie to "/". For example:

```
Response.Cookies("city").Path = "/"
```

The cookie will then be sent by the browser during each request for a page in your Web application.

You can set other attributes for cookies, such as a cookie's expiration date:

```
Response.Cookies("Type").Expires = "July 31, 1998"
```

Using Cookies

The browser will send cookies to the appropriate pages in your Web application. To read the value of a cookie, you use the Cookies collection of the **Request** object.

For example, if the HTTP request sends a cookie with the city set to Redmond, then the following example code will retrieve the value of Redmond:

```
<%= Request.Cookies("city") %>
```

For more information about cookies, search for "Cookies" in Visual InterDev Help.

To see a sample site and VBScript code that uses cookies to store user-supplied information, go to http://msdn.microsoft.com/workshop/essentials/webmen/webmen0527.asp#cookies.

Using COM Components

You can run COM components (formerly known as Automation servers) on a Web server in response to a user request. These components enable you to extend the functionality of an Active Server Page with any resource, such as a database, located on the Web server.

In this section, you will learn how to use COM components in your Web application.

Creating Component Instances

To use a server component, you first need to understand how to create an instance of a component, or an object. There are two ways to create an object. You can use:

♦ The <OBJECT> tag
♦ Server.CreateObject syntax

Using the <OBJECT> Tag

You can use the <OBJECT> tag to create a component that runs on the Web server.

To use the <OBJECT> tag, you set the **RUNAT** attribute to **Server**. You can set the scope of the component by setting the **SCOPE** attribute to **Application** or **Session**. If you do not set the **SCOPE** attribute, the component will have page scope, meaning it can only be referenced on the current page. To specify the type of component to be created, you can use either its registered name, PROGID, or its registered number, CLASSID.

In the following example code, the registered name (PROGID) is used to create a session-scope instance of the fictitious component:

```
<OBJECT RUNAT=Server SCOPE=Session ID=MyComp
PROGID="MS.MyComponent">
</OBJECT>
```

In the following example code, the registered number (CLASSID) method is used to create an application-scope instance of MyComponent:

```
<OBJECT RUNAT=Server SCOPE=Application ID=MyComp
CLASSID="Clsid:00000293-0000-0010-8000-00AA006D2EA4"></OBJECT>
```

When you use the <OBJECT> tag to declare a session-scope or application-scope instance of a component, the variable you assign to the component is stored in the session or application namespace. You do not need to use the **Session** or **Application** objects to access the instance of the component.

The following example code opens the instance of MyComponent that has been declared in the previous example code:

```
<%= MyComp.GetSomething("some.txt") %>
```

Note When you drag a component from the Server Objects tab of the Toolbox, Visual InterDev adds an <OBJECT> tag for the component to your ASP page. It does not set the **SCOPE** attribute in the tag, so components created this way will have page scope.

Using the CreateObject Method

You can also use the **CreateObject** method of the **Server** object to create an instance of a component.

The following example code creates a reference to the Browser Capabilities component using its PROGID.

```
<% Set bc = Server.CreateObject("MSWC.BrowserType") %>
```

Using Installable Components Provided for ASP

To help you create Web applications, IIS 4.0 provides a large number of COM components that are available on the **Server Objects** tab of the Toolbox.

The following table describes several of these server objects.

Server objects	Description
ADO Command, ADO Connection, and ADO Recordset	ActiveX Data Objects (ADO) that access information stored in a database or other tabular data structures.
Ad Rotator	Automatically rotates advertisements displayed on a Web page, according to a specified schedule.
Browser Capabilities	Determines the capabilities, type, and version of a user's browser.
Content Linking	Creates a table of contents for Web pages, and links them sequentially, like pages in a book.
CDONTS NewMail and CDONTS Session	Collaboration Data Objects for NTS.
File Access	Uses the **FileSystemObject** object to retrieve and modify information stored in a text file on the server.

COM components enable you to package and reuse common functions, such as accessing a database and writing information to text files in an ASP application.

You can access the components installed on a Web server by using an .asp file with the **CreateObject** method of the **Server** object.

For information about using the Database Access component, see Chapter 6, "Understanding Data Access Technologies" on page 277.

For information about using the rest of these COM components, see Visual InterDev Help.

For additional components, see the IIS Web site and the IIS Resource Kit as well as the Site Builder Network web site.

The Browser Capabilities Component

The Browser Capabilities component enables you to determine the capabilities of the user's browser.

How the Browser Capabilities Component Works

The Browser Capabilities component compares the browser type and version number provided in the header of the HTTP request to entries contained in the Browscap.ini file stored on the Web server. By default the Browscap.ini file is found in the Windows\Winnt\System32\inetsrv folder.

If a match is found, the component uses the capabilities for that particular browser. If a match is not found, the component uses default capabilities in the Browscap.ini file.

Customizing the Browscap.ini File

You can declare property definitions for multiple browsers in the Browscap.ini file. You can also set default values that will be used when a browser that is not listed in the Browscap.ini file makes an HTTP request.

For each browser definition, you provide an HTTP User Agent header, along with the properties and values you want to associate with that header. For information about the format of an HTTP User Agent header, go to the HTTP Specification Web site at http://www.w3.org/pub/WWW/Protocols/Specs.html.

The following sample code shows a sample Browscap.ini file that lists only Microsoft Internet Explorer, Netscape Navigator, and default entries for all other browsers. To copy this code for use in your own project, see "Browscap.ini" on the accompanying CD-ROM.

```
; Last update 16-Jun-97
;;;;;;;;;;;;;;;;;;;;;;;;;;
;;; Microsoft Browsers ;;;
;;;;;;;;;;;;;;;;;;;;;;;;;;

;;;;;;;;;;;;;;;;;;;;;;;;;;;;;;;;;;;;;;;;;; IE 4.x
[IE 4.0]
browser=IE
Version=4.0
majorver=4
minorver=0
frames=TRUE
tables=TRUE
cookies=TRUE
backgroundsounds=TRUE
vbscript=TRUE
javascript=TRUE
javaapplets=TRUE
ActiveXControls=TRUE
Win16=False
beta=False
AK=False
SK=False
AOL=False
crawler=False
cdf=True


;;;;;;;;;;;;;;;;;;;;;;;;
;;; Netscape Browsers ;;;
;;;;;;;;;;;;;;;;;;;;;;;;

;;;;;;;;;;;;;;;;;;;;;;;;;;;;;;;;;;;;;;;;;; Navigator 4.x
[Netscape 4.00]
browser=Netscape
version=4.00
majorver=4
minorver=00
frames=TRUE
tables=TRUE
cookies=TRUE
backgroundsounds=FALSE
vbscript=FALSE
javascript=TRUE
javaapplets=TRUE
ActiveXControls=FALSE
beta=True
```

code continued on next page

```
code continued from previous page

;;;;;;;;;;;;;;;;;;;;;;;;;;;;;
;;; Default Browser      ;;;
;;;;;;;;;;;;;;;;;;;;;;;;;;;;;
[Default Browser Capability Settings]
browser=Default
Version=0.0
majorver=#0
minorver=#0
frames=False
tables=True
cookies=False
backgroundsounds=False
vbscript=False
javascript=False
javaapplets=False
activexcontrols=False
AK=False
SK=False
AOL=False
beta=False
Win16=False
Crawler=False
CDF=False
AuthenticodeUpdate=
```

For more information about customizing the Browscap.ini file, see Visual
InterDev Help.

Using the Browser Capabilities Component

You check values of properties of the Browser Capabilities component to present
Web content in a format that is appropriate for a specific browser.

The following table describes some possible properties of the Browser Capabilities
component.

Property	Description
ActiveXControls	Specifies whether the browser supports ActiveX controls.
Backgroundsounds	Specifies whether the browser supports background sounds.

table continued on next page

Property	Description
Beta	Specifies whether the browser is beta software.
Browser	Specifies the name of the browser.
cdf	Specifies whether the browser supports the Channel Definition Format for Webcasting.
Cookies	Specifies whether the browser supports cookies.
Frames	Specifies whether the browser supports frames.
Javaapplets	Specifies whether the browser supports Java applets.
Javascript	Specifies whether the browser supports JScript.
Platform	Specifies the platform on which the browser runs.
Tables	Specifies whether the browser supports tables.
VBscript	Specifies whether the browser supports VBScript.
Version	Specifies the version number of the browser.

In the following example code, the Browser Capabilities component is used to determine whether a browser supports ActiveX controls. If it does, an HTTP response that contains ActiveX controls will be sent.

```
<% Set objBrowser = Server.CreateObject("MSWC.BrowserType")
If objBrowser.ActiveXControls = "True" Then
  'Insert ActiveX Control here
Else
  'Handle Without Control
End If %>
```

The File Access Component

You can use the File Access component in your Web application to create and read from any text file stored on the Web server.

With text files, you can store the state of your Web application when the Web server shuts down.

Creating and Opening Text Files

The File Access component contains the **FileSystemObject** object, which you use to open or create a text file.

To open a text file, create a **TextStream** object by using the **OpenTextFile** method of the **FileSystemObject** object.

To create a text file, create a **TextStream** object by using the **CreateTextFile** method of the **FileSystemObject** object.

The following example code creates a **TextStream** object and opens a text file:

```
' Creates a FileSystem Object
Set fsVisitors = Server.CreateObject("Scripting.FileSystemObject")
' Creates a TextStream Object and opens a text file
Set fileVisitors = fsVisitors.CreateTextFile("c:\visitors.txt",
True)
```

If a text file already exists, the **CreateTextFile** method will overwrite the existing file if the overwrite argument is equal to **True**.

Reading and Writing Text

After you have created a **TextStream** object with either the **CreateTextFile** or **OpenTextFile** method, you can use the methods of the **TextStream** object to read and write text.

You can use the **ReadLine** and **WriteLine** methods of the **TextStream** object to read from and write to a text file.

The following example code sets an **Application** object value equal to the value read from a text file with the **ReadLine** method:

```
Application("visitors") = fileVisitors.ReadLine
```

The following sample code uses the events of the **Session** and **Application** objects to count the number of visitors to the Web site and stores that number in a text file. To copy this code for use in your own project, see "Reading and Writing Text" on the accompanying CD-ROM.

```
'when application starts, read hit counter information
'from a text file
Sub Application_OnStart
  Dim fsVisitors    'FileSystemObject object
  Dim fileVisitors 'TextStream object

  Set fsVisitors =
Server.CreateObject("Scripting.FileSystemObject")
  Set fileVisitors = fsVisitors.OpenTextFile("c:\visitors.txt")
  'Read counter value from text file
  Application("visitors") = fileVisitors.ReadLine
  fileVisitors.Close
End Sub

'when application ends, save hit counter in a text file
Sub Application_OnEnd
  Dim fsVisitors    'FileSystemObject object
  Dim fileVisitors 'TextStream object

  Set fsVisitors =
Server.CreateObject("Scripting.FileSystemObject")
  Set fileVisitors = fsVisitors.CreateTextFile("c:\visitors.txt",
True)
  'Write counter value to text file
  fileVisitors.Writeline(Application("visitors"))
  fileVisitors.Close
End Sub

'when session starts, increment the hit counter
Sub Session_OnStart
  Application.Lock
  'Increment counter
  Application("visitors") = Application("visitors") + 1
  Application.Unlock
End Sub
```

The preceding code sample ensures that the number of visitors to the Web site is retained even when the Web server shuts down and the Web application ends.

Practice: Using the Browser Capabilities Component

In this practice exercise, you will create an instance of the Browser Capabilities component on an Active Server Page. You will use the properties of the component to determine if the user's browser supports ActiveX controls, and then display the result.

▶ **Determine if the browser supports ActiveX controls**

1. Create a new ASP file in Visual InterDev.

2. From the **Server Objects** tab on the Toolbox, drag a **Browser Capabilities** server object to the ASP file. Make sure that it is not positioned within a script block.

   This will insert an <OBJECT> tag for the Browser Capabilities component.

3. Insert a server script block in the file.

4. Add script that will display the response "ActiveX is not dead" if the **ActiveXControls** property of the Browser Capabilities component is set to **True**.

5. View the ASP file in the browser to test your work.

Using Page Objects

A page object is an ASP page that contains server script that you use in your application. The functions or subroutines on the page can become methods for the page object.

Creating Page Objects

Using design-time controls and the scripting object model in Visual InterDev allows you to create and script a Web page using standard object-oriented techniques. You can specify any ASP page as a page object. To do so, you use the **PageObject** design-time control.

A page object is an ASP page that contains server script that you use in your application. The functions or subroutines on the page can become methods for the page object. Page objects also allow you to create properties, which maintain state over multiple round trips to the server.

Page objects enable the following:

◆ Simplified navigation.

◆ An easy way to execute specific script on another page.

◆ A means of maintaining state information.

◆ A way to execute server script from a page displayed in the browser.

For more information about the scripting object model, see "Using the Scripting Object Model" on page 261 in Chapter 5, "Accessing Databases."

▶ **To specify a page as an object**

1. Create or open an .asp file in the HTML editor.

2. Enable the scripting object model for the page.

    a. Right-click anywhere in the page away from an object or control, choose **Properties,** and then choose the **General** tab.

    b. Under **ASP settings,** choose **Enable scripting object model.** The HTML editor adds the scripting object model framework to the page in <META> tags. You should not alter the content of these tags.

Make sure that you have set options to view controls graphically. From the **View** menu, choose **View Controls Graphically.** To set this option as the default, use the **HTML** node of the **Options** dialog box.

3. From the **Design-Time Controls** tab of the Toolbox, drag a **PageObject** control onto your page. You can drag the control anywhere on the page, although it must be inside the framework of the scripting object model blocks.

4. In the **Name** box on the **PageObject** control, type a name for the page object. This will be the name that you can use to reference the object in script.

The name you give your page object is registered in your Web project so that it is available to any other page. Even if you move the page to another location, its page object name remains the same.

Defining Methods and Properties

Once you have added a **PageObject** control to an ASP page, you can define methods and properties for the page.

Defining Methods

Page objects can define two types of methods, as described in the following table.

Type of method	Description
Navigate	Called by a client page to load the ASP page and run a procedure on the page. A common use for navigate methods is to process a form.
Execute	Called by a client page to run a procedure on the ASP page, without leaving the current page. A common use for execute methods is to validate a user-entered value by looking it up in a database.

All page objects have a default navigate method called **Show**, which displays the contents of the page.

▶ **To define a method for a page object**

1. If the page does not already have one, add a **PageObject** control to the page and give the control a name.

2. Write the procedures in a script block that has the attribute **RUNAT=SERVER**. Procedures can take any number of parameters, but all are passed by value.

Note Parameters are converted to strings when you call a page object method so that they can be successfully passed across the Web. In your page object scripts, you should convert parameter values to the appropriate data type as required.

3. Right-click the **PageObject** control, and then choose **Properties** to display the **Property Pages** dialog box.

4. Determine whether the method will be available via navigation or execution. Then in the list under either **Navigate methods** or **Execute methods**, find the first blank line. From the drop-down list box, select the procedure that you want to define as a method for the page object.

Defining Properties

Page object properties have lifetime and visibility features, as described in the following table.

Feature	Settings	Description
Lifetime	Application	Available to any page of your application. Application values use application variables to store values.
	Page	Available to scripts anywhere on the page until you navigate to another page.
	Session	Available to any page in your application for the current session. Session values use session variables to store values.
Visibility	Client	None, Read, Read/Write
	Server	None, Read/Write

▶ **To define a property for a page object**

1. If the page does not already have one, add a **PageObject** control to the page and give the control a name.

2. Right-click the **PageObject** control, choose **Properties** to display the **Property Pages** dialog box, and then click the **Properties** tab.

3. In the Name column, find the first blank line, and then enter the name of the property you want to create.

4. Select the characteristics for the new property from the **Lifetime, Client,** and **Server** columns.

To make properties accessible to your scripts, page objects implement **get** and **set** methods. For example, if you define a property called **Color**, you can read its value using the method **getColor( )** method and set it using the **setColor( )** method.

Using Methods and Properties

To access the methods or properties of another page object, you must first create a reference to that page on the current page.

▶ **To reference another page object**

1. If the page does not already have one, add a **PageObject** control to the page and give the control a name. If your scripting target is **Server**, the scripting object model must be enabled for the page.

2. Right-click the **PageObject** control, choose **Properties** to display the **Property Pages** dialog box, and then choose the **References** tab.

3. In the Name column, click the three-dot button to display the **Create URL** dialog box.

4. Select the .ASP file that you want to reference as a page object. Enter options for how to call the page object, and then click **OK**.

Calling Page Object Methods

Page objects support two types of methods—**Navigate** methods and **Execute** methods. Each method is called according to the following general syntax:

pageObject.*navigate*.methodName*(parameters)*

pageObject.*execute*.methodName*(parameters)*

However, there are additional considerations for calling **Execute** methods, which can be called in two ways:

Calling Method	Definition
Synchronously	Your script calls the remote procedure and waits for it to return. This is useful if you need the results of the remote procedure before you proceed.
Asynchronously	Your script makes the call to a remote script, and then continues processing. The page remains available to users. Asynchronous calls are useful in Web applications because a remote procedure can take a long time while the request goes to the server and back.

When you call an **Execute** method either synchronously or asynchronously, it will not return a single value as you might expect. Instead, it returns a call object, which is an object that contains return and status information about the method that you called.

The most commonly used property of the call object is **return_value**. It contains the single value calculated or looked up by the method. Other call object properties allow you to retrieve more information about the state of the method call.

For more information about calling page object methods, and remote scripting which is the technology that supports execute methods, see Visual InterDev Help.

Accessing Page Object Properties

When you define a property for a page object, the scripting object model creates a **get** method and a **set** method that you use to access the property. For example, if you have defined a property called UserName, you can read the value of the property using the method getUserName, and set it using setUserName, as shown in the following example:

```
newUser = PageObj1.Navigate.getUserName()
PageObj1.Navigate.setUserName(txtUserName.Value)
```

When working with properties, you need to be aware of their lifetimes. For example, if you have defined the property's lifetime as "page," you can get and set its value only until you leave the page and display another one. (Calling the same page again to execute a method retains property values scoped to the page.) However, after you navigate to another page, the property is reset.

Note You can call methods and use properties on the current page using the default page object name of **thisPage**.

Practice: Using Page Objects

In this practice exercise, you will create a page object method on an Active Server Page, and call the method from another page.

▶ **Define a Navigate method for a page object**

1. Create a new ASP file named Callme.asp in Visual InterDev.

2. Insert a server script block.

3. Create a procedure named **Test** that displays the response "Hi, my name is Test."

4. From the **Design-Time Controls** tab of the Toolbox, drag a **PageObject** control to the ASP file.

   If you are prompted to enable the scripting object model on the page, click **Yes**.

5. Right-click the page object control on the page, and click **Properties**.

6. On the **Methods** tab of the **PageObject Properties** dialog box, select **Test** in the **Navigate methods** list box, and then click **Close**.

   The procedure you created named Test is now defined as a **Navigate** method for the page object.

▶ **Refer to the page object from another page**

1. Add another ASP file named Caller.asp.

2. From the **Design-Time Controls** tab of the Toolbox, drag a **PageObject** control to the ASP file.

   If you are prompted to enable the scripting object model on the page, click **Yes**.

3. Right-click the page object control on the page, and click **Properties**.

4. On the **References** tab of the **PageObject Properties** dialog box, click the ellipsis (...) button, and select **Callme.asp**, the ASP file you created in the previous procedure.

▶ **Call the method from another page**

1. Insert a server script block in the Caller.asp file.

2. Add script to call the **Test** method of the page object named Callme, which is contained in the ASP file named Callme.asp. Remember that it is a **Navigate** method.

3. View Caller.asp in the browser and verify that the message from the **Test** procedure in Callme.asp is displayed.

Security Issues in ASP

In this section, you will learn about security issues as they relate to ASP pages. There are four levels of security:

◆ ASP application security supported through Visual InterDev

◆ IIS level security

◆ Operating system file-level security

◆ SQL database-level security

Security Overview

The main Web security issues are:

◆ Authenticating user identify.

◆ Controlling user access to files and resources.

The following table identifies these security issues, the location for their control, their purpose, and the options available for managing them.

Issue	Location	Purpose	Security Option
User authentication	Web server	Identify the user requesting files in a Web application.	Basic Authentication Anonymous Logon Windows NT Challenge/ Response
File permissions	Web server	Control access to files in the application.	Read, write, script, and execute permissions for files and folders
File permissions	Web application	Control access to files in the application.	FrontPage Server Extensions
File permissions	Operating system	Control access to files in the application.	Access Control Lists in NTFS
Database permissions	Database	Control access to objects in the database.	Standard Security Integrated Security

The rest of this section shows you how to set up Web application, Web server, and operating system-level security. For more information on SQL Server security levels, see "Setting SQL Server Login Authentication" on page 236 in Chapter 5, "Accessing Databases," and in the SQL Server documentation.

For more information on user authentication, guidelines for design-time and run-time security, and securing HTTP transactions using SSL, see "Security" in Visual InterDev Help.

Web Application Security

Every Web application on a Web server has permission settings that identify authorized users and specify their privileges. These settings are specified from the **Settings** tab of the **Permissions** dialog box. The following illustration shows this tab.

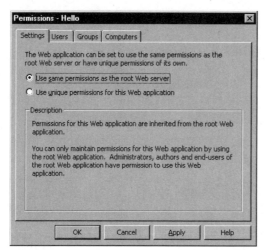

By default, a new Web application inherits the same permissions as the root Web server. You can customize these permissions, and then control the permissions for individual users and groups.

▶ To set unique permissions for a Web application

1. In the Project Explorer window, select the project for which you want to set permissions.

2. From the **Project** menu, choose **Web Project** and then **Web Permissions**.

3. On the **Settings** tab, select **Use unique permissions for this Web application.** This specifies that the current Web application does not inherit its permissions setting from the root Web application.

4. Choose **Apply.**

You can also limit browse access to the Web application from this dialog box by clicking the **Only registered users have browse access** option on the bottom of the **Users** tab in the **Permissions** dialog box.

In Microsoft Visual InterDev, you can set one of three levels of user permissions. The following table lists these choices and specifies which of these are design-time or run-time permissions.

User permission level	Type of permission
Browse	Design-time and run-time
Author	Design-time only
Administer	Design-time and run-time

Note In order to set Web application security in Windows NT, the Web application files must be stored on a disk using the NTFS file system, not FAT.

For more information on setting design-time security for your Web application, see "Setting Web Application Permissions" in Visual InterDev Help.

Web application security uses FrontPage Server Extensions, and Microsoft provides a resource kit for FrontPage Server Extensions. For more information, see www.microsoft.com/frontpage/wpp/serk/default.htm.

Setting IIS Permissions

You use the Internet Service Manager to set the access permission on the virtual directories of your Web site. The Internet Service Manager is a snap-in component of the Microsoft Management Console (MMC).

There are five possible levels of permission that you can grant for a virtual directory. The following table describes the differences among these settings.

Setting	Description
Read	Enables Web clients to read or download files stored in a home directory or a virtual directory. Give Read access permission only to directories containing information to publish (HTML files, for example). Disable Read permission for directories containing Common Gateway Interface (CGI) applications and Internet Server Application Program Interface (ISAPI) DLLs to prevent clients from downloading the application files.
Write	Enables Web clients to upload files to the enabled directory, or to change the content in a write-enabled file.
Script	Enables applications mapped to a script engine to run in this directory without having Execute permission set. Use Script application permission for directories that contain ASP scripts, Internet Database Connector (IDC) scripts, or other scripts. Script permission is safer than Execute permission because you can limit the applications that can be run in the directory.
Execute	Enables any application to run in this directory, including applications mapped to script engines as well as .dll and .exe files.
None	Do not allow any programs or scripts to run in this directory.

If the directory is on a Windows NT File System (NTFS) drive, the NTFS settings for the directory must match these settings. If the settings do not match, the most restrictive settings take effect. For example, if you give a directory Write permission in this property sheet but give a particular user group only Read access permissions in NTFS, those users cannot write files to the directory because the Read permission is more restrictive.

▶ **To set access permissions on virtual directories**

1. Click **Microsoft Internet Information Server**.
2. Click **Internet Service Manager**.

   This starts Microsoft Management Console.

3. Click **Properties**.

4. Click the **Home Directory** tab.

5. Set the appropriate access permissions for the virtual directory.

Allowing Anonymous Logon

Windows NT requires assigned user accounts and passwords. If you want to allow everybody to access your Web server, you must either provide a valid Windows NT account for every user or allow anonymous logon.

Anonymous logon allows users to access your Web server without providing a user ID and password. When an IIS Web server receives an anonymous request, it maps the user to a special anonymous logon account, referred to as the Internet Guest account. The user receives the access rights that have been granted to this account.

▶ **To enable anonymous logon**

1. Click **Microsoft Internet Information Server**.

2. Click **Internet Service Manager**.

    This starts Microsoft Management Console.

3. Within the virtual root, right-click **Default Web Site**.

4. Click **Properties**.

5. Select the **Directory Security** tab.

6. Click **Edit** in the **Anonymous Access and Authentication Control** group box.

7. Click the **Allow Anonymous Access** check box.

Setting the Account Used for Anonymous Access

When you install IIS, it creates an account named IUSR_*computername*. For example, if the computer name is "marketing", the account name will be IUSR_marketing. By default, this account is used for anonymous Internet logons.

IIS adds the IUSR_*computername* account to the Guests group and receives any permissions assigned to that group. You should review the settings for the Guests group to ensure that they are appropriate for the IUSR_*computername* account.

▶ **To change the account name and/or password used for anonymous logon**

1. Click **Microsoft Internet Information Server.**

2. Click **Internet Service Manager.**

   This starts Microsoft Management Console.

3. Within the virtual root, right-click **Default Web Site.**

4. Click **Properties.**

5. Select the **Directory Security** tab.

6. Click **Edit** in the **Anonymous Access and Authentication Control** group box.

7. Click the **Allow Anonymous Access** check box and disable the **Basic Authenti-cation** and **Windows NT Challenge/Response** options.

8. Click **Edit.**

9. Disable **Enable Automatic Password Synchronization.**

10. Set the **Username** and **Password** text boxes to the values that you want.

11. Click **OK, OK,** and **OK.**

Preventing Anonymous Logon

If you prevent anonymous logon, each request made to your Web server must include a valid Windows NT logon ID and password. To obtain this information, the browser will prompt the user for an account name and password.

▶ **To prevent anonymous logon**

1. From the Microsoft Management Console, under the virtual root, right-click **Default Web Site.**

2. Click **Properties.**

3. Select the **Directory Security** tab.

4. Click **Edit** in the **Anonymous Access and Authentication Control** group box.

5. Disable **Allow Anonymous Access.**

6. Enable **Basic Authentication, Windows NT Challenge/Response,** or both.

7. Click **OK** and **OK.**

Authentication Methods

You can specify how the logon information is sent from the Web browser to the Web server by setting the authentication method.

Basic Authentication

If you select **Basic Authentication**, the user name and password is sent from the Web browser to the Web server as plain text. This method is useful because it is generally supported by all Web browsers.

Windows NT Challenge/Response

Windows NT Challenge/Response authentication (often called NTLM authentication) is the most secure form of authentication because the user name and password are not sent across the network. Instead, the Windows Security Provider interface is used to provide an encrypted challenge/response handshake mechanism that is functionally unbreakable. This method of authentication is supported by Microsoft Internet Explorer version 4.0 and later.

Note This type of authentication is really only practical on an intranet.

Using Both Basic Authentication and Windows NT Challenge/Response

If you select both **Basic Authentication** and **Windows NT Challenge/Response** authentication, Windows NT Challenge/Response will be used if it is supported by the browser. Otherwise, Basic Authentication will be used.

If you select all three methods of authentication (Anonymous, Basic, and Windows NT Challenge/Response), every request to a Web page will attempt to access the page as anonymous. If the request fails, the user will be prompted for a login ID and the request will be attempted again.

Setting NTFS Permissions

You should place your Web pages and data files on an NTFS partition. When you use an NTFS partition, you can set permissions for users or groups of users on individual files and folders.

▶ **To set permissions on files and folders**

1. Start Windows NT Explorer.

2. Right-click the file or directory for which you want to set permissions.

3. Click **Properties**.

4. Select the **Sharing** tab.

5. Enable **Shared As** and give the folder or directory a **Share Name**.

6. Click **Permissions**.

7. Add or remove users and specify the type of access allowed for each user.

You can use a combination of IIS settings, NTFS permissions, and server script to protect your Web pages.

For example, if you want to allow all users to access most of your Web site—but restrict a few pages to certain users—you can configure your Web site as follows:

◆ In Internet Service Manager, enable **Allow Anonymous, Basic Authentication,** and **Windows NT Challenge/Response**.

For more information on these security settings, see "Preventing Anonymous Logon" on page 218.

◆ For the pages you want to restrict, use Windows NTFS file permissions to remove the Anonymous account IUSR_*computername* from the access list, and then add the users for whom you want to allow access.

When a user requests a Web page, the user is logged on as anonymous and IIS attempts to access the Web page. If access is denied, the user will then be prompted for a login ID and password. Only users who provide a valid login ID and password will be able to access the restricted page.

Lab 4: Using Active Server Pages

In this lab, you will create an ASP page that reads the student ID, name, and major data from the HTML form on the Profile page and saves the data in session variables. You will then write an event procedure for the **Session** object that routes all users to the Profile page to prompt them for their student data before they can access other pages on the State University Web site. Finally, you will write script that stores the student data in cookies and retrieves them on session start-up.

To see the demonstration "Lab 4 Solution," see the accompanying CD-ROM.

The following diagram shows how the files you edit in this lab will fit into the State University Web site.

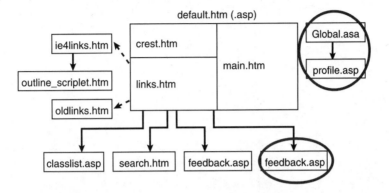

Estimated time to complete this lab: **60 minutes**

To complete the exercises in this lab, you must have the required software. For detailed information about the labs and setup for the labs, see "Labs" in "About This Course."

The solution code for this lab is located in the folder \Labs\Lab04\Solution.

Objectives

After completing this lab, you will be able to:

◆ Process form data using an ASP page.

◆ Save data in session variables.

◆ Add code to the **Session_OnStart** event procedure.

◆ Use cookies to store and retrieve data.

Prerequisites

Before working on this lab, you should be familiar with the following:

◆ Adding files to Web projects in Visual InterDev.

◆ Editing project files in Visual InterDev.

◆ Creating and debugging scripts in Visual InterDev.

Exercises

The following exercises provide practice working with the concepts and techniques covered in this chapter:

◆ Exercise 1: Reading Form Data

In this exercise, you will create an Active Server Page that reads the student ID, name, and major data from the HTML form on the Profile page and saves the data in session variables that will be used by other pages on the State University Web site.

◆ Exercise 2: Starting a Session

In this exercise, you will write an event procedure for the **Session** object that routes all users to the Profile page to prompt them for their student data before they can access other pages on the State University Web site.

◆ Exercise 3: Using Cookies

In this exercise, you will write script that stores the student data in cookies. You will then write script to retrieve the cookies on session start-up, and use them to set values for session variables used by other pages on the State University Web site.

Exercise 1: Reading Form Data

In this exercise, you will create an Active Server Page that reads the student ID, name, and major data from the HTML form on the Profile page and saves the data in session variables that will be used by other pages on the State University Web site.

▶ **Read the form data**

1. Add the file Profile.asp in the \Labs\Lab04\New folder to the project.

2. Open the file for editing, and switch to Source view.

3. At the top of the page, before the <HTML> tag, add the following server script to test whether the data on the form has been filled in:

```
<% If Not (IsEmpty(Request.Form("txtID"))) Then
...
    End If %>
<HTML>
...
```

If this test is **True**, the page was requested by clicking the **Submit** button on the form. If it is **False**, the page was requested by going to a page in a Web browser.

4. If the form data is filled in:

   a. Add server script that reads the values of all controls sent from the form on the page Profile.asp.

   For information about reading form data, see "Using the Form Collection" on page 184 in this chapter.

   b. Display a message that includes the values from the **txtName** and **txtMajor** controls.

To see an illustration of how your code should look, see Lab Hint 4.1 in Appendix B.

5. Save your changes, and view Profile.asp in the browser. Enter data in the form fields, and click **Submit**. Verify that the page returned includes the message you added in the previous step.

▶ **Save the form data in session variables**

To make the form data available to other pages in the State University Web site, save the data in session variables.

- After saving the form data in local variables, add server script to Profile.asp to save the form data in session variables.

For information about saving user data, see "The Session Object" on page 192 in this chapter.

To see an illustration of how your code should look, see Lab Hint 4.2 in Appendix B.

▶ **Use session variables in another file**

1. Add the file Transcript.asp in the \Labs\Lab04\New folder to the project.

2. Open the file for editing, and switch to Source view.

3. Write script to use the information stored in the **Session** object variables to display the user's student ID in the header for the page. Include the value within the <H3> tag on the page.

To see an illustration of how your code should look, see Lab Hint 4.3 in Appendix B.

4. Save your changes, and view Profile.asp in the browser. Enter data in the form fields, and click **Submit**.

5. View Transcript.asp in the browser and verify that the student ID you entered appears in the header of the page.

Exercise 2: Starting a Session

In this exercise, you will write an event procedure for the **Session** object that routes all users to the Profile page to prompt them for their student data before they can access other pages on the State University Web site.

▶ **Rename the default page for the State University Web site**

- Rename Default.htm to Default.asp. This will make it easier to test your work with Global.asa.

▶ **Redirect all users to the Profile page**

1. Open the Global.asa file for the project.

2. Add script to the **Session_OnStart** event procedure that redirects the user to Profile.asp if they attempt to start the session with a different page.

a. Save the name of the Profile page in a local variable.

 Tip Remember that profile.asp is in the StateU virtual directory.

b. Save the name of the requested page in a local variable.

The server variable SCRIPT_NAME contains the name of the page that is requested.

c. Use the **strcomp** function to determine if the user is requesting the Profile page.

The **strcomp** function does a case-insensitive string comparison.

d. If the user is not requesting the Profile page, redirect the user to that page.

For information about redirecting a user to a different Web page, see "The Redirect Method" on page 189.

 To see an illustration of how your code should look, see Lab Hint 4.4 in Appendix B.

3. Save your changes to Global.asa.

4. Test your code by trying to view any .asp file on the State University Web site other than Profile.asp in the browser. Verify that you get redirected to Profile.asp.

Note You need to start a new session each time you want to test the script in Profile.asp. To start a new session, start a new instance of the browser.

▶ **Redirect users to the page they originally requested**

Add code to the files Global.asa and Profile.asp to send users to the start page they requested after they entered their user information in Profile.asp.

1. In Global.asa, add script to the **Session_OnStart** event procedure that saves the name of the requested page in a session variable named requestedPage.

   To see an illustration of how your code should look, see Lab Hint 4.5 in Appendix B.

2. Save your changes to Global.asa.

3. Open Profile.asp.

4. In the script you added in Exercise 1, add more script to redirect users to the page they originally requested, or to Default.asp if they originally requested Profile.asp.

   Compare the session variable named requestedPage with the string "profile", using the VBScript function **InStr**.

   To see an illustration of how your code should look, see Lab Hint 4.6 in Appendix B.

5. Save your changes to Profile.asp.

6. Test your code in the browser by trying to view any .asp file on the State University Web site other than Profile.asp.

   a. Verify that you get redirected to Profile.asp.

   b. Enter the student data on the Profile page, enter **4** for the student ID, and submit the form.

   c. Verify that you get redirected to the page you originally requested.

Exercise 3: Using Cookies

In this exercise, you will write script that stores the student data in cookies. You will then write script to retrieve the cookies on session start-up, and use them to set values for session variables used by other pages on the State University Web site.

▶ **Store the student data in cookies**

1. Open Profile.asp in Visual InterDev, and locate the section of script you added at the top of the page in the previous exercises.

2. After the script that stores the form data in session variables, add script to store the same data in cookies as part of the response. Create cookies for the student's ID, name, and major.

Tip You could also store the data in one cookie using keys within the cookie. For more information about using keys within cookies with Active Server Pages, see the product documentation.

For more information about using cookies with the **Response** object, see "Using Cookies" on page 195 in this chapter.

3. For each cookie, set its path to the StateU virtual root, and set its expiration date to be a year from the current date.

Tip Make sure the case of the characters is correct in the path you specify for the StateU Web site. The browser will only send the cookie back to the server if there is an exact match in the path.

To see an example of how your code should look, see Lab Hint 4.7 in Appendix B.

▶ **Check for the cookies when a session starts**

1. Open Global.asa in Visual InterDev.

2. In the **Session_OnStart** event procedure, add an **If...Then** statement that only redirects the user to the Profile page if there are no cookies for ID, name, and major in the request. If those cookies are part of the request, set session variables equal to the value for each cookie. By doing so, the student data can be used by other pages on the StateU Web site.

For more information about using cookies with the **Request** object, see "Using Cookies" on page 195 in this chapter.

To see an example of how your code should look, see Lab Hint 4.8 in Appendix B.

▶ **Test your work**

1. Start a new instance of the browser and try to view an .asp file on the State University Web site other than Profile.asp. Verify that you get redirected to the Profile page.

2. Enter the student data on the Profile page, enter **4** for the student ID, and submit the form.

3. Verify that you get redirected to the page you originally requested.

4. Close the browser to end the session.

5. Start a new instance of the browser, and try to view Transcript.asp. In this case you should not get redirected, since the student data is being retrieved from a cookie. The student ID you previously entered on the Profile page should be displayed in header of the table.

Note For testing purposes, you may want to delete the cookie that is created on your computer. To do this, go to the Winnt\Profiles\<*username*>\Cookies folder, and delete the text file that has a name like <*username*>@StateU.txt.

Self-Check Questions

To see the answers to the Self-Check Questions, see Appendix A.

1. Which Active Server Pages built-in object would you use in your Web application to extract information from an HTTP request message?

A. The **Request** object

B. The **Response** object

C. The **Session** object

D. The **Server** object

2. When is a Session object created to indicate the start of a new user session?

A. When a user requests a Web page from a Web application.

B. When a user logs on to a Web server.

C. When a user requests an Active Server Page from a Web application.

D. When the WWW service starts.

3. Which event procedure always runs when a Web server is shut down?

A. Session_OnStart

B. Session_OnEnd

C. Application_OnStart

D. Application_OnEnd

4. Which of the following statements about cookies and session variables is false?

A. Cookies are sent with the HTTP request; session variables are not.

B. Cookies save information on the user's computer; session variables are saved on the Web server.

C. Cookies can be created with server-side script; session variables cannot be created with server-side script.

D. Cookies are destroyed automatically by the Web browser; session variables are destroyed by the Web server.

5. What should you do to access the properties and methods of a COM component in an Active Server Page?

A. Set a reference to the component's type library, and use the **New** keyword when you declare a variable of that type.

B. Install the COM component on the Web server, and create a variable with the **New** keyword.

C. Install the COM component on the Web server, and use the **CreateObject** method of the **Server** object.

D. Install the COM component on the user's computer, and use the <OBJECT> tag.

6. Which of the following tags sets the default language for server-side script?

A. <% LANGUAGE="VBScript" %>

B. <SCRIPT LANGUAGE="VBScript">

C. <LANGUAGE="VBScript">

D. <%@ LANGUAGE="VBScript" %>

7. If you have disabled Anonymous logon on your Web server, who can access your Web site?

A. Users with accounts that you have added to a database on your Web server.

B. Users with valid Windows NT accounts.

C. Users who log on with the account IUSR_*computername*.

D. No one can access the Web site.

8. If you have enabled Anonymous, Basic, and NT Challenge/Response authentication for your Web server, what authentication process occurs when a user requests a Web page?

A. The Web browser tries Anonymous authentication. If that fails, the user will not be able to access the page and receives an error message.

B. If the browser supports NT Challenge/Response authentication, the browser tries to use it. Otherwise, the browser uses Basic authentication.

C. If the browser supports Basic authentication, the browser uses it. Otherwise, the browser uses NT Challenge/Response authentication.

D. The Web browser tries to use Anonymous authentication, but if that fails, the user must provide a valid logon ID and password. Then, if the browser supports NT Challenge/Response authentication, that method is used. Otherwise, the browser uses Basic authentication.

9. If you want to restrict access to the page private.asp on your Web site, but also enable all users to access other pages on your Web site, what should you do?

A. Configure the hard drive partition, where the Web site files are located, to use the FAT file system.

B. Enable Anonymous and Basic authentication for the Web server, and then remove the Internet Guest account from the access control list for the file Private.asp.

C. Enable the Guest account, and then remove the Guest account from the access control list for the file Private.asp.

D. Set the HIDDEN attribute of the file Private.asp.

10. Which server-side script retrieves the name of the logon account that is used to access the Web site?

A. Request.Server("LOGON_USER")

B. Request.ClientCertificates("LOGON_USER")

C. Request.ServerVariables("LOGON_USER")

D. Session("LOGON_USER")

Chapter 5:
Accessing Databases

 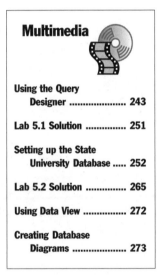
In this chapter, you will learn how to display data from a database in an ASP page. You will find out how to add a data environment to your Visual InterDev project and how to view and use data from the database in the Data View window. You will also be introduced to Database Designer, a tool for creating and manipulating database tables, and Query Designer, a tool for creating SQL queries.

The following illustration highlights the technologies you will learn about in this chapter.

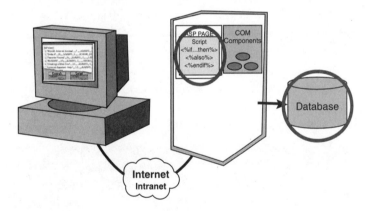

Objectives

After completing this chapter, you will be able to:

◆ Add a data source name to your project.

◆ Add a data connection to your project.

◆ Add a data command to your project.

◆ Connect the properties for a data-bound control to a **Recordset** object.

- ◆ Use Query Designer to create SQL queries.
- ◆ Use Database Designer to create a database.
- ◆ Use the **FormManager** design-time control to create a data input form.

Assumed Skills

Before beginning this chapter, you should be able to:

- ◆ Use objects from an object model.
- ◆ Write simple server-side and client-side scripts.

Accessing Data

Data access in Visual InterDev is easier than ever before. You simply add controls to a page, connect a source for data to your project, and connect the data to the controls.

The following table outlines the steps for displaying data from a database in an ASP page. These steps are discussed in further detail in later topics.

Location	Activity	Tool
First, in your project	Add an object to hold information about the connection to the database.	A data connection
	Connect to a database by creating a data source name.	A data source name to identify a database
	Add an object to hold information about what data to retrieve.	A data command
Second, in your ASP page	Add a control that will connect the data in the database to the data-bound controls on the form.	A **Recordset** control

table continued on next page

Location	Activity	Tool
Second, in your ASP page	Add a data-bound control to display data from the database.	Any of the data-bound controls on the **Toolbox**
	Set the properties of the data-bound control so it displays the data.	The properties sheet of the data-bound control.
	Add a control that lets users scroll the displayed data.	A **RecordsetNavbar** control

The steps outlined in the previous table assume that the structure of the database is finished before you begin. However if you want to design or manipulate the tables in a database, you can use the Database Designer.

Note   Features of the Visual Database Tools that allow you to alter the structure of a database are available only in the Enterprise Edition of Visual InterDev.

For more information on the Data View window, Database Designer, and Query Designer, see "Managing Databases" on page 270 in this chapter.

Adding a Data Connection

In this section, you will learn how to add a data connection to your Visual InterDev project.

When you add a data connection to a project, Visual InterDev creates a Data View window on that data. You use this window to view the objects in your database and to determine which objects from the database you want to use in a data command.

Using the Data Environment

The data environment is the focal point and repository for storing and reusing data connections and data commands in a Visual InterDev project.

A data environment holds the information required to access data in a database. It contains one or more data connections. Each data connection can contain one or more data commands that represent a method for querying or modifying a database.

The first time you add a data connection to your project, Visual InterDev creates a DataEnvironment folder as a subfolder of the Global.asa file. It is located here because data connection information is stored in application level variables in Global.asa and can be used by multiple ASP pages.

The following illustration shows you the location of the data environment within a project.

Creating a Data Source Name

As part of creating a data connection, you need to add the name of a source for data. A data source name (DSN) stores information about how to connect to a specific data provider.

Features of Data Source Names

A DSN specifies:

- The physical location of the database.
- The type of driver used for accessing the database.
- Any other parameters needed by a driver to access the database.

There are two ways to create a DSN for a Visual InterDev project.

- Create one while adding a data connection to your project.

◆ Use the **ODBC Data Source Administrator** in **Control Panel** before you begin a project.

In the practice exercise at the end of this topic, you will see how to create a DSN while adding a data connection to your project.

Types of Data Source Names

There are two different types of DSNs: machine DSNs and file DSNs. A machine DSN stores information for a database in the system registry. A file DSN is a text file that contains connection information for a database. This file is saved on your computer.

The following table outlines the scenarios in which each DSN type is used.

Scenario	DSN type
The production version of the database is not on the local computer	File DSN
The production version of the database is on the local computer	Machine DSN

Setting Up a Data Source Name

You can add a DSN to a project when adding a data connection. You do this from the **Select Data Source** dialog box.

The following steps outline the process for creating a new DSN when adding a data connection.

1. Start the process of creating a new data source. You do this by clicking **New** in the **Select Data Source** dialog box.

2. Set the driver for the data source. You do this by selecting **Select the database driver name** in the **Create a New Data Source** dialog box.

3. Locate the data source that you want to connect to your project. You do this by browsing available data source locations and selecting the appropriate name. This creates a file with the extension .dsn.

Setting SQL Server Login Authentication

As part of the process of creating a new data source to a SQL server, you are given two options for verifying the authenticity of a user login ID. The following table describes your two choices.

Choice	Name	Description
Windows NT authentication using the network login ID of the user	Integrated Security	User is given guest account privileges on the database server based on user's Windows NT login ID.
SQL authentication using a login ID and password entered by the user	Standard Security	User is given specific account privileges on the database server based on user's SQL Server login ID and password.

For more information on these two types of security, see "Integrated Security" and "Standard Security" in Visual InterDev Help.

Standard vs. Integrated Security

When a Web user requests an Active Server Page that connects to a Microsoft SQL Server database on a separate computer running Windows NT, the user is first logged on to the computer running Windows NT, and then on to the SQL Server.

This illustration shows the logon process from a Web browser to a SQL Server.

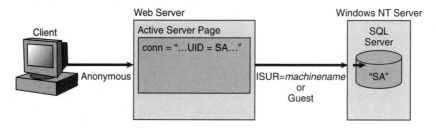

The following steps outline the logon process that occurs when a user requests an Active Server Page that connects to a SQL Server database.

1. If the Web server allows anonymous log on, the user is mapped to the anonymous account.

2. The .asp file runs script to connect to a SQL Server database.

3. For the .asp file to connect to the SQL Server database, the user is first logged on to the Windows NT-based computer where SQL Server is installed.

4. Finally, the user is logged on to the SQL Server itself.

Setting Data Connection Properties

To access data in a database for use on an ASP page, you need to add a data connection to your Visual InterDev project. A data connection tells the project how to access the database, and usually contains information about:

◆ The type of database to be accessed (for example, Microsoft SQL Server) and the server name (if appropriate)

◆ The name of the database (for example, pubs)

◆ A user name

◆ A password

The following illustration shows you the location of the data connection within a project.

You can add as many data connections to a project as you need. For example, if your application requires access to two different databases, you would add two data connections.

When you create a data connection, Visual InterDev reads connection information from a DSN on your computer. In addition, Visual InterDev creates a Data View window through which you can view and select data from a database.

▶ **To add a data connection to your project**

1. On the **Project** menu, click **Add Data Connection**.

2. Add the name of a data source.

3. Set the **Connection Name** and **Connection String** properties for the connection.

Note You can also add a data connection or a data command to your project by right-clicking **Data Environment** and using the popup menu.

The following illustration shows you an example of a Data View window.

For more information about the Data View window, see "Using the Data View Window" on page 271 in this chapter.

Run-time vs. Design-Time Authentication

Visual InterDev 6 offers a new feature that lets you easily test database access during development. You can quickly switch between design-time and run-time authentication from the **Authentication** tab on the **Connection Properties** dialog box.

The following illustration shows you the two types of authentication that are available.

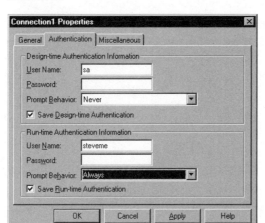

Scenarios for Design-Time and Run-Time Authorization

When specifying design-time authorization, you choose the type of security for your authorization. For maximum security, you can choose to be prompted for a password each time you connect to the database. For less stringent security, you can choose not to be prompted. In this case, Visual InterDev encrypts your password and stores it in the project.

When you specify run-time authorization, you do not have this choice: You cannot prompt users for a password because the prompting would occur on the Web server. Therefore, you must include the password with the user name. The password is encrypted and stored in the project so it can be passed to the database each time a user connects to the database when the application is running.

Practice: Adding Connections and DSNs to a Project

In this first practice exercise, you will learn how to create a data source name for an SQL Server database.

In the following set of practice exercises you will build an ASP page that displays the first and last names of the authors listed in the pubs database using the data tools available in Visual InterDev.

▶ Add a data connection and file DSN to your project

1. From the **Project** menu, click **Add Data Connection**.

2. In the **File Data Source** tab, click **New**.

3. In the **Create New Data Source** dialog box, click **SQL Server**, and then click **Next**.

4. In the text box, add a name for the DSN that you are creating—**authors**—and click **Next**.

5. In the **Create New Data Source** dialog box, verify the type of data source, its name, and the driver for the data source. Click **Finish**.

6. In the **Create a New Data Source to SQL Server** dialog box, type your local server name in the **Server** dropdown list box and click **Next**.

7. Accept the default values for Windows NT and SQL Server authentication, and click **Next**.

8. Select **Change the default database to,** and then select **pubs** from the dropdown list box. Accept all of the other default settings, and click **Next**.

9. Accept all of the default values for character set translation, and click **Next**.

10. Accept both of the default values for logging on, and click **Finish**.

11. If you want to check the data source connection that you have created, click **Test Data Source**. Otherwise, click **OK**.

12. In the **Select Data Source** dialog box, select **authors**, then click **OK**.

13. In the **Connection1 Properties** dialog box, accept the default values, then click **OK**.

Note In subsequent practice exercises, you will add a grid control and other objects to complete other ASP functionalities.

Adding a Data Command

In this section you will learn how to add a data command to an ASP page that displays and uses data from a database.

Creating a Data Command

A data command contains information about accessing a particular database object. For example, a data command might query the authors table of the pubs database so that you can display the contents of that table in a Web page. A data command can run a SQL statement or a stored procedure.

The following illustration shows you the **Property** dialog box for the authors data command.

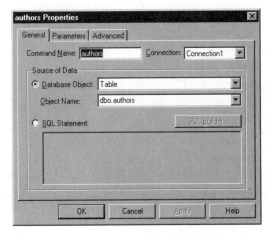

There are four ways to create a data command:

◆ You can move a database object from the Data View window to the data environment. This will automatically create a data command in the data environment.

◆ You can create a data command using the **Data Command** dialog box and selecting a database object.

◆ You can create a data command using the **Data Command** dialog box and typing in a SQL statement.

◆ You can create a data command using the **Data Command** dialog box and clicking **SQL Builder**. This invokes Query Designer.

Note When you move a data command onto an HTML page or Active Server Page, a **Recordset** control is added to the page.

For more information about using Query Designer, see "Using Query Designer" in the following section.

Using Query Designer

The Microsoft Query Designer is a graphical tool for creating SQL commands. You can create complex, multi-table queries by dropping tables into your query, setting options, and entering values.

Query Designer is aware of the differences between databases such as Microsoft SQL Server and Oracle, so it can generate and recognize database-specific SQL commands.

Queries created in Query Designer can both return data using SQL SELECT commands and create queries that update, add, or delete records in a database, using UPDATE, INSERT, and DELETE.

Query Designer consists of four panes, which are described in the following table.

Pane	Function
Diagram pane	Displays the input sources — the tables or views — that you are querying
Grid pane	Displays your specific query options: Which data column to display What rows to select How to group rows
SQL pane	Displays the SQL statement for the current query
Results pane	Displays the results of the most recently executed query

▶ **To open and use Query Designer**

1. Right-click the **Command** object.

2. Click **Properties**.

3. Select **SQL Statement**.

4. Click **SQL Builder**.

5. From the Data View window, drop the table or tables that you want to include in the query into the Diagram pane.

The following illustration shows the Query Designer window.

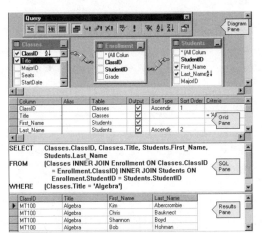

To see the demonstration "Using the Query Designer," see the accompanying CD-ROM.

For more information about this tool, see Query Designer in Visual InterDev Help.

Practice: Adding a Data Command

In this practice exercise you will add a data command to a project. This exercise assumes that you have already added a **Connection1** object and an authors data source name to your project. If you have not done this, see Practice, "Adding Connections and DSNs to a Project" on page 239 in this chapter.

▶ **Add a command to your project**

- From the Data View window, move the authors table from the pubs data connection and drop it on the data environment in the Project Explorer window. This creates a data command in the data environment named authors.

▶ **See the SQL query that was generated**

1. Right-click the authors **Data Command** object, and click **Open**.

2. On the **Query Builder** toolbar, click **SQL**.

3. Inspect the SQL command.

Adding Data-Bound Controls

In this section, you will learn about the data-bound controls that are available in Microsoft Visual InterDev. This version contains a wide selection of data-bound controls that make data access, display, and manipulation easy.

Types of Controls

Data-bound controls are user interface elements, such as labels, text boxes, and option groups, that can display the contents of a database. They are connected, or bound, to the database through a **Recordset** control.

Data-bound controls are located on the **Design-Time Controls** tab on the **Toolbox**.

To add a control to an ASP page, click and drag the control name onto the page.

For purposes of discussion, data-bound controls can be divided into two categories —data display controls and data manipulation controls. Data display controls include labels, text boxes, and list boxes. Experienced Windows developers should be familiar with these types of data-bound controls.

Data manipulation controls include **Recordset**, **RecordsetNavBar**, and other controls.

The following are types of data display controls:

- Button
- Checkbox
- Text box
- OptionGroup
- Grid
- Label
- List box

For more information about these data display controls, see Visual InterDev Help.

Data Manipulation Controls

The following table describes the types of data manipulation controls.

Control name	Description
Recordset	A data source for data-bound design-time controls. The **Recordset** control connects controls on an ASP page with fields in the tables of a database. **Recordset** controls do not appear on an ASP page.

table continued on next page

Control name	Description
RecordsetNavBar	Creates a set of forward and backward buttons that lets users navigate the data being displayed on an ASP page.
FormManager	Creates sets of event-driven forms, such as a data-entry form with Browse, Edit, and Insert modes. For more information, see "Using the FormManager Control" on page 263 in this chapter.

How Data-Bound Controls Work

Data-bound controls in Visual InterDev are a special form of a design-time control (DTC) that support data binding. You bind fields in a database to the control by setting the control's design-time properties.

How Do Design-Time Controls Work?

A design-time control is a user interface element that you use to create application functionality. By setting properties of a design-time control it generates script that executes at run-time. For example, when you need to get text information from a user, you place a design-time text box control on the form to receive the data.

At design time, these controls act just like controls that you put on a form in an environment such as Visual Basic. You set their properties to specify their appearance and behavior. However, when you change a property, you also change the script that is executed when the page runs.

For more information on design-time controls and the script objects that they create, see "The Scripting Object Model" in Visual InterDev Help.

Advantage of Using Design-Time Controls

The key advantage to using design-time controls is their flexibility in targeting— you do not need to write one script for client side processing and another for server-side processing. For example, if you want to Web application to run on many different browsers, you target the server as the platform, and all of the generated code will run on the server. However, if you want your Web application to take advantage of Internet Explorer's client-side data binding capability you can generate script that will run on the client.

Connecting Controls to the Data

In this section, you will learn how to connect the fields in a database to the data-bound controls on an ASP page. You will also learn about a number of **Recordset** control features and practice adding a data command, a data-bound grid control, and a **Recordset** control to your project. You will also practice placing fields in a database onto a grid control.

Using the Recordset Control

The key to data access in ASP pages is the **Recordset** control. The **Recordset** control does not appear as a part of the user interface. Instead the **Recordset** control connects items in a database to data-bound controls on an ASP page.

The **Recordset** control specifies:

- A **Data Connection** object
- A database object within that connection or a SQL statement querying the database.
- Other properties that determine how data is read from and written to a database, such as cursor type and cursor location.

Adding a Recordset Control to a Page

There are a number of ways to add a **Recordset** control to an ASP page. The recommended method is to drag a **Data Command** object onto a page. Visual InterDev automatically creates the control and binds it to the DE, or **Data Environment**, object.

You can bind a **Recordset** control to:

- A **Data** Command object
- A stored procedure
- A table
- A view

You can also manually add the **Recordset** control from the **Toolbox**.

The following illustration contains an example of a **Recordset** control on an ASP page.

Recordset Control Properties

Recordset controls have a number of properties that you can manipulate. The following table describes some of the important choices. All of them are found on the **Advanced** tab of the **Recordset Property** dialog box.

Recordset feature	Description
Cursor type	Sets the types of cursor that will be used to view and manipulate the data. Default setting is 3 - Static. For more information on cursor types, see "Retrieving Records" on page 286 in Chapter 6, "Understanding Data Access Technologies."
Cursor location	Sets the location for the cursor, either client-side or server-side. Default setting is client-side cursor.
Lock type	Sets the type of record locking that takes place when several users try to access records simultaneously. Default setting is 3 - Optimistic. For more information on lock type, see "Retrieving Records" on page 286 in Chapter 6, "Understanding Data Access Technologies."
Cache size	Sets the size of the cache that will be used for the recordset. Default setting is 100KB.
Command timeout duration	Sets the amount of time, in seconds, that is allotted for a command to execute before processing is stopped and the timeout message is returned from the database.
Maximum records to display	Sets the maximum number of records that will be dis played in the browser. For more information on this topic, see "Adding Recordset Navigation" on page 249 in this chapter.

Client- vs. Server-Based Access

When setting the properties for a **Recordset** control, you can specify either the server-side (Server ASP) or client-side (IE 4.0 DHTML) scripting platform.

You can change the setting at anytime, and Visual InterDev will automatically generate the appropriate code to populate the recordset and its related data-bound controls. The following table outlines the two types of targeting options you have and which data access technology they use

Scenario	Client or Server	Technology
Target non-Microsoft browsers	Server	Active Data Objects (ADO)
Target Microsoft browser only and reduce the number of round trips to the server	Client	Remote Data Service (RDS)

For more information on ADO and RDS, see "Universal Data Access" on page 278 in Chapter 6, "Understanding Data Access Technologies."

The following illustration contains the **Implementation** tab from the Recordset **Property Pages** dialog box.

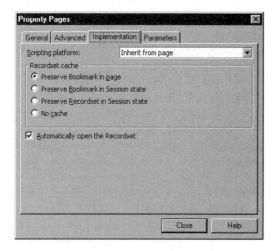

Note When you change the scripting platform for the **Recordset** control, all the controls that are bound to it automatically inherit the scripting platform.

Recordset Cache Properties

On the **Implementation** tab you can also set how much of the recordset is maintained in memory and which record appears when the recordset is opened.

For more information on managing the recordset cache, see "Implementation Tab (Recordset Properties Dialog Box)" in Visual InterDev Help.

Adding Recordset Navigation

To make an ASP page user friendly, you will want to limit the number of records displayed on the page. You can do this in one of two ways:

♦ If you are displaying data from a database in individual data-bound controls, use the **RecordNavBar** control.

♦ If you are displaying data from a database in a grid control, use the settings on the **Navigation** tab of the **Property Pages** dialog box for the grid.

The **RecordsetNavbar** control is located on the **Design-Time Controls** tab of the **Toolbox**. You add it to your page as you would any other design-time control, but you need to add it after you have placed all the controls that it will be handling.

▶ **To use the RecordsetNavbar control on your ASP page**

1. Add the design-time controls that will contain data from the database to your ASP page.

2. Add the **RecordsetNavBar** control to the page below the controls that it will be using.

3. On the **General** tab of the RecordsetNavbar **Property Pages** dialog box, set the **Recordset** data property to the name of the appropriate recordset.

4. Check to see that the **Recordset** data properties for each of the data-bound controls on the page are set to the appropriate values.

Practice: Adding the Recordset and Grid Controls

A grid allows you to easily display tables of information from a database. In this practice exercise, you will add a grid control to display the first and last names of authors listed in the pubs database.

▶ **Add a data command and a grid control to your ASP page and set its properties**

1. Drag the authors data command from the data environment to your ASP page to create the **Recordset** control.

2. From the **Design-Time Controls** tab of the **Toolbox**, drag a grid control onto the ASP page and drop it below the **Recordset** control.

3. Right-click the grid control and select **Properties** to display the **Properties Pages** dialog box.

4. Click the **Data** tab, and then select **Recordset1** in the **Recordset** dropdown list box.

5. In the **Available Fields** list box, click **au_fname** to provide data for the first column of the grid, and then click **au_lname** to provide data for the second column.

6. In the **Header** text box, provide an appropriate header for the au_fname column, **First Name,** and then click **Update**.

7. In the **Header** text box, provide an appropriate header for the au_lname column, **Last Name,** and then click **Update**.

The following table lists other grid control properties and their tab locations.

Property	Tab
Border styles	Border tab
Cell alignment	Font tab
Cell font type, size, and color	Format tab
Grid lines	Border tab
Grid width	General tab
Page navigation enabling/disabling	Navigation tab
Page numbering enabling/disabling	Navigation tab
Row colors	Font tab

Lab 5.1: Accessing Data

In this lab, you will set up the State University database on Microsoft SQL Server. You will then create a data connection for the database. Using the data connection, you will create a data command that queries the database for a list of classes. Finally, you will add a **Recordset** control and a data-bound **Grid** control to the class list page in order to display the list of available classes at State University.

To see the demonstration "Lab 5.1 Solution," see the accompanying CD-ROM.

The following diagram shows how the files you edit in this lab will fit into the State University Web site.

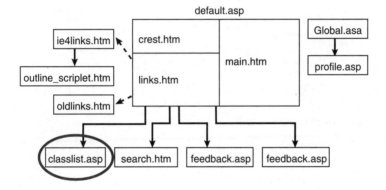

Estimated time to complete this lab: **60 minutes**

To complete the exercises in this lab, you must have the required software. For detailed information about the labs and setup for the labs, see "Labs" in "About This Course."

The solution code for this lab is located in the folder \Labs\Lab05.1\Solution.

Objectives

After completing this lab, you will be able to:

◆ Set up a database on Microsoft SQL Server.

◆ Add a data connection to a Web project.

◆ Add a data command to a Web project.

◆ Use Query Designer to build a SQL statement for a data command.

- ◆ Add a **Recordset** control to a Web page.
- ◆ Include a data-bound **Grid** control on a Web page, associate it with a **Recordset** control, and set other properties to affect its appearance and behavior.

Prerequisites

Before working on this lab, you should be familiar with the following:

- ◆ Opening Web projects in Visual InterDev, and adding Web pages to the project.
- ◆ Creating and editing Web pages in Visual InterDev.

Exercises

The following exercises provide practice working with the concepts and techniques covered in this chapter:

- ◆ Exercise 1: Setting Up the Database

  In this exercise, you will set up the State University database using Microsoft SQL Server.

- ◆ Exercise 2: Adding a Data Connection

  In this exercise, you will add a data connection to the State University database in your Web project. As the first step in creating the data connection, you will create a new data source name (DSN) for the State University database.

- ◆ Exercise 3: Adding a Data Command

  In this exercise, you will add a data command to the State University Web project. You will then build the SQL statement for the data command using Query Designer.

- ◆ Exercise 4: Using a Data-Bound Grid Control

  In this exercise, you will build a class list page for the State University Web site. You will add a data-bound **Grid** control to the page, and use the data command created in Exercise 3 to add database records to the grid.

Exercise 1: Setting Up the Database

In this exercise, you will set up the State University database using Microsoft SQL Server.

To see the demonstration "Setting Up the State University Database," see the accompanying CD-ROM.

▶ **Register your SQL Server if necessary**

1. Run the SQL Enterprise Manager from the Microsoft SQL Server 6.5 Programs folder. This folder can be accessed from the Windows NT **Start** menu.

2. To open the SQL Server within the SQL Enterprise Manager, click the plus sign (+) next to the server name.

   If your server does not appear, you will need to register your server in the SQL Enterprise Manager. To do this, click **Register Server** on the **Server** menu, select the server, and then type a valid login and password.

   If your server does not start, right-click the traffic signal and then click **Start**.

▶ **Create the State University database device**

1. To create a database device for the StateU Web project, right-click the Database Devices folder, and then click **New Device**.

2. To name the new device, type **StateU** in the **Name** field.

3. In the **Size** field, type **5 MB**.

4. To create the StateU database device, click **Create Now**.

▶ **Create the State University database**

1. To create the database, right-click the Databases folder, and then click **New Database**.

2. To name the new database, type **StateU** in the **Name** field.

3. In the **Data Device** field, select the StateU device.

4. In the **Size** field, type **5 MB**.

5. To create the StateU database, click **Create Now**.

▶ **Create the tables and load the data for the State University database**

1. In the SQL Enterprise Manager, click **SQL Query Tool** on the **Tools** menu.

2. Click the **Load SQL Script** button on the toolbar.

3. Select the StateU.sql file from the folder \Labs\Lab05.1\New, and then click **Open**.

4. To run the SQL script, click **Execute** on the **Query** menu.

   This script creates tables, and adds data to the tables. The script is complete when the **Execute Query** button changes from a black arrow to a green arrow.

5. Close the Query Tool window, and then click **Yes** when prompted if the window should be closed.

The following illustration shows how the SQL Enterprise Manager should look after creating the State University database.

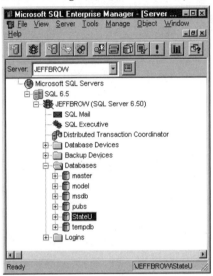

Exercise 2: Adding a Data Connection

In this exercise, you will add a data connection to the State University database in your Web project. As the first step in creating the data connection, you will create a new data source name (DSN) for the State University database.

▶ Create a DSN for the State University database

1. Open the State University Web project if it is not already open in Visual InterDev.

2. In the **Project Explorer** window select the StateU project.

3. Right click to open the context menu then click **Add Data Connection**.

4. On the **File Data Source** tab of the **Select Data Source** dialog box, click **New** to create a new DSN.

For more information about DSNs, see "Creating a Data Source Name" on page 234 in this chapter.

5. In the **Create New Data Source** dialog box, select **SQL Server** from the list of database drivers, then click **Next**.

6. Type in **StateU** as the name for the data source, then click **Next**.

7. Click **Finish** in the dialog box.

▶ **Enter the database connection information**

1. In the **Create a New Data Source to SQL Server** dialog, select (**local**) or the name of your SQL Server from the **Server** list box, then click **Next**.

2. Select the **SQL Server authentication** option in the dialog box.

3. Type in **sa** for **Login ID** and type the password you have set for this user account in SQL Server. Then click **Next**.

   For more information about SQL Server authentication, see "Setting SQL Server Login Authentication" on page 236 in this chapter.

4. Select the **Change the default database** to check box, and select StateU from the list box, then click **Next**.

5. Click **Next** in the dialog box.

6. Click **Finish** in the dialog box. Verify the settings that are displayed in the dialog box.

7. Click **Test Data Source** to test out the newly created DSN, then click **OK**.

   The **Select Data Source** dialog box should be displayed again.

▶ **Select the State University DSN for the data connection**

1. In the **Select Data Source** dialog box, select StateU from the **Data Sources** list box, then click **OK**.

2. You will be prompted to enter the security information again. Enter **sa** for **Login ID** and the password you have set for this user account in SQL Server.

3. In the **Properties** dialog box for the newly created data connection, type in **StateU** for the **Connection Name**, then click **OK**.

   The new data connection should be created and added to your Web project.

4. In the Project Explorer window, verify that there is an icon for the StateU data connection listed within the DataEnvironment subfolder of Global.asa in the Project Explorer window. There should also be an icon for the StateU data connection in the Data View window.

The following illustration shows how your Project Explorer and Data View windows should look.

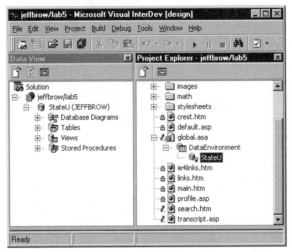

Exercise 3: Adding a Data Command

In this exercise, you will add a data command to the State University Web project. You will then build the SQL statement for the data command using Query Designer.

▶ **Add a data command to the data environment**

1. In the Project Explorer window, expand the DataEnvironment subfolder of Global.asa within the project.

2. Select the StateU data connection that you created in Exercise 2.

3. Right-click to open the context menu, then click **Add Data Command**.

4. On the **General** tab in the **Command Properties** dialog box, type in **classlist** for the **Command Name**.

5. Make sure the StateU data connection is selected in the **Connection** list box.

The following illustration shows how the **Command Properties** dialog box should look.

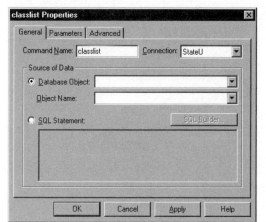

6. Select the **SQL Statement** option, then click **SQL Builder**.

This will start Query Designer so you can build the SQL statement that the data command will store.

For more information about data commands, see "Adding a Data Command" on page 240 in this chapter.

For more information about Query Designer, see "Using Query Designer" on page 242 in this chapter.

▶ **Build the SQL statement for the command using Query Designer**

1. Drag the Classes and Majors tables from the Data View window to the Design pane of Query Designer.

   Query Designer will recognize the relationship between the tables automatically, and will add a join line between them.

2. In the Classes table, select the Title and ClassID fields.

3. In the Majors table, select the Description field.

4. Sort the query on the ClassID field in ascending order.

The following illustration shows how the query should look.

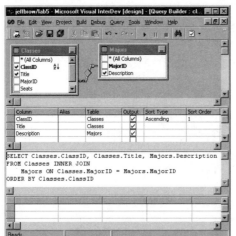

5. Close the Query Designer window, and click **Yes** to save the query.

The data command should be created and added to the project.

6. In the Project Explorer window, verify that there is an icon for the data command named classlist listed within the StateU data connection within the DataEnvironment subfolder of Global.asa.

The following illustration shows how your Project Explorer window should look.

Exercise 4: Using a Data-Bound Grid Control

In this exercise, you will build a class list page for the State University Web site. You will add a data-bound **Grid** control to the page, and use the data command created in Exercise 3 to add database records to the grid.

▶ **Add a Recordset control to the class list page**

1. Add the file Classlist.asp from the \Labs\Lab05.1\New folder to the project.

2. Open the file for editing, and switch to Source view.

3. Drag the data command you created in Exercise 3 named classlist from the Project Explorer window to the page. Place it after the <BODY> tag on the page.

   This should create a **Recordset** control on the page named Recordset1.

   The following illustration shows how the page should look.

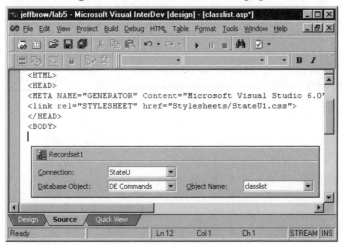

For more information about the **Recordset** control, see "Using the Recordset Control" on page 246 in this chapter.

▶ **Add a data-bound Grid control**

1. Move the insertion point to a line that follows the </H3> tag on the page.

2. Drag a **Grid** control from the Toolbox onto the page.

3. Select the **Grid** control, right click, and click **Properties** on the context menu.

4. On the **General** tab in the **Grid Properties** sheet, type in 90 and select **Percentage** in the **Width** list box.

5. On the **Data** tab in the **Grid Properties** sheet, select **Recordset1** in the **Recordset** list box.

   This will bind the **Grid** control to database records produced by the classlist data command.

6. In the **Available fields** list box select all the fields.

7. Change the settings for the ClassID and Description fields so they use "Number" and "Major", respectively, for their column header. Leave the settings for the Title field as they are.

   Do this by selecting the column in the **Grid columns** list box, typing the new header in the **Header** text box and clicking **Update**.

   The following illustration shows how the **Data** tab should look.

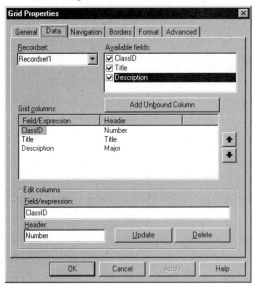

8. On the **Navigation** tab, under **Page navigation**, type in **10** in the **Records/Page** dialog box.

   This will limit the number of records the grid will display on the page.

9. Click **OK** to close the **Grid Properties** sheet.

The following illustration shows how the completed class list page should look.

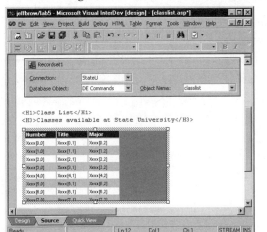

For more information about data-bound controls, see "Adding Data-Bound Controls" on page 244 in this chapter.

▶ **Test your work**

1. Save Classlist.asp so the changes you made are reflected on the Web server.

2. View the page in the browser and view the output in the **Grid** control.

3. Verify that the column headers are labeled correctly, and use the navigation buttons to navigate through the records.

Customizing Database Access

In this section, you will learn how to customize database access using FormManager to create data input forms. You will also learn how to use the scripting object model.

Using the Scripting Object Model

In this chapter you have been adding design-time controls to a page and implicitly using Visual InterDev scripting objects. In this topic you will learn how to use a scripting object programmatically.

What Is the Scripting Object Model?

Script objects are part of the scripting object model, which defines a set of objects with events, properties, and methods that you use to create Web applications. When you add a design-time control to your Web application and set its properties, you are actually creating and manipulating script objects.

Visual InterDev provides you with the script objects found in the following table:

- Button
- Checkbox
- Grid
- Label
- Listbox
- OptionGroup
- PageObject
- Recordset
- RecordsetNavbar
- Textbox

Each of these script objects has specific properties, methods, and events. However, the **Onchange** event is common to all of these objects.

Each of these script objects also has a common method—the **Advise** method. With the **Advise** method, you can extend the set of events available to an object by "advising" for an event, or registering the object to be notified when the event occurs. After you have advised for an event, you can write event handlers for that event for that object as you would for any other event.

Using Script Objects

The following example code shows how to use some methods and properties of the **Listbox** and **Recordset** script objects:

```
Sub Listbox1_onchange()
   ' make the current record be the class the user selected
   Recordset1.moveAbsolute(Listbox1.selectedIndex+1)
End Sub
```

Advantages of Using Scripting Objects

Script objects provide the following advantages:

- Browser and platform independence
- Data binding

- Simplified page navigation
- Remote scripting

Enabling the Scripting Object Model

Before you can use the scripting object model, you must enable it so that it can construct the scripting object model framework for the page.

Note Visual InterDev design-time controls require the scripting object model. If you add a design-time control to a page that does not already have the scripting object model enabled, Visual InterDev prompts you to enable it.

▶ **To enable the scripting object model for a page**

1. Right-click anywhere in the page away from an object or control, choose **Properties**, and then choose the **General** tab.

2. Under **ASP settings**, choose **Enable scripting object model**. The HTML editor adds the scripting object model framework to the page in <META> tags. You should not alter the content of these tags.

Note Script objects are available only in Visual InterDev.

Using the FormManager Control

FormManager is a design-time control that facilitates the creation of data input forms. You add the controls that you need; and **FormManager** generates the script that enables and disables the buttons, and updates or cancels changes to the recordset. All you need to do is set values for methods and properties for the controls on the form. **FormManager** handles most of the other operations.

Instead of writing script, you specify modes that handle property settings for controls and events on the page.

To see an example that uses **FormManager** to change the display mode for an online university class registration form, see the lab solution demonstration in Lab 5.2, "Creating an Event-Driven Form."

▶ **To create an input form using FormManager**

1. Create the data entry ASP form in a project.

2. Add a **Data Connection** object to the project, along with a data source name.

3. Create a **Recordset** control.

4. Leave the **Lock Type** on the default **3 - Optimistic** or any setting other than read-only.

5. Add data-bound controls that will display the fields in the database and make sure that the **Recordset** property points to the recordset that you added previously.

6. If you use separate data-bound controls to display the contents of the database, add a **RecordsetNavbar** control, and set the **Recordset** property to the recordset that you added previously.

7. Add the command buttons — such as add, delete, or save — that will implement the different modes that your page will have.

8. Add a **FormManager** control at the bottom of your page.

▶ **To specify the modes that your page will use**

1. Identify each mode and specify the property settings and methods for the control while the mode is active.

2. Specify the transition events between the modes that trigger specific actions.

3. Add the actions that occur after the transition event is triggered but before the transition is complete.

Note In order to validate user input, you will need to develop and call separate validation functions.

For more information on using **FormManager**, see "Simplifying Data Entry Pages" and "Creating Event-Driven Forms" in Visual InterDev Help.

Lab 5.2: Creating an Event-Driven Form

In this lab, you will modify the Registration page of the State University Web site to make it an interactive form. You will write an event handler and use properties and methods for script objects in response to the user selecting classes in the list box on the page. You will also modify properties of the **FormManager** control on the page to define an additional form mode, actions, and mode transitions.

To see the demonstration "Lab 5.2 Solution," see the accompanying CD-ROM.

The followng diagram shows how the files you edit in this lab will fit into the State University Web site.

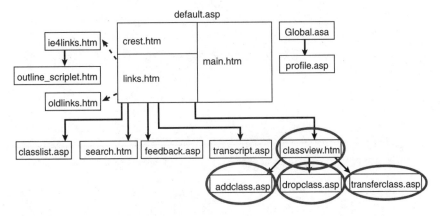

Estimated time to complete this lab: **60 minutes**

To complete the exercises in this lab, you must have the required software. For detailed information about the labs and setup for the labs, see "Labs" in "About This Course."

The solution code for this lab is located in the folder \Labs\Lab05.2\Solution.

Objectives

After completing this lab, you will be able to:

◆ Write script to handle events and use properties and methods of script objects.

◆ Set properties of the **FormManager** control to define form modes, actions, and mode transitions.

Prerequisites

Before working on this lab, you should be familiar with the following:

◆ Opening Web projects in Visual InterDev, and adding Web pages to the project.

◆ Creating and editing Web pages in Visual InterDev.

Exercises

The following exercises provide practice working with the concepts and techniques covered in this chapter:

◆ Exercise 1: Using Script Objects

In this exercise, you will write an event handler and use properties and methods for script objects in response to the user selecting classes in the list box on the Registration page.

◆ Exercise 2: Using the FormManager Control

In this exercise, you will modify properties of the **FormManager** control on the Registration page to define an additional form mode, actions, and mode transitions for the page.

Exercise 1: Using Script Objects

In this exercise, you will write an event handler and use properties and methods for script objects in response to the user selecting classes in the list box on the Registration page.

▶ **Add the Registration page to the project**

1. Add the file Classview.htm from the \Labs\Lab05.2\New folder to the project.

2. Open the file for editing, and examine the existing controls on the page, and their properties.

    a. Notice the data-bound list box named Listbox1.

    b. Notice there are four data-bound text boxes: **classid**, **title**, **startdate**, and **seats**.

    c. All of these controls are bound to the **Recordset** control on the page named Recordset1.

The **Recordset** control is dependent on having a data connection in your project named StateU. If you have not set up the data connection, see Lab 5.1, "Accessing Data" on page 251 in this chapter.

The page also uses client-side database targeting. For more information about client-side database targeting, see "Client vs. Server-Based Access" on page 248 in this chapter.

All of the design-time controls on the page create corresponding script objects that you can manipulate at run-time. For more information about script objects, see "Using the Scripting Object Model" on page 261 in this chapter.

▶ **Change the current record to the selected item in the list box**

1. Add an **onchange** event handler for Listbox1.

2. Write script to change the current record of Recordset1 on the page.

    a. Use the **selectedIndex** property of the Listbox1 to determine what item the user clicked.

    b. Add 1 to the value. This is necessary because list box item numbers start at 0 whereas record numbers start at 1.

    c. Use the **moveAbsolute** method of Recordset1 to move the current record to be the record number of the class the user clicked.

To see an example of how your code should look, see Lab Hint 5.1 in Appendix B.

3. Test your work by viewing Classview.htm in the browser. You should see that when you click a class number in the list box, all the data-bound controls on the page are updated with the appropriate data for the record.

Exercise 2: Using the FormManager Control

In this exercise, you will modify properties of the **FormManager** control on the Registration page to define an additional form mode, actions, and mode transitions for the page.

The Registration page allows the user to select a class number, and then click the **Add, Drop,** or **Transfer** buttons to add, drop, or transfer classes. Clicking one of the buttons will trigger a transition to the appropriate form mode. The controls and message on the page will change in response to the mode transitions.

The actions for the **FormManager** control include calls to custom methods on the page that in turn call methods on other ASP using page objects. In later labs, you will implement these remote page methods to enable the user to add, drop, and transfer classes using the Registration page.

▶ **Add pages with remote methods to the project**

1. Add the files Addclass.asp, Dropclass.asp, and Transferclass.asp from the \Labs\Lab05.2\New folder to the project.

   The script in Classview.htm calls methods on these pages using page objects.

2. Open Classview.htm and examine the **Page Object** control at the bottom of the page named classview.

   If its name is highlighted in red, indicating an error in its property settings, you will need to reset its properties. The page objects that classview refers to are addclass, dropclass, and transferclass. These page objects correspond to the ASP files Addclass.asp, Dropclass.asp, and Transferclass.asp, respectively. You need to reset the URL for the pages on the **References** tab of the **PageObject Properties** sheet. For information about how to set page object properties to refer to other page objects, see "Using Methods and Properties" on page 210 in Chapter 4, "Using Active Server Pages."

▶ **Examine the property settings of the FormManager control on the page**

1. Select the **FormManager** control on the page named FormManager1, right click, then click **Properties** on the context menu.

2. In the **FormManager Properties** sheet, examine the settings on the **Form Mode** tab.

   Notice that modes named Browse, Drop, TransferSetup, TransferAdd, and TransferDrop have already been defined. By selecting the mode name in the **Form Mode** list box you will see that actions for those modes also have been defined.

3. Examine the settings on the **Action** tab.

   Notice that several mode transitions have already been defined in the **Form Mode Transitions** list box.

   For more information about the **FormManager** control, see "Using the FormManager Control" on page 263 in this chapter.

▶ **Create a new form mode named Add**

1. On the **Form Mode** tab in the **FormManager Properties** sheet, type in **Add** in the **New Mode** text box, and click the **>** button.

   A new mode named Add should be displayed in the **Form Mode** list box.

2. Make sure Browse is still the default mode by selecting it in the **Default Mode** list box.

▶ **Enter the actions for Add mode**

1. On the **Form Mode** tab in the **FormManager Properties** sheet, select **Add** in the **Form Mode** list box.

2. Add the following sequence of actions in the **Actions Performed For Mode** list box.

   a. Call the custom method named **addClass,** and pass the value of the **classid** text box as the argument.

   To call a custom method, you type in its name in the **Member** column and type in any arguments in the **Value** column. The arguments need to be surrounded by parentheses.

   b. Hide the **Add** button.

   To set properties or call a method for a control on the page, you select it in the **Object** column, select its property or method in the **Member** column, then enter any values or arguments in the **Value** column. Arguments to methods need to be surrounded by parentheses.

   c. Hide the **Drop** button.

   d. Hide the **Transfer** button.

   e. Show the **Reset** button.

▶ **Enter the mode transitions for Add mode**

1. Select the **Action** tab in the **FormManager Properties** sheet.

2. Enter a new row in the **Form Mode Transitions** list box.

   Do this by going to the end of the list, and then typing in the new data in the last row.

3. Enter the mode transition data.

Select the mode to transition from in the **Current Mode** column. Select the object that triggers the transition in the **Object** column. Select the event that triggers the transition in the **Event** column. Finally, select the mode to transition to in the **Next Mode** column.

    a. Transition from Browse mode to Add mode when the user clicks the **Add** button.

    b. Transition from Add mode to Browse mode when the user clicks the **Reset** button.

4. Click **Close** to close the **FormManager Properties** sheet, and save all the property settings you have made to FormManager1 in the previous steps and procedures.

▶ **Test your work**

- View Classview.htm in the browser and verify that Add mode works as expected.

    a. Select a class number in the list box.

    b. Click **Add**.

    Verify that the **Add, Drop,** and **Transfer** buttons are not visible, and that the **Reset** button is now visible. Also, the message displayed at the top page should indicate the class was added.

    c. Click **Reset**.

    The page should now return to its original state, with the **Add, Drop,** and **Transfer** buttons visible.

Managing Databases

In this section, you will learn about several of the database management tools that are available with Microsoft Visual InterDev, particularly the Data View window and Database Designer.

Database Tools In Visual InterDev

Visual InterDev offers a suite of database integration features. The following table describes these features and their capabilities.

Feature	Description
Database projects	A type of project that you can add to your Visual InterDev solution that includes tools required to build and manage your database as a separate component from Web pages.
Data View window	A window that provides a live view of the data to which your database or Web project is currently connected.
Visual Database tools	A set of tools for managing and querying your database. Includes Database Designer and Query Designer.
Data environment	A repository in your Web project for information required to connect to and access data in a database.
Data-bound controls	Controls such as text boxes and buttons that you can put on your Web page and that can be bound to specific fields in a database record.

Using the Data View Window

The Data View window is a graphical environment for creating, viewing, and editing database objects. It is your starting point for managing database objects such as database diagrams, tables, stored procedures, and more in any ODBC-compliant database.

The following illustration contains a sample Data View window.

The Data View window is visible when a data connection has been established for your database or Web project. When you move a database object from the Data View window to the data environment, Visual InterDev automatically creates a data command that represents that database object.

Note Some databases have objects different from those listed here. For more information about the objects available from your databases, consult its documentation.

To see the demonstration "Using Data View," see the accompanying CD-ROM.

For more information about editing and saving changes to the structure of a database, see "Managing Database Diagrams in Data View" in Visual InterDev Help.

Creating Database Projects

A database project is a collection of one or more data connections which contain a database and the information needed to access it. When you create a database project, you can connect to one or more databases through ODBC and view components through a graphical user interface.

The following illustration shows the location of a database project in Project Explorer.

▶ **To create a database project**

1. Start Visual InterDev.

2. Under **Visual Studio**, click **Database Projects**.

3. Give your project a name and click **Open**.

4. In the **Select Data Source** dialog box, you will be queried to select or create a new data source. Click **OK**.

Note You can also create a database project by clicking **New Project** from the **File** menu.

Using the Database Designer

Database Designer is a visual tool that allows you to create, edit, and delete database objects in databases while you are connected to those databases.

You interact with the server database using database diagrams. Database diagrams graphically represent the tables in your database. These tables display the columns they contain and the relationships between the tables.

Database Diagrams

You use database diagrams to:

◆ View the tables and their relationships in your database.

◆ Alter the physical structure of your database.

Changing the structure of a database diagram does not automatically change the structure of the underlying database. Changes to the database are not saved until you save the table or database diagram that you have created.

Saving Changes to Database Diagrams

You have two choices for saving changes:

◆ Save the changes to the selected tables or the database diagram and have the changes modify the server database.

◆ Save a change script that contains the SQL code generated by your changes to the diagram. With a change script, you can edit the change script in a text editor and then apply the modified script to the server database.

To see the demonstration "Creating Database Diagrams," see the accompanying CD-ROM.

For more information on the Database Designer tool, see "Database Designer" in Visual InterDev Help. For more information on database diagrams, see "Working in Database Diagrams" also in Visual InterDev Help.

Other Database Tools

Stored procedures can make managing your database and displaying information about that database and its users very easy. Stored procedures are a precompiled collection of SQL statements and optional control-of-flow statements stored under a name and processed as a unit.

What Are Stored Procedures?

Stored procedures are stored within a database and can be executed with one call from an application. They allow user-declared variables, conditional execution, and other powerful programming features.

Stored procedures can contain program flow, logic, and queries against the database. They can accept parameters, output parameters, return single or multiple result sets, and return values.

A stored procedure executes faster than individual SQL statements because it is compiled on the server when it is created.

When you create a stored procedure in Microsoft Visual Database Tools, the stored procedure appears in the Stored Procedures folder in Data View. You can expand a stored procedure in Data View to see a list of the parameters it contains.

A detailed discussion of stored procedures is beyond the scope of this chapter, but their use is covered in the documentation. The following table shows you the skills you need for using stored procedures and where they are discussed in Visual InterDev Help.

Skill	Topic in Visual InterDev Help
Create stored procedures to be executed from the database	"Creating a Stored Procedure"
Set execute permissions to allow access to the stored procedures by specific users	"Setting Execute Permissions on Stored Procedures "
Use parameters in stored procedures	"Using Parameters in Stored Procedures"
Open a stored procedure to view or edit its text	"Opening a Stored Procedure"

table continued on next page

Skill	Topic in Visual InterDev Help
Save stored procedures	"Saving a Stored Procedure"
Delete stored procedures	"Deleting a Stored Procedure"
Copy stored procedures	"Copying a Stored Procedure"
Run stored procedures against your database	"Running a Stored Procedure"

Self-Check Questions

To see the answers to the Self-Check Questions, see Appendix A.

1. When you add a data connection to a Visual InterDev project, how will your Web project be modified?

A. Script will be added to the global.asa file.

B. The **Data Command** control will be added to all of your existing ASP pages.

C. Script will be added to all existing ASP pages.

D. Script will be added to the default ASP page.

2. What does a data environment hold?

A. The name of the database server to be accessed.

B. The physical location of the database.

C. Information required to access data in a database.

D. The type of driver used for accessing the database.

3. Where is a file DSN stored?

A. On the computer where the database is located.

B. On the developer's computer.

C. On the computer where the browser is located.

D. On the end-user's computer.

4. When you create a data connection, Visual InterDev reads connection information from what source?

A. From the data environment.

B. From the **Recordset** object.

C. From the **Command** object.

D. From the data source name stored on your computer.

5. Where is the password for run-time authentication stored?

A. The run-time authentication password is stored with the project.

B. The password for run-time authentication is stored in an SQL database.

C. The password for run-time authentication is stored in a machine DSN.

D. The password for run-time authentication is stored with a command object.

6. What does a data command always refer to?

A. A data connection

B. An SQL table

C. A stored procedure

D. An SQL statement

7. What mechanism handles the communication between a design-time control and a database when the contents of the control are changed?

A. The recordset

B. DCOM

C. PageNavbar

D. ActiveX

8. How can you limit database access to users of your Web site?

A. Create a logon ID for your database that has limited rights, and use that ID to access the database.

B. Add records in a new SQL database for each user who needs access to the Windows NT Server and SQL Server.

C. Hard code the SQL system administration account and password into the ActiveX Data Objects (ADO) connection string.

D. Disable the Internet Guest account and the Guest account.

Chapter 6:
Understanding Data Access Technologies

In this chapter, you will learn how to create Web pages that retrieve and update information in a database by using ActiveX Data Objects and the Remote Data Service.

The following illustration shows the technologies that you will learn about in this chapter.

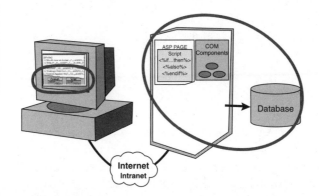

Objectives

After completing this chapter, you will be able to:

◆ Describe the Microsoft Universal Data Access platform.

◆ Define ActiveX Data Objects and Remote Data Service, and explain the relationship between them.

◆ Use ActiveX Data Objects to retrieve and update data and to handle errors returned from a data source.

◆ Discuss the data-binding capabilities of Internet Explorer 4.0.

◆ Explain how to use the Remote Data Service and data binding in Internet Explorer 4.0 to connect page elements to a data source.

Assumed Skills

Before beginning this chapter, you should be able to:

◆ Write client-side script.

◆ Write server-side script.

◆ Use methods and properties exposed by an object.

Note In Chapter 5 you learned how to use Visual InterDev tools for data access. In this chapter, you will learn about the underlying data access technologies.

In Chapter 7 you will learn how to build a separate component for handling database access. At this point you will need to write the code that accesses databases.

In Chapter 8 you will learn how to secure database transactions that use Microsoft Transaction Server.

Universal Data Access

Microsoft Universal Data Access is a platform for developing multi-tier enterprise applications that access diverse relational or non-relational data sources across intranets or the Internet. Universal Data Access consists of a collection of software components that interact with each other using a common set of system-level interfaces defined by OLE DB.

OLE DB is a Microsoft system-level programming interface to diverse data sources. OLE DB specifies a set of Microsoft COM interfaces that contain database management system services. These interfaces enable you to create software components that implement the Universal Data Access platform.

Universal Data Access components consist of:

◆ Data providers, which contain and expose data

◆ Consumers, which use data

◆ Services, which process and transform data

The following illustration depicts the structure of the Universal Data Access platform.

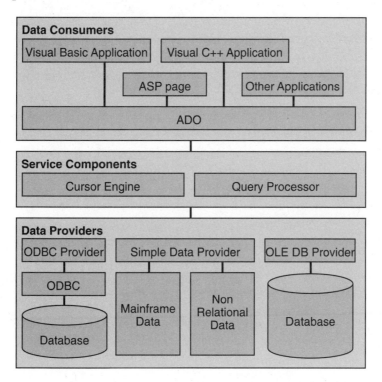

To see the expert point-of-view "Universal Data Access," see the accompanying CD-ROM.

Universal Data Access is supported by two related data access technologies — ActiveX Data Objects and Remote Data Service.

ActiveX Data Objects

ActiveX Data Objects (ADO) is the application-level programming interface that allows you to write applications that access data from OLE DB data sources, including ODBC data sources. It is based on Automation. When using ADO with Active Server Pages, all data access and manipulation is done on the server.

Remote Data Service

Remote Data Service (RDS) allows you to access data on a server and manipulate it on the client, reducing the number of round trips to the server. RDS extends ADO.

Both ADO and RDS are collections of COM objects. They are installed with the Windows NT Option Pack as part of Microsoft Data Access Components.

For more information about using these data access technologies, see "Client- vs. Server-Based Access" on page 248 in Chapter 5, "Accessing Data in Visual InterDev."

Microsoft Data Access Components

The Microsoft Data Access Components (MDAC) are the key technologies that enable Universal Data Access. MDAC 1.5 includes the latest versions of the following components:

- ActiveX Data Objects (which includes Remote Data Service)
- OLE DB Provider for ODBC
- ODBC Driver Manager
- Updated ODBC drivers for Microsoft SQL Server, Microsoft Access and Oracle.

The client components of MDAC ship with Internet Explorer 4.0. The server components ship with the Windows NT Option Pack.

For more information on Universal Data Access, go to the Microsoft Universal Data Access Web site at www.microsoft.com/data/.

ActiveX Data Objects Overview

In this section, you will learn about several data access models and the object hierarchy provided by ADO. You will also learn how ADO communicate with a database.

ADO Architecture

ADO provides a layer between your Active Server Page and the underlying database. To work with a database, you write code that sets properties and invokes methods of ADO objects.

ADO communicates with databases using OLE DB. OLE DB can access both SQL and non-SQL databases or data sources. If a database vendor supplies an OLE DB

Provider for ODBC, ADO uses the Provider to communicate with the database. If a database vendor supplies an OLE DB Provider, ADO communicates directly with the database. The Provider for ODBC is the default.

The following illustration shows how ADO communicates with databases.

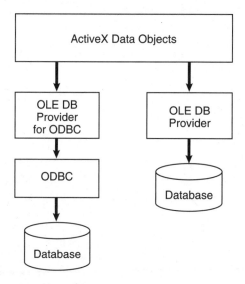

ADO Object Model

ADO is made up of three top-level objects: the **Connection, Command,** and **Recordset** objects. Each of these objects is created and destroyed independently of one another.

The following illustration shows the relationship among these objects.

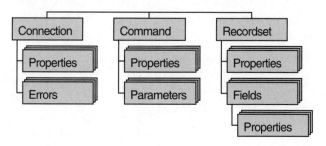

Note ADO allows you to create objects independently, which enables you to write simpler code and create only the objects you need for the task at hand. This means that you no longer have to navigate through a hierarchy to create objects. You can create and track only the objects you need, which results in fewer ADO objects and a smaller working set.

To see the animation "ActiveX Data Objects," see the accompanying CD-ROM.

Connection

The **Connection** object encapsulates the OLE DB **Data Source** and **Session** objects. It represents a single session with the data source. The **Connection** object:

◆ Defines properties of the connection.

◆ Assigns the scope of local transactions.

◆ Provides a central location for retrieving errors.

◆ Provides a point for executing queries.

Command

The **Command** object encapsulates the OLE DB **Command** object. The **Command** object:

◆ Specifies the data-definition or data-manipulation statement to be executed. In the case of a relational provider, this is an SQL statement.

◆ Allows you to specify parameters and customize the behavior of the statement to be executed. A collection of **Parameter** objects exposes the parameters.

◆ Contains a collection of **Parameter** objects used for parameterized queries or stored-procedure arguments.

Recordset

The ADO **Recordset** object encapsulates the OLE DB **Rowset** object. The **Recordset** object is the actual interface to the data, whether it is the result of a query or was generated in a different manner. The **Recordset** object:

◆ Provides control over the locking mechanism used.

◆ Specifies the type of cursor to be used.

◆ Specifies the number of rows to access at a time.

The **Recordset** object exposes a collection of **Field** objects that contain information about the columns in the recordset (such as name, type, length, and precision) as well as the actual data values themselves.

Use the **Recordset** object to navigate through records and change data (assuming that the underlying provider can be updated).

Using ActiveX Data Objects

In this section, you will learn how to use ADO objects to create a connection from a Web page to a data source, retrieve and modify data, run stored procedures, and handle errors.

Establishing a Database Connection

A **Connection** object represents an open connection to a data source or OLE DB provider. You can use the **Connection** object to run commands or queries on the data source. When a recordset is retrieved from the database, it is stored in a **Recordset** object.

Opening a Connection

To define the connection, you set properties for the **Connection** object. The following steps describe how to create an ADO connection.

▶ **To establish a connection with a data source**

1. Create a **Connection** object by calling **CreateObject** and passing it the **ADODB.Connection** parameter.

2. Set the **ConnectionTimeout** property of the **Connection** object. **ConnectionTimeout** determines, in seconds, how long the object will wait before timing out when connecting to a data source.

3. Set, in seconds, the **CommandTimeout** property of the **Command** object. **CommandTimeout** determines, in seconds, how long the object will wait for the results of a command or query.

4. Use the **Open** method to connect to the data source.

The syntax for the **Open** method is as follows.

connection.*Open* ConnectionString, User, Password

The **Open** method takes the following arguments:

♦ ConnectionString

Information, such as the data source name, used for establishing a connection to a data source. The information required for a connection string is defined by the OLE DB provider.

♦ User

A string that contains the user name for establishing a connection.

♦ Password

A string that contains the password for establishing a connection.

After the **Open** method succeeds in connecting to the data source, you can run queries.

The following example code creates a **Connection** object, opens a connection to the StateU data source:

```
Set conn = Server.CreateObject("ADODB.Connection")
conn.ConnectionTimeout = 10
conn.CommandTimeout = 20
conn.Open "DSN=StateU;DATABASE=StateU", "SA", ""
```

The following methods are important features of the **Connection** object:

♦ The **Execute** method runs an SQL query.

♦ The **BeginTrans** method initiates a transaction between the client and the database.

♦ The **CommitTrans** method ensures a transaction will occur.

♦ The **RollbackTrans** method returns a database to its original state if the transaction fails.

Using Connection Information

Rather than using literal values for the **Connection** object properties, you can use application variables. When you use Visual InterDev to add a data connection to a Web project, it adds script to the Global.asa file that stores information about the connection in application variables. You can access these application variables from code in an .asp file.

The advantage to using application variables when creating a connection is that you can change the value of the variables in the Global.asa file, and the new values will be used by any of your .asp files that refer to the variables. If you change the properties of a data connection in Visual InterDev, it modifies the script in the Global.asa file to set the variables to the new values.

The following example code shows how you can use application variables to create a connection:

```
Set conn = Server.CreateObject("ADODB.Connection")
conn.ConnectionTimeout = Application("StateU_ConnectionTimeout")
conn.CommandTimeout = Application("StateU_CommandTimeout")
conn.Open Application("StateU_ConnectionString"), _
        Application("StateU_RuntimeUserName"), _
        Application("StateU_RuntimePassword")
```

Closing a Connection

When you have finished working with the database, you use the **Close** method of the **Connection** object to free any associated system resources. Using the **Close** method does not remove the object from memory. To completely remove an object from memory, you set the object variable to **Nothing**.

The following example code closes a data connection and sets the object variable to **Nothing**:

```
conn.Close
Set conn = Nothing
```

Connection Pooling

Web database applications that frequently establish and terminate database connections can reduce database server performance. IIS supports efficient connection management by using the connection pooling feature of ODBC 3.5.

Connection pooling maintains open database connections and manages connection sharing across different user requests to maximize performance. On each connection request, the connection pool first determines if there is an idle connection in the pool. If so, the connection pool returns that connection instead of making a new connection to the database.

If you want your ODBC driver to participate in connection pooling, you must set the driver's CPTimeout property in the Windows registry. The CPTimeout property determines the length of time that a connection remains in the connection pool. If the connection remains in the pool longer than the duration set by CPTimeout, the connection is closed and removed from the pool.

You can selectively set the CPTimeout property to enable connection pooling for a specific ODBC database driver by creating a registry key with the following settings:

```
\HKEY_LOCAL_MACHINE\SOFTWARE\ODBC\ODBCINST.INI\driver-
name\CPTimeout = timeout (REG_SZ, units are in seconds)
```

Note By default, IIS activates connection pooling for SQL Server by setting CPTimeout to 60 seconds.

Retrieving Records

To retrieve records from a database, you create a **Recordset** object. You use properties and methods of the **Recordset** object to manipulate the data in the recordset. This topic shows you how to create a recordset. It also discusses four different kinds of cursors.

Creating a Recordset Using CreateObject

The following steps explain how to create a **Recordset** object.

▶ **To create a Recordset object**

1. Define a **Recordset** object variable by passing **ADODB.Recordset** as an argument to **CreateObject**.

2. Call the **Open** method of the **Recordset** object.

The **Open** method uses the following syntax.

recordset.**Open** Source, ActiveConnection, CursorType, LockType, Options

◆ Source

Optional argument. A **Command** object variable name, an SQL statement, a table name, or a stored procedure call.

◆ ActiveConnection

Optional argument. A **Connection** object or a string that contains connection information.

◆ CursorType

A constant that indicates the type of cursor to create.

- adOpenForwardOnly = forward-only cursor
- adOpenKeyset = keyset cursor
- adOpenDynamic = dynamic cursor
- adOpenStatic = static cursor

◆ LockType

A constant that indicates what type of locking should be used.

- adLockReadOnly = Read-only
- adLockPessimistic = Pessimistic
- adLockOptimistic = Optimistic
- adLockBatchOptimistic = Batch Optimistic

◆ Options

A numeric value that indicates how the **Source** argument should be interpreted if it is not a **Connection** object.

- adCmdText = Evaluate Source as a text definition of a command, such as an SQL statement.
- adCmdTable = Evaluate Source as a table name.
- adCmdStoredProc = Evaluate Source as a stored procedure.
- adCmdUnknown = The type of command in the **Source** argument is not known.

Note You can include a file named adovbs.inc in your Active Server Pages that use ADO. The file enables you to use VBScript constants for ADO option parameters, so you do not need to remember the numeric value for the option. The file is installed in the \Program Files\Common Files\system\ado folder of the Web server by the Windows NT Option Pack Setup program.

The following example code uses the **CreateObject** function to define a **Recordset** object variable and then uses the **Open** method to create the **Recordset** object. The example passes a connection string when invoking the **Open** method of the **Recordset** object:

```
Const adOpenKeyset = 1
Const adLockOptimistic = 3

Set rs = Server.CreateObject ("ADODB.Recordset")
rs.Open "Select * from students", "DSN=StateU;UID=SA;PWD", _
    adOpenKeyset, adLockOptimistic
```

When you pass a connection string to the **Open** method of the **Recordset** object, a connection will be created. However, a separate connection is opened for each recordset you create using this method.

If you want to share a connection with multiple recordsets, create the **Connection** object first, and then pass the **Connection** object variable, rather than a literal string, when invoking the **Open** method of a **Recordset** object, as shown in the following example code:

```
Set conn = Server.CreateObject ("ADODB.Connection")
conn.Open "DSN=StateU;DATABASE=StateU", "SA", ""

Set rs = Server.CreateObject ("ADODB.Recordset")
rs.Open "Select * from students", conn, _
        adOpenKeyset, adLockOptimistic
```

Creating a Recordset Using the Execute Method

There are two other ways to create a recordset:

◆ **Execute** method on a **Connection** object

◆ **Execute** method on a **Command** object

For information about using the **Execute** method of the **Command** object, see "Executing a Command" on page 292 in this chapter. For information about using the **Execute** method of the **Connection** object, see the Visual InterDev Help.

Cursor Types

When you open a recordset, it contains a cursor. A cursor points to the current record. When you call a navigation method such as **MoveNext**, you move the cursor. When you create a recordset, you can specify which type of cursor to create. Each cursor type supports different functions. To determine your cursor type, identify the features you need and which cursor types are included by your database provider.

The following table describes the features of the different cursor types.

Cursor Type	Cursor Features
Forward-only	Lets users move forward through read-only data
Static	Lets users move back and forth through read-only data
Keyset	Lets users move back and forth through read/write data and see modifications and deletions made by other users
Dynamic	Lets users move back and forth through read/write data and see additions, modifications, and deletions made by other users

Note Forward-only cursors are the fastest cursors, but they include only one view of the data.

Types of Locking Modes

The following table outlines your choices for types of locking modes.

Locking Mode	Scenario
Optimistic locking	Locks a record in a data source at the last possible moment, during a call to the **Update** function
Pessimistic locking	Locks a record at the earliest possible moment, during a call to the **Edit** function and not unlock it until after the call to the Update function

Navigating Records

In any recordset, there is one current record (unless the recordset is empty). To change the current record, you use one of the **Move** methods of the **Recordset** object.

The **BOF** (beginning of file) or **EOF** (end of file) properties are **True** if you are at the beginning or the end of the recordset, respectively. If there are no records in a recordset, both the **BOF** and **EOF** properties are **True**. As you move through a recordset, check the value of the **BOF** and **EOF** properties to determine when you reach the end of the recordset.

Tip If a recordset supports bookmarks (the cursor type is keyset or static), the **RecordCount** property of a recordset will return the number of records in the recordset.

If a recordset does not support bookmarks (the cursor type is forward only or dynamic), the **RecordCount** property will always return **-1**.

The following illustration shows a recordset.

Error	
BOF	
1	Shannon
2	Chris
3	Kari
EOF	
Error	

The following example code moves through all the records in a recordset:

```
Do Until rs.EOF
  ' while not at end of recordset,
  ' move to the next record
  rs.MoveNext
Loop
```

To retrieve data from a field in the current record, use the **Fields** collection, and specify the name of the field, as in the following example code:

```
customer = rs.Fields("First_Name")
```

You can also use the **Fields** collection to loop through all fields in the current record. The following example code displays all fields from the current record:

```
For i = 0 to rs.Fields.Count -1
  Response.Write rs.fields(i)
Next
```

Modifying Data

To add, modify, and delete records from a recordset, you can use methods of the **Recordset** object.

Adding Records

To add a record to a database, use the **AddNew** method of the **Recordset** object, set values for the record, and then use the **Update** method to save the record.

The following example code retrieves values from the **Request** object in an .asp file and adds a new record to the Majors table:

```
rsMajors.Addnew
  rsMajors("MajorID")= Request("MajorID")
  rsMajors("Description")= Request("Description")
rsMajors.Update
```

If you invoke the **AddNew** method, and then move from the current record, or you invoke another **AddNew** method before calling **Update**, ADO will automatically update the record.

To cancel an update, call the **CancelUpdate** method.

Updating Records

To change the values of the current record, set the appropriate fields and then use the **Update** method to save the changes.

The following example code changes the description of the current record to Science, and saves the changes:

```
rsMajors("Description") = "Science"
rsMajors.Update
```

Note If you have opened the recordset with a lock type of **adLockBatchOptimistic**, you must call the **UpdateBatch** method to save changes.

Deleting Records

To delete the current record, use the **Delete** method of the **Recordset** object. After you delete a record, invoke a **Move** method to move to the next record. Otherwise the current record pointer points to an empty record.

The following example code deletes the current record in the rsStudents recordset.

```
rsStudents.Delete
rsStudents.MoveNext
```

Executing a Command

You do not need to create a **Recordset** object to open a database and query on it. You can use a **Command** object and execute an SQL **Insert**, **Update**, or **Delete** statement to add or modify records. Using a SQL statement is more efficient than creating a recordset and using recordset methods.

The collections, methods, and properties of the **Command** object vary, depending on the database provider.

Creating a Command Object

To create a **Command** object, you pass *ADODB.Command* as an argument to the **CreateObject** function.

▶ **To create a Command object**

1. Create a **Command** object by calling **CreateObject** and passing it the **ADODB.Command** parameter.

2. Set the **CommandText** property equal to the text that you want to have executed.

3. Set, in seconds, the **CommandTimeOut** property of the **Command** object. The **CommandTimeOut** property determines how long the object will wait for the results of a command.

4. Make the **Command** object the active connection for the data source.

5. Call the **Execute** method to run the command.

The following example code retrieves a value from the **Request** object in an .asp file, creates a **Command** object, sets properties for the command, and then runs it:

```
frmClassID = Request("classID")
Set cmd = Server.CreateObject("ADODB.Command")
cmd.CommandText = "exec ClassList " & frmClassID
cmd.CommandTimeOut = 30
cmd.ActiveConnection = conn ' use existing Connection object
cmd.Execute
```

The syntax for the **Execute** method is as follows.

command.***Execute*** RecordsAffected, Parameters, Options

◆ RecordsAffected

Optional argument. A Long variable to which the database provider returns the number of records affected by the SQL command that was executed.

◆ Parameters

Optional argument. An array of values used as parameters for the command.

◆ Options

Optional argument. A numeric value that indicates the type of command, such as an SQL string, a stored procedure, or a table name.

- adCmdText, 1 = Evaluate CommandText as a text definition of a command.

- adCmdTable, 2 = Evaluate CommandText as a table name.

- adCmdStoredProc, 4 = Evaluate CommandText as a stored procedure.

- adCmdUnknown, 8 = The type of command in the CommandText argument is not known.

> **Note** If Options, is not explicitly stated, it will default to 8 - adCmdUnknown, and try each option type one at a time against the command until it finds one that will run. This will slow execution time. Specify the option if you know it so the command will execute immediately.

The following example code runs an SQL command that changes a student's last name. The code then displays the number of records affected by the update.

```
sql= "UPDATE Students SET Last_Name= " & _
     "'" & frmNewName &"'" & _
     " WHERE StudentID = " & frmStudentid
cmd.CommandText = sql
cmd.Execute iRecordsAffected, , adCmdText

Response.Write "Number of Records updated = " &  iRecordsAffected
```

To execute an SQL command that returns a recordset, save the return value from the **Execute** method in a **Recordset** object variable. This example code runs the stored procedure **ClassList**, which returns a recordset.

```
cmd.CommandText = "Exec ClassList " & frmClassID
Set rs = cmd.Execute
```

> **Note** Recordsets created from the Cmd.Execute method will have a forward-only cursor, and will be of type Read-only. If you need a different cursor type or write access, create a **Recordset** object independently and specify the cursor type in the **Open** method.

Running Stored Procedures with Parameters

To run a stored procedure that accepts parameters, you can create a **Parameter** object for each parameter, and then append the **Parameter** object to the **Parameters** collection of the **Command** object.

To create a **Parameter** object, you invoke the **CreateParameter** method of the **Command** object.

The syntax of the **CreateParameter** method is as follows.

command.*CreateParameter* Name, Type, Direction, Size, Value

◆ Name

Optional argument. A string representing the name of the **Parameter** object.

◆ Type

Optional argument. A Long value specifying the data type of the **Parameter** object.

◆ Direction

Optional argument. A Long value specifying whether the **Parameter** object represents input, output, or both.

◆ Size

Optional argument. A Long value specifying the maximum length for the parameter value in characters or bytes.

◆ Value

Optional argument. A Variant value specifying the value for the **Parameter** object.

The following sample code runs a command with parameters. To copy this code for use in your own project, see "Calling Parameterized Queries" on the accompanying CD-ROM.

```
'This code runs a stored procedure that requires parameters
cmd.CommandText = "GetStudentGPA"
cmd.CommandType = adCmdStoredProc
set parm =
cmd.CreateParameter("StudentID",adInteger,adParamInput,4,1)
cmd.Parameters.Append parm
set parm = cmd.CreateParameter("GPA",adSingle,adParamOutput,4)
cmd.Parameters.Append parm
cmd.Execute
response.write cmd.Parameters("GPA")
```

> **Note** You can pass parameters by assigning values to the **Parameters** collection without using **CreateParameter**. However, the disadvantage to this method is that each assignment causes the **Command** object to query the data source for the type of the parameter.
>
> Using **CreateParameter** to create parameters explicitly, and then appending the **Parameter** objects to the **Command** object, requires a few more lines of code but will avoid extra network trips to the database.

If a stored procedure returns an output parameter and a recordset, you must read the output parameters before accessing the recordset. Once you access the recordset, the output parameters can no longer be read.

Handling Errors

When you create Web applications that access a database, you should anticipate possible database errors and include error-handling code in your script. For general information on how to write error-handling code in VBScript, see "Handling Run-Time Errors in Client Script" on page 112 in Chapter 3, "Using Dynamic HTML."

Error-Handling Strategy

The best strategy for handling errors is to provide code that attempts to correct the error. For example, if a database connection fails to open, you can write code that connects to a back-up database. If this works, the user doesn't need to know that an error has occurred.

You can also try to prevent errors. For example, if you have a form in which the user enters a date range, you can place validation code on the form to verify the dates before the form is submitted.

If an error cannot be corrected or prevented, you can return an informative message to the user. One way to supply a message is to redirect the user to another Web page that will display the message.

To redirect the user to another Web page, you call the **Redirect** method of the **Response** object. However, **Redirect** will work only if it has been placed in the server script before the <HTML> tag is read. By placing all of the server script before the <HTML> tag, you can trap errors and display a different Web page if necessary. For more information on using **Redirect**, see "The Redirect Method" on page 189 in Chapter 4, "Using Active Server Pages."

The following sample code checks for a database error and redirects the user to another Web page that displays an error message. To copy this code for use in your own project, see "Error Handling by Redirecting" on the accompanying CD-ROM.

```
'This code is placed before the <HTML> tag
'Run code to perform work here
If err.number <> 0 Then
    session("ErrorTitle") = "Error Title to be Displayed"
    session("ErrorText") = "Description of Error"
    'Redirect to custom built error page that will display the
session variables
    response.redirect "error.asp"
End If
```

The Errors Collection

The **Connection** object provides an **Errors** collection that contains information on database errors. To determine if an error occurred, you can use the **Err** object provided by VBScript or the **Errors** collection.

The advantage of using the **Errors** collection is that if multiple errors occur during a single database operation, all of the errors will be stored in the collection. The **Err** object contains information only on the last error returned.

Performance Considerations for ADO

The following paragraphs describe some issues to consider when using ADO in your applications.

Use SQL Commands Instead of a Recordset

When you create an ADO **Recordset** object, the recordset is created on the server. This is referred to as a server-side cursor. This is an expensive operation because it consumes server system resources.

To update a database, you can use SQL commands, instead of creating a recordset and using methods of the **Recordset** object. For example, to insert a record into a table, you can execute an SQL Insert command rather than creating a recordset and using the **AddNew** and **Update** methods. When you use the SQL Insert command, no recordset is created.

Manage Recordset Size for Efficiency

If the records returned from a query can be displayed on one Web page, you can write server-side script that creates a recordset, scrolls through the recordset, returns all the data as HTML text, and then closes the recordset. In this case, you can set the cursor type for the recordset to forward-only. This is the fastest type of cursor.

If the records returned from a query do not fit on one Web page, you can provide command buttons on the Web page for the user to request another page of records. To do this, you have several choices.

◆ When you create the initial recordset, you can store the **Recordset** object in a session variable. When the user requests a new page of records, you use the stored **Recordset** object to retrieve the next set of records. Storing a **Recordset** object consumes server resources. Therefore, this approach may not be practical if your Web site has many concurrent users.

◆ Another approach is to save only the number of the current record in a session variable. In this case, you create a recordset, return one page of records, save the number of the last record returned, and then close the recordset.

When the user requests the next page of records, you query the database again, use the saved recordset number to return the next page of records, and then close the recordset again. This approach reduces data server resources because no recordsets are kept open during a session.

◆ A third alternative is to use RDS instead of using ADO. RDS stores a recordset on the client workstation rather than on the server. For more information on using RDS, see "Using the Remote Data Service" on page 307 in this chapter.

Place Data Updates in Business Objects

The best approach to working with data updates is to place the update code in business objects rather than directly in .asp files. The .asp file can then create an instance of the business object and invoke methods to perform an update. You can use ADO in Visual Basic to implement business objects.

There are several reasons to place code for data updates in business objects.

♦ You can create multiple business objects, each one responsible for a discrete task. Breaking an application into discrete components simplifies maintenance and testing.

♦ Business logic should be isolated from the user interface, which is provided by the .asp file. Business logic determines how a database can be modified based on rules of the business. For example, at a university, there may be a rule that a student who has a grade point average below 2.0 cannot enroll in any new classes. When you write code to add a record to an enrollment table, you must ensure the student meets the required grade point average. By placing this logic in a business object, you isolate the code. If the business rule changes, you modify the business object rather than redesign the .asp file.

♦ A business object can be invoked by many types of clients, such as .asp files and Visual Basic or Visual C++ applications. If you have a general business object that updates a database, many applications can use the object. Code in .asp files works only with browser clients.

♦ If a business object fails, the error is isolated. It will not cause the failure of the entire Web server.

For more information about creating business objects, see Chapter 7, "Creating COM Components" on page 319, and Chapter 8, "Using Microsoft Transaction Server" on page 353.

Lab 6: Using ActiveX Data Objects

In this lab, you will use ADO code in Active Server Pages to retrieve and update a database. You will also add code to handle possible database errors.

To see the demonstration "Lab 6 Solution," see the accompanying CD-ROM.

The following diagram shows how the files you edit in this lab will fit into the State University Web site.

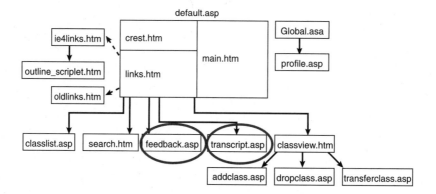

Estimated time to complete this lab: **60 minutes**

To complete the exercises in this lab, you must have the required software. For detailed information about the labs and setup for the labs, see "Labs" in "About This Course."

The solution code for this lab is located in the \Labs\Lab06\Solution folder.

Objectives

After completing this lab, you will be able to:

◆ Create a connection to a database using the ADO **Connection** object.

◆ Create an ADO **Recordset** object and retrieve records.

◆ Add new records to a database using ADO objects.

Prerequisites

Before working on this lab, you should be familiar with the following:

◆ Adding files to Web projects in Visual InterDev.

◆ Editing project files in Visual InterDev.

◆ Creating and debugging scripts in Visual InterDev.

Exercises

The following exercises provide practice working with the concepts and techniques covered in this chapter:

◆ Exercise 1: Retrieving Records

In this exercise, you will create the transcript page that retrieves the classes and grades for a student. You will use ADO to establish a connection to the State University database, retrieve the transcript for the student into a recordset, and then display the records in a table.

◆ Exercise 2: Adding Records

In this exercise, you will add ADO code to the Feedback page to add data to the Feedback table in the State University database

◆ Exercise 3: Handling Database Errors

In this exercise, you will modify the Feedback page to handle errors that occur when adding a new record.

Exercise 1: Retrieving Records

In this exercise, you will create the Transcript page that retrieves the classes and grades for a student. You will use ADO to establish a connection to the State University database, retrieve the transcript for the student into a recordset, and then display the records in a table.

▶ Create the data connection

1. In the file Transcript.asp, just before the <HTML> tag, add server script that sets the value of a variable named frmStudentID equal to the student ID session variable.

   This is the session variable you created and used in Lab 4.

2. On the line following the </H3> tag, add some more server script.

3. Create an ADO **Connection** object named conn by using the **CreateObject** function.

4. Using the application variables stored in Global.asa for the StateU data connection set the **ConnectionTimeout** and **CommandTimeout** properties for the object.

Note These application variables will only exist in Global.asa if you have added a data connection in your project to the State University database. For more information, see Lab 5.1, "Accessing Data" on page 251.

5. Add a call to the **Open** method to establish the connection. Use the application values stored in Global.asa to set the connection string, user name, and password.

   For more information about using the **Connection** object, see "Establishing a Database Connection" on page 251 in this chapter.

   To see an example of how your code should look, see Lab Hint 6.1 in Appendix B.

▶ **Retrieve the transcript records**

1. Use the **CreateObject** method to create a **Recordset** object variable named rsTranscript.

2. Set the **ActiveConnection** property of rsTranscript to the conn **Connection** object.

3. To retrieve the transcript records for the student ID, invoke the **Open** method of rsTranscript.

   The query should retrieve the classid, title, and grade fields from the Enrollment table and Classes table, where StudentID equals frmStudentID.

   For more information about using the **Recordset** object, see "Retrieving Records" on page 286 and "Navigating Records" on page 290 in this chapter.

   To see an example of how your code should look, see Lab Hint 6.2 in Appendix B.

▶ **Display the transcript records**

1. In Transcript.asp, after the server script from the previous procedure, create an HTML table that has one row and three columns. Enter the following column headers: Class Number, Title, and Grade.

   To see an example of how your code should look, see Lab Hint 6.3 in Appendix B.

2. After the first row of the table, add script that defines a **Do Until...Loop** statement to loop through the recordset. Use the **EOF** property of the recordset to determine when to exit the loop.

3. In the loop, add script that creates a new table row by writing a <TR> tag, then display the ClassID and Title fields from the rsTranscript recordset. Use the beginning and ending <TD> tags around the fields in the table columns.

4. To convert the Grade field from a number to a letter before displaying them, add a **Select Case** statement that converts 4, 3, 2, 1, 0 to A, B, C, D, and F, respectively, and then display the letter grade in the third column. Include a **Case Else** clause to check for a no grade, and display "In Progress" if there is no numeric value for the grade.

5. In the last step of the loop, write a </TR> tag to end the table row.

6. Add script to move to the next record in the rsTranscript recordset.

To see an example of how your code should look, see Lab Hint 6.4 in Appendix B.

7. Test your work by viewing Transcript.asp in the browser.

You should see the student ID listed in the header of the page, and the table displaying class number, title, and grades for any courses the student has attended.

Note The Transcript.asp file uses the student ID provided on the Profile page, Profile.asp. You may need to first view Profile.asp and enter the information on the form before viewing Transcript.asp. To get data for an existing student in the State University database, enter **4** for the student ID on the Profile page.

Exercise 2: Adding Records

In this exercise, you will add ADO code to the Feedback page to add data to the Feedback table in the State University database.

▶ Store the form values in variables

1. Open the file Feedback.asp in Visual InterDev.

2. Remove any server script that you added to the page in Lab 2.

3. At the beginning of the page, add server script that reads the form values from the **Request** object.

4. Store the values passed for the controls in the form — **restime, ease, interactive,** and **useful** — in variables named frmRestime, frmEase, frmInteractive, and frmUseful, respectively.

To see an example of how your code should look, see Lab Hint 6.5 in Appendix B.

▶ **Add the data only if the user entered data in the form**

1. After the script you created in the previous procedure, add the following **If...Then...Else** statement that checks to see if the all the variables for the form controls have values:

```
If Not IsEmpty(frmRestime) And _
    Not IsEmpty(frmEase) And _
    Not IsEmpty(frmInteractive) And _
    Not IsEmpty(frmUseful) Then
```

If all the variables have values, then the feedback data can be added to the State University database. If they are empty, then the feedback page including the form should be redisplayed.

2. Surround the HTML content of the page in an **Else** clause. The **Else** clause should be the last server script statement before the <HTML> tag in the page, like the following code:

```
...
Else %>
<HTML>
...
```

3. At the end of the page after the </HTML> tag, add the **End If** statement, like the following code:

```
</HTML>
<% End If %>
```

Note The script you create in subsequent procedures should be added between the **Then** and **Else** clause of the statements you added in the previous procedure.

▶ **Create the data connection**

1. Add to the script you created in the previous procedure, and create an ADO **Connection** object named conn by using the **CreateObject** function.

2. Using the application variables stored in Global.asa for the State University data connection, set the **ConnectionTimeout** and **CommandTimeout** properties for the object.

> **Note** These application variables will only exist in Global.asa if you have added a data connection in your project to the State University database. For more information, see Lab 5.1, "Accessing Data" on page 251.

3. Add a call to the **Open** method to establish the connection. Use the application values stored in Global.asa to set the connection string, user name, and password.

    For more information about using the **Connection** object, see "Establishing a Database Connection" on page 283 in this chapter.

    To see an example of how your code should look, see Lab Hint 6.6 in Appendix B.

▶ **Add a new record and acknowledge the student's feedback**

1. To add a new record, call the **Execute** method on the **Connection** object to run an SQL query that inserts the form parameters into the database. Add the following code for the SQL query to execute:

```
strSQL = "INSERT INTO feedback " & _
    "(Response, Useful, Interactive, Ease)" & _
    " VALUES (" & frmResponse & "," & frmUseful & _
    "," & frmInteractive & "," & frmEase & ")"
```

2. Display a message to acknowledge the feedback using **Response.Write.**

3. Send back the response using **Response.End.**

    Use this method in order to send back the response to the browser immediately without including the rest of the HTML content in Feedback.asp.

    To see an example of how your code should look, see Lab Hint 6.7 in Appendix B.

▶ **Test your work**

1. Save your changes, and view Feedback.asp in the browser.

2. Enter data in the feedback form, and click **Submit**. Verify that you get a response acknowledging that your feedback was recorded.

3. In the Data View window, open the Feedback table and verify that the new record has been added.

Exercise 3: Handling Database Errors

In this exercise, you will modify the Feedback page to handle errors when adding a new record.

> **Note** This exercise demonstrates a simple error-handling approach for the State University Web site. However, in a real-world application, you may want to use more powerful techniques, such as logging errors to a Web server log or taking different actions based on the error.

▶ **Check for errors when adding a new record**

1. Add the file Error.asp from the \Labs\Lab06\New folder to the State University Web project.

2. Open the file Feedback.asp in Visual InterDev.

3. To change the default error-handling behavior, add the statement **On Error Resume Next** just before the statement that establishes a database connection.

4. Locate the server script that adds the new record with the SQL **INSERT** statement.

5. After the **Execute** method is called to run the SQL statement, add an **If** statement to check if an error has occurred.

6. If an error has occurred:

   a. Set the ErrorTitle session variable to Feedback Form.

   b. Set the ErrorText session variable to the **Description** property of the **Err** object.

   c. Call the **Response.Redirect** method to redirect to Error.asp.

   For information about using the **Redirect** method of the **Response** object, see "The Redirect Method" on page 189 in Chapter 4, "Using Active Server Pages."

   To see an example of how your code should look, see Lab Hint 6.8 in Appendix B.

▶ **Test your work**

1. Save your changes.

2. For testing purposes, start the SQL Service Manager, and pause your server by double-clicking **Pause**.

3. View Feedback.asp in the browser. Verify that you get redirected to Error.asp, and it displays the cause of the error.

4. Go to SQL Service Manager, and restart your server by double-clicking **Start**.

Using the Remote Data Service

In this section, you will learn how to use RDS to create Web pages that retrieve and update information in a database.

RDS is a set of components that you can use to build Web applications for accessing ODBC-compliant databases. RDS binds the data from a recordset to data-aware HTML elements or ActiveX controls on a Web page.

To use RDS, you work with COM components, HTML, and client-side script. You add the **RDS.DataControl** object to an HTML document, and set properties to indicate the data to retrieve. You then set attributes on HTML elements to bind them to the **RDS.DataControl** object.

You can also write client-side script to request a new set of records or submit changes to the database at run time.

RDS Component Overview

The components of RDS are divided into client-side components and server-side components.

To see the animation "How RDS Works," see the accompanying CD-ROM.

Client-Side Components

RDS client-side components run in an HTML document to provide dynamic data to the user. These components are not visible in the HTML document. Instead, they provide data from a recordset in data-bound ActiveX controls that are visible. The following list describes the RDS client components.

◆ RDS.DataControl

The **RDS.DataControl** object runs queries and makes the resulting recordsets available to the data-bound controls on an HTML document. You set properties for the object to identify the Web server, data source, and SQL statement to retrieve records.

◆ RDS.DataSpace

The **RDS.DataSpace** object creates instances of business objects that reside on a Web server.

You can write client-side script to use these objects to invoke instances of your own custom business objects on the Web server.

◆ ADOR.Recordset

The **RDS.DataSpace** object creates an **ADOR.Recordset** object when it retrieves records. This type of recordset object is similar to the ADO **Recordset** object, but does not include all of the same features. Because it includes fewer features, it is smaller and can download quickly.

Server-Side Components

The server-side components of RDS include the **RDSServer.DataFactory** object.

◆ RDSServer.DataFactory

The **RDSServer.DataFactory** object is a business object that has been implemented as a COM server component. This is the default object used by the **RDS.DataControl** object to run queries.

How RDS Displays a Recordset

The following list outlines the sequence of events that occurs when RDS displays a recordset.

1. User submits a query on an HTML document.

2. The client-side script assigns the query to the **RDS.DataControl** object and calls the **Refresh** method.

3. The **RDS.DataControl** object submits the query by using HTTP to the Web server.

4. RDS routes the query to the **RDSServer.DataFactory** object, which runs the query against the data source.

5. Resulting recordset is sent back to the **RDS.DataControl** object by using HTTP.

6. The data-bound controls on the HTML document display records from the recordset.

7. The recordset is cached on the client side.

8. When a user moves through the recordset, the controls display the data without making another trip to the Web server.

Binding Data to an Element

Data binding is based on a component architecture that consists of four major pieces:

♦ Data source objects, which provide the data to a page

♦ Data consumers, which are data-consuming HTML elements that display data

♦ Binding agents, which ensure that both provider and consumer are synchronized

♦ The table repetition agent, which works with tabular data consumers to provide a data set

Internet Explorer 4.0 supports data binding and the use of data source objects. RDS is simply one more data source object.

To see the expert point-of-view "Data Binding," see the accompanying CD-ROM.

Data Source Objects

To bind data to the elements of an HTML page in Internet Explorer 4.0, a data source object (DSO) must be present on that page. A DSO implements an open specification that allows the DSO developer to determine the following:

♦ How the data is transmitted to the page. A DSO can use any transport protocol it chooses. This might be a standard Internet protocol such as HTTP or simple file I/O.

♦ Whether the transmission occurs synchronously or asynchronously. Asynchronous transmission is preferred, as it provides the most immediate interactivity to the user.

♦ How the data set is specified. A DSO might require an ODBC connection string and an SQL statement, or it might accept a simple URL.

- How the data is manipulated through scripts. Since a DSO maintains data on the client, it also manages how the data is sorted and filtered.
- Whether updates are allowed.

Data Consumers

Data consumers are elements on the HTML page capable of rendering data supplied by a DSO. Elements include many of those intrinsic to HTML, as well as custom objects implemented as Java applets or ActiveX Controls. Internet Explorer 4.0 supports HTML extensions to allow authors to bind an element to a specific column of data in a data set exposed by a DSO. Applets and ActiveX Controls support additional binding semantics.

Binding Agents

Binding agents perform the following two functions:

- When a page is first loaded, the binding agent finds the DSOs and the data consumers among those elements on the page.
- The binding agent also maintains the synchronization of the data that flows between all DSOs and data consumers. For example, when the DSO receives more data from its source, the binding agent transmits the new data to the consumers. Conversely, when a user updates a data bound element on the page, the binding agent notifies the DSO.

Table Repetition Agents

The repetition agents work with tabular data consumers (such as the HTML TABLE element) to repeat the entire data set supplied by a DSO.

Note Individual elements in the table are synchronized through interaction with the binding agent.

Using a Data Source Object

To use a data source object on a page:

1. Insert the data source object onto a page using the OBJECT tag.

2. Set the DATASRC attribute/property of the HTML element to which you want to bind data equal to the ID of the data source object you inserted.

3. Set the DATAFLD attribute/property equal to the column of the data source from which you want data.

Inserting the RDS.DataControl Object

The **RDS.DataControl** functions like a recordset in ADO. It provides data to a data-bound elements, like a text box control, on an HTML page in a Web application.

The **RDS.DataControl** object runs queries and makes the resulting recordset available to data-bound elements on an HTML page. You bind data from the **RDS.DataControl** to data-aware controls by setting attributes of the elements.

In order to use the **RDS.DataControl** in your Web application, you add the ActiveX control to your Web page.

▶ **To add the RDS.DataControl to your page**

1. Add the following object tag anywhere on the page:

```
<OBJECT classid="clsid:BD96C556-65A3-11D0-983A-00C04FC29E33"
    ID=myDataSource Width=1 Height=1>
    <PARAM NAME="SERVER" VALUE="http://example.microsoft.com">
    <PARAM NAME="CONNECT" VALUE="dsn=sample">
</OBJECT>
```

2. Set the ID attribute, for example myDataSource.

Setting Attributes

The following table describes the attributes you set for the **RDS.DataControl** object.

Attribute	Description
SQL	Specifies the SQL statement to retrieve records.
CONNECT	Specifies the data source name, user ID, and password.
SERVER	If you are using HTTP, ServerName is the name of the Web server computer.

▶ **To use the RDS.DataControl object**

1. Add the appropriate HTML controls to your HTML document.

2. Set the DATASRC attribute to the ID of the RDS.DataControl and place a # in front of it. For example:

```
<TABLE DATASRC=#myDataSource>
```

3. Set the DATAFLD attribute of the HTML control to a field in the DATASRC.

```
<TD DATAFLD=Name>
```

Scripting the Control

You can add client-side script to your HTML document to change properties of the **RDS.DataControl** object and submit a new query to the Web server at run time.

Sending a New Query

To send a new query to RDS, you modify the SQL property of the **RDS.DataControl** object and use the **Refresh** method to run the query. A new set of records will be retrieved and the data-bound controls will be updated automatically with the new data.

The following example code sets the SQL property of the **RDS.DataControl** object based on input from a user, then queries the database again:

```
Sub cmdFind_OnClick
  ADC.SQL = "exec classlist " & "'" & txtid.value & "'"
  ADC.Refresh
End Sub
```

Changing the Current Record

The **RDS.DataControl** object uses a recordset that always specifies a current record. The current record is displayed in the data-bound controls.

To change the current record, you run script that uses one of the move methods of the **RDS.DataControl** object. The data-bound controls will display the new current record. Because the recordset is cached on the client workstation, a user can browse a large recordset without sending additional requests to the Web server for new data.

The following example code moves the current record forward one record:

```
Sub cmdMoveNext_OnClick
  ADC.MoveNext
End Sub
```

Changing Data

Data-bound controls enable the user to visually edit, add, or delete records. All changes made by the user are stored locally until the user explicitly submits or cancels the update.

Tip For some ActiveX controls, you must set a property to allow editing. For example, you must set the **AllowUpdate** and **AllowAddNew** properties of the data-bound Grid control to allow the user to edit and add data in the control.

Note To enable the user to change data on data-bound controls, you add the **For Browse** statement to the end of the query. Currently, only Microsoft SQL Server supports this statement.

To submit changes, invoke the **SubmitChanges** method of the **RDS.DataControl** object. To cancel changes, invoke the **CancelUpdate** method.

The following example code shows how an **Update** button and a **Cancel** button can be used to submit or cancel changes to a recordset:

```
Sub Update_OnClick
  ADC.SubmitChanges
End Sub

Sub Cancel_OnClick
  ADC.CancelUpdate
End Sub
```

Using the RDSServer.DataFactory

In most cases, you will not need to use the **RDSServer.DataFactory** object directly. When you use the **RDS.DataControl** object, it invokes the **RDSServer.DataFactory** object for you.

However, when you use the **RDS.DataControl** object to create a recordset, you cannot write script that reads the data in the recordset programmatically. If you need to read the data in a recordset programmatically, you can use **RDS.DataSpace** and **RDSServer.DataFactory** objects to create the recordset.

You will need to programmatically read data in a recordset if you want to display the data from the recordset in controls that are not data-aware. In this case, you must write script to read the recordset and then set the value of the controls.

▶ **To create a recordset using the RDSServer.DataFactory object**

1. Insert the **RDS.DataSpace** control on your HTML document.

2. Create an instance of the **RDSServer.DataFactory** object by invoking the **CreateRecordset** method of the **RDS.DataSpace** object.

3. Create a recordset by invoking the **Query** method of the **RDSServer.DataFactory** object.

4. Assign data from the current record to HTML text box controls.

The following example code creates an **RDSServer.DataFactory** object, queries the State University database for a list of all students, and then assigns the first and last names from the current record to HTML controls.

```
set ADF = ADS1.CreateObject("AdvancedDataFactory","http://
myserver")
set myRS = ADF.Query("DSN=stateu;UID=sa;PWD=;","select * from
students")
txtFirstName.value = myRS.fields("First_Name")
txtLastName.value = myRS.fields("Last_Name")
```

If you also want to display the data from the recordset in data-aware controls, you can insert the **RDS.DataControl** object in your HTML document and add the data-aware controls. Then, you set the **Recordset** property of the **RDS.DataControl** object to the recordset object returned by **RDSServer.DataFactory**. The following example code sets the **Recordset** property of the **RDS.DataControl** to the recordset variable myRs.

```
ADC.Recordset = myRS
```

Some data-bound controls enable users to scroll through records. Depending on the purpose of your HTML document, you may want to update other controls in response to a user moving through the recordset. You can set the **Bookmark** property of a **Recordset** object to reposition the current record.

The following example code shows a data-bound list box that displays a list of student IDs. When a user selects a student ID in the list box, the script sets the **Bookmark** property of the recordset to the selected item from the list box and updates the HTML text boxes.

```
Sub DBList_Click()
    myRS.BookMark = DBList.selecteditem
    txtFirstName.value = myRS.fields("First_Name")
    txtLastName.value = myRS.fields("Last_Name")
End Sub
```

Performance Considerations for RDS

With RDS, you can create efficient Web applications. This topic summarizes some of the advantages of using RDS to design and build applications that enable data retrieval and updates on your Web site.

Data Retrieval

RDS is ideal for retrieving and displaying records from both small and large recordsets. RDS caches records on the user's computer, which enables the user to browse all of the records in a recordset without having to retrieve additional HTML documents from the Web server.

Data Updates

Your Web site will be easier to maintain and will serve a larger number of users if you isolate the data updates in business objects instead of placing the data update code directly in HTML documents. You use a tool such as Visual Basic or Visual C++ to create business objects. In the business object, you define methods that update the database.

From an HTML document, you can use the **RDS.DataSpace** object to create an instance of your custom business objects and then invoke methods of the object.

Platform and Browser Compatibility

Currently, RDS works only in Microsoft Internet Explorer 4.0 running on an Intel platform in Windows 95 or Windows NT 4.0.

Self-Check Questions

To see the answers to the Self-Check Questions, see Appendix A.

1. Which ADO objects can you create with the CreateObject method?

A. Only the **Connection** object

B. Only the **Connection** and **Command** objects

C. Only the **Command** and **Recordset** objects

D. The Connection, Command, and Recordset objects

2. Assume that conn is a valid Connection object, and rsStudents is a valid Recordset object. Which statement will retrieve all of the records from the Students table?

A. Set rsStudents = conn.OpenRecordset "select * from students"

B. rsStudents.OpenRecordset "select * from students", conn

C. rsStudents.Open "select * from students", conn

D. Set rsStudents = CreateObject ("ADODB.Recordset", "select * from students", conn)

3. How is an ADO database error handled in an Active Server Page that does not have an error handler?

A. The error is ignored and processing continues. No message is returned to the user.

B. An HTML document containing nothing but the error message from the database is returned to the user.

C. The Web browser displays a dialog box with the message "Error processing Web page."

D. The error message from the database is included at the bottom of the HTML document returned to the user.

4. When you use RDS to retrieve records, where are the records cached?

A. On the Web client

B. In a business object on the Web server or Web client

C. On the Web server

D. On the database server

5. When you use the RDS.DataControl object, what properties do you set to specify the source of the data and the records to be retrieved?

A. Set the BINDINGS attribute of the **RDS.DataControl** object to the names of the data-bound controls in which the data will be displayed.

B. Set the DATASOURCE attribute of the data-bound controls in which the data will be displayed to the name of the **RDS.DataControl** object.

C. Set the BINDINGS attribute of the data-bound controls in which the data will be displayed to the name of the **RDS.DataControl** object.

D. Set the **Server, Connect,** and **SQL** properties.

6. What attributes of an HTML element do you set to bind it to a data source and fields within the data source?

A. sqlsc and sqlfld

B. datasrc and datafld

C. datasql and sqlfld

D. None of the above.

Student Notes:

Chapter 7:
Creating COM Components

In Chapter 1, "Planning a Web Site," you saw the importance of designing a Web site to accommodate the requirements of three different logical entities: user services, business services, and data services. In this chapter, you will learn how to create business services that can run on a Web server.

You will also learn how to use Visual Basic version 6 to build COM components that contain business rules, and how to call these COM components from a Web page.

The following illustration highlights the technologies you will learn about in this chapter.

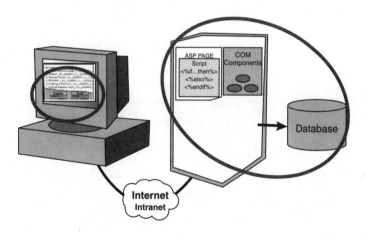

Objectives

After completing this chapter, you will be able to:

♦ Explain how to implement business services as middle-tier automation servers.

♦ Describe the development problems associated with building a three-tier solution.

♦ List the advantages of creating business objects as COM components.

♦ Build a COM component using Visual Basic 6.

♦ Call a COM component from an Active Server Page.

Overview of Business Services

In this section, you will learn how business rules in server components can increase your Web site's efficiency. You will also learn about the attributes used to create business objects.

Business Rules and Business Processes

In this topic, you will learn about two basic concepts of business services: business rules and business processes. You can process a number of business rules together as part of a business service.

The following illustration shows how business rules can be used together to carry out a process.

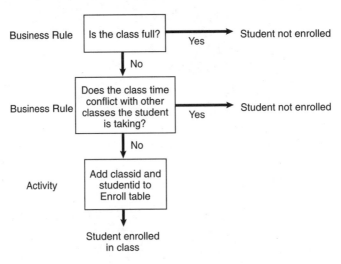

Business Rules

A business rule is an algorithm that determines how information is processed. For example, if a credit card number is entered into a form, one business rule may check the credit card number for the limit available in that account. If the available credit limit exceeds the transaction, credit will be granted and the transaction will proceed.

Business Processes

A business process is a sequence of related tasks that produces a specific response to a user's request. For example, when a user submits an order form to purchase a product from an online catalog, a transaction is executed. This is a business process.

Other examples of business processes include activities such as opening a new bank account, retrieving customer information, or retrieving benefit options for a specific employee. For each of these examples, a business process acts on a business rule.

The following illustration highlights the business processes for the State University Web Site.

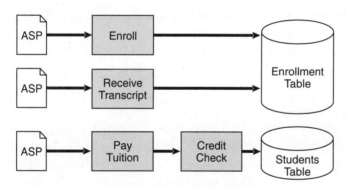

Business Objects and COM

Business processes are commonly represented as middle-tier objects. By using this approach, you can represent and implement business processes in an object-oriented environment as you plan your Web site. Furthermore, business services can be implemented as COM components and encapsulate a set of business functionalities.

Using Business Objects

There are several advantages to using an object-oriented model to create business processes.

◆ Simplification of complex processes

You can simplify a complex business process by breaking its individual parts into smaller pieces, or objects. Conceptually, you can think of each part of the process as a specific object, where an object performs a specific function of the process.

◆ Natural modeling techniques

Because object-oriented methodology reflects a natural way of looking at real-world objects and processes, components are often easier to analyze, design, and develop with object-oriented techniques. Furthermore, such objects tend to be more maintainable and reusable once they are developed.

◆ Encapsulation

Each business object encapsulates the data and functionality needed to accomplish its task. A business object exposes only those methods needed by other business objects. By encapsulating only specific data and functionality in each object, business objects are self-contained and isolated from changes made to other objects.

Implementing Business Objects as COM Components

A COM component is a unit of code that provides a specific, predefined functionality. By breaking your code into components, you can decide later how to most effectively distribute your application.

COM components offer several benefits:

◆ They provide a standard method of creating reusable, higher-level components.

◆ They can be created with and used from a variety of programming languages such as Visual Basic, Visual J++, and C++. COM guarantees interoperability regardless of the language used to implement the components.

◆ Scriptlets can also be modified to create COM components (more specifically, ActiveX controls). For more information about scriptlets, go to the Microsoft Scripting Technologies Web site at msdn.microsoft.com/scripting.

◆ They work with MTS. For information about MTS, see Chapter 8, "Using Microsoft Transaction Server" on page 353.

◆ COM components can be installed and used on both the server and the client.

However, because they run machine-dependent code, use on the client requires a rather homogenous client environment, which is not generally the case on a Web site. Nonetheless, COM components can be effectively used on servers running Win32 operating systems, as well as on Macintosh systems and certain types of UNIX systems.

The following illustration shows how the State University Web site will implement business services as COM components.

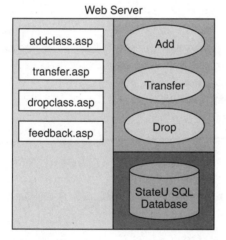

Creating COM Components in Visual Basic

In this section, you will learn how to create a new ActiveX DLL project in Visual Basic 6.0.

You will learn how to add class modules to create objects that encapsulate the internal functionality of a COM component. You will also learn how to expose methods from objects to make the COM components interoperable with other components and applications.

Choosing the Type of Component

With Visual Basic, you can build and run in-process or out-of-process components. In-process components are ActiveX DLLs. Out-of-process components are ActiveX EXEs.

The following table lists the advantages and disadvantages of using in-process and out-of-process components.

Type of component	Advantages	Disadvantages
In-process DLL	Faster access to objects	Less fault-tolerant; if the DLL fails, the entire executable fails.
Out-of-process EXE	Fault-tolerant; if the EXE fails, other processes in the system will not fail. Can be retained in memory as independent process.	Slower because of marshaling.

Note Starting with version 4.0, IIS allows you to run server applications in a process separate from the Web server. For more information, see "Isolating Applications" in the Windows NT Option Pack Help.

For more information about the differences between in-process and out-of-process components, search for "How Marshaling Affects ActiveX Component Performance" in Visual Basic Books Online.

MTS Constraints for Components

In Chapter 8, business objects of the State University application will be migrated to run under MTS. MTS places certain restraints and requirements on COM components that run under it. Components:

◆ Must be compiled as an ActiveX DLL (in-process COM component).

◆ Must provide a type library that describes their interfaces.

◆ Must be self-registering.

Fortunately, Visual Basic satisfies the last two options automatically when building COM components.

Note This chapter will focus on using ActiveX DLL projects in Visual Basic to build components, and not ActiveX EXE projects. This chapter and lab require you to use COM in-process DLLs. In addition, MTS components must be in-process DLLs. For more information about MTS components, see Chapter 8, "Using Microsoft Transaction Server" on page 353.

Project Templates

When you create a new project in Visual Basic, you first choose a template. To create a COM component, you choose either the ActiveX EXE or the ActiveX DLL template in the **New Project** dialog box. Selecting either type of template sets a number of default values that are important for creating code components.

Tip You can change the project type later by changing the project properties.

The following illustration shows the standard Visual Basic templates.

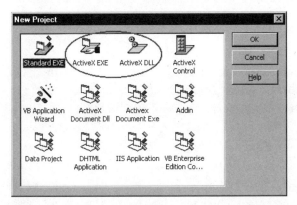

Setting Properties for Projects

When you create a new ActiveX DLL or ActiveX EXE project, you also set properties that affect how your component runs.

Project Properties

You set properties for a project by clicking *<projectname>* **Properties** on the **Project** menu. Then, you click the **General** tab of the **Project Properties** sheet to select the options you want. The following table describes the options you typically set for a new ActiveX DLL or ActiveX EXE project.

Option	Description
Project type	Provides the four template options: Standard EXE, ActiveX EXE, ActiveX DLL, and ActiveX Control. When you create a new ActiveX DLL or ActiveX EXE project, Visual Basic automatically sets the Project Type property. The project type determines how other project options can be set. For example, options on the Component tab are not available when the project type is set to Standard EXE.
Startup object	Sets which form or Sub Main procedure in the current project runs first. For most ActiveX EXEs and ActiveX DLLs, you set the Startup Object field to (None). If you want initialization code to run when the component is loaded, set the Startup Object property to Sub Main. If you want initialization code to run when an instance of a class is created, use the Class_Initialize event.
Project name	Specifies the component name to which the client application refers.
Project description	Enables you to enter a brief description of the COM component, along with the objects it provides. The contents of this field will appear in the References dialog box when you select references for other Visual Basic projects. The text also appears in the Description pane at the bottom of the Object Browser.
Unattended execution	Specifies whether the component will run without user interaction. Unattended components do not have a user interface. Any run-time functions, such as messages that normally result in user interaction, are written to an event log. If this box is checked, the project will be built to use the threading apartment model. Using this model will make your objects run more efficiently.
Threading model	The threading model list box is only activated for ActiveX DLL and ActiveX Control projects. The only options are single-threaded and apartment-threaded.

The business service objects created in this chapter will be built as ActiveX DLLs.

Using Class Modules

Visual Basic provides a type of module called a class module. Each class module defines one type of object.

A class module represents a logical object in your component. In an application, you can have several class modules. At run time, you create an object by creating an instance of a class. A class is a template for an object. An object is an instance of a class.

For example, you can create an **Employee** class that has properties such as **LastName** and **FirstName**, and a method such as **Hire**.

Adding a Class Module to a Project

When you create a new ActiveX DLL project, by choosing the ActiveX DLL template in the **New Project** dialog box, Visual Basic creates a project with one class module.

To see the animation "Creating an Instance of a Class," see the accompanying CD-ROM.

You can add a new class module by clicking **Add Class Module** on the Visual Basic **Project** menu. You can then add methods, properties, and events to the class.

Creating an Instance of a Class

To create an instance of a class in the project that defines the class, you use the **Dim** and **Set** statements. This example code creates an instance of the **Customer** class:

```
Dim objCustomer as Customer
Set ObjCustomer = New Customer
```

You can also use the more compact syntax such as **Dim ObjCustomer As New Customer** instead of using the **Set** statement.

Once you have created an object, you can use methods and properties of the object. This example code invokes the **Add** method of the **Customer** object.

```
ObjCustomer.Add "Joe", "Programmer", 31
```

Setting Properties for Class Modules

To determine the behavior of a component, you set properties for each class module in the component. The **Name** and the **Instancing** properties provide classes with information about components, which client applications use to instantiate objects.

Name Property

To create a name for the class, set the **Name** property in the Properties window. This name will be used by the client application to create an instance of an object.

For example, the following code creates an instance of a class named **MyClass**, which is defined in the project named **Project1**.

```
Dim x
Set x = CreateObject ("Project1.MyClass")
```

The class name is combined with the name of the component to produce a fully qualified class name, also referred to as a *programmatic ID* or *ProgID*. In the previous example code, the fully qualified class name of the **MyClass** class is Project1.MyClass.

Instancing Property

The **Instancing** property determines whether applications outside of the Visual Basic project that defines the class can create new instances of the class, and if so, how those instances are created.

The available **Instancing** property settings are different for ActiveX EXE and ActiveX DLL projects in Visual Basic. The following illustration shows the **Instancing** property settings for an ActiveX DLL project.

When you create a business object, set the **Instancing** property to MultiUse.

The following table describes each of the **Instancing** property settings.

Setting	Description
Private	Other applications are not allowed access to type library information about the class and cannot create instances of it. **Private** objects are used only within the project that defines the class.
PublicNotCreatable	Other applications can use objects of this class only if the component creates the objects first. Other applications cannot use the **CreateObject** method or the **New** operator to create objects of this class. Set the **Instancing** property to this value when you want to create dependent objects.
MultiUse	Multiple clients can use the same instance of the component. If multiple clients create objects from the component, the same instance of the component is used for all clients.
GlobalMultiUse	Similar to MultiUse except that properties and methods of the class can be invoked as though they were global functions. It is not necessary to create an explicit instance of a class because one will automatically be created.

Creating and Using Methods

For classes to be useful, they must contain methods that implement the functionality required of your component, such as business services. For every class module you create, Visual Basic automatically supplies two built-in event handlers called Initialize and Terminate (also known as event procedures) for which you can supply handler methods. You must add other general methods manually.

 To see the demonstration "Adding a Method to a Class Module," see the accompanying CD-ROM.

Note Keep in mind that these methods will be the interfaces of the COM components running as part of the IIS server process. As a general rule, server processes should not have a user interface (UI). Therefore you must not call Windows GUI interface methods, like **MsgBox,** in the methods you create.

Initialize and Terminate Event Handlers

To add code to a class module event, you open a Visual Basic code window for the class, and then click **Class** in the **Object** drop-down list box.

Initialize Event

The **Initialize** event occurs when an instance of a class is created, but before any properties have been set. You use the **Initialize** event handler to initialize any data used by the class, as shown in the following example code:

```
Private Sub Class_Initialize()
  'All methods in this class use a global Log object
  'to record each method call
  Set objLog = New Log
  objLog.Write "Object Initialized"
End Sub
```

Terminate Event

The **Terminate** event occurs when an object variable goes out of scope or is set to **Nothing.** You use the **Terminate** event handler to save information, unload forms, and perform tasks that you want to occur only when the class terminates, as shown in the following example code:

```
Private Sub Class_Terminate()
  objLog.Write "Object Terminated"
  Set objLog = Nothing
End Sub
```

For information about adding code to the **Initialize** and **Terminate** events, search for "Coding Robust Initialize and Terminate Events" in Visual Basic Books Online, and then click "Adding Classes to Components."

General Methods

To add methods to an object, you create public **Sub** or **Function** procedures within the class module for that object. The public **Sub** and **Function** procedures will be exposed as methods for the object.

> **Note** You must add the **Public** keyword before Sub or Function to make the procedure available to other objects and applications. Otherwise, the procedure is private and can be accessed only from the object.

To create a method for an object, you can either type the procedure heading directly in the code window, or click **Add Procedure** on the **Tools** menu and complete the dialog box.

The following example code creates a method that accepts a number and then returns the number squared:

```
Public Function SquareIt (Num As Integer) _
  As Integer
  SquareIt = Num * Num
End Function
```

To view the properties and methods you have defined for an object, you can use the Object Browser. For information about using the Object Browser, see "Object Browser" in Visual Basic Help.

Practice: Creating a COM Component

In this practice exercise, you will create an ActiveX DLL project containing a class with a method that calculates the square of a number. You will also compile the project to create a DLL.

▶ **Create an ActiveX DLL project**

1. Open Visual Basic 6.

2. In the **New Project** dialog box, select **ActiveX DLL**, and click **Open**.

3. On the **Project** menu, click **Project1 Properties**.

4. Type **Math** as the project name and **Math Object** as the project description.

5. Select **Unattended Execution** and click **OK**.

6. In the Properties window, change the default class name to **Square**.

▶ **Create a method**

1. In the Code window for the **Square** class, type the following function:

```
Public Function SquareIt(Num As Integer)As Integer
    SquareIt = Num * Num
End Function
```

2. On the **File** menu, click **Save Project**. Save the Class file as Square.cls and the Project file as Math.vbp.

3. On the **File** menu, click **Make Math.dll** to compile the project.

Practice: Testing a COM Component

You can use Visual Basic to test a COM component before using the component on a Web server. To test an ActiveX DLL project, you create another project within the same instance of Visual Basic. To test an ActiveX EXE project, you must run a second copy of the Visual Basic development environment because this type of component runs in a separate process.

In this practice, you will create a project group in Visual Basic and use a Standard EXE project to test the component you created in the previous practice exercise.

▶ **Create a project group**

1. On the **File** menu, click **Add Project**, and in the **New** tab, double-click **Standard.EXE**.

   This will add a new project to the Project Group window.

2. To make it the start-up project, right-click the new project, and then click **Set as Start Up**.

   Whenever you run the component, your new project will start first.

3. In the new project, add a reference to the Math DLL project that you created in the previous exercise, by clicking **References** on the **Project** menu, and then selecting Math.

▶ **Add code to call a method**

1. Add a **Command** button to the form.

2. In the **Click** event for the **Command** button, add the following code to create an instance of the class defined in the ActiveX DLL:

```
Dim x
Set x = New Math.Square
```

3. Call the **SquareIt** method to test the component, as shown in the following example code:

```
Print x.SquareIt(5)
```

▶ **Set a breakpoint**

1. Place the cursor in the following line of code:

```
Print x.SquareIt(5)
```

2. On the **Debug** menu, click **Toggle Breakpoint**.

   The line of code is highlighted in red to indicate that it is a breakpoint and that the code will suspend execution when the program reaches this line.

▶ **Trace the source code of the method**

1. On the **Run** menu, click **Start**.

2. Click the **Command** button on the form.

   The program stops at the highlighted line of code.

3. On the **Debug** menu, click **Step Into**.

   The program steps directly into the **SquareIt** function as it is called.

4. Hold the mouse over the variables in the code to see the values that are currently in the variables.

   The current value of **SquareIt** is zero. As you continue stepping into the code, the value of **SquareIt** changes to 25.

5. Click the **Continue** button to continue execution, and then click the **Command** button on the form.

   The program prints the value 25 to the form.

For information about debugging and testing COM components, search for "Creating ActiveX Components" in the Component Tools Guide in Visual Basic Books Online.

Working with COM Components

Having created a business component, you can work with it in a variety of scenarios to enhance a Web site's functionality.

In this section, you will learn how to call COM components from a Web page and how to include them directly in a Microsoft Visual InterDev project. In addition, you will learn how to register a component and how to set version compatibility options from within Visual Basic.

Registering a Component

Before you can use a COM component, it must be registered. Registration ensures that a component is recognized by the Windows operating system. This process creates entries in the Windows registration database.

Registering a Component

There are three ways to register an in-process (DLL) component:

◆ Build the DLL

On the development computer, Visual Basic will automatically register the component as part of a successful build process.

◆ Run Regsvr32.exe.

Regsvr32 is a utility that will register a DLL. Pass the DLL file name as an argument to the Regsvr32 utility as shown in the following example:

```
Regsvr32.exe mydll.dll
```

◆ Create a setup program.

When you run the setup program, the component is registered.

Unregistering the Component

When a component is no longer needed, it can be unregistered, using either of the following mechanisms:

◆ To remove a DLL entry from the registry, run Regsvr32.exe, including the /u option and the name of the DLL file, as shown in the following code:

```
Regsvr32.exe /u mydll.dll
```

◆ If the component was installed by a setup program, it should be able to be uninstalled by the Add/Remove Programs applet in the Control Panel.

Registering a Server Component from Visual InterDev

If a component in your Web application is designed to run on the server, you must make sure it is registered on the production server. In a Microsoft Visual InterDev Web project, you can designate a component to be registered as a server component. When you use the Copy Web Application feature in Visual InterDev, your component will be automatically registered on the server.

For more information about registering components from Visual InterDev, search for "Registering Server Components" in Visual InterDev Online Help.

▶ **To mark a server component for registration**

1. In Project Explorer, add the component to your Web project.

2. Select the component you want to register on the server.

3. In the Properties grid, select **Custom**.

4. In the **Component Installation** tab of the **Custom** property page, select **Register on server,** and then choose **OK**.

Integrating a Component in a Web Solution

You can deploy COM components as part of your Web project directly from Project Explorer in Microsoft Visual InterDev 6. This enables you to distribute an integrated solution that includes files created using other Visual Studio tools. For example, you can integrate a .dll file created with Visual Basic into your Visual InterDev project. If a component is designed to run on the server, you must specify that the component be registered on the server. For more information about this procedure, see "Registering a Component" on page 334 in this chapter.

Note The deployment of a Web application with components requires the Microsoft FrontPage Server Extensions on the production server. For more information about this deployment method, search for "Deploying an Integrated Web Solution" in Visual InterDev Help.

▶ **To deploy a Web application with components**

1. In Project Explorer, select the project that points to the Web application you want to deploy.

2. On the **Project** menu, click **Web Project,** and then click **Copy Web Application.**

3. In the **Copy Project** dialog box, choose the copy of the application you want to deploy.

Note If you work on a team, you typically deploy the master version because it includes the updated files from the team members.

4. In the **Server Name** box, enter the name of the Web server you want to use.

5. In the **Web project** box, enter the name you want the users to type for the URL.

6. Select **Register server components** and click **OK.**

Visual InterDev adds a new application to the destination Web server and copies the files in the Web application to that new folder. The name you specified in the **Copy Web Application** dialog box becomes part of the application's URL. You can now test the application on the production server.

The following illustration shows the **Copy Project** dialog box:

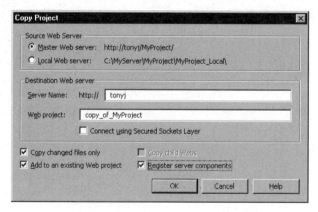

Calling a Component from an Active Server Page

In an Active Server Page, you can create an instance of a COM component by using the **CreateObject** method. Once you have created an instance of a component, you can access its properties and methods.

To see the demonstration "Calling a Server-based COM Component," see the accompanying CD-ROM.

The following example code shows how to use the **CreateObject** method, and then output the return value of a method to an HTML response:

```
<% Set bc = Server.CreateObject ("MyServer.MyObject") %>
<% Response.Write bc.method( ) %>
```

When you build your COM component, you should specify that all parameters be passed using ByVal. This is the most efficient way to pass a parameter to a COM component.

Note If you pass parameters using ByRef, you must convert each parameter into the data type that the method expects. This is because Visual Basic Scripting Edition (VBScript) uses variants for all variable types. If you call a method of a COM component that does not accept parameters of type variant, then you must explicitly convert the arguments to the correct type.

The following example code shows how to call the **SquareIt** method on the **Math** object. It also shows how to convert the argument to an integer data type and print the result to an HTML response.

```
<% Set mathobj = Server.CreateObject ("Math.Object") %>
<%= mathobj.SquareIt (cint(5)) %>
```

Note Once you have created a COM component by using the **CreateObject** method, its corresponding DLL will remain loaded in memory by IIS until it stops running. If you are testing the DLL, you will not be able to recompile until the DLL is freed from memory. To force IIS to free the DLL, stop and restart the Web service in the Internet Service Manager.

For more information about calling an object from an Active Server Page, see "Creating Component Instances" on page 197 in Chapter 4.

Using RDS to Create a Remote Business Object

In "Using the RDSServer.DataFactory" on page 313 in Chapter 6, you learned that the RDS of ADO allows a client to create instances of remote business objects.

Creating an Instance of a Remote Business Object

To create an instance of a remote business object, you insert the **RDS.DataSpace** object into an HTML document and then call the **CreateObject** method of the **RDS.DataSpace** object.

CreateObject creates an instance of the business object on a Web server. In the case of an out-of-process component, it creates a proxy on the client to marshal method calls to the object. **CreateObject** returns an object reference, which you use to invoke methods of the business object.

The syntax of the **CreateObject** method is as follows.

RDS.DataSpace.*CreateObject* ProgID, ServerName

◆ ProgID

A string identifying a server-side business object that implements the rules and methods for the client application.

◆ ServerName

A string that identifies the Web server where an instance of the server-side business object is created.

The following example code uses the **CreateObject** function to create an instance of the **StateU.Enroll** business object using DCOM. Then it invokes the **Add** method of the object to enroll a student in a class.

```
set objEnroll = ADS1.CreateObject("StateU.Enroll","myserver")
objEnroll.Add (classID, stuID)
```

Client vs. Server

There are several reasons for creating an instance of a business object by using the **RDS.DataSpace** object on the client rather than by using an Active Server Page on the server. **RDS.DataSpace** provides the following advantages:

◆ The ability to call multiple business objects from a single Web page without retrieving new pages.

This permits more flexibility in the design of a Web page. Active Server Pages can also call multiple business objects; however, they can only get information from a submitted HTML form, which is more limiting.

◆ The ability to use the **RDS.DataSpace** object to retrieve the data and cache it on the client.

This improves performance by reducing the load on the server, and is especially useful if business objects return a large amount of data.

However, you should use an Active Server Page instead of **RDS.DataSpace** in the following situations:

◆ Business objects that must perform secure transactions.

Using the **RDS.DataSpace** object would expose the code of the business objects by creating them on a Web page, where it could be misused. When the code is placed in server-side script in an Active Server Page, it will never be returned to a client.

◆ The client cannot run ActiveX controls.

Controlling Version Compatibility

When you compile a project, Visual Basic creates a unique class identifier (CLSID), a unique interface identifier (IID), and a unique type library ID. Applications using your component use these identifiers to create and use objects. If these identifiers change in a new version of a component, existing applications will not be able to use the new version.

Type Library IDs

A COM component stores its data type information and object characteristics, including descriptions of methods and properties, in a type library. When a COM component is registered with Microsoft Windows, an entry is created under

HKEY_CLASSES_ROOT\TypeLib in the registry, associating a globally unique identifier (GUID) with its type library data. By providing access to an object's type library through a unique type library ID, a client can manipulate the methods and properties of the object.

Version Compatibility

Version compatibility is very important when building components for use in a distributed environment. When you compile an ActiveX EXE or ActiveX DLL project, its classes expose methods that clients will use. If at some point you change a class in a component by deleting or changing the signature of a property or method, that component will no longer work with old clients. When you next compile the component, a new type library ID will be created, which will be incompatible with existing versions of the component used by clients.

Setting Version Compatibility Options

Visual Basic provides three options to help control version compatibility. To set the version compatibility, click **Project Properties** on the **Project** menu. In the **Project Properties** sheet, click the **Component** tab and set the **Version Compatibility** option.

If you make any change to the component (for example, if you delete a property) that is incompatible with the version on your Web server specified in the Project Compatibility field, Visual Basic displays a warning message and generates a new type library ID.

This illustration shows the **Component** tab of the **Project Properties** sheet.

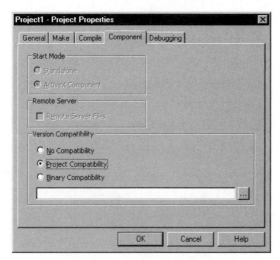

There are three options for version compatibility:

Option	Description
No compatibility	Each time you compile the component, the type library ID, CLSIDs, and IIDs are re-created. Because none of these identifiers match the ones existing clients are using, backward compatibility is not possible.
Project compatibility	Each time you compile the component, the CLSIDs and IIDs are re-created, but the type library remains constant. This is useful for test projects so you can maintain references to the component project. However, each compilation is not backward compatible with existing clients. This is the default setting for a component.
Binary compatibility	Each time you compile the component, Visual Basic keeps the type library ID, CLSIDs, and IIDs the same. This maintains backward compatibility with existing clients. However if you attempt to delete a method from a class, or change a method's name or parameter types, Visual Basic will warn you that your changes will make the new version incompatible with previously compiled applications. If you ignore the warning, Visual Basic will create new CLSIDs and IIDs for the component, breaking its backward compatibility.

Lab 7: Creating COM Components

In this lab, you will create the **Enrollment** business object in Microsoft Visual Basic, and implement the Add, Drop, and Transfer business services within it. You will also modify the Web project file Addclass.asp to test this business object and its services.

To see the demonstration "Lab 7 Solution," see the accompanying CD-ROM.

The following diagram shows how the files you edit in this lab will fit into the State University Web site.

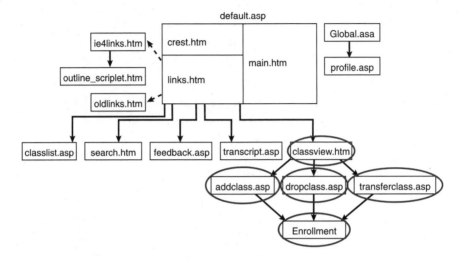

Estimated time to complete this lab: **90 minutes**

To complete the exercises in this lab, you must have the required software. For detailed information about the labs and setup for the labs, see "Labs" in "About This Course."

Objectives

After completing this lab, you will be able to:

◆ Create a COM component using Visual Basic 6.

◆ Add methods to a COM component.

◆ Call a COM component from an Active Server Page.

Prerequisites

Before working on this lab, you should be able to do the following:

◆ Use Visual Basic 6 to create a new ActiveX DLL project.

◆ Write server-side script in an Active Server Page.

Exercises

The following exercises provide practice working with the concepts and techniques covered in this chapter.

◆ Exercise 1: Creating the COM Component

In this exercise, you will create a COM component that implements enrollment business processes for the State University Web application. To add a student to a class, you will use the **Add** method in this component. You will create and invoke this component from the Addclass.asp page.

◆ Exercise 2: Adding New Business Processes

In this exercise, you will add two additional methods, **Drop** and **Transfer**, to the enrollment COM component. The **Drop** method will drop a student from a class, and the **Transfer** method will drop a student from one class and add the student to another class. As in the previous exercise, you will test your work from the Addclass.asp page.

Exercise 1: Creating the COM Component

In this exercise, you will open an existing Visual Basic 6 project, examine its single Enrollment class module, and then compile the project into a COM server component. In the second part of the exercise you will create an **Enrollment** object and invoke its **Add** method from an Active Server Page.

You will use the ClassView.htm file, which you worked on in Lab 5.2, to test your work by adding classes. The following illustration shows how ClassView.htm looks.

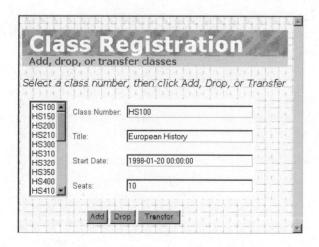

▶ **Add the Visual Basic project to the Web site**

1. Using Desktop Explorer, copy the folder \MWD6\Lab\Lab07\New_busobjects under the Web project's root folder (typically C:\InetPub\Wwwroot\StateU).

2. In the Visual InterDev Project Explorer window, click **Refresh Project View**.

   Note that in Project Explorer, this new folder and its content are displayed in light gray, indicating that these files exist in this folder, but are not a part of the local StateU Web project.

3. In Project Explorer, right-click this new folder node, and click **Get Latest Version**.

   The _busobjects folder will be added to the project and local copies of the files will be created.

▶ **Build the Add COM component in Visual Basic**

1. Start Visual Basic 6 (or later). Open the Enroll.vbp project located in the new _busobjects folder. (If your Web and local files are located on the same machine, open the VB project file located under the Internet publishing folder; if your Visual InterDev project is located on a separate machine, open the local copy.)

2. Examine the properties and contents of this project:

   - The name of the project is **Enroll**.

   - It contains a single class module named **Enrollment**.

   - **Enrollment** contains one public method named **Add**. View the **Add** method code to see how it enrolls a student in a class.

Note The **Add** method creates a connection to the StateU ODBC database using a connection string (see the following) reflecting setup done in Lab 5.1. If you have installed the StateU data source differently, then you will need to modify this string.

```
"DRIVER=SQL Server;SERVER=(local);UID=sa;DATABASE=StateU"
```

   - **Enrollment** also contains two private methods named **OverEnrolled** and **ClassCompleted** that check to see if the student is at the class limit or has already taken the class, respectively. (These are both examples of implementation of business rules for this domain.)

3. Add a reference to ActiveX Data Objects (ADO) by clicking **References** on the **Project** menu. Select **Microsoft ActiveX Data Objects 2.0 Library,** and then click **OK.**

4. Save the Visual Basic project.

5. Build the Enroll.dll file by choosing **Make Enroll.dll** from the **File** menu.

6. Synchronize the project and Web files by clicking the Synchronize Files toolbar button in the Project Explorer Window.

7. If you are deploying the State University Web site on a remote Web server, you register the Enrollment component by marking its custom property.

   a. In the Visual InterDev Project Explorer window, right-click on the Enroll.dll node and click **Get Working Copy** to add Enroll.dll to the Web project.

   b. In the Properties window, click the **Custom** property to display the **Property Pages** dialog box.

   c. Click the **Component Installation** tab. In the **Server Component** group box, select the **Register On Server** option.

Note If you are developing the Enrollment component on a computer running IIS, explicitly registering the component on the server is redundant because Visual Basic registers the COM component when you build it.

▶ **Call the StateU Enrollment object from an Active Server Page**

In this procedure, you will modify the file AddClass.asp so that when the user registers for a new class, the following process occurs:

♦ AddClass.asp creates an **Enrollment** COM object.

♦ AddClass.asp invokes the **Add** public method of this object to add a student to a class.

♦ Control is returned to Classview.htm, which informs the user that the class registration was successful.

The following illustration shows AddClass.asp looks when returned to the student.

Class Registration

Add, drop, or transfer classes

Class HS300 was added, click Reset Form

HS100 ▲ HS150	Class Number:	HS300
HS200 HS210	Title:	World Wars
HS300 HS310 HS320	Start Date:	1997-05-01 00:00:00
HS350 HS400 HS410 ▼	Seats:	100

[Reset Form]

1. Open AddClass.asp for editing in Visual InterDev, and locate the function **DoAdd**.

   This is a remote scripting method called by ClassView.htm. Note that this method takes a single argument, the class ID, and contains a first statement that retrieves the student ID from a session variable.

2. As the first line of the function, add a statement that creates an **Enrollment** object named **enrollObj**.

3. Next, call the **Add** method and pass **lngStudentID** and **strClassID** as arguments. Store the return value from the **Add** method in a variable named **errEnrollment**.

4. Change the return value of **DoAdd** from zero (0) to **errEnrollment**.

   To see an illustration of how your code should look, see Lab Hint 7.1 in Appendix B.

   For more information on calling components, see "Calling a Component from an Active Server Page" on page 337.

5. Save your changes to AddClass.asp, and test the page by opening ClassView.htm in the browser.

6. Log on to the profile with a student ID of 1 and try adding classes.

   a. First try adding a class, such as HS100 course. You should receive the message, displayed above the form, *Class HS100 was added, click Reset Form*.

   b. Click the Reset Form button to reset the form.

   c. Try adding the same class a second time. The business rule will catch this mistake and an error message will be displayed.

7. Use the DataView window to verify that the SQL Enrollment table has been updated correctly when classes are added.

Alternately, you can verify that classes have been properly added by browsing to the Transcript.asp file.

Exercise 2: Adding New Business Processes

In this exercise, you will add the **Drop** and **Transfer** methods to the **Enroll** business object, and call these methods of the object from Active Server Pages, DropClass.asp and TransferClass.asp respectively.

As in the first exercise, these changes are effected by the end user via the ClassView.htm page.

▶ **Create the Drop method**

In contrast to the **Add** method, the **Drop** method will remove a student from a class in which he or she is currently registered.

1. In Visual Basic, open the Enroll project, and then open the **Enrollment** class module.

2. Create a new **Public** function named **Drop**.

The **Drop** function accepts the fields **lngStudentID** and **strClassID** as parameters, and returns an **Integer** data type. Declare the parameters as **ByVal**.

For more information on creating methods, see "Creating and Using Methods" on page 329.

3. In the **Drop** function, set the default return value to zero (0). If zero is returned, it indicates that no errors have occurred.

4. Add code to drop the student from a class.

   a. Add the following code to create a connection to the State University database.

```
Set conn = CreateObject("ADODB.Connection")
conn.Open "DRIVER=SQL
Server;SERVER=(local);UID=sa;DATABASE=StateU"
```

   b. Next, add the following code to call the **ClassCompleted** function. This statement implements a business rule that checks whether the student has already completed the class. If the student has completed the class, the student is not allowed to drop it. In this case the return value is set to 1, and the function exits.

```
If ClassCompleted(conn, lngStudentID, strClassID) Then
    Drop = 1
    Exit Function
End If
```

    c. Add the following code to create a transaction and execute an SQL statement that drops the student from the class.

```
strSQL = "DELETE FROM enrollment where ClassID = '" &
strClassID & "' AND StudentID = " & lngStudentID
conn.BeginTrans
conn.Execute strSQL
conn.CommitTrans
```

    d. Close the connection.

5. Add an error handler named **ErrorHandler** that rolls back the transaction by calling **RollbackTrans** and sets the return value to 1.

6. Turn on error handling at the beginning of the function by adding an **On Error** statement.

To see an illustration of how the code for the **Drop** method should look, see Lab Hint 7.2 in Appendix B.

▶ **Create the Transfer method**

As its name implies, the **Transfer** method implements the process of transferring a student between classes, as allowed by appropriate checks.

1. Open the file \MWD6\Labs\Lab07\Transfer.txt. Copy the code for the **Transfer** method in this file to the **Enrollment** class module.

2. Examine the **Transfer** method. Note the following properties, many of which it shares with the **Add** and **Drop** methods:

    • The signature of this public method accepts the fields **lngStudentID, strSrcClassID,** and **strDstClassID** as parameters, and returns an **Integer** data type. The parameters are passed by value.

    • It returns a value of zero (0) if successful and one (1) if there is an error.

- It uses standard ADO statements and SQL commands to manipulate the StateU database.

- It contains an error handler that rolls back the transaction by calling **RollbackTrans** and sets the return value to 1.

3. Save the changes to the project.

4. Rebuild Enroll.dll.

> **Note** If you get access error message when you try to update Enroll.dll, it is because this file has been locked in memory by IIS. To successfully update this file, you must reboot the machine.

5. In Visual InterDev's Project Explorer, synchronize the files between the local and web folders.

To see an illustration of how your code for the **Transfer** method should look, see Lab Hint 7.3 in Appendix B.

▶ **Modify the Drop Web page**

In this procedure, you will modify the DropClass.asp page to create an **Enrollment** object and invoke its **Drop** method. This exactly parallels the changes you made to AddClass.asp in exercise 1.

1. Open the file DropClass.asp, and locate the remote method **DoDrop**.

2. In this function, add script that creates the StateU **Enrollment** object.

3. Call the **Drop** method and pass the **lngStudentID** and **strClassID** as arguments. Store the return value from the **Drop** method in a variable named **errEnrollment**.

4. On the next line, return the value of **errEnrollment** from **DoDrop**.

5. Save your changes to the file Dropclass.asp.

▶ **Test the Drop Web page**

1. In the browser, view the page Classview.htm.

2. Log in to the profile with a student ID of 1. You should be able to drop from all classes except for MT100, which has already been completed by student ID 1.

3. Use DataView to verify that the Enrollment table was updated correctly when classes were dropped. You can also verify that classes are dropped by retrieving the Transcript.asp file.

Note If you drop a class in which the current student ID is not enrolled, the drop will still succeed. This is because the **Drop** method uses the **SQL DE-LETE** statement to remove records from the Enrollment table. The **SQL DELETE** statement will succeed even if the record does not exist.

▶ **Modify and test the Transfer Web page**

Edit TransferClass.asp using the same process as in DropClass.asp. You may want to copy the code body from the **DoDrop** method in DropClass.asp, but substitute the **Transfer** method call for the **Drop** method call, including the correct parameters.

1. Open the file TransferClass.asp, and locate the remote method **DoTransfer**.

    a. Create the StateU **Enrollment** object.

    b. Call the **Transfer** method in this new object.

    c. Return the error code.

2. In the browser, view the page Classview.htm.

3. Log in to the profile with a student ID of 1 and try to transfer between classes. As student 1, you should be able to transfer from any class except MT100, which is already completed.

4. Use DataView to verify that the Enrollment table has been updated correctly. You can also verify that classes are transferred by retrieving the Transcript.asp file.

Self-Check Questions

To see the answers to the Self-Check Questions, see Appendix A.

1. **Which Visual Basic project template would you use to build an in-process COM component?**

    A. ActiveX Control

    B. ActiveX DLL

    C. ActiveX EXE

    D. Standard EXE

2. **Assume that a business process is used to take customer orders. Before placing the order, the Inventory table must be checked to make sure the item is in stock. If it is, a new record must be added to the Shipping table to make sure the item gets shipped. Which of the following strategies should you use to implement this business process?**

    A. Create a new ActiveX server component that implements the business process with an object named **Customer.Order,** and call it from an Active Server Page.

    B. Create a new Active Server Page that uses ActiveX Data Objects (ADO) to implement the business process.

    C. Create a stored procedure named customerorder that implements the business process, and call it from an Active Server Page.

    D. Create an .exe file as a COM component on the server to hold this business process as well as other processes.

3. **How do you export a method from a class module in Visual Basic 6?**

    A. Mark the Visual Basic project for unattended execution.

    B. Set the **Instancing** property to MultiUse.

    C. Add the **Public** keyword before the method.

    D. Set the Visual Basic project type to ActiveX DLL.

4. **What are all of the ways in which an in-process component can be registered?**

   A. During Setup, by using the file RegSvr32.exe, and when compiling the component with Visual Basic 6.

   B. During Setup, and when compiling the component with Visual Basic 6.

   C. By using the file RegSvr32.exe, and when compiling the component with Visual Basic 6.

   D. During Setup, and by using the file RegSvr32.exe.

5. **What is defined as an algorithm that determines how a piece of information should be processed?**

   A. A business rule

   B. A business process

   C. A COM component

   D. A business object

Chapter 8:
Using Microsoft Transaction Server

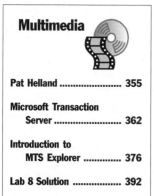
In Chapter 7, "Creating COM Components," you learned how to build COM components that implement business rules for business processes.

In this chapter, you will learn about MTS, an application that provides transaction and resource management for server-based COM components. You will also learn how to create Microsoft Transaction Server components, which are COM components that work within the MTS architecture.

The following illustration highlights the technologies you will learn about in this chapter.

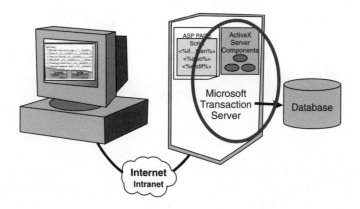

Objectives

After completing this chapter, you will be able to:

- Explain what a transaction is and why it must conform to the ACID test.
- Explain how the two-phase commit process works.
- Describe the architecture of MTS.
- Describe how business objects work with MTS.
- Explain how transactions are handled by Microsoft Distributed Transaction Coordinator.
- Use Microsoft Transaction Server Explorer to create a package and add components to it.
- Add transactional support to a business object.
- Use transactional ASP to integrate business objects.
- Use Microsoft Transaction Server Explorer to implement security for middle-tier business components.

Assumed Skills

Before you begin this chapter, you should be able to:

- Write client-side script.
- Write server-side script.
- Use methods and properties exposed by an object.

Overview

Historically, the transition from simple, single-user desktop applications to distributed multi-user, three-tier applications has been a difficult and time-consuming activity. A significant amount of development time must be spent to merely create the application architecture under which distributed multi-user, three-tier applications can run.

MTS eases the transition from single-user to multi-user development by providing the application infrastructure and administrative support for building scalable, robust enterprise applications.

To see the expert point-of-view "Pat Helland," see the accompanying CD-ROM.

In this section, you will learn about the benefits, architecture, and overall operation of MTS. You will also learn about the basic concepts of transactions and see how they are supported by MTS.

Benefits of Microsoft Transaction Server

Microsoft Transaction Server (MTS) is a component-based transaction processing system for building, deploying, and administering server applications. MTS defines a programming model, and provides a run-time environment and graphical administration tool for managing enterprise applications.

MTS provides the solution developer and server administrator with the following benefits and services:

◆ Transaction support

Transactions provide an all-or-nothing simple model for managing work. Either all of the objects succeed and all of the work is committed, or one or more of the objects fail and none of the work is committed.

MTS provides much of the infrastructure to automatically support transactions for components. MTS will also automatically handle cleanup and rollback of a failed transaction. You do not have to write any transaction management code in your components.

◆ A simple concurrency model

In a multi-user environment, a component can receive simultaneous calls from multiple clients. In addition, a distributed application can have its business logic running in multiple processes on more than one computer. Synchronization of object services must be implemented in order to avoid problems such as deadlocks and race conditions.

MTS provides a simple concurrency model based on activities. An activity is the path of execution that occurs from the time a client calls an MTS object, until that object completes the client request.

◆ Fault tolerance and isolation

MTS performs extensive internal integrity and consistency checks. If MTS encounters an unexpected internal error condition, it immediately terminates the process. This policy, called failfast, facilitates fault containment and results in more reliable, robust systems.

Components can be run in Windows NT server processes separate from Microsoft Internet Information Server (IIS) or the client application. In this manner, if a component catastrophically fails (throws an unhandled exception), it will not cause the client process to terminate as well.

◆ Resource Management

As an application scales to a larger number of clients, system resources (such as network connections, database connections, memory, and disk-space) must be utilized effectively. To improve scalability, objects in the application must share resources and use them only when necessary.

MTS maximizes resources by using a number of techniques such as thread management, just-in-time (JIT) object activation, resource pooling, and in future versions, object pooling.

◆ Security

Because more than one client can use an application, a method of authentication and authorization must be used to ensure that only authorized users can access business logic.

MTS provides declarative security by allowing the developer to define roles. A role defines a logical set of users (Windows NT user accounts) that are allowed to invoke components through their interfaces.

◆ Distributed computing support

A transaction typically uses many different server components that may reside on different computers. A transaction can also access multiple databases. Microsoft Transaction Server tracks components on multiple computers, and manages distributed transactions for those components automatically.

◆ Business object platform

MTS provides an infrastructure for developing middle-tier business objects.

Some of the services and benefits previously listed require that the solution developer create components using special requirements and techniques. These requirements are outlined later in this chapter in the section "Creating MTS Components" on page 364.

MTS is fully supported on the Microsoft Windows NT operating system, and a subset of its functionality is available on Windows 95. MTS will form a core piece of the COM+ run-time service initiative. Visit the Microsoft COM home page, which contains many resources, at http://www.microsoft.com/com.

Transaction Processing Concepts

From a business point of view, a transaction is an action that changes the state of an enterprise. For example, a customer depositing money in a checking account constitutes a banking transaction.

In the following illustration, three business objects work together to transfer money from one account to another. The **Debit** object debits an account and the **Credit** object credits an account. The **Transfer** object calls the **Debit** and **Credit** objects to transfer the money.

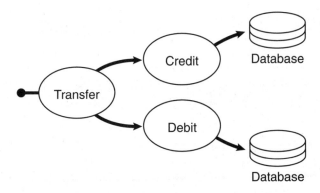

The ACID Test

A transaction changes a set of data from one state to another. For a transaction to succeed, it must have the following properties, commonly known as the ACID (Atomicity, Consistency, Isolation, and Durability) test.

- Atomicity means that a transaction is an indivisible unit of work: all of its actions succeed or they all fail.

- Consistency means that after a transaction executes, it must leave the system in a correct state or it must abort. If the transaction cannot achieve a stable end state, it must return the system to its initial state.

  In the transaction described earlier, money can be debited from one account and not yet credited to the other account during the transfer process. When the transaction is finished and able to commit, either both the debit and credit occur, or neither occurs.

◆ Isolation ensures that concurrent transactions are not aware of each other's partial and uncommitted results. Otherwise, they might create inconsistencies in the application state.

For example, in the transaction of transferring money, if two transfers occur at the same time, neither will know of the partial debit or credit from an incomplete transfer.

◆ Durability ensures that committed updates to managed resources (such as database records) survive communication, process, and server system failures. Transactional logging enables you to recover the durable state after failures.

Together these properties ensure that a transaction does not create problematic changes to data between the time that the transaction begins and the time that it must commit.

This period of a transaction constitutes one part of a two-phase commit process. The second phase occurs when all the business objects used in a transaction process are successful and can proceed with the commitment.

Two-Phase Commit Process

When transactions are processed on more than one server, a two-phase commit process ensures that the transactions are processed and completed either on all of the servers or on none of the servers.

There are two phases to this process: prepare and commit. You can use the analogy of a business contract to illustrate the two-phase commit process.

In the prepare phase, each party involved in the contract commits by reading and agreeing to sign the contract. In the commit phase, each party signs the contract. The contract is not official until both parties have made a commitment. If one party does not commit, the contract is invalid.

MTS coordinates and supports the two-phase commit process, ensuring that all objects of the transaction can commit and that the transaction commits correctly.

Commit or Abort

Transactions provide an all-or-nothing simple model for managing work. Either all of the objects succeed and all of the work is committed, or one or more of the objects fail and all of the work is aborted. For example, in the transaction described earlier in this topic, both databases must be changed successfully or the entire transaction will fail and the objects will be rolled back to their previous states. In either scenario, any database tables or files affected by the work will either all be changed, or not changed at all. They will not be left in an inconsistent state.

MTS Architecture

MTS introduces a new programming and run-time environment model that is an extension of the Microsoft standard COM. The basic structure of the MTS run-time environment involves several parts working together to handle transaction-based components.

MTS and the Supporting Environment

The MTS architecture comprises one or more clients, application components, and a set of system services. The application components model the activity of a business by implementing business rules and providing the objects that clients request at run-time. Components that share resources can be packaged to enable efficient use of server resources.

The following diagram shows the structure of the MTS run-time environment (including the MTS components) and the system services that support transactions.

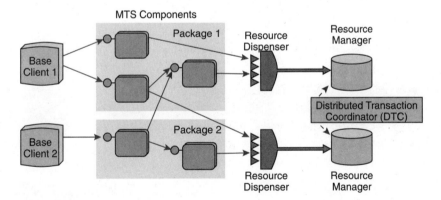

Base Client

The base client is the application that invokes a COM component running under the MTS environment. The base client could be a Visual Basic .EXE file running on the same Windows NT server computer, or running on a client computer that communicates through a network. In this course, the base client is an active server page (.ASP) running under IIS on behalf of an Internet user.

Note A base client never runs under the MTS environment.

MTS Components

MTS components are COM components that are registered to run in the MTS environment. These COM components must be created as in-process dynamic link libraries (DLL), although more than one COM component can be placed in a single DLL.

COM components created specifically for the MTS environment commonly contain special code that takes advantage of transactions, security, and other MTS capabilities. The process of creating transaction components is explained in the section "Creating MTS Components" on page 364 in this chapter.

System Services

This previous diagram illustrates several important parts of MTS:

◆ Resource managers are system services that manage durable data. Resource managers work in cooperation with Microsoft Distributed Transaction Coordinator to guarantee atomicity and isolation of an application.

◆ Resource dispensers manage non-durable shared state on behalf of the application components within a process. Resource dispensers are similar to resource managers, but without the guarantee of durability. Resource dispensers are responsible for database connection pooling.

MTS provides two resource dispensers: the ODBC resource dispenser (for ODBC databases) and the Shared Property Manager for synchronized access to application-defined, process-wide properties (variables).

◆ Microsoft Distributed Transaction Coordinator is a system service that coordinates transactions among resource managers. Work can be committed as an atomic transaction even if it spans multiple resource managers on separate computers.

MTS Executive (not shown in the diagram) is the DLL that provides run-time services for MTS components, including thread and context management. This DLL loads into the processes that host application components and runs in the background.

MTS Packages

A package is a container for a set of components that perform related application functions. All components in a package run together in the same MTS server process. A package is both a trust boundary that defines when security credentials are verified, and a deployment unit for a set of components.

MTS Explorer is typically used to register COM components as MTS components through a two-step process. First, an MTS package is created. Then the COM components are added to the package. This process is described in the section "Using MTS Explorer" on page 375 in this chapter.

Package Location

Components in a package can be located on the same computer as Microsoft Transaction Server on which they are being registered, or they can be distributed across multiple computers. Components in the same DLL can be registered in different MTS packages. Note the following limitations and recommendations:

◆ A COM component can only be added to one package per computer.

◆ Because COM components in the same DLL can share programmatic and operating system resources, place related COM components in the same DLL.

◆ Because MTS components in the same package share the same MTS security level and resources, place related MTS components in the same package.

Package Guidelines

The following relationships between the MTS parts are important to note:

◆ Packages typically define separate process boundaries. Whenever a method call in an activity crosses such a boundary, security checking and fault isolation occur.

◆ Components can call across package boundaries to components in other packages. Such calls can access existing components or create new components.

◆ On a single computer, an MTS component may only be installed once. The same component cannot exist in multiple packages in the same machine. However, multiple copies (objects) of the same component can be created and can exist at any time.

For more information about the architecture of MTS, search for "How Does MTS Work?" in the MTS online documentation.

MTS Concepts and Processes

As a programmer or Web developer, you can use popular tools such as Visual Basic, Visual C++, or Visual J++ to easily build server applications that run within the MTS environment. The MTS architecture utilizes several important concepts and processes to implement the complexity behind transaction processing in a distributed enterprise system.

To see the animation "Microsoft Transaction Server," see the accompanying CD-ROM.

> **Note** The animation uses the term *ActiveX Server component*, which was used in a previous version of this course. This course uses the term *COM component* instead of *ActiveX Server component*.

Activities

All MTS objects run in activities. An activity is a set of objects that run on behalf of a base client application to completely fulfill its request. When an object runs in an activity, it can create additional objects to perform work. All of these objects will run within the same activity and can be viewed as running on a single logical thread. The objects in an activity can be distributed across one or more processes, and can execute on one or more computers.

Every MTS object belongs to one activity. This is an intrinsic property of the object and is recorded in the object's context. The association between an object and an activity cannot be changed. MTS tracks the flow of execution through each activity, preventing inadvertent parallelism from corrupting the application state. This simplifies writing components for Microsoft Transaction Server.

Contexts

A context is an object associated with another object. It is a programmatic and run-time entity that is used to keep track of the state and support processing of its associated object. The MTS run-time environment manages a context for each object.

MTS Context Objects

MTS creates a context object for each MTS server component. As the component runs within the activity, the context object tracks properties of that component, including the activation state, its security information, and transaction state (if any). This frees the object from tracking its own state.

Transaction Context Objects

When multiple objects participate in a single transaction, the associated context objects work together to track the transaction. MTS uses a transaction context object to ensure that the transaction is consistent for all objects. The transaction context object, in conjunction with each of the individual context objects, guarantees that the whole transaction either commits or aborts.

MTS maintains the relationship between transaction server components and their associated context objects.

Server Process

A server process is a system process that hosts the execution of one or more MTS components. A server process can service tens, hundreds, or potentially thousands of clients.

Each package has an associated activation property that determines whether the components in the package run (as a group) in a separate, new server process (a server package) or run in their caller's process (a library package).

Note Some MTS capabilities, such as security checking and fault tolerance, are only enabled for server package activation.

Automatic Transactions

MTS supports both objects that need transactions and objects that do not.

If an object requires a transaction, MTS creates the transaction when the object is called. When the object returns to the client, the transaction either commits or aborts. When you place components in MTS, all of the infrastructure for processing and managing a transaction is provided for you.

Just-in-Time Activation

Just-in-time activation is the ability for transactional MTS objects to be activated only as needed for executing requests from clients. Objects can be deactivated even while clients hold references to them, allowing otherwise idle server resources to be used more productively. A deactivated object may be completely discarded from memory and created anew when required by another call from the client.

Creating MTS Components

In this section, you will learn about the requirements of MTS components. You will also learn how to add transactional support to your business objects.

You will learn how to obtain access to context objects, and how to indicate that a transaction has been completed or aborted. You will also learn about the importance of creating stateless objects for transactions.

Requirements for an MTS Component

MTS components are COM components that have been registered in the MTS environment. These components have the following requirements and restrictions:

♦ MTS components must be implemented as in-process dynamically linked libraries (DLLs). Components that are implemented as executable files (.exe files) cannot execute in the MTS run-time environment.

♦ MTS components should follow proper COM conventions including a standard class factory, a complete type library, and should use standard marshaling.

Fortunately, COM components built with Visual Basic using the procedure described in Chapter 7, "Creating COM Components" automatically meet these requirements. For other languages, see the MTS online topic "MTS Reference" for more information.

♦ MTS components should be designed as single threaded or apartment threaded. Apartment-threaded components are more scalable than single-threaded ones.

♦ MTS components should neither create threads nor terminate threads. This is a strong recommendation because MTS manages threads and synchronizes MTS activities for you automatically.

In addition, the following strong recommendations apply for MTS components:

◆ An MTS component should not programmatically alter its process security. The declarative security features of MTS should be used instead.

◆ MTS components should be stateless; they should not maintain local data between client calls. Stateless objects are more scalable than stateful ones.

Declarative security and package identity are discussed in "Security Issues: MTS Declarative Security" later on page 384 in this chapter.

For more information on statelessness, see "Creating Efficient Objects" on page 371 in this chapter.

Packaging Components for MTS

In "Integrating a Component in a Web Solution" on page 335 in Chapter 7, "Creating COM Components," you saw how to integrate components directly into a Visual InterDev Web project. You can also deploy components that are controlled by MTS to the server using Visual InterDev.

▶ **To package components for MTS**

1. In the Project Explorer window, right-click the component you want to add to the package.

2. On the shortcut menu, click **Properties**.

3. In the **Component Installation** tab, choose **Add to Microsoft Transaction Server package**.

4. In the **Package name** box, type the name of the package to which you are adding the component.

5. Select the **Transaction support** option appropriate for your component.

   Typically the component's objects inherit the transaction specified by the client. You can set these options to specify otherwise.

For more information about the **Transaction** options, search for "Deploying an integrated Integrated Web Solution" in Visual InterDev Help.

The following illustration shows the **Component Installation** tab in the **Property Pages** dialog box:

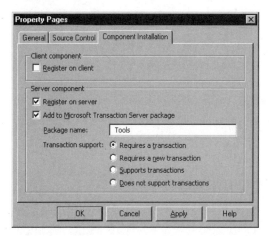

Adding Transactional Support

You can easily modify your existing business components so that they become part of a transaction as server-based MTS components.

Support for Transactions

You can use MTS to modify an object so that it supports transactions. In the MTS transaction processing model, each object simply reports to MTS whether it was successful in completing its client's request. MTS handles the complexity of synchronizing activities and transaction processing (committing or aborting the transaction). MTS eliminates the need to call any transaction functions, such as **BeginTrans** or **EndTrans**.

When an object is created, Microsoft Transaction Server creates a corresponding context object. **ObjectContext** supplies methods through the **IObjectContext** interface. Commonly used methods include:

♦ SetComplete

The **SetComplete** method informs the context object that it can commit transaction updates and can release the state of the object along with any resources that are being held. If and only if all other objects involved in the transaction also call **SetComplete,** the context object will commit the transaction updates of all objects.

◆ SetAbort

The **SetAbort** method signifies that the operation failed. **SetAbort** informs the **ObjectContext** object that the transaction updates must be rolled back to their original states. If one or more MTS objects in an activity call **SetAbort,** the transaction will roll back even if other objects have called the **SetComplete** method. Typically, **SetAbort** is called just prior to a (MTS object's) method exiting.

◆ CreateInstance

The **CreateInstance** method is used by the MTS component to create another object.

For more information about all **IObjectContext** interface methods, search for "IObjectContext" in MTS Help.

Adding Transactions to an MTS Object

To add transactional support to an MTS component, use the following procedure:

1. Using the **GetObjectContext** function, obtain a reference to the component's corresponding context object, as in the following Visual Basic 6 example code:

```
Dim ctxObject As ObjectContext
Set ctxObject = GetObjectContext()
```

Note To call the **GetObjectContext** function in Visual Basic 6, you must set a reference to Microsoft Transaction Server Type Library (mtxas.dll) by clicking **References** on the **Project** menu.

2. After the component has executed its logic, determine the outcome of that process.

   a. If the component was successful, call the context object's **SetComplete** method.

   The following example code adds a new customer record to the Customers table in the database, and calls **SetComplete** to indicate it has completed work successfully:

```
Dim ctxObject As ObjectContext
Set ctxObject = GetObjectContext()
Set conn = CreateObject("ADODB.connection")
conn.Open "DSN=dbcentral;UID=User;PWD=password;"
conn.Execute sqlstr 'sqlstr is SQL that adds the new customer
ctxObject.SetComplete
```

Warning Do not use the **New** keyword in Visual Basic to create MTS objects. This mechanism currently creates the object outside of the MTS environment.

–Or–

b. If a component was unsuccessful, call the context object's **SetAbort** method.

The following example code checks if a customer is considered a credit risk. If he is, then the current public method cannot complete its work successfully. The example calls the **SetAbort** method to abort all parts of the current transaction.

```
If InArears(customerid) Then
    ctxObject.SetAbort
    Exit Function
End If
```

3. As normally expected, return a value from the method, if required.

The following Visual Basic example code creates a new **Account** object that credits a checking account with $500.00:

```
Set CheckAccount = ctxObject.CreateInstance("Checking.Account")
CheckAccount.Credit(500)
```

In this example, if the component that creates the **Account** object fails and calls the **SetAbort** method, the crediting of the checking account will roll back.

Note that these steps are often implemented for each public method of an MTS component.

Handling Errors

MTS performs extensive internal integrity and consistency checks. In this way, MTS automatically provides fault isolation to maximize the robustness of applications. However, as a component developer, you may want to design your components to take a more active role in error handling.

Unhandled Errors in MTS Components

MTS does not allow unhandled errors to propagate outside of an MTS component. If an error occurs while executing within an MTS context and the component doesn't catch the error before returning from the context, MTS catches the error and terminates the process. Using the failfast policy in this case is based on the assumption that the exceptional condition has put the process into an indeterminate state—it is not safe to continue processing.

MTS interprets all aborted processes as exceptional conditions. If the transaction aborts and you do not raise an error to the client, MTS will force an error to be raised. It will set the HRESULT return value to CONTEXT_E_ABORTED informing the client that the call aborted. However, if an MTS object has set an HRESULT error code, MTS never changes this returned value.

Types of Errors

There are three types of errors that can occur in an MTS application: business rule errors, internal errors, and Windows exceptions.

Business Rule Errors

When an activity performs an operation that violates business rules, the activity causes a business rule error. This would be an error such as a client attempting to withdraw money from an empty account. These types of errors must be detected by the MTS objects that you write. They enforce the business rules by checking client actions against existing business rules. For example, a **Debit** object should check an account balance before withdrawing money.

Business rules can also be enforced in the database itself. For example, if a client attempts to withdraw money from an empty account, it may be the database that catches and raises the error (back to the **Debit** object).

In either case, you may want to take the following two actions:

1. Abort the current transaction by calling **SetAbort**.

2. Report the error to the MTS client. To report the error back to the client, raise the error using the **Err.Raise** method, typically with a custom error you have defined.

The client application, whether an ASP page, Visual Basic, or other client, must be able to interpret the error that you raise to display the proper message to the user. In the debit example, this might mean transferring money from other funds into the account.

Internal Errors

Internal errors are unexpected errors that occur while objects are working on behalf of a client. For example, a file could be missing, network problems could prevent connecting to a database, or creation of a dependent COM component could fail.

In Visual Basic, these errors will be detected and raised by Visual Basic itself. Like business rules errors, you can write code to trap these errors, and then attempt to correct them or abort the transaction.

Optionally, you may want to raise the error to the client using the **Err.Raise** method to pass the same error back. This will inform the client that an error occurred, and that it must display an appropriate error message. The client should take appropriate action, for example by displaying a friendly error message to the user, or by recording the error in an event log.

Windows Exceptions

If for some reason your MTS object causes a Windows exception (a crash), MTS will shut down the process that hosts the object and log an error event in the NT event log. As previously described, this process is called failfast. When failfast occurs, the process hosting the object is terminated. An HRESULT indicating the type of error will be returned to the client.

The MTS run time can also raise exceptions that cause your object to fail. In this case, your object automatically aborts. The following table gives a description of the standard MTS error codes.

MTS error code	Description
S_OK	The call succeeded.
E_INVALIDARG	One or more of the arguments passed in is invalid.
E_UNEXPECTED	An unexpected error occurred.
CONTEXT_E_NOCONTEXT	The current object doesn't have a context associated with it. This is probably either because its component hasn't been installed in a package or it wasn't created with one of the MTS CreateInstance methods.

table continued on next page

MTS error code	Description
CONTEXT_E_ROLENOTFOUND	The role specified in the szRole parameter in the **IObjectContext::IsCallerInRole** method does not exist.
E_OUTOFMEMORY	There's not enough memory available to instantiate the object. This error code can be returned by **IObjectContext::CreateInstance** or **ITransactionContext::CreateInstance**.
REGDB_E_CLASSNOTREG	There's not enough memory available to instantiate the object. This error code can be returned by **IObjectContext::CreateInstance** or **ITransactionContext::CreateInstance**.
DISP_E_ARRAYISLOCKED	One or more of the arguments passed in contains an array that is locked. This error code can be returned by the **ISharedProperty::put_Value** method.
DISP_E_BADVARTYPE	One or more of the arguments passed in isn't a valid VARIANT type. This error code can be returned by the **ISharedProperty::put_Value** method.

For more information about error handling, see the following recommendations:

◆ For general information on Visual Basic error handling, see "Debugging Your Code and Handling Errors" in the product documentation.

◆ For more information on how error handling occurs in MTS, see "Error Handling" in the Windows NT Option Pack Help.

Creating Efficient Objects

Transaction components place a heavy demand on server resources, but certain programming techniques enable you to gain the maximum efficiency from transaction components. You need to consider the network, database, and processing resources used by the component in the transaction, and how long an object will be active.

Stateless Objects

While an object is active, it maintains data. An object is referred to as "stateful" if data is maintained across multiple client calls. An object is "stateless" if the data is reset with each client call. In general, Microsoft Transaction Server objects should be stateless. Using stateless objects provides the following benefits:

◆ Helps ensure transaction isolation and database consistency by not introducing data from one transaction to another.

◆ Reduces the server load by not storing data indefinitely.

◆ Improves scalability because of the reduced server load and because there are fewer internal data dependencies in the stateless object.

Components built with Visual Basic have **Initialize** and **Terminate** events that you can use to create and free resources that the component needs to run. Data created in the **Initialize** event and maintained across multiple client calls is stateful data and should be avoided. If the component requires localized data to be created during startup, the component should expose the **Activate** and **DeActivate** methods instead.

For more information on the **Activate** and **DeActivate** methods, search for **Activate** and **DeActivate** in the Windows NT Option Pack Help.

Persistent state shared between objects can be implemented in a database or through the shared property manager. For information on the latter, see the topic "Sharing State" in the Windows NT Option Pack Help.

Maximizing Performance

There are a number of ways in which you can improve the efficiency of the objects you manage using Microsoft Transaction Server.

◆ Pass arguments by value (**ByVal**) whenever possible. The **ByVal** keyword minimizes trips across networks.

◆ Use methods that accept all of the property values as arguments. Avoid exposing object properties. Each time a client accesses an object property, it makes at least one round-trip call across the network.

- Avoid passing or returning objects. Passing object references across process and network boundaries wastes time.

- Avoid creating database cursors. Cursors create a large amount of overhead. Whenever you create a **Recordset** object, ActiveX Data Objects (ADO) creates a cursor. Instead of creating **Recordset** objects, run SQL commands whenever possible.

- When making updates keep resources locked for as short of a time as possible. This will maximize the availability of resources to other objects.

- Enable Microsoft Transaction Server to run simultaneous client requests through objects by making them apartment threaded. In Visual Basic 6, you make objects apartment threaded by selecting the **Apartment Threaded** option in the Project Properties dialog box. (Since these are typically server-based objects, you'll also want to select the **Unattended Execution** option.)

MTS and Active Server Pages

Web-based business applications often need to run both scripts and components within the same transaction. Starting with IIS 4.0 and MTS 2.0, support has been added for including ASP pages within MTS transactions.

Using MTS Components from an ASP Page

In Chapter 4, you learned how to invoke COM components from an ASP page using the following two techniques:

- Use the **CreateObject** method of the built-in ASP **Server** object.

- Use the HTML <OBJECT> tag and supply the **RUNAT**, **ID**, and **PROGID** (or **CLSID**) attributes.

MTS components should only be created from ASP clients using the first technique, **Server.CreateObject**. Using the <OBJECT> tag will currently cause the created object to run outside of the MTS environment.

For more information about invoking COM components from an ASP page, see "Creating Component Instances" on page 197 in Chapter 4, "Using Active Server Pages."

Creating Transactional Scripts

Beginning with Microsoft IIS 4.0, ASP pages can take part directly in MTS transactions. To code a transactional ASP page, use the following process:

1. Declare the page to be transactional with the @TRANSACTION directive. This creates a new MTS transaction.

2. Optionally, add code to interact with the transaction, either completing or aborting it, or handling transaction events.

MTS components created and used by the page will be enlisted automatically in the page's transaction. Because a single ASP page can create multiple components, you can use transactional ASP pages to associate unrelated MTS components programmatically into the same transaction.

A transaction can only involve one ASP page.

Determining Transactional Status of an ASP Page

A transaction associated with an ASP page completes when all the script on the page executes. If any transactional MTS components are created, the transaction completes successfully only if *all* the components call **SetComplete**.

The transaction aborts if there is a script processing error (such as syntax error) on the page; the page times out; or **ObjectContext.SetAbort** is invoked.

Declaring a Transactional Script

To declare an ASP page to be transactional, place the following line as the very first line of the page:

```
<%@ TRANSACTION = Required %>
```

Coding to a Transaction

You can interact with an MTS transaction from an ASP script through the following methods and events of the **ObjectContext** object:

♦ **SetAbort** and **SetComplete** methods. Calling **SetComplete** is optional, since this is equivalent to the script on the ASP page completing successfully.

♦ **OnTransactionCommit** and **OnTransactionAbort** events (for which you can supply handlers).

The following sample code uses the **SetAbort** method and the **OnTransactionCommit** and **OnTransactionAbort** events of the **ObjectContext** object in an ASP script. To copy this code for use in your own project, see "Coding to a Transaction from ASP" on the accompanying CD-ROM.

```
<%@ TRANSACTION = Required %>
' ...
<% ' ...
If Result <> True Then ObjectContext.SetAbort
' ...
'Called when either the script has sucessfully completed,
' or the ObjectContext.SetComplete method was called.
Sub OnTransactionCommit()
Response.Write "<br>Your Transaction has committed."
end sub

'Called when the script either encounters some kind of processing
' error, or the ObjectContext.SetAbort method was called.
Sub OnTransactionAbort()
Response.Write "<br>Your Transaction was aborted."
end sub
%>
```

Since there is currently no resource manager associated with ASP pages or built-in IIS components, any work accomplished directly by your ASP page must be explicitly rolled back manually, typically in the **OnTransactionAbort** event handler.

For more information about transactional ASP pages, search for "Creating Transactional Scripts" in the Microsoft Internet Information Server online documentation.

Using MTS Explorer

In this section, you will learn how to use MTS Explorer to create packages and install MTS components on Microsoft Transaction Server.

Introduction to MTS Explorer

Microsoft Transaction Server Explorer is a snap-in component of Microsoft Management Console (MMC). It is the graphical interface that you use to create, distribute, install, export, import, maintain, and manage MTS packages and their components.

To see the demonstration "Introduction to MTS Explorer," see the accompanying CD-ROM.

MTS Explorer helps the following computer professionals to work with transactions:

◆ Programmer (MTS component developer)—creates packages, adds MTS components to packages, creates roles; and helps monitor and debug MTS components.

◆ Web developer—installs, imports, and exports packages; assigns identities to packages; maps roles to NT users; troubleshoots and profiles MTS activities.

◆ Web administrator—updates and maintains packages, manages NT users mapped to roles, monitors MTS transactions, and manually resolves transactions under failure conditions.

For more information about MTS Explorer, search for the "Microsoft Transaction Server Administrator's Guide" in the MTS online documentation.

Creating a Package

To run a transaction on MTS, you must first create a new package to hold all components of a transaction. For more information about packages, see "MTS Architecture" on page 359 in this chapter.

▶ **To create a new, empty package**

1. In the left pane of the MTS Explorer window, select the computer for which you want to create a new package.

2. Expand the tree under that computer and select the Packages Installed folder.

3. Start the Package Wizard by performing one of the following:

   a. On the **Action** menu, click **New,** and then click **Package.**

   b. Right-click the **Installed Packages** icon. Click **New,** and then click **Package.**

   c. Click on the **Create a new object** button on the MTS toolbar.

4. In the Package Wizard, click the **Create an Empty Package** button.

5. Enter a name for the new package, and then click **Next.**

6. In the **Set Package Identity** dialog box, select either the **Interactive User** or specify an existing NT user account.

The default selection for package identity is **Interactive User**. The interactive user is the user that logged on to the server computer on which the package is running. Use this setting during the development of MTS components.

For more information about declarative identity and security, see "Declarative Security: Roles and Identities" on page 384 in this chapter.

Setting Package Properties

Once you have created a package, you can set package properties, such as how the package is accessed, how it participates in the security system, and how it ends when the system is shut down.

> **Tip** If you need to force package processes to shut down, you can do so by right-clicking **My Computer** and choosing **Shutdown Server Processes**. One common reason you would do this, is to replace one or more of the MTS components with a newer version. Shutting down the server processes forces the MTS runtime to unload DLLs from memory.

To set properties for a package, right-click the package in Microsoft Transaction Server Explorer, and then click **Properties**. The **Package Properties** dialog boxes will be displayed.

The following illustration shows the **Package Properties** dialog box.

General Package Properties

The following table describes the basic package properties and lists under which tab they can be set:

Property	Description	Tab
Name	Friendly name of the package (ID number is also listed)	General
Description	Displays a description of the package.	General
Authorization	Enables Microsoft Transaction Server to check the security credentials of any client that calls the package.	Security
Process Shutdown	Determines whether the server process associated with a package always runs, or whether it shuts down after a specified period of idle time.	Advanced
Account	Specifies the identity of the package. This is set during package creation.	Identity
Activation Type	Specifies either Library or Server activation for the package.	Activation

Activation Property

You use an activation property of a transaction server package to specify the process where the package's components will run when activated. The activation property determines whether the components in a package will run (as a group) in a separate, new server process (a server package) or will run in their caller's process (a library package). MTS security and fault tolerance are only available for server packages.

The following table describes the activation property settings for a transaction server component.

Setting	Description	Advantage
Library Package	Will run in the same process as the client that creates it.	Minimum overhead

table continued on next page

Setting	Description	Advantage
Server Package	Will run in its separate process; shared by all the components in the current package.	Fault tolerance, package security enabled

During development, a component should be generally activated as a server package to prevent any faults that may occur from crashing other processes.

> **Tip** For changes to the activation property to take effect, you must restart the server process. To restart the server process, right-click the computer icon in the Microsoft Transaction Server Explorer, and then click **Shutdown Server Processes.**

Adding Components to a Package

Once you have created a new package, you can add components to manage related business services. A component can be included only in one package on a single computer, so you must decide how to combine components into packages.

▶ **To add a component to a package**

1. In the left pane of the MTS Explorer window, open the Packages Installed folder, and then expand the package for which you want to install a component.

2. Select the Components folder (under the Packages Installed folder).

3. Drag the file containing the component(s) from the Windows Explorer window to the right pane of the MTS Explorer window.

   –Or–

   Start the Component Wizard by performing one of the following:

   a. On the **Action** menu, click **New**, and then click **Component**.

   b. Right-click the Installed Packages icon, click **New**, and then click **Package**.

   c. Click on the **Create a new object** button on the MTS toolbar.

4. Click the **Install New Component(s)** button.

5. In the **Install Components** dialog box, click **Add Files** to select the component.

   The component should include all of the files that are used to implement the component. If the component has an external type library or proxy/stub DLL, also add those files.

6. In the **Select Files to Install** dialog box, select the files you want to add, and then click **Open**.

7. In the **Install Components** dialog box, click **Finish**.

Component Location and Versioning Issues

Only proper COM in-process components with type library information are recognized by MTS. Other files are ignored.

Adding a component to a package does not physically copy or move the implementation file (usually a DLL) from its original folder location; it simply registers it with MTS. You can force package processes to shut down, which is common when replacing one or more MTS components with a newer version. Shutting down the server processes forces the MTS run time to unload DLLs from memory.

To shut down a package process, right-click **My Computer** in the left pane of the MTS Explorer window and click **Shutdown Server Processes**.

Note If later you change the name or physical location of the component implementation file, or you replace it with a newer component implementation with a different type library, you must re-register the component in MTS. MTS does not track file changes automatically.

Tip An easy way to ensure that Transaction Server is using the latest component information is to select the **Refresh All Components** command from the **Tools** menu.

Setting Component Properties

When you set the properties of a component at design time, you:

◆ Determine the process in which the component will run.

◆ Define the component's role with respect to the current transaction.

To set the properties of a component, right-click the component in the MTS Explorer window, and then click **Properties**.

Transaction Property

Each transaction server component has a transaction property. Whenever an instance of a component is created, MTS checks the transaction property of the component to determine whether it needs a transaction to do its work.

Most MTS components are marked either **Supports Transactions** or **Requires a Transaction**.

Tip MTS uses Visual Basic's **MTSTransactionMode** property during object creation to determine whether the object should be created to execute within a transaction, and whether a transaction is required or optional.

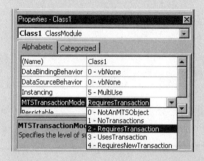

For more information about the **MTSTransactionMode** property settings, search for "MTSTransactionMode" in Visual Basic online Help.

The following illustration shows the different options for setting transaction options on the **Transaction** tab on the **Math.Square Property** sheet.

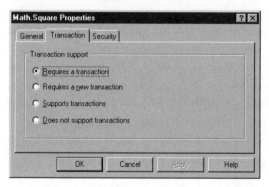

This specifies that the component must execute within the scope of a transaction. When a new object is created, the context of the object inherits the transaction from the context of the client. If the client does not have a transaction, Microsoft Transaction Server automatically creates a new transaction for the object.

This specifies that the component must always run within its own transaction. When a new object is created, Microsoft Transaction Server automatically creates a new transaction for the object, regardless of whether its client has a transaction.

This specifies that the components in a package will run within the scope of their client's transactions. When a new object is created, its context inherits the transaction from the context of the client. If the client does not have a transaction, the context will be created without one.

This specifies that the components in a package should not run within a transaction.

Practice: Using MTS Explorer to Create a Package

In this practice exercise, you will use MTS Explorer to create a new package (Math) that contains one component (Math). You will also set properties for the Math package.

Note For this exercise, you will need to copy the file Math.dll from the Practice folder on the CD-ROM to your hard disk.

▶ **Create a new package**

1. Start the MTS Explorer. On the **Start** menu, choose **Programs**, and **Windows NT 4.0 Option Pack**. Then choose **Microsoft Transaction Server**, and **Transaction Server Explorer**.

2. In the left pane of the MTS Explorer window, select My Computer.

3. Double-click the Packages Installed folder.

4. On the **Action** menu, click **New**, and then click **Package**.

5. In the Package Wizard, click the **Create an Empty Package** button.

6. Type **Math** as the name for the new package, and then click **Next**.

7. In the **Set Package Identity** dialog box, leave **Interactive user - the current logged on user** as the default setting, and then click **Finish**.

▶ **Add a component to a package**

1. Double-click the Packages Installed folder, and then double-click the Math package you just created.

2. Select the Components folder.

3. On the **Action** menu, click **New**, and then click **Component**.

4. Click the **Install New Component(s)** button.

5. In the **Install Components** dialog box, click **Add Files** to select the component.

   The component should include all of the files that are used to implement the component.

6. In the **Select files to install** dialog box, navigate to the folder in which you copied the practice file for this exercise, select **Math.dll**, and then click **Open**.

7. In the **Install Components** dialog box, click **Finish**.

Tip An easy way to ensure that Transaction Server is using the latest component information is to select the **Refresh All Components** command from the **Tools** menu.

▶ **Set package properties**

1. In the left pane of the MTS Explorer window, right-click the Math package, and then click **Properties**.

2. In the **General** property sheet, enter a description for the Math package.

3. In the **Advanced** property sheet, change the length of time a server process can be idle before being shut down.

4. Select **Disable deletion** and **Disable changes**, and then click **OK**.

   When you attempt to delete the Math package or any of its components, a warning appears informing you that one or more items selected cannot be deleted. Also, all settings in the **Math Properties** dialog box are disabled, with the exception of **Disable deletion** and **Disable changes**.

5. Right-click the Math package in the MTS Explorer window, and then click **Properties**.

6. In the **Advanced** property sheet, clear **Disable deletion** and **Disable changes**.

   A subsequent practice exercise requires that these options be cleared.

Security Issues: MTS Declarative Security and Identity

In this section, you will learn about the declarative security model of MTS. You will also learn how to use MTS Explorer to set the security properties of packages and components.

Declarative Security: Roles and Identities

The traditional approach to file security in the Windows NT operating system is to define users and user groups (typically with the User Manager for Domains administrative tool), and then set access permissions for a file (typically with Windows Explorer).

Because of security considerations at both the development and distribution phases of a project, MTS extends the traditional approach to security through *declarative security*. With this approach, security is configured directly with MTS Explorer. In declarative security, MTS introduces the concept of package roles.

Tip MTS provides also supports programmatic security in MTS components. Programmatic security is used to define access privileges on a more granular level than that offered by declarative security. Using programmatic security, you can control user access to any part of your code. It can also be is also used to dynamically configure security of MTS components.

For more information about MTS programmatic security, search for "Programmatic Security" in the MTS online documentation.

MTS Roles

A role is a logical group of users that defines security access to the components of a package. Roles are created at development time by the component programmer or Web developer. Roles are subsequently mapped onto actual NT users and user groups during package deployment, by the Web developer or administrator.

The following list describes two important consequences of the role architecture:

◆ Packages define security boundaries.

   MTS uses roles to determine who can use an MTS component any time a call is made into the package. Method calls from one component to another inside a package are not checked because components in the same package trust each other.

◆ Security is checked for each method call that crosses packages boundaries.

MTS checks security on each method call because it is possible for one client (that is authorized) to pass an interface pointer to another client (that may not be authorized). MTS also checks security when a client creates an object from outside of the package.

Note Because declarative security uses Windows NT accounts for authentication, you cannot use declarative security for a package running on a computer that uses the Windows 95 operating system.

MTS Package Identity

By default, components take on, or impersonate, the process identity of the calling client. For example, if a process started by the NT guest account calls a component, then that component operates with the security privileges of the guest account. MTS introduces the new concept of package identities to give components a separate, independent security identification.

Rather than impersonate the client, MTS packages typically use declarative identity features of MTS to associate themselves with an NT user account. Therefore, when any component in the package accesses resources such as files or databases, the component's access rights correspond to this identity.

Package identities are set during deployment.

Setting Package Security

Using declarative security to set MTS package roles is a three-step process:

1. During package creation, associate one or more roles with the package.

    Existing roles can be used or new roles can be created at this time.

2. During deployment time, map Windows NT users and groups to roles.

    Note that this gives the Web administrator great flexibility in determining access to MTS activities.

3. Enable security at the package and component level.

    If you do not enable security for the package, then roles for the component or interface will not be checked by MTS. In addition, if you do not have security enabled for a component, MTS will not check roles for the component's interface.

Creating and Assigning Security Roles

After you have created a package and added components to it, you can create roles for that package. Roles are defined at the package level and once created, are mapped to components or interfaces within the package.

▶ **To create a new role**

1. In the left pane of the MTS Explorer window, select the package that will include the role.

2. Double-click the Roles folder.

3. On the **Action** menu, click **New,** and then click **Role.**

   –Or–

   Right-click the Roles folder, click **New,** and then click **Role.**

4. Type the name of the new role, and then click **OK.**

The following illustration shows the **New Role** dialog box:

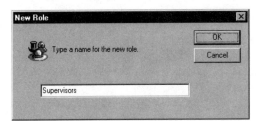

▶ **To assign roles to a component or interface**

1. In the left pane of the MTS Explorer, select the component or interface that will include the role.

2. Double-click the Role Membership folder.

3. On the **Action** menu, click **New,** and then click **Role.**

   – Or –

   Right-click the Roles folder, click **New,** and then click **Role.**

4. In the **Select Roles** dialog box, select the roles you want to add to the component and click **OK.**

Mapping Users to Roles

When you install and deploy your application, you must map Windows NT users and groups to any existing roles. The roles you map users to determine what components and interfaces those users can access.

▶ **To assign users to roles**

1. In the left pane of the MTS Explorer window, open the package in which you will assign users to roles.

2. Open the Roles folder and double-click the role to which you want to assign users.

3. Open the Users folder.

4. On the **Action** menu, click **New,** and then click **Users.**

   –Or–

   Right-click the Users folder, select **New,** and then click **Users.**

5. In the **Add Users and Groups to Role** dialog box, add user names or groups to the role.

6. Use the **Show Users** and **Search** buttons to locate a user account and then click **OK.**

The following illustration shows the **Add Users and Groups to Role** dialog box.

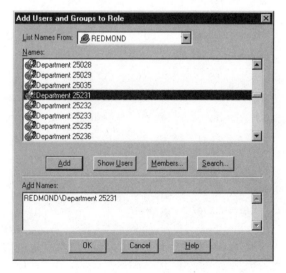

Enabling Security

There are two levels at which security is enabled: package-level security and component-level security. Package-level security is set once at the package level. Component-level security is set at the component level for each component in the package.

This table shows the implications of enabling or disabling authorization checking for packages and components.

Package security	Component security	Result
Enabled	Enabled	Security is enabled for the component.
Enabled	Disabled	Security is disabled for the component, but will be enabled for other components that have security enabled.
Disabled	Enabled or Disabled	Security is disabled for all components.

Tip You can make it easier to test packages by disabling security at the package level. This disables security regardless of the security settings at the component level. Then you can test the components without the complication of security checks. However, disabling security at the package level or component level will not disable programmatic security in the components.

▶ **To enable or disable authorization checking for packages or components**

1. In the left pane of the MTS Explorer window, click the package or component.

2. Right-click the package or component, and click **Properties**.

3. Click the **Security** property sheet.

4. Select or clear **Enable authorization checking**.

For more information about setting properties for packages and components, see "Using MTS Explorer" on page 375 in this chapter.

Tip The MTS environment contains a built-in package called the System Package. This package contains components MTS uses for internal functions. Mapping users to this package allows them access to MTS Explorer functionality. When MTS is installed, security on the System package is disabled. For a secure site, you will probably want to enable security for this package and map users into its roles.

For more information about the System Package and how to administer it, search for "Enabling MTS Package Security" in the MTS online documentation.

Setting Package Identity

There are two general identity types a package can assume:

◆ The interactive user (the default)

This setting allows the package to assume the identity of the currently logged on user. However, if no user is logged on to the server when a client accesses the package, the package will fail to create a server process. This identity is often used for development testing purposes.

◆ A specific Windows NT user account

This setting assigns a specific Windows NT user account to the package. When a client accesses the package, it creates a server process using this account as its identity. All components running in the package share this identity.

▶ **To set package identity**

1. Select the package whose identity you want to change.

2. On the **Action** menu, click **Properties** and select the **Identity** tab.

   – Or –

   Right-click the package and click **Properties**. Then, select the **Identity** tab.

3. To set the identity to a user account, select **This user** and enter the user domain followed by a backslash (\), user name, and password for the Windows NT user account.

4. Or, to set the identity to Interactive User, select the **Interactive User** option.

The following illustration shows the **Identity** tab of the **Properties** sheet.

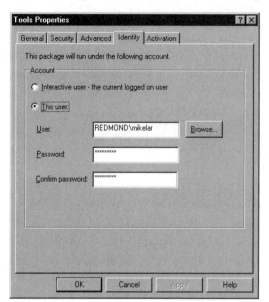

Package Identity and Database Access

Package identity is important when your MTS components access databases because database connections can be pooled. Connections are pooled based on userids and passwords, so if a process has many connections using the same userid and password, they can be pooled. If components impersonate clients, each userid is different and the connections cannot be pooled. By using package identity, each component can use the same userid and each connection can be pooled.

> **Note** If you want to use package identity to restrict access to a database, you must set database access privileges for the user account of that package.

Practice: Setting Package Security and Identity

In this practice exercise, you will create a new role called Students for the Math package you created in the last practice exercise. You will assign the Students role to the Math component and then map a user group to Students. Finally, you will set security for the Math package and Math component, and add a specific user identity for the Math package.

Creating and Assigning Security Roles

▶ **Create a new role**

1. In the left pane of the MTS Explorer window, navigate to the Roles folder (node) under the Math package.

2. Click the Roles folder to select it.

3. On the **Action** menu, click **New**, and then click **Role**.

   – Or –

   Right-click the Roles folder, click **New**, and then click **Role**.

4. Type **Students** as the name of the new role and click **OK**.

▶ **Assign a role to a component**

1. In the left pane of the MTS Explorer window, navigate to the Components folder under the Math package.

2. Navigate to the Math.Square component under the Components folder, and then navigate to the Role Membership folder.

3. On the **Action** menu, click **New**, and then click **Role**.

   – Or –

   Right-click the Role Membership folder, click **New**, and then click **Role**.

4. In the **Select Roles** dialog box, select **Students** and click **OK**.

Mapping Users to Roles

▶ **Assign users to roles**

1. In the left pane of the MTS Explorer window, navigate to the Roles folder under the Math package.

2. Double-click the Roles folder to open it, and select Students.

3. Double-click Students and select the Users folder.

4. On the **Action** menu, click **New**, and then click **User**.

   –Or–

   Right-click the Users folder, select **New**, and then click **User**.

5. In the **Add Users and Groups to Role** dialog box, add user names or groups to the role and then click **OK**. Assign the users and groups who will be accessing the Math.Square object to the Student role.

You can use the **Show Users** and **Search** buttons to locate a user account.

Enabling Security

▶ **To enable or disable authorization checking the component**

1. In the left pane of the MTS Explorer window, select the Math component.

2. Right-click the Math component, and click **Properties**.

3. Click the **Security** tab.

4. Select or clear **Enable authorization checking**.

Setting Package Identity

▶ **To set package identity**

1. Select the Math package.

2. On the **Action** menu, click **Properties** and select the **Identity** tab.

   – Or –

   Right-click the package and click **Properties**. Then, select the **Identity** tab.

3. To set the identity to Interactive User, select the **Interactive User** option.

   This is the default selection by which components in the package acquire the access privilege of their parent process.

4. Or, to set the identity to a specific, existing user account, select **This user** and enter the user domain followed by a backslash (\), user name, and password for the Windows NT user account.

Lab 8: Using Microsoft Transaction Server

In this lab, you will add transactional support to the State University Web site by creating MTS packages and components that are called from ASP pages. You will also use MTS Explorer to configure the packages and components.

To see the demonstration "Lab 8 Solution," see the accompanying CD-ROM.

The following diagram shows how the files you edit in this lab will fit into the State University Web site.

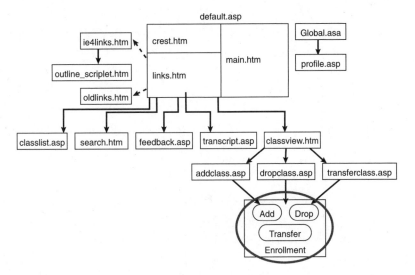

Estimated time to complete this lab: **90 minutes**

Objectives

After completing this lab, you will be able to:

♦ Create a new package using MTS Explorer.

♦ Add components to a package, and set their properties using MTS Explorer.

♦ Monitor transaction statistics using MTS Explorer.

♦ Create a component that supports MTS transactions and calls either the **SetComplete** or **SetAbort** method, or both.

♦ Use the MTS **Context** object to create other components in the same transaction.

♦ Create an ASP page that participates in an MTS transaction.

Prerequisites

Before working on this lab, you should be able to do the following:

♦ Create Web pages, including ASP files, and projects in Microsoft Visual InterDev.

♦ Create a COM component using Visual Basic 6 or later.

♦ Call a server-based COM component from an ASP file.

This lab continues the work you did in Lab 7. If you did not complete Lab 7 you will need to check that you have the following software installed and properly configured:

◆ The Visual InterDev State University project loaded in Visual InterDev.

◆ Microsoft SQL Server 6.0 or later installed with the State University SQL database loaded.

◆ Visual Basic 6 or later.

Exercises

The following exercises provide practice working with the concepts and techniques covered in this chapter:

◆ Exercise 1: Creating the State University Package

In this exercise, you will examine and build a new version of Enroll.dll that contains three business objects for StateU called **Add, Drop,** and **Transfer.** You will then create a new MTS package to contain these business components. Finally, you will add these components to the MTS package you created and test the Add component by calling it from an ASP file.

◆ Exercise 2: Adding Transaction Support to COM Components

In this exercise, you will modify the **Drop** object to call **SetComplete** or **SetAbort,** which enables transaction support in Microsoft Transaction Server. You will also modify the **Transfer** object to create the **Add** and **Drop** objects using **CreateInstance.** The **Transfer** object will then call the **Add** and **Drop** objects to perform the work of transferring a student. Finally, you will test these components by calling them from ASP files.

◆ Exercise 3: Adding Transaction Support to an ASP Page

In this exercise, you will modify the AddClass.asp page so that it participates in the MTS transaction responsible for adding a student to the appropriate class in the StateU database.

Exercise 1: Creating the State University Package

In this exercise, you will examine and build a new version of Enroll.dll that contains three business objects for StateU called **Add, Drop,** and **Transfer.** You will then create a new MTS package to contain these server-based COM components.

Finally, you will add the three components to the MTS package you created and test it by calling the Add component from an ASP file.

You will use the Classview.htm file to add and drop classes. The following illustration shows how Classview.htm looks.

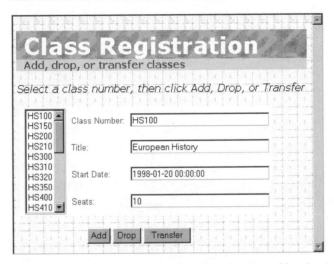

When you add a class using the classview.htm file, the Addclass.asp file calls the **Add** object to add a student to a class. The following illustration shows how Addclass.asp looks when returned to the student.

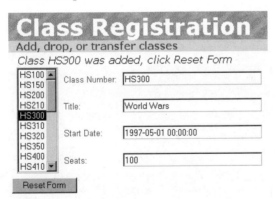

▶ Add newer files to the StateU Web project

1. In Visual InterDev, release working copies of all files in the StateU Web project.

2. Uninstall the enrollment component through the following steps:

   a. Close Visual Basic if you have it running.

   b. Unregister the Enroll.dll component through one of the following procedures:

      • If you installed this component through Visual InterDev, right-click on the Enroll.dll node and choose the Properties command from the context menu. In the properties dialog box, click on the Component Installation tab, then deselect any registration check boxes. Click OK to unregister the component.

      • Otherwise, start a command-line session and navigate to the Visual Basic enrollment project directory. Issue the following command:

      ```
      Regsvr32 /u enroll.dll
      ```

3. Delete the existing business object subfolder. In Visual InterDev's Project Explorer Window, right-click on the _busobjects node and choose the delete command from the context menu. Answer Yes to any prompt.

4. Locate the folder \MWD6\Labs\Lab08\New. Select all the contents of this folder.

5. Drag the contents of the New folder and drop them on the StateU node in Visual InterDev's Project Explorer Window. Answer yes to prompts to overwrite existing files.

6. Get latest versions of all files in the _busobjects folder.

▶ **Examine the code changes in the new files**

1. Build the new enrollment component.

   a. Start Visual Basic and open the _busObjects\Enroll.vbp project.

   b. From the Project menu, choose the References command. Add a reference to the **Microsoft Transaction Server Type Library**.

   c. Make the file Enroll.dll.

2. In the Project Explorer window of Visual Basic, expand the Project node. Note that the previous lab had only one class module (Enroll), whereas this lab has three class modules (Add, Drop, and Transfer).

   The corresponding logic for these three business processes has been separated into individual modules so that finer transactional support can be applied to each.

3. Open the Add (Add.cls) module in the editor. Note that this module contains only the logic for adding a class, entailed in the **Add** and **OverEnrolled** procedures. Also note the following alterations in the **Add** function:

- A new local variable of type ObjectContext is declared. A new reference to Microsoft Transaction Server Type Library in the project allows this process.

- A context object is being created through a call to **GetObjectContext**.

- The context object is used to call the MTS transaction methods **SetComplete** and **SetAbort** when the transaction succeeds or fails, respectively.

4. In Visual InterDev, open AddClass.asp in the editor. Locate the **DoAdd** function. Note that the argument to the call to **CreateObject** has changed from Enroll.Enrollment to the more specific Enroll.Add. Similar changes have been made to the DropClass.asp and TransferClass.asp files.

▶ Create the State University package and add components to it

1. Open MTS Explorer.

2. Create a new package named State University. When prompted for the package identity, set it to **Interactive user**.

   a. Expand the nodes in the left pane until you find the Packages Installed node.

   b. Right-click this node, and click the **New** submenu. Then choose **Package**. The Package Wizard should be displayed.

   c. In the first step, click **Create an Empty Package**.

   d. In the second step, type **State University**.

   e. In the third step, select the **Interactive user** option, and then click **Finish**.

3. Set the **Activation** property for the State University package to **Server Package**.

   a. In MTS Explorer, select the State University Package node.

   b. Right-click the State University package, and choose **Properties**.

   c. In the **State University Properties** dialog box, click the **Activation** tab.

   d. Select the **Server Package** option (the default.) Click **OK**.

For more information on creating packages, see "Creating a Package" on page 376.

4. Add the component Enroll.dll to the State University package by using one of the following techniques:

- Drag the file from the Windows Explorer or the Visual InterDev Project Explorer window to the Components folder of the State University package in MTS Explorer.

- In MTS Explorer, right-click the Components folder, click **New**, and then click **Component**. Use the Component Wizard to add the file Enroll.dll.

- In the Visual InterDev Project Explorer window, do the following:

    a. In the _busobjects subfolder, right-click the Enroll.dll node, and then choose **Properties**.

    b. In the **IDispWebFile Properties** dialog box, click the **Component Installation** tab.

    c. Select the **Register on Server** and **Add to MTS Package** options.

    d. Enter the MTS package name, "State University", in the text box.

    e. Leave the transaction level at **Requires a Transaction**, and then click **OK**.

5. In MTS Explorer, expand the new State University package. You should see three new components: Add, Drop, and Transfer.

For more information on adding components, see "Adding Components to a Package" on page 379 in this Chapter.

▶ Set and test transaction properties for the component

1. If you have not already done so, set the transaction properties for the Add component to **Requires a transaction**.

    a. In MTS Explorer, expand the State University package node.

    b. Expand the Components node and locate the Add component.

    c. Right-click the Add component, and then choose **Properties**.

    d. In the **State University Properties** dialog box, click the **Transaction** tab. Select the **Requires a transaction** option. Click **OK**.

2. Repeat step 1 for the Drop and Transfer components.

3. In MTS Explorer, click the Transaction Statistics node to display information on currently running transactions.

4. Test the **Add** object by opening ClassView.htm in the browser. Log in to the profile using student ID 1 or any other valid student ID, and try adding yourself to classes.

5. View the transaction statistics in MTS Explorer.

If you attempt to add yourself to a class in which you are not enrolled, the transaction will complete successfully and the statistics will show that a transaction completed.

If you attempt to add yourself to a class in which you are already enrolled, the transaction will fail and the statistics will show that a transaction aborted.

6. Use DataView to verify that the Enrollment table has been updated correctly when classes are added. You can also verify that classes are added by browsing to the Transcript.asp file.

Exercise 2: Adding Transaction Support to COM Components

In this exercise, you will modify the Drop component to call the **SetComplete** and **SetAbort** methods. You will also modify the Transfer component to use the **CreateInstance** method so that it can create the **Add** and **Drop** objects. The **Transfer** object will then call the **Add** and **Drop** objects to perform the work of transferring a student.

Finally, you will test these components by creating objects of these types and invoking their methods from ASP pages DropClass.asp and TransferClass.asp, respectively.

For example, you will use ClassView.htm to submit a form that transfers a student. The following illustration shows how Classview.htm looks.

When you transfer a student, the TransferClass.asp file calls the **Transfer** object to transfer a student. The following illustration shows how TransferClass.asp looks when returned to the student.

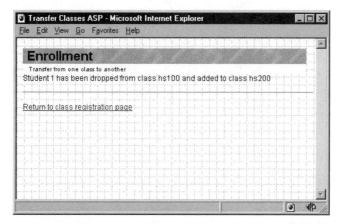

▶ Modify the Drop object to call SetComplete or SetAbort

The changes required to update the Drop component are very similar to those you examined in the Add component in the previous exercise.

1. If not already open in Visual Basic, open the Enroll project from the \busobjects folder.

2. Open the class module Drop (Drop.cls).

3. At the beginning of the **Drop** function, assign the **Drop** function 0 as a default return value.

   The return value is used by the .asp file that calls the object to determine if it was successful.

4. Add code to retrieve the **Context** object from the MTS run-time environment.

   To see an example of how your code should look, see Lab Hint 8.1 in Appendix B.

5. Locate the call to the **ClassCompleted** function. Add a line of code to call **SetAbort** if **ClassCompleted** is **True**.

   If the function returns a value of **True**, it indicates that the student has completed the class, so the **Drop** function aborts.

6. In the error handler, add code to call the **SetAbort** method to indicate that any changes made by the **Drop** function should be undone.

7. After the **conn.close** statement, add a statement that calls the **SetComplete** method.

   For more information on the **SetComplete** and **SetAbort** methods, see "Adding Transactional Support" on page 366 in this Chapter.

8. Save your changes, and then remake Enroll.dll.

   If Visual Basic reports an error while trying to remake this file, you will have to temporarily shut down the State University package to unload the DLL from memory.

   a. In the MTS Explorer, locate the State University package node.

   b. Right-click on this node and choose the **Shut Down** command.

   The next time one of StateU's components is accessed, MTS will automatically reload this DLL.

▶ **Test the Drop component of the State University Package**

1. If not already open, open the MTS Explorer and locate the My Computer node.

2. Right-click on the node and choose the **Refresh All Components** command.

3. Click on the Transaction Statistics node.

4. Test the Drop component by opening the file ClassView.htm in the browser. Log in to the profile using student ID 1 and try dropping the MT100 class.

   The attempt should fail because the class is already completed. The failure should be logged as an aborted transaction.

   Try dropping other classes. These drops should succeed and be logged as completed transactions.

5. Use DataView to verify that the Enrollment table has been updated correctly when classes are dropped. You can also verify that classes are dropped by retrieving the Transcript.asp file.

Note If you drop a class in which the current student ID is not enrolled, the drop will still succeed. This is because the **Drop** method uses the SQL DE-LETE statement to remove records from the enrollment table. The SQL DELETE statement will succeed even if the record does not exist.

▶ **Modify the Transfer object to create the Add and Drop objects**

In this procedure you will update the implementation of the Transfer component with prepared code, and then examine the changes made.

1. Open the class module Transfer.cls for editing in Visual Basic.

2. Open the file \MWD6\Labs\Lab08\Update_Transfer.txt.

3. Replace the contents of the Transfer class module with the contents of Update_Transfer.txt.

4. Examine the contents of the class module. There are update comments denoting new or altered code lines. The following changes have been made to the **Transfer** function:

   - Declaring an ObjectContext variable.

   - Declaring variables of type Enroll.Add and Enroll.Drop.

   - Obtaining the current object's context with the **GetObjectContext** method.

   - Using **ObjectContext.CreateInstance** to create instances of the Add and Drop components.

   - Calling **ObjectContext.SetComplete** when the method is successful, or otherwise calling **ObjectContext.SetAbort**.

5. Save the changes and remake Enroll.dll.

6. In the MTS Explorer, refresh this component again.

▶ **Test the Transfer component of the State University package**

1. Test the **Transfer** object by opening ClassView.htm in the browser. Log in to the profile using student ID 1 and try transferring to a class in which that student is already enrolled.

   The transfer should fail and be logged as an aborted transaction.

   Then, try transferring between valid classes. The transfer should succeed and be logged as a completed transaction.

2. Use DataView to verify that the Enrollment table has been updated correctly. You can also verify that classes are transferred by retrieving the Transcript.asp file.

Exercise 3: Adding Transaction Support to an ASP Page

In this exercise, you will modify the AddClass.asp page so that it participates in the MTS transaction responsible for adding a student to the appropriate class in the StateU database. Specifically, you will add an event handler for the **Abort** event and code to display an error message to the user.

▶ **Alter the ASP page to participate in MTS transactions**

1. Open the AddClass.asp file for editing.

2. Find the @ command at the top of the file indicating that the language being used is VBScript. Extend this command by indicating that the page requires a transaction:

```
<%@ LANGUAGE=VBScript TRANSACTION=Required %>
```

Any MTS components created by addclass.asp and marked as **Requires a Transaction** activation will now be recruited in the same transaction.

For more information about adding transaction support to Active Server Pages, see "MTS and Active Server Pages" on page 373 in this Chapter.

▶ **Handle the Transaction Abort event**

Although there is already code in the AddClass.asp page to handle an error returned from the **Add** object, there is still the possibility that a critical exception or time-out will occur before the component has a chance to return. To guard against these possibilities, you will add a handler for a **Transaction Abort** event.

1. After the function **DoAdd**, but before the ending </Script> tag, add a server-side VBScript subroutine called **OnTransactionAbort**.

2. As the first statement in this subroutine, use the **Clear** method of the **Response** object to erase any previously buffered HTML.

3. Use a series of **Response.Write** method calls to output a short HTML page informing the student that the transaction has aborted, to try again later, and if the problem persists to e-mail the Webmaster (webmaster@stateu.edu).

4. In the last statement of this handler, flush the HTML page to the output.

To see an example of how your code should look, see Lab Hint 8.2 in Appendix B.

Self-Check Questions

To see the answers to the Self-Check Questions, see Appendix A.

1. What is the ACID test?

A. Properties that a transaction should have so it does not fail.

B. A test that you can perform to determine whether a transaction failed.

C. The change in the state of data.

D. A test that can be performed on components before they are placed on a Web server.

2. How do you set a Microsoft Transaction Server component to require a transaction?

A. Set the transaction property of the component's package to require a transaction.

B. Set the transaction property of the component to support a transaction.

C. Set the transaction property of the component to require a transaction.

D. Write the component so that it calls the transaction functions **BeginTrans**, **EndTrans**, and **Rollback**.

3. How do you enable a COM component to participate in transactions on Microsoft Transaction Server?

A. Call the transaction functions **BeginTrans**, **CommitTrans**, and **Rollback**.

B. Modify the component to call the methods **SetComplete** and **SetAbort**.

C. Place the component in Microsoft Transaction Server Explorer.

D. Create the public methods **SetComplete** and **SetAbort** for the component.

4. What are the advantages of stateless objects?

A. They reduce the server load.

B. They ensure transaction isolation and database consistency.

C. They reduce the internal data dependencies of objects.

D. All of the above.

5. How do you get a reference to a context object created by Microsoft Transaction Server for a component?

A. Call the GetObjectContext API.

B. Call **CreateObject** ("object.context").

C. Microsoft Transaction Server will automatically pass the parameter that gets the context object.

D. Call **GetObject** ("object.context").

6. Which of the following statements correctly describes package roles?

A. Roles are applied at the package level.

B. Roles allow bypassing of security checks for method calls that cross process boundaries.

C. Roles can be created only when a component is deployed.

D. Roles can be configured dynamically using MTS Explorer.

Student Notes:

Chapter 9:
Integrating Other Server-Side Technologies

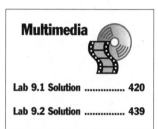

Multimedia

As Web applications become more mission-critical to corporations, it becomes a requirement that a complete Web solution integrate well with existing services.

In this chapter, you will learn how to use the Simple Mail Transport Protocol (SMTP) service of Microsoft Internet Information Server (IIS) 4.0 to send e-mail from a Web site. You will also learn how to enable custom search capabilities for a Web site.

Objectives

After completing this chapter, you will be able to:

◆ Use SMTP to send e-mail from a Web site.

◆ Use Microsoft Index Server to add search capabilities to a Web page.

Overview of Server-Side Technologies

Web developers can use various server-side technologies to enhance their Web sites and provide users with richer functionality. This topic provides an overview of the server-side technologies and products that are discussed in this chapter.

Mail Services

Through its support for standard interfaces and protocols such as MAPI, SMTP, and Collaboration Data Objects (CDO), Windows NT provides an extensive messaging infrastructure that can benefit both developers and users.

The ability to use a simpler, non-API-based object library with a Simple Mail Transport Protocol (SMTP) service is particularly useful for the Web developer, whose primary concern is to generate and deliver simple e-mail messages (notifications) in a Web site. If more advanced functionality is required, for example workgroup and collaboration capabilities, then the Collaboration Data Objects (CDO) 1.2 library and Microsoft Exchange Server 5.5 can be combined to provide more sophisticated messaging functionality.

Index Server

Microsoft Index Server 2.0, a component of Internet Information Server (IIS) 4.0, adds powerful searching and indexing capabilities to IIS Web sites. Organizations can create Web sites that contain a broad range of document formats, which can then be indexed and queried by users. Web developers can use Visual Basic, VBScript, C, C++, Java, and JavaScript to create dynamic, flexible, customized query and result forms. Because Index Server is integrated with the Windows NT file and security system, it provides automatic indexing of content that follows the security policies set by the Web and Windows NT Server administrators. Administrators do not need to manually update or manage indices.

Integrating Mail Services

Web developers can enhance the usefulness of their Web sites by integrating messaging capabilities that enable users to send and receive e-mail, participate in threaded news discussions, and perform other messaging tasks. Windows NT provides an ideal platform to accomplish this because of its broad range of messaging support, particularly for the SMTP service of IIS 4.0 and Microsoft Exchange Server 5.5.

In this section, you will learn how to use an ASP script with an SMTP server to create and send e-mail from a Web site.

Mail Services for Windows NT

Windows NT provides a robust and flexible messaging platform with comprehensive mail service support that includes mail servers and programmability options. Web developers can use the mail services offered through Windows NT to enable messaging for their Web sites.

Mail Servers

Mail servers constitute a primary element of an electronic messaging system's infrastructure. Windows NT supports different server options for implementing a messaging system, depending on the functionality required by users of the system.

Standard Internet Mail Services

Internet users who want only to send and receive e-mail should use the following two server programs:

◆ A SMTP server, which is used in a TCP/IP network to transport mail between mail nodes—typically POP3 and end user nodes—on the Internet. SMTP is often referred to as a delivery service since it is only concerned with moving e-mail from one node to another. User services such as log in and mailbox creation are not supported. For more information about SMTP, see "How SMTP Service Works" on page 411 in this chapter.

◆ A Post Office Protocol (POP or POP3) server, which supplies the e-mail store and administrative and user services. Mail users interact directly with POP3 services to log in, access mail, create new messages and mail folders, and perform other messaging tasks. Internet Message Access Protocol (IMAP) is a specification for newer, more powerful Internet post office services.

For information about POP3, go to the Standards Track for the POP3 specification at src.doc.ic.ac.uk/computing/internet/rfc/rfc1939.txt.

For information about IMAP services, go to the Standards Track for the IMAP specification at src.doc.ic.ac.uk/computing/internet/rfc/rfc2060.txt.

SMTP Service of IIS

The Windows NT Option Pack contains Microsoft SMTP Service, a commercial-grade implementation of SMTP designed to meet the needs of high-traffic loads required by mission-critical applications. Microsoft SMTP Service is implemented as an extension to Internet Information Server 4.0. It is based on the open Internet specification (RFC) 821.

For more information about Microsoft SMTP Service for IIS, search for "Operating Microsoft SMTP Service" in Microsoft NT Option Pack Help.

Microsoft Exchange Server

Microsoft Exchange Server 5.5, a component of the Microsoft BackOffice suite, provides a messaging platform that extends rich messaging and collaboration capabilities to businesses of all sizes. In addition to providing high performance and high availability, Microsoft Exchange 5.5 is fully compatible with the existing Internet standards, including POP3, IMAP, LDAP, NNTP, and MAPI, and provides tools for developers to create Active Server Pages.

For more information about Exchange Mail Service features, go to the Microsoft Exchange Server Web site at www.microsoft.com/exchange/default.htm.

Mail Access Technologies

In addition to providing support for different messaging server options, Windows NT supports options for creating programmable messaging objects in the form of a messaging API and various libraries. These libraries can be used by clients such as Microsoft Visual Basic, C and C++, Microsoft Visual C++, and Visual Basic Scripting Edition (VBScript) applications. The following table describes some types of mail access technologies and provides links to relevant Web sites for more information.

Access technology

◆ Messaging API (MAPI)

Industry-standard C-level mail and messaging interface. Enables multiple applications to interact with multiple messaging systems across a variety of hardware platforms. For more information, see the web site at msdn.microsoft.com/isapi/msdnlib.idc?theURL=/library/sdkdoc/mapi/book_9jqc.htm.

◆ Collaborative Data Objects (CDO)

A COM-based set of technologies that enables any MAPI-based application to act as the Exchange data store. The CDO library, included with Exchange 5.5, defines a set of objects that supports calendaring, collaboration, and workflow capabilities. (CDO supercedes the Microsoft Active Messaging 1.1 library for Exchange.) For more information, see the web site at msdn.microsoft.com/isapi/msdnlib.idc?theURL=/library/sdkdoc/cdo/kluaover_34a7.htm.

◆ CDO Rendering Objects

A component of CDO that can be used to display Exchange data in HTML format. This library increases the efficiency and manageability of similar approaches using ASP scripting. For more information, see the web site at msdn.microsoft.com/isapi/msdnlib.idc?theURL=/library/sdkdoc/cdo/kluaover_34a7.htm.

◆ CDO for Windows NT Server (CDONTS).

This subset of the CDO library is used for building simple, scalable applications, based on the SMTP mail protocol. This library runs in both Internet Information Server 4.0 (with the SMTP mail service) and Exchange 5.5 environments. For more information, see the web site at msdn.microsoft.com/isapi/msdnlib.idc?theURL=/library/sdkdoc/cdo/kluaover_34a7.htm.

For more information about CDO for Windows NT Server, see "Collaboration Data Objects for Windows NT Server (CDONTS)" on page 414 in this chapter.

How SMTP Service Works

An SMTP server functions as a gateway that enables disparate clients to interact with the same messaging backbone. The SMTP protocol is layered on top of the standard TCP protocol on which much of the Internet is based.

Message Transmission Process

SMTP defines a simple process for transporting messages. An e-mail message is created, typically by a user of a mail package, and then delivered to the SMTP server of the user's domain. The SMTP server relays the messages to another SMTP node—either another SMTP server or the final mail recipient. Through a process called "hopping," a message may pass through several SMTP servers before it is delivered.

Microsoft SMTP Service uses a designated TCP port (port 25 by default) for delivering and sending messages. You can use the Internet Service Manager snap-in program to configure delivery, security, domain, and other administrative options.

Delivering Messages (Inbound)

Microsoft SMTP Service uses the following process to deliver inbound messages:

1. A message arrives via the designated inbound TCP port.

2. It is placed in the Queue directory \INetPub\mailroot\Queue.

   - If the message recipients are local to that domain, the message is placed in the Drop directory designated for the default domain.

   - If the recipients are not local, the message is processed for remote delivery. These messages are placed in the Queue directory for delivery. At this stage they are equivalent to queued outbound messages.

   - If a message can neither be delivered nor returned to the sender, it is placed in the BadMail directory.

Sending Messages (Outbound)

Microsoft SMTP Service uses the following process to deliver outbound messages:

1. An outbound message that is created as a text file is placed in the Pickup directory \INetPub\mailroot\Pickup.

2. Microsoft SMTP Service collects the message and initiates delivery.

   - If the message recipients are local (to the current domain), the message is placed in the Drop directory designated for the current domain.

   - All other outbound messages are sent directly to the Queue directory for delivery.

   - If a message can neither be delivered nor returned to the sender, it is placed in the BadMail directory.

3. Queued messages are transmitted through the designated outbound TCP port to a receiving mail server for the designated remote domain.

The following illustration shows the process of sending and delivering messages through the SMTP Service.

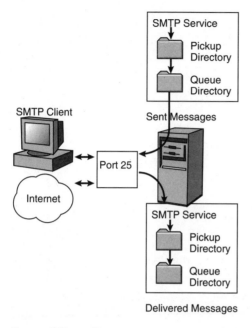

Specifications

For information about the status of the SMTP protocol specification, go to the page "Current Internet Drafts" at ftp://isi.edu/internet-drafts/1id-abstracts.txt.

Microsoft SMTP Service is compliant with the open Internet specifications in Request for Comments (RFC) 821 and RFC 822. For information, go to the RFC 821 specification page at ftp://isi.edu/internet-drafts/draft-ietf-drums-smtpupd-10.txt.

Note The SMTP protocol specification is referred to as an Internet Draft. Internet Drafts are working documents of the Internet Engineering Task Force (IETF).

Collaboration Data Objects for Windows NT Server (CDONTS)

Collaboration Data Objects for Windows NT Server (CDONTS) is a smaller and faster subset of CDO 1.2, available only on Internet Information Server for Windows NT Server. CDONTS also contains an object model and exposes messaging objects for use by Microsoft Visual Basic, C and C++, Microsoft Visual C++, and ActiveX Scripting (such as VBScript and JScript) applications.

Functionality

CDONTS has no underlying MAPI infrastructure. Instead it works by itself on Internet Information Server or on a combination of Internet Information Server and Microsoft Exchange. CDONTS supports the sending of anonymous e-mail through a system-wide inbox drop directory under Internet Information Server 4.0. CDO 1.2 provides support for anonymous messaging, but only at the public folder level.

Like CDO 1.2, CDONTS supports the following types of message content:

- Plain text
- HTML and MHTML
- UUEncoded or Base64 content
- File-attachment encoding
- The creation of large bodies of text from files
- URLs

CDONTS also supports the standard COM interface, IStream, enabling developers to create Web-based applications that read message content directly from a hard drive or from in-memory objects.

CDONTS Object Model

The CDONTS object model is organized as a log-on session with a top-level **Session** object. Creating a **Session** object is necessary in order to use any other objects in CDONTS. Under the **Session** object are other objects, collections of objects, properties, and methods.

The following illustration shows the object model for the CDONTS library.

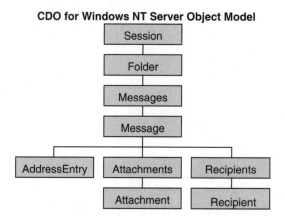

CDO for Windows NT Server Object Model

For more information on CDO for NT Server, search for "Collaboration Data Objects for NTS Component" in the Windows NT Option Pack online documentation.

Sending E-mail from an ASP Script

For workgroup applications that require advanced collaboration functionality such as scheduling, calendaring, and folder administration, CDO 1.2 provides programmatic access to a broad range of standard mail server functionality. However, the most commonly desired capability for Web developers is the ability to create and send e-mail messages. CDONTS, with its SMTP-based messaging support, enables quick and easy e-mail notification from an ASP script.

Using the NewMail Object

The **NewMail** object enables the generation and sending of an automatic e-mail notification to a variety of independent messaging systems. The **NewMail** object is self-contained and independent of the CDONTS object hierarchy. There is no need to log on to a session or deal with a folder or a Messages collection.

Note The CDO component is only available with Windows NT Server and is installed with the SMTP Service for IIS.

▶ **To use the CDONTS component to send e-mail**

1. Create an instance of a **NewMail** object.

2. Set properties, such as **To, From, Cc,** and **Subject**.

3. Use the **Send** method to send the message.

4. Remove the **NewMail** object from memory by setting it to **Nothing**.

The following example code shows how to use the CDONTS component to send a simple e-mail message:

```
Set objNewMail = Server.CreateObject("CDONTS.NewMail")
objNewMail.Send "me@company.com",_
  "you@companya.com; someone@companyb.com", _
  "Testing 1,2,3 ", _1
```

When the **Send** method completes successfully, the **NewMail** object is invalidated but not removed from memory. Therefore, after you send a message, you should do one of the following:

◆ If you do not intend to send another message with this object, set it to **Nothing** to remove it from memory, as shown in the following example code:

```
Set objNewMail = Nothing ' cannot reuse it for another message
```

◆ If you want to send another message with this object, reassign it to another **NewMail** object, as shown in the following example code:

```
Set MyMail = CreateObject("CDONTS.NewMail")
'...
```

The **Send** method sends the **NewMail** object to the specified recipients. It uses the following syntax:

*objNewMail.**Send**([From] [, To] [, Subject] [, Body] [, Importance])*

The following table describes each syntax element:

Syntax element	Description
objNewMail (required)	This NewMail object.
From (string — optional)	The full messaging address to be identified as the sender.

table continued on next page

Syntax element	Description
To (string — optional)	A list of full messaging addresses of recipients. The individual recipient addresses are separated by semicolons.
Subject (string — optional)	The subject line for the message.
Body (**IStream** object or string — optional)	The text of the message.
Importance (Long — optional)	The importance associated with the message.

Remarks

The *From*, *To*, *Subject*, *Body*, and *Importance* parameters correspond to the **From**, **To**, **Subject**, **Body**, and **Importance** properties on the **NewMail** object.

If both the **To** property and the *To* parameter of the **Send** method are supplied, the **NewMail** object is sent to all recipients on both lists.

Only C/C++ and Java programs can use an **IStream** object for the *Body* parameter. They should pass an **IUnknown** object that returns an **IStream** interface in response to **QueryInterface**. Microsoft Visual Basic supports the **IDispatch** interface and not **IUnknown**, so it cannot use an **IStream** object.

The **NewMail** object becomes invalid upon successful completion of the **Send** method, and you cannot reuse it for another message. You should **Set** it to **Nothing** to release the memory. Attempted access to a sent **NewMail** object results in a return of **CdoE_INVALID_OBJECT**.

Limitations of the NewMail Object

Because the **NewMail** object is designed to send notification mail from a Windows NT service, there is no user interface and no user interaction during the creation and sending of the mail. Also, it is not possible to remove attachments or recipients that have been added to the **NewMail** object, nor can the **NewMail** object itself be deleted.

For more information on the **NewMail** object and its members, search for the NT Option Pack online documentation topic "NewMail Object (CDONTS Library)."

The following sample code shows how to use the objects provided by the CDONTS component from within an ASP script. To copy this code for use in your own project, see "Sending Email from an ASP Script" on the accompanying CD-ROM.

This sample first uses the **Server.CreateObject** method to create an instance of the **NewMail** object. Next, the most important **NewMail** properties are set, including the **From, To, Subject,** and **Body** properties. Finally, the **Send** method of the **NewMail** object is invoked to send the message to the specified destination.

```
<% @Language=VBScript %>
<% Option Explicit %>

<HTML>
<HEAD>
<TITLE>CDO Component</TITLE>
</HEAD>
<BODY bgcolor="white" topmargin="10" leftmargin="10">

<!- Display Header ->

<font size="4" face="Arial, Helvetica">
<b>CDO Component</b></font><p>

This sample demonstrates how to use the Collaboration
Data Objects for NTS Component to send a simple
e-mail message.

<p>To actually send the message, you must
have the SMTP Server that comes with the
Windows NT Option Pack Installed.

<%
Dim myMail
Set myMail = Server.CreateObject("CDONTS.NewMail")

' For demonstration proposes, both From and To
' properties are set to the same address.

myMail.From = "someone@Microsoft.com"
myMail.To = "someone@Microsoft.com"

myMail.Subject = "Sample"
myMail.Body = "I hope you like the sample"
```

code continued on next page

```
code continued from previous page

myMail.Send
%>
</BODY>
</HTML>
```

Sending Mail through Exchange Server

Using CDO 1.2 with Microsoft Exchange Server 5.5 to send e-mail differs from using CDONTS with the SMTP server provided with the Windows NT Option Pack. Because the **NewMail** object is not available in CDO 1.2 for Microsoft Exchange Server 5.5, you must first establish a MAPI session before any MAPI functionality is available to you.

For more information about using CDO 1.2 with Microsoft Exchange Server 5.5, go to the "Introduction to Collaboration Data Objects" page at the MSDN Web site at msdn.microsoft.com/isapi/msdnlib.idc?theURL=/library/sdkdoc/cdo/kluaover_34a7.htm.

Microsoft Exchange Server version 5.5 comes with several extensive examples on how to use scripting—both inside a Web application and within the Exchange Server environment—to create messaging solutions. For example, the "Full Send" example application demonstrates how to create a browser-based client capable of composing and sending messages.

Sending E-mail Via the Pickup Directory

Although CDONTS provides the best approach for generating e-mail messages for most ASP applications, Microsoft SMTP Service provides a second, file-based technique for creating messages using the Pickup directory.

Using this method technique, you simply create the text-based e-mail message, then place it in a file in the SMTP server's Pickup directory. To the server, this new message is indistinguishable from any other message that has been queued in the Pickup directory by other mail processes for delivery. (In fact, this simple pickup mechanism forms the basis of how SMTP sends and relays e-mail messages.)

▶ **To send a message using the Pickup directory**

1. Compose a plain text message using an editor or word-processing program, or programmatically through standard file and string library calls.

The top of the message must have the appropriate mail headers such as the "x-sender", "x-receiver," and so on. After a carriage return/line feed (CRLF) pair, the body of the message is entered. The following sample code is an example of such a message. To copy this code for use in your own project, see "Using the Pickup Directory to Send and Receive Email" on the accompanying CD-ROM.

```
x-sender: johns@CompanyA.com
x-receiver: mariab@CompanyB.com
From: johns@CompanyA.com
To: mariab@CompanyB.com
Subject: Hello from John

Hello, how have you been?
```

For information about mail headers, search for "Using the Pickup Directory for Message Delivery" in the Windows NT Option Pack online documentation.

2. Save this message as a file in a temporary directory.

3. Move or copy this file to the SMTP service's Pickup directory. By default, this directory's location is \InetPub\MailRoot\PickUp.

   Microsoft SMTP Service periodically searches this directory for messages. When it finds a new message in the Pickup directory, it moves it to the Queue subdirectory where it processes it for immediate delivery.

Note The two methods of creating e-mail messages—using the **NewMail** object and creating a file in the Pickup folder—are equivalent because the **NewMail** object simply generates a file in the Pickup folder.

Lab 9.1: Sending E-mail

In this lab, you will extend the State University Web application so that when a student registers for a new course, the student receives an e-mail confirmation.

To see the demonstration "Lab 9.1 Solution," see the accompanying CD-ROM.

Estimated time to complete this lab: **30 minutes**

To complete the exercises in this lab, you must have the required software. In particular you must have installed the optional Microsoft SMTP Service for Internet

Information Server (IIS). For detailed information about the labs and setup for the labs, see "Labs" in "About This Course."

Note As the SMTP Service for IIS is only available for the Windows NT Server operating system, this lab can only be accomplished on a machine running Windows NT Server.

Objectives

After completing this lab, you will be able to:

◆ Use the Internet Service Manager snap-in program to investigate and administer the SMTP Service for IIS.

◆ Write an ASP script that uses Collaborative Data Objects for Windows NT Server (CDONTS) to create e-mail messages.

Prerequisites

Before working on this lab, you should be familiar with the following:

◆ Operating the Microsoft Management Console (MMC) and the Internet Service Manager snap-in program.

◆ Creating server-side scripts using Visual Basic, Scripting Edition (VBScript).

Exercises

The following exercises provide practice working with the concepts and techniques covered in this chapter:

◆ Exercise 1: Exploring the SMTP Service

In this exercise, you will use the Internet Service Manager (MMC snap-in version) to explore and administer the Microsoft SMTP Service for IIS. You will browse the service, start and stop the service, and change some of its properties.

◆ Exercise 2: Sending E-mail Using the NewMail Object

In this exercise, you will modify the addclass.asp page so that it generates a confirmation e-mail message to students when they successfully register for classes. To accomplish this, you will write an OnTransactionCommit handler that creates a **NewMail** object and then invokes its **Send** method.

Exercise 1: Exploring the SMTP Service

In this exercise, you will use the Internet Service Manager (MMC snap-in version) to explore and administer the Microsoft SMTP Service for IIS. You will browse the service, start and stop the service, and change some of its properties.

▶ **Browse the SMTP Service**

1. Start the Internet Service Manager snap-in program for the Microsoft Management Console (MMC). This program should be located in the Microsoft Internet Information Server folder.

2. In the left pane, expand the Internet Information Server node, and then the current computer node. Select and expand the Default SMTP Site node. If you do not see this node, then the SMTP Service for IIS was not installed.

   When the SMTP Service is installed, it creates a local SMTP domain with the same name as the computer.

3. View the properties for the Default SMTP Site by performing one of the following:

   - On the **Action** menu, click **Properties**.
   - Right-click on the Default SMTP Site node. On the context menu, click **Properties**.
   - Click the **Properties** toolbar button.

   Briefly view the options available on each tab on the **Default SMTP Site Properties** sheet. Windows Help is available for each property sheet by pressing F1.

Note If you receive errors when you try to access the SMTP Service, log on as the local administrator account and try again.

▶ **Start and stop the service**

1. Select the Default SMTP Site node if it is not already selected. On the toolbar, click the **Stop** button to stop the service.

   If you select the Current Sessions node, you will receive a dialog box explaining that the service is not running.

2. Select the Default SMTP Site node again. Click the **Start** button to restart the service.

Tip Another method you can use to show and modify the status of the SMTP service, as well as to modify its startup type is through the Services applet of the Control Panel. This service is listed under the name "Microsoft SMTP Service."

▶ **Edit the Service Properties**

Because you are using the SMTP Service on the State University Web site only to generate e-mail, you can make a number of simplifications, optimizations, and security enhancements to this service.

1. Display the **Default SMTP Site Properties** sheet for the SMTP Service again.

2. On the **SMTP Site** tab, make the following changes:

    • Set the incoming connection limit to 10 simultaneous connections.

    • Set the incoming and outgoing connection timeout to 100 seconds.

    • Deselect the **Enable Logging** check box.

    As this service will be used mainly to send out short, low-priority confirmation messages, these changes increase outgoing mail efficiency.

3. Click the **Messages** tab and set the maximum message size to 10 KB. Confirmation messages should be relatively short.

4. Click the **Delivery** tab and set the maximum retries to 24. Since confirmation messages are low priority, you will limit the time allowed to send them to one day.

5. Click the **Directory Security** tab and then click the **Edit** button in the **Relay Restrictions** box. In the **Relay Restrictions** dialog box, select **Not allowed to relay** to prevent other computers from using this service to relay their mail.

For more information on how to administer the SMTP Service for IIS, search for "Microsoft SMTP Service" in the Windows NT Option Pack online documentation.

Exercise 2: Sending E-mail Using the NewMail Object

In this exercise, you will modify the addclass.asp page so that it generates a confirmation e-mail message to students when they successfully register for classes. To accomplish this, you will write an **OnTransactionCommit** handler that creates a **NewMail** object and then invokes its **Send** method. You will then invoke this new server-side script and view the generated e-mail message.

For simplicity, assume that the e-mail address of each student is the student's ID concatenated with the string "@stateu.edu".

▶ Edit the existing server script

Before adding the handler for the transaction commit event, you will need to modify the existing script so that this new method will have access to the required information.

1. Open the file Addclass.asp in Visual InterDev for editing. Locate the following line:

```
<SCRIPT LANGUAGE=vbscript RUNAT=Server>
```

2. After this line, insert the following declaration:

```
Dim lngStudentID, strClassID
```

3. Make the following changes to the **DoAdd** function:

   - Change the name of the parameter to this method from strClassID to strpClassID to differentiate it from the global variable you just added.

   - Insert the following line at the beginning of **DoAdd**:

   ```
   strClassID = strpClassID
   ```

▶ Add the OnTransactionCommit handler

In Exercise 3 of Lab 8, "Adding Transactional Support to an ASP Page," you added a handler for the **OnTransactionAbort** event to the Addclass.asp file to alert the user about critical failures of the Web application. In this procedure, you'll add an event handler for completed transactions.

1. After the OnTransactionAbort handler, create an empty **OnTransactionCommit** subroutine.

2. Code the body of the event handler to create an enrollment confirmation message as described in the following steps. If you need assistance, see "Sending E-mail from an ASP Script" on page 415 in this chapter.

   a. Create a new **NewMail** object.

   b. Invoke the **Send** method on this object. Supply the following four parameters and values:

Parameter	Type	Value
Sender	String	"registrar@stateu.edu"
Recipient	String	Concatenation of Student ID and "@stateu.edu"
Subject	String	"Class Enrollment Confirmation"
Body	String	Compose a short message that explains the student has been registered, and include the actual course ID in this message.
Importance (optional)	Long	normal (default value)

   c. Set your **NewMail** object to **Nothing** to release it.

   Remember that the underscore character, _ , is used to continue a statement in Visual Basic. The student and course IDs have been stored in local page variables in previous labs.

   To see an example of how your code should look, see Lab Hint 9.1 in Appendix B.

3. Save the changes to Addclass.asp.

▶ **Test the page**

The SMTP Service will prepare the e-mail for delivery to a POP3-compliant e-mail server such as Microsoft Exchange 5.5 or later. This procedure assumes that you have not yet configured the SMTP Service to deliver the generated mail to such a server. Therefore, the message you prepared in the previous procedure will be viewed in the Queue directory.

1. In Internet Explorer, view the page Classview.htm (using an http:// URL). If you are beginning a new session, you will be required to fill out the student profile form.

2. Enroll in a new class. (If you receive an ASP syntax error in Addclass.asp, please review the previous section.)

3. With the Windows Explorer, browse to the \InetPub\MailRoot\Queue folder and locate the file with the .eml extension.

4. Double-click this file to open it in your default Internet e-mail reader. Confirm that the information you supplied is represented correctly by this e-mail message.

   The following example shows a confirmation message, as viewed in Microsoft Outlook Express.

5. Use Notepad to view the .eml file. Note that the **Send** method you coded in Addclass.asp generated a text-based file similar to the type discussed in "Sending E-mail Via the Pickup Directory" on page 419 in this chapter.

Adding Search Services

Many organizations are now creating intranets to provide their employees with documents that have the same ease of use as the World Wide Web. Because organizations may produce large amounts of information, they need to utilize indexing and searching technology to help their users find the right documents quickly.

In this section, you will learn how to use Microsoft Index Server 2.0 in conjunction with the Windows NT Server operating system to provide search capabilities for an intranet or Internet site.

The FrontPage Search Bot

Microsoft Visual InterDev 6 uses a FrontPage 98 WebBot component to provide a default search form that users can use to search a Web site. This functionality relies upon the FrontPage Server Extensions, which can be obtained in one of the following ways:

◆ From the Visual InterDev Server Setup program

◆ As a part of the Minimum and Typical IIS 4.0 setup

◆ As separate downloadable components

When a user submits a search form that contains words to locate, the search bot performs a full-text search over all pages in a Web site and returns hyperlinks to all pages that contain the words.

How the Search Bot Works

The FrontPage search bot is a convenient interface to the actual search engine located on the Web server. The FrontPage search bot can use either of two following search engines:

◆ Wide Area Information Server (WAIS)

   The WAIS search engine is an implementation of an older, Internet-standard search service. It is the default search engine included with the FrontPage Server Extensions, but is not installed as part of Visual InterDev or the Windows NT Option Pack.

◆ Index Server

   Microsoft Index Server version 2.0 is a content-indexing and search component included with Microsoft IIS 4.0. If Index Server has been installed as part of IIS, the search bot uses Index Server instead of the WAIS search engine.

For more information about the FrontPage search bot, see the FrontPage 98 Server Extensions Resource Kit at officeupdate.microsoft.com/frontpage/SERK/.

Introduction to Microsoft Index Server

Microsoft Index Server 2.0 is a standard extension component of IIS 4.0 that indexes the content of a Web site and allows queries against that content. Index

Server enables any client using an HTML browser to search a Web site by using a normal HTML form.

Index Server Features

Index Server combines flexible search techniques with support for multiple document formats. In addition, it is fully integrated with Windows NT and IIS security, logging, and administration facilities. By indexing the contents and properties of documents on a single Web site, you can enable clients to search the contents of that site.

Flexible Search Strategies

Clients can search an indexed Web site using several query types, as described in the following table.

Query type	Description
Basic query	Enables the user to search for multiple separate words and phrases.
Complex query	Boolean, UNIX-like regular expression matching, weighted, and fuzzy word capabilities enable the user to search with wild cards, regular expression matching, and linguistic stemming to find all tenses of a verb.
Free text query	Enables the user to express a search as a question. For example: "How do I sign up for a math course?"
Document property query	Enables the user to query against file size, time stamp, author's name, HTML meta parameters, and so on.

Filtering Proprietary Document Formats

Index Server is designed to work directly on text and HTML files, and also includes filters for Microsoft Office formats (Word, Excel, and so on). Other companies may also provide filters for their file formats. For example, Adobe Systems has announced plans to create a filter for its popular Portable Document Format (PDF) files.

You can create custom filters for other document formats by implementing the IFilter COM interface. For more information about creating filters for proprietary document formats, search for "Filtering" in the Window NT Option Pack online documentation. You can download the IFilter SDK from the Microsoft BackOffice Download and Trial Center page. Go to this page at www.microsoft.com/backoffice/downloads.htm.

Consistent and Integrated Security, Logging, and Administration

The following table describes how Index Server uses the security, logging, and administration features of Windows NT and IIS.

Feature	Index Server implementation
Security	Uses Access Control List (ACL) security built into Windows NT. Clients may only find information about and access files or directories for which they have proper permission.
Logging	Logs system errors to the application event log; these can be viewed with the Event Viewer administration tool. If logging is enabled in IIS, user search requests are recorded by the standard IIS logging mechanism.
Administration	Administered through a snap-in component of Microsoft Management Console (MMC). This tool provides a simplified way to create, adjust, and monitor catalogs and directories.

How Index Server Works

With Index Server, you typically use the following process to add search capabilities to a Web site:

1. After Microsoft Index Server is installed, the Content Index service is started and begins indexing all the documents in a computer's virtual directories. This process creates a master index, which along with some process information, is written to a file called the *default catalog*.

2. To enable users to utilize Index Server's search capabilities, a query form is created and published on the Web site. Users fill out fields on the form and submit their queries to the Web server.

3. IIS passes the query information to Index Server. Index Server reconciles most queries against the master index, returning the results as one or more HTML pages.

The following illustration depicts the process of passing a query from a client browser to the Web server, and shows how Index Server returns the results of the query to the client.

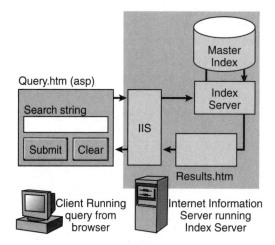

For information about how IIS and Index Server communicate, see "Integrating Index Server into a Web Site" in the following section.

Integrating Index Server into a Web Site

There are three techniques for integrating Index Server into a Web site:

◆ Active Server Pages can be used to create and process query forms, and to directly access the search capabilities of Index Server through its built-in query and utility objects.

◆ SQL queries can be used in applications to query Index Server. Since an OLE DB provider is supplied for Microsoft Index Server, other applications can use ActiveX Data Objects (ADO) to query Index Server. The SQL used with Index Server consists of extensions to the subset of SQL-92 and SQL3 that is detailed in the Windows NT Option Pack online help.

For example, in an ASP page, you can use the SQL Extensions to form the query, ADO to retrieve the data, and a scripting language to display the data.

◆ Index Server extension files - involves the creation and publication of three related files: an HTML search form, an Internet data query (.IDQ) file that defines query parameters, and an HTML extension (.HTX) file that acts as a template for the result.

This technique closely parallels that used by the Internet Database Connector (IDC) of IIS, and was the only available technique in the first release of Index Server. Although it is the best-performing technique, it is the least flexible.

Using ASP to Query Index Server

Active Server Pages typically offer the most general and flexible method of integrating Index Server into a Web application. Using this method has several advantages; it allows you to:

◆ Integrate searching with your ASP applications.

◆ Create search criteria dynamically.

◆ Format and manipulate search results before they are presented to the user.

General Procedure for Accessing Index Server through ASP

To enable query processing in an ASP page, use the following procedure:

1. Create a query form, an HTML form that allows the Web client to specify the search that should be performed. The ACTION parameter of the form should be set to the ASP page created in the next step.

   Note that the intrinsic HTML controls on the query form are typically named after the conventional URL tags recognized by Index Server.

   The following table lists the conventional tags, recognized by Index Server, used to form a query.

Tag	Description
qu	Full text of the query. Associated with the Query property.
so	Sort in ascending order on this field. Associated with the SortBy property.
sd	Sort down (in descending order). Associated with the SortBy property.
ct	Specify the (non-default) catalog. Associated with the Catalog property.
mh	Specify the maximum hits returned. Associated with the MaxRecords property.

table continued on next page

Tag	Description
ae	Allow enumeration. Associated with the AllowEnumeration property. If set to a nonzero digit, enumeration is allowed.
op	Optimize for. Associated with the OptimizeFor property. The first character of the value can be x for "performance" or r for "recall."

A simple example of a URL sent by a form might be:

```
http://www.stateu.edu/search.htm?qu=statistics&mh=50
```

2. Create an ASP page to process the request, submit a query to Index Server, and format and return the query results.

Index Server provides two server-side objects — the query object and the utility object — that greatly aid the ASP writer in performing these tasks. For more information, see "Using Server-Side Objects to Perform Queries" in the following section.

3. As an optional step, store the query and results of the search in Step 2 as session variables so that they can be reused.

Using Server-Side Objects to Perform Queries

Index Server provides two server-side objects (SSO)—the query object and the utility object—for building and enhancing Index Server queries. Both the query and utility objects are COM objects that provide late binding through their support of the IDispatch interface. The query object is used to form and submit the basic query, while the utility object adds miscellaneous functionality, such as query refinement, and helper functions for working with the query and query result.

Processing a Search Request with the Query Object

Typically, an ASP page will perform the following minimum number of steps to satisfy a user search request:

1. Create an instance of the query object. If Index Server has not been installed properly on the Web server, this step will fail.

2. Obtain the QUERY_STRING from the request URL by using the **Request.ServerVariables** or **Request.QueryString** methods. For more information, see "The Request Object" on page 181 in Chapter 4, "Using Active Server Pages."

3. Parse the request URL to form a valid Index Server query. The query object provides the **SetQueryFromURL** method for this purpose.

4. Submit the query to Index Server and accept the returned ADO recordset as provided by the **CreateRecordSet** method of the query object.

5. Format the results and return them to the user. Optionally, the ASP script can choose to further manipulate the information, for example by filtering it for additional security, usefulness, or user preference reasons.

The following example code shows a simple version of the previous procedure:

```
<!- Using ASP to process a simple Index Server query. ->
<% ClsQry = Server.CreateObject("IXSSO.Query") %>
<% if IsObject(ClsQry) = FALSE then %>
  The Web server's query support is not working
  correctly. Please contact the StateU Site
  Administrator at webmaster@stateu.edu .
<% else
    iRequest = Request.ServerVariables("QUERY_STRING")
    ClsQry.SetQueryFromURL(iRequest)
    RS=ClsQry .CreateRecordSet("nonsequential")
%>
<% end if %>
<!- Now Format and return results ->
<%NextRecordNumber = 1%>
<% Do While Not RS.EOF%>
<%=NextRecordNumber %> <%=RS("FileName")%>
<A HREF="http::<%=RS("vpath")%>"><%=RS("vpath")%></A><BR>
<% RS.MoveNext NextRecordNumber = NextRecordNumber+1 Loop%>
```

The query object contains several properties and methods to aid the script writer in processing a request. The following tables lists these properties and methods

Properties

The following table lists and describes the query object properties used in building .asp files.

Name	Description
AllowEnumeration	Specifies whether to allow searches other than on the content index, for example directly on Web files and folders.
Catalog	Provides the catalog name on a local computer.
Columns	Specifies the columns for each record to be retrieved from the content index result set. This property is supplied as a string containing comma-separated column names, for example "Author, Location, Title".
LocaleID	Specifies the language code and optional country code used for a search.
MaxRecords	Limits the number of records that a provider returns from a data source.
OptimizeFor	Modifies the number of hits in the result set of a query, based on the security and scope restrictions of the query.
Query	Determines the number of documents to be returned in a search.
SortBy	Specifies the Index Server properties to sort by in a search. Result sets can be ordered in ascending or descending order.

Methods

The following table lists and describes the query object methods used in building .asp files.

Name	Description
CreateRecordSet	Executes a query and creates an ADO **RecordSet** object for navigating through query results.

table continued on next page

Name	Description
DefineColumn	Defines a new friendly name for a column in a result set.
QueryToURL	Produces a uniform resource locator (URL) string reflecting the state of the query object.
Reset	Resets the state of the query object.
SetQueryFromURL	Allows search criteria to be set from a string passed by the Web client.

In addition, there are numerous search properties, such as vpath and FileName in the previous example code, that you can use to refine and format the search request. The following table lists the most common search properties.

Name	Description
A_HRef	Text of HTML HREF. Can be queried but not retrieved.
ClassId	Class ID of object, for example, WordPerfect, Word, and so on.
Characterization	Characterization, or abstract, of document. Computed by Index Server.
Contents	Main contents of file. Can be queried but not retrieved.
Directory	Physical path to the file, not including the file name. See also Path, VPath.
DocAuthor	Author of the document.
DocCharCount	Number of characters in the document.
DocCreatedTm	Time that document was created.
DocLastSavedTm	Time of last document save (update). See also Write.
DocLineCount	Number of lines contained in a document.
DocPageCount	Number of pages in document.
DocParaCount	Number of paragraphs in a document.

table continued on next page

Name	Description
DocRevNumber	Current version number of the document.
DocSubject	Subject of the document.
DocTitle	Title of the document.
DocWordCount	Number of words in the document.
FileIndex	Unique ID of file as used by NT.
FileName	Name of the file.
HitCount	Number of hits (words matching query) in file.
HtmlHRef	Text of HTML HREF. Can be queried but not retrieved
Path	Full physical path to file, including file name. See also Directory, VPath.
Rank	Rank of row. Ranges from 0 to 1000. Larger numbers indicate better matches.
Size	Size of file, in bytes.
VPath	Full virtual path to file, including file name. If more than one possible path, then the best match for the specific query is chosen.
WorkID	Internal ID for file. Used within Index Server.
Write	Time stamp of last file update. See also DocLastSavedTm.

To see a complete list of search properties, see "List of Property Names" in the Windows NT Option Pack Help.

Utility Object

You can use the utility object to further customize your search. For example, you can use the methods of the utility object to restrict the scope of a query specification, or to specify the language that will be used in the query.

The following table describes some of the methods of the utility object.

Method	Description
AddScopeToQuery	Adds a scope restriction to a query specification. A scope can either cover only the named folder or all its subfolders.
LocaleIDToISO	Converts an ISO 639 language code into a Win32 locale identifier (LCID), allowing the user some control over the language used in the query.
TruncateToWhitespace	Ends a string at the maximum specified length and at a whitespace (whole word). Helpful in creating shortened abstracts.

For more information about the query and utility objects and for more examples, see "Active Server Pages" and "Creating an ASP Query Form" in Windows NT Option Pack Help. For information about errors that are returned by the query and utility objects, see "IXSSO Errors" in Windows NT Option Pack Help.

Administering Index Server

Like other new Windows NT and Microsoft BackOffice servers and services, Microsoft Index Server can be administered through the use of the Index Server Manager, a snap-in program to the Microsoft Management Console (MMC).

Common administrative functions that can be performed using the Index Server Manager include:

◆ Stopping or starting the Index Server service.

◆ Obtaining status and statistics on the current index.

◆ Specifying the index operation behavior—for example, whether unknown file types are included in the content index, whether document summaries are created, and so on.

◆ Specifying which directories, if any, under virtual roots to exclude from indexing.

Once Index Server has been installed, it typically requires minimum day-to-day administration. For more information about administering Index Server, search for "Basic Administration" in Windows NT Option Pack Help.

You can further customize how Index Server works by changing settings for Registry parameters. For more information about individual Registry parameters and their settings, search for "Main Registry Parameters" in Windows NT Option Pack Help.

Updating the Content Index

The inherently changing nature of the Web life cycle results in frequent and ongoing changes to Web content. Therefore, it is important that users can obtain current results when querying an index on a Web server. Index Server enables indices to be refreshed in the following ways:

- Automatically

  Index server automatically updates the content index in two different scenarios:

  - Index Server's content index is updated as a background system process as the result of automatic change notification by the Windows NT file system. Index Server may not index the document right away, but waits until there are sufficient computer resources available to do the indexing without adversely affecting overall system performance.

  - When you add a new virtual root to IIS through the Internet Service Manager, Index Server is notified of the change and adds the new directory to its corpus. Consequently, Index Server will immediately index the files in this new virtual directory.

- Administratively

  If a site undergoes a large structural change (for example, if content is replaced, a new content filter is added, or a backup version is used for restoration), then you will probably want to force a manual updating of the content index. This can be accomplished through the Index Server Manager.

 Tip The following procedure is used to manually update a content index.

▶ **To force Index Server to rescan (update) a directory**

1. In the left pane of MMC, under the catalog where the virtual directory is located, double-click **Directories**.

2. In the right frame, right-click the directory you want to scan.

3. Select **Rescan**.

4. In the **Full Rescan** dialog box, click **Yes** for a full rescan, or click **No** for an incremental rescan.

◆ Programmatically

You can produce special administrative scripts to obtain service status, force index merges, and update virtual roots. These administrative scripts are very similar to .idq queries, except that they use the .ida file extension. For more information on administrative scripts, see the online topic "Writing IDA Scripts" in the Windows NT Option Pack.

Lab 9.2: Adding Search Services

In this lab, you will begin by examining the default search capabilities supplied by a Visual InterDev Web project working in conjunction with Microsoft Index Server. In the second part of the lab, you will replace the default search page with a page that accesses the indexing service through server-side script.

To see the demonstration "Lab 9.2 Solution," see the accompanying CD-ROM.

Estimated time to complete this lab: **35 minutes**

To complete the exercises in this lab, you must have the required software. For detailed information about the labs and setup for the labs, see "Labs" in "About This Course."

Objectives

After completing this lab, you will be able to:

◆ Issue simple search queries from an HTML page.

◆ Monitor and administer the indexing service through the Index Server Manager snap-in program to the MMC.

◆ Access Index Server services through an ASP script.

Prerequisites

Before working on this lab, you should be familiar with the following:

◆ The general interface and function of the MMC.

◆ Creating ASP using VBScript.

Exercises

The following exercises provide practice working with the concepts and techniques covered in this chapter:

◆ Exercise 1: Exploring the Default Search Capabilities

In this exercise, you will first examine the default search capabilities of a Visual InterDev Web application by using the Index Server Manager to explore the indexing service. You will then issue search requests using the project's auto-generated search page, Search.htm. Finally you will examine the code behind this page.

◆ Exercise 2: Integrating Index Server with ASP

In this exercise, you will replace the default search page, Search.htm, which accesses the indexing service through a FrontPage Webbot, with an ASP page, SResults.asp, which accesses this service though server-side VBScript. You will code the portions of this new page that instantiate and access the COM Query component.

Exercise 1: Exploring the Default Search Capabilities

In this exercise, you will first examine the default search capabilities of a Visual InterDev Web application by using the Index Server Manager to explore the indexing service. You will then issue search requests using the project's auto-generated search page, Search.htm. Finally, you will examine the code behind this page.

▶ **Verify the index service is installed and running**

Microsoft Index Server is an optional component of the Windows NT Option pack that must be installed to perform searches on a Web site.

1. On the Web server machine, start the Services Control Panel applet.

2. In the **Service** list box, locate the Content Index entry.

   If this entry is not listed in the list, then you must rerun the setup for the Windows NT Option Pack to install the Index Server component.

3. Verify that its status is **Started** and the Startup type is **Automatic**. If these properties are not set to these values, change them accordingly.

4. Close the Services applet.

▶ **Examine the indexing service in Index Server Manager**

1. Start the Index Server Manager application. On the **Start** menu, choose **Programs**, and **Windows NT 4.0 Option Pack**. Then choose **Microsoft Index Server**, and **Index Server Manager**.

2. In the left pane, expand the tree until you see the Web node. Right-click this node and choose **Properties**. The **Web Properties** dialog box should be displayed.

3. Notice that the **Web Properties** dialog box has three property pages:

   - **Location** displays the following read-only information: name, location, and number of indexed virtual roots.

   - **Web** determines which specific directories and directory types will be indexed.

   - **Generation** allows you to alter the indexing process by choosing whether to index unknown file types and to determine the existence and size of the file characterization (the generated abstract).

4. Click the Directories node in the left pane. All the indexed directories will be displayed in the right pane. The following example shows what the Index Server Manager should look like at this point.

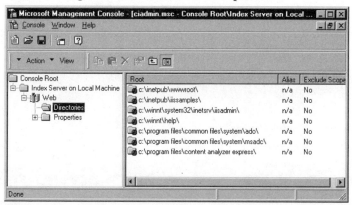

Many of the indexed directories, such as C:\Winnt\Help, support the Find functionality of the online documentation for Windows NT Option Pack components.

Note You can exclude one or more of the listed directories from being indexed through the Internet Information Manager snap-in program. In the **Properties** dialog box for a directory, click on the Virtual Directory tab, then clear the **Index This Directory** option.

5. Right-click one of the directories in the right pane, and from the context menu, choose **Rescan**. This causes Index Server to immediately re-index the content in the selected directory.

▶ **Explore the default search page**

1. Start Internet Explorer and navigate to the StateU home page, Default.htm. Expand the Site Services node and then click the **Search The Site** link in the lower left frame to navigate to the default search page.

2. In the **Search For** text box, type in a word or phrase for which you would like to search in the StateU Web site (for example "Math*"). The returned page should contain all the hits for that text.

   For the default search page to work properly, you must have the FrontPage Server Extensions installed, and your Web project must have generated the _vti_bin and _derived folders for you. (The Web Project Wizard creates the required folders and files when you check the **Create search.htm to enable full text searching** option in Step 2 of 4.)

3. View the source for the search page, Search.htm. Locate the line that contains the string "Webbot".

   This line is an HTML comment that the FrontPage Server interprets as a request to access the FP Search Component.

In the next exercise, you will replace the default search page with an ASP page, to which you will add additional code.

Exercise 2: Integrating Index Server with ASP

In this exercise, you will replace the default search page, Search.htm, which accesses the indexing service through a FrontPage Webbot, with an ASP page, SResults.asp, which accesses this service though server-side VBScript. You will code the portions of this new page that instantiate and access the COM Query component.

▶ **Replace the existing search page**

1. Open the StateU Web project in Visual InterDev if it is not already open.

2. Rename the file Search.htm to OldSearch.htm. Answer No when asked if you want to update the links that refer to this file.

3. Add the files Search.htm and SResults.asp, located in \MWD6\Labs\Lab09.2\New, to the StateU project. Search.htm replaces the old file.

4. Open the new files for editing.

▶ **Examine the new project files**

1. Examine the file Search.htm in both Source and Design modes. Note the following:

   - It contains a simple form to take a search string supplied by the user. The action target of this form is the SResults.asp page.

   - It contains a simple expanding <DIV> section that explains the query language used to form a search request.

2. Examine SResults.asp in Source mode and note the following:

   - The body contains two main parts: an initial server-side script section that prepares and executes the query, and a subsequent section that formats the results in a table for return to the user.

   - There are a number to ToDo comments in the first section.

▶ **Completing the search query script**

In this procedure you will complete the server-side script that interfaces with the content indexing service.

1. Locate the first ToDo comment. Replace the comment with a line of code that sets the **Query** property of the query object to the text the user supplied in the **Search For** text box of the file Search.htm.

2. Replace the next ToDo with a statement that sets the **Columns** property of the query object to the search properties to be retrieved: filename, vpath, size, and characterization.

3. Replace the next ToDo with a statement that sets the **MaxRecords** property to 50.

4. Replace the next ToDo comment with a declaration for an Index Server utility object named SUUtil.

The next statement, which already exists, calls **AddScopeToQuery** to limit the scope of the search to the StateU Web site.

To see an example of how your code should look, see Lab Hint 9.2 in Appendix B.

For more information on scripting search queries, see the topic "Using Server-Side Objects to Perform Queries" on page 432.

▶ **Testing your new search page**

1. View Search.htm in Internet Explorer.

2. Enter the same search string as you did in the Exercise 1. If you did not make any coding errors, the results that are returned should be similar.

In this exercise, you essentially duplicated the functionality of the Search Webbot. Keep in mind that scripting allows much more powerful and flexible integration of search capabilities within your Web application.

Other Microsoft Server-Side Technologies

Microsoft has developed various server-side technologies and products that can be grouped under several broad categories, such as communications, integration, security, and extensibility. While this course does not cover every Microsoft server-side technology, the following table highlights the main Microsoft server- and Web-based technologies and products, and includes references to the relevant Web sites for more information.

Communications

◆ Microsoft Exchange Server

An e-mail server that embraces Internet standards and extends rich messaging and collaboration to businesses of all sizes. See www.microsoft.com/exchange/default.asp for more information.

◆ Microsoft Message Queue Server (MSMQ)

A store and forward service for Windows NT Server, Enterprise Edition, providing loosely coupled and reliable network communications services based on a message queuing model. Additional MSMQ components include the MSMQ Exchange Connector, which enables MSMQ to send, receive, and transport

Exchange messages and forms, and the MAPI Transport Provider, which enables MAPI-enabled applications to communicate via MSMQ. See www.microsoft.com/ntserver/appservice/default.as for more information.

Integration

♦ Microsoft SNA Server

A comprehensive gateway and application integration platform that provides a means of adopting Internet, intranet, and client/server technologies while preserving investments in existing AS/400- and mainframe-based systems. See www.microsoft.com/sna/default.asp for more information.

♦ COM Transaction Integrator for CICS and IMS

The COM Transaction Integrator for CICS and IMS feature, formerly known as "Cedar," provides developers with a tool for creating COM objects that run on the MTS, providing a bridge between Automation and mainframe programs. See www.microsoft.com/sna/guide/comti.asp?A=2&B=2 for more information.

♦ Microsoft Site Server

A comprehensive Web site environment for enhancing, deploying, and managing intranet sites on Windows NT Server and Internet Information Server. See http://www.microsoft.com/siteserver for more information.

♦ Microsoft Commercial Internet System

Part of the Microsoft BackOffice family of server products, a comprehensive set of standards-based, commercial-grade server components that enhance the Internet services and Web sites of commercial service providers (for example, ISPs, telecommunications carriers, and cable network operators). See www.microsoft.com/mcis/default.asp for more information.

Security

♦ Microsoft Proxy Server

An extensible firewall and Web cache server that provides secure Internet access while improving network response time and efficiency. See www.microsoft.com/proxy/default.asp for more information.

◆ Microsoft Certificate Server

A standard extension component of IIS 4.0. It runs as a customizable Windows NT service that processes certificate requests and also creates, issues, revokes, and renews digital certificates. See www.microsoft.com/security/products/certserver.asp for more information.

Extensibility

◆ Windows Media Player

Windows NT Server uses Media Player services to stream audio and video over the Internet or corporate intranets, delivering a high-quality end-user experience over a wide range of bandwidths. See www.microsoft.com/windows/windowsmedia/default.asp for more information.

◆ Microsoft English Query

A powerful, flexible search specification mechanism that enables users to ask questions about data in plain English in database-driven Web sites and applications. See www.microsoft.com/SQL/70/gen/eq.htm for more information.

Self-Check Questions

To see the answers to the Self-Check Questions, see Appendix A.

1. **Which of the following services is required for Internet users to send and receive e-mail?**

   A. An IMAP server.

   B. An LDAP Directory Service.

   C. An NNTP server.

   D. An SMTP server (and a POP3 server).

2. **Which of the following mail access technologies is appropriate for building simple e-mail functionality based on the SMTP protocol?**

   A. CDO

   B. MAPI

   C. CDONTS

   D. CDO Rendering Objects

3. **Which search engine does the FrontPage98 search WebBot use when it is installed with Visual InterDev 6 and IIS 4.0?**

   A. The WAIS search engine.

   B. Index Server 2.0.

   C. FrontPage98 Server Extensions.

   D. Dependent on whether Index Server is running on the Web server.

4. **What mechanism does Index Server use to implement automatic index updates?**

   A. A change notification is provided through the file system (NTFS only).

   B. An administrator must create an initial script for the update process to become automatic.

   C. A change notification is provided through the file system (FAT or NTFS).

   D. This is controlled through the ForcedNetPathScanInterval registry parameter.

Student Notes:

Appendix A:
Self-Check Answers

Chapter 1

1. Which of the following is an example of a business service?

A. An ActiveX control that displays a calendar on the screen.
   Incorrect

   This is an example of a user service, not a business service.

B. A stored procedure in an SQL Server.
   Incorrect

   This is an example of a data service, not a business service.

C. A database table that stores payroll information.
   Incorrect

   This is an example of a data service, not a business service.

D. A COM component that can place an order in a database.
   Correct

   This is an example of a business service.

For more information, see *The Services Model*, page 7.

2. Which service provides the application with its graphical interface?

A. User services

Correct

User services provide the application with its graphical interface.

B. Business services

Incorrect

Business services implement the business rules for an application.

C. Data services

Incorrect

Data services provide low-level manipulation of data in the database.

For more information, see *The Services Model,* page 7.

3. Which member of a Web development team is responsible for creating code that invokes COM components?

A. Web developer

Correct

The Web Developer is responsible for adding server-side script to Active Server Pages. The script invokes components and controls that are created by the Programmer.

B. Programmer

Incorrect

The Programmer creates COM components. The Web Developer is responsible for adding server-side script to Active Server Pages. The script invokes COM components.

C. HTML author

Incorrect

The HTML Author creates the content in a Web site by adding HTML tags and hyperlinks.

D. Graphic artist

Incorrect

The Graphic Artist creates images that are included in Web pages.

For more information, see *Web Site Development Team,* page 12.

4. Which member of a Web development team is responsible for defining the architecture of a Web site?

A. Web developer

Correct

The Web Developer defines the Web site architecture.

B. Programmer

Incorrect

The Web Developer defines the Web site architecture.

C. HTML author

Incorrect

The Web Developer defines the Web site architecture.

D. Graphic artist

Incorrect

The Web Developer defines the Web site architecture.

For more information, see *Web Site Development Team*, page 12.

5. Which programming tool enables the programmer to create COM components and ActiveX controls?

A. Visual InterDev

Incorrect

Visual InterDev is a tool that you use to create HTML pages and Active Server Pages for Web sites.

B. Visual Basic

Correct

Visual Basic is a programming tool that you can use to create COM components and ActiveX controls.

C. Microsoft Transaction Server

Incorrect

Microsoft Transaction Server is not a programming tool. Microsoft Transaction Server is an application that provides transaction and resource management for COM components.

D. Microsoft SQL Server

Incorrect

Microsoft SQL Server is not a programming tool. Microsoft SQL Server is a database management system.

For more information, see *Web Site Development Team*, page 12.

6. Which tool provides transaction and resource management for COM components?

A. Visual InterDev

Incorrect

Visual InterDev is a tool that you use to create and manage the HTML pages and Active Server Pages in a Web site.

B. Visual Basic

Incorrect

Visual Basic is a programming tool that you can use to create COM components.

C. Microsoft Transaction Server

Correct

Microsoft Transaction Server provides transaction and resource management for COM components.

D. Microsoft SQL Server

Incorrect

Microsoft SQL Server is a database management system that you can use to create and manage databases.

For more information, see *Web Site Development Team*, page 12.

Chapter 2

1. What is a Visual InterDev Web project?

A. An autonomous Web site.

Incorrect

A Visual InterDev Web project is not a Web site. It keeps track of the files that make up a Web site.

B. A container of files that create a Web site.

Correct

A Visual InterDev Web project contains all of the files used to create a Web site.

C. A container for .gif and .jpg files used in a Web site.

Incorrect

A Visual InterDev Web project contains all of the files used to create a Web site, not just the .gif and .jpg files.

D. A container for .asp files used in a Web site.

Incorrect

A Visual InterDev Web project contains all of the files used to create a Web site, not just the .asp files.

For more information, see *Project Explorer Window*, page 54.

2. How are Active Server Pages different from HTML pages?

A. Active Server Pages contain only server-side script; HTML pages contain only client-side script.

Incorrect

Active Server Pages can contain both server-side and client-side script.

B. HTML pages can contain <SCRIPT> sections; Active Server Pages can only contain in-line script.

Incorrect

Active Server Pages can contain HTML <SCRIPT> sections with client-side script. They can also contain <SCRIPT> sections with the RUNAT attribute set to Server that contain server-side script.

C. Active Server Pages are processed by the server before being returned to the client; HTML pages are sent to the client without being processed.

Correct

Active Server Pages let you dynamically add content to a page before it is returned from the server. HTML pages are static with no processing by the Web server before they are returned to the client.

D. Active Server Pages can be edited with the Visual InterDev Source Editor; HTML pages can be edited with the FrontPage Editor.

Incorrect

The FrontPage Editor cannot be used to edit Active Server Pages.

For more information, see *Adding a Site Diagram*, page 45.

3. **Which view lets you work with design-time controls, Java applets, and most other objects using the visual representation they will have in the browser?**

A. Data view.

Incorrect

The Source view lets you work with objects as they will appear in the browser.

B. Design view.

Incorrect

The Source view lets you work with objects as they will appear in the browser.

C. Source view.

Correct

The Source view lets you work with objects as they will appear in the browser.

D. Quick view.

Incorrect

The Source view lets you work with objects as they will appear in the browser.

For more information, see *HTML Editor Window*, page 58.

4. Which HTML tag would you use to create a nested frame?

A. <FRAMESET>

Correct

A <FRAMESET> tag placed inside a <FRAMESET> tag creates a nested frame.

B. <FRAME>

Incorrect

A <FRAME> tag defines the source file for a frame in a <FRAMESET> tag.

C. <IFRAME>

Incorrect

The <IFRAME> tag defines a floating frame outside of a <FRAMESET> tag.

D. None of the above

Incorrect

A <FRAMESET> tag placed inside a <FRAMESET> tag creates a nested frame.

For more information, see *Using Frames*, page 69.

5. What is the purpose of using forms?

A. To contain license information about controls on a Web page.

Incorrect

License Package (.lpk) files contain license information about the ActiveX controls that are used in a Web page.

B. To group standard HTML controls visually on a Web page.

Incorrect

Forms are not visible to Web browsers.

C. To place controls in a file so they can be included with the same layout in other Web pages.

Incorrect

HTML Layout (.alx) files contain layout information about the placement of controls. An .alx file can be used in multiple source files.

D. To send information to a Web server.

Correct

When a user clicks the **Submit** button, forms automatically send the data in controls to the Web server.

For more information, see *Creating HTML Forms*, page 75.

6. Which of the following is not a standard HTML control?

A. Multi-select list box

Incorrect

You create a multi-select list box with the <SELECT MULTIPLE ...> tag.

B. Frame

Correct

The standard HTML controls are text box, two types of list boxes, check box, option button, hidden control, and three types of buttons.

C. Check box

Incorrect

You create a check box by using the HTML <INPUT TYPE=CHECKBOX ...> tag.

D. Command button

Incorrect

You create a command button with the HTML <INPUT TYPE=BUTTON ...> tag.

For more information, see *Adding Standard HTML Controls*, page 75.

7. Which type of file can you edit with the source editor?

A. .gif file

Incorrect

You can edit .gif files with an image editor such as Microsoft Image Composer.

For more information, see *HTML Editor Window*, page 58.

B. .sln file

Incorrect

You change .sln files from the Visual InterDev Project Explorer window.

For more information, see *Web Server and Site Structure*, page 40.

C. .ocx file

Incorrect

You can create .ocx files by using Microsoft Visual C++.

For more information, see *HTML Editor Window*, page 58.

D. .htm file

Correct

You can edit HTML files by using the HTML Editor.

For more information, see *HTML Editor Window*, page 58.

8. Which of the following is the correct syntax for a hyperlink?

A. <ANCHOR="finance.htm">ABC Co. Financial Statement</A>

Incorrect

Anchors are done with the syntax <A HREF="www.SomeSite.com">SomeSite</A>.

B. <A="finance.htm">ABC Co. Financial Statement</A>

Incorrect

Anchors are done with the syntax <A HREF="www.SomeSite.com">SomeSite</A>.

C. <A HREF="finance.htm">ABC Co. Financial Statement<A>

Incorrect

Anchors are done with the syntax <A HREF="www.SomeSite.com">SomeSite</A>.

D. <A HREF="finance.htm">ABC Co. Financial Statement</A>

Correct

Anchors are done with the syntax <A HREF="www.SomeSite.com">SomeSite</A>.

For more information on adding hyperlinks to a page, see *Adding Hyperlinks*, page 68.

Chapter 3

1. Assume you have an object defined in your Web page as follows:

```
<INPUT TYPE="BUTTON" NAME="ValidateOrder" VALUE="Order">
```

When a user clicks the button, you want to display a Validating Order message box. What do you need to do?

A. In a <SCRIPT> section of your Web page, create a procedure named **ValidateOrder_OnClick**, and add the appropriate code.

Correct

The control is named ValidateOrder, and the name of the event is OnClick. When you name a procedure ValidateOrder_OnClick, it runs automatically when the user clicks the control.

B. In a <SCRIPT> section of your Web page, create a procedure named **Order_OnClick**, and add the appropriate code.

Incorrect

The name of the event procedure must include the name of the control that is set with the NAME attribute of the <INPUT> tag.

C. Before you close the <INPUT> tag, create a procedure named **OnClick**, and add the appropriate code.

Incorrect

You can add code, but not a procedure, in the <INPUT> tag. A procedure must be placed in a <SCRIPT> section of a Web page, and referenced by the <INPUT> tag.

D. In an <EVENTS> section of your Web page, create a procedure named **Button_Click**, and add the appropriate code.

Incorrect

All client-side script is placed in a <SCRIPT> section of a Web page.

For more information, see *Writing Event Procedures*, page 127.

2. Which of the following is NOT a part of the browser object hierarchy?

A. Screen

Incorrect

The Screen object is a part of the browser object hierarchy.

B. Forms

Correct

Forms are not a part of the browser object hierarchy.

C. Frames

Incorrect

The Frames collection is a part of the browser object hierarchy.

D. Document

Incorrect

The Document object is a part of the browser object hierarchy.

For more information, see *Using Browser Objects*, page 117

3. The Visual InterDev Debugger can be used for which of the following activities?

A. Debugging server-side script only.

Incorrect

The Visual InterDev debugger can use used to debug both client and server script.

B. Debugging client-side script only.

Incorrect

The Visual InterDev debugger can use used to debug both client and server script.

C. Viewing the relationships of files that comprise frames.

Incorrect

The Visual InterDev debugger can use used to debug both client and server script.

D. Debugging server and client scripts.

Correct

The Visual InterDev debugger can use used to debug both client and server script.

For more information, see *Debugging Client Script*, page 110.

4. What types of procedures can you create with JavaScript?

A. Functions

Incorrect

You can create functions, sub-procedures, and event handlers in JavaScript.

B. Sub-procedures

Incorrect

You can create functions, sub-procedures, and event handlers in JavaScript.

C. Event procedures

Incorrect

You can create functions, sub-procedures, and event handlers in JavaScript.

D. All of the above

Correct

You can create functions, sub-procedures, and event handlers in JavaScript.

For more information, see *Scripting Languages*, page 105.

5. Why should you enclose client script in HTML comment tags (<!— —>)?

A. Script-enabled browsers require that you use comment tags to distinguish script code from HTML code.

Incorrect

Use comments to prevent browsers that do not support the <SCRIPT> tag from displaying the script in the HTML page.

B. To hide the script from users.

Incorrect

Use comments to prevent browsers that do not support the <SCRIPT> tag from displaying the script in the HTML page.

C. To prevent browsers that do not support the <SCRIPT> tag from displaying the script in the HTML page.

Correct

Use comments to prevent browsers that do not support the <SCRIPT> tag from displaying the script in the HTML page.

D. To help programmers understand the script code.

Incorrect

Use comments to prevent browsers that do not support the <SCRIPT> tag from displaying the script in the HTML page.

For more information, see *Scripting Languages*, page 105.

6. Which kind of scriptlets are normally used as visual controls?

A. Active scriptlets.

Incorrect

There are two kinds of scriptlets: DHTML and automation scriptlets.

B. DHTML scriptlets.

Correct

DHTML scriptlets are used as visual controls in an application.

C. Automation scriptlets

Incorrect

There are two kinds of scriptlets: DHTML and automation scriptlets.

D. COM scriptlets.

Incorrect

There are two kinds of scriptlets: DHTML and automation scriptlets.

For more information, see *Introducing Scriptlets*, page 151.

7. In order to create a readable property function you need to?

A. Define a function with the prefix public_put_.

Incorrect

Create a readable function property using public_get_.

B. Create a **Public_Description** function.

Incorrect

Create a readable function property using public_get_.

C. Define a function with the prefix public_.

Incorrect

Create a readable function property using public_get_.

D. Define a function with the prefix public_get_.

Correct

Create a readable function property using public_get_.

For more information, see *Exposing Methods and Properties*, page 160.

8. Which statement about absolute positioning is True?

A. Takes elements out of the default flow of text.

Correct

Absolute positioning takes the element out of the default flow of text.

B. Specifies the exact x, y position of the element relative to previous elements.

Incorrect

Absolute positioning takes the element out of the default flow of text.

C. Reflows content on the Web page as necessary.

Incorrect

Absolute positioning takes the element out of the default flow of text.

D. None of the above.

Incorrect

Absolute positioning takes the element out of the default flow of text.

For more information, see *Dynamic Positioning*, page 136.

9. Which step below is not part of the process needed to send a custom event in a scriptlet to a host application?

A. Call the **Scriptlet** event.

Correct

In order to send a custom event to a host application, you need to check the scriptlet's frozen property, call its raiseEvent method, and create an event handler.

B. Call the scriptlet's **raiseEvent** method.

Incorrect

In order to send a custom event to a host application, you need to check the scriptlet's frozen property, call its raiseEvent method, and create an event handler.

C. Create an event handler for the **onscriptletevent** event.

Incorrect

In order to send a custom event to a host application, you need to check the scriptlet's frozen property, call its raiseEvent method, and create an event handler.

D. Check the scriptlet's **Frozen** property.

Incorrect

In order to send a custom event to a host application, you need to check the scriptlet's frozen property, call its raiseEvent method, and create an event handler.

For more information, see *Exposing Events*, **page 154**.

Chapter 4

1. Which Active Server Pages built-in object would you use in your Web application to extract information from an HTTP request message?

A. The **Request** object

Correct

The **Request** object retrieves values from the user's browser, and passes the information to the Web server in an HTTP request message.

B. The **Response** object

Incorrect

The **Response** object controls what information is sent to a user in the HTTP response message.

C. The **Session** object

Incorrect

The **Session** object stores information about a particular user session.

D. The **Server** object

Incorrect

The **Server** object provides access to resources that run on a Web server.

For more information, see *ASP Built-In Objects*, **page 174**.

2. When is a Session object created to indicate the start of a new user session?

A. When a user requests a Web page from a Web application.

   Incorrect

   A **Session** object is created when a user requests an Active Server Page from the Web application.

B. When a user logs on to a Web server.

   Incorrect

   A **Session** object is created when a user requests an Active Server Page from the Web application.

C. When a user requests an Active Server Page from a Web application.

   Correct

   A **Session** object is created when a user requests an Active Server Page from the Web application.

D. When the WWW service starts.

   Incorrect

   A **Session** object is created when a user requests an Active Server Page from the Web application.

For more information, see *The Session Object*, page 192.

3. Which event procedure always runs when a Web server is shut down?

A. Session_OnStart

   Incorrect

   The Session_OnStart event procedure runs when a user requests an Active Server Page from your Web application.

B. Session_OnEnd

   Incorrect

   The Session_OnEnd procedure will run only if there is an active session when you shut down the WWW service of your Web server.

C. Application_OnStart

   Incorrect

   The Application_OnStart event procedure runs when you start the WWW service of your Web server.

D. Application_OnEnd

Correct

The Application_OnEnd event procedure runs when you shut down the WWW service of your Web server.

For more information, see *Handling Application and Session Events*, page 194.

4. Which of the following statements about cookies and session variables is false?

A. Cookies are sent with the HTTP request; session variables are not.

Incorrect

Cookies are sent by the Web browser as part of an HTTP request; session variables reside on the Web server.

B. Cookies save information on the user's computer; session variables are saved on the Web server.

Incorrect

Cookies are saved in a file on the user's computer; session variables are saved on the Web server.

C. Cookies can be created with server-side script; session variables cannot be created with server-side script.

Correct

You can create both cookies and session variables with server-side script.

D. Cookies are destroyed automatically by the Web browser; session variables are destroyed by the Web server.

Incorrect

You can specify an expiration time for a cookie. The browser will destroy it when the time expires. Session variables are destroyed when the session ends.

For more information, see *Using Cookies*, page 195.

5. What should you do to access the properties and methods of a COM component in an Active Server Page?

   A. Set a reference to the component's type library, and use the **New** keyword when you declare a variable of that type.

     Incorrect

     You cannot use the **New** keyword in server-side script.

   B. Install the COM component on the Web server, and create a variable with the **New** keyword.

     Incorrect

     Installing a COM component is the first step in accessing properties and methods. However, you cannot use the **New** keyword in server-side script.

   C. Install the COM component on the Web server, and use the **CreateObject** method of the **Server** object.

     Correct

     Install the COM component, and use the **CreateObject** method of the **Server** object to instantiate an ActiveX server component.

   D. Install the COM component on the user's computer, and use the <OBJECT> tag.

     Incorrect

     COM components are installed and run on the Web Server, not the user's computer.

For more information, see *Creating Component Instances*, page 197.

6. Which of the following tags sets the default language for server-side script?

   A. <% LANGUAGE="VBScript" %>

     Incorrect

     The <% %> tag is used for a statement that will run on the Web server.

   B. <SCRIPT LANGUAGE="VBScript">

     Incorrect

     The <SCRIPT> tag creates client-side script, unless you set the RUNAT attribute to Server.

   C. <LANGUAGE="VBScript">

     Incorrect

     To set the language for server-side script, you must use the <%@ %> tag.

D. <%@ LANGUAGE="VBScript" %>

Correct

To set the language for server-side script, you must use the <%@ %> tag.

For more information, see *Introduction to Active Server Pages*, page 172.

7. If you have disabled Anonymous logon on your Web server, who can access your Web site?

A. Users with accounts that you have added to a database on your Web server.

Incorrect

The users will need valid NT accounts.

B. Users with valid Windows NT accounts.

Correct

If you turn off Anonymous logon, only users with valid NT accounts can access your Web site.

C. Users who log on with the account IUSR_*computername*.

Incorrect

If users know the password for the IUSR_*computername* account, they can view your Web site because it is a valid NT account. However, the password is generated by IIS and cannot be found easily.

D. No one can access the Web site.

Incorrect

Any user who logs on with a valid NT account will be able to see the pages of your Web site.

For more information, see *Preventing Anonymous Logon*, page 218.

8. If you have enabled Anonymous, Basic, and NT Challenge/Response authentication for your Web server, what authentication process occurs when a user requests a Web page?

A. The Web browser tries Anonymous authentication. If that fails, the user will not be able to access the page and receives an error message.

Incorrect

The Web browser tries Anonymous authentication, but several other types of authentication are also tried in order to gain access.

B. If the browser supports NT Challenge/Response authentication, the browser tries to use it. Otherwise, the browser uses Basic authentication.

Incorrect

Anonymous authentication is tried first.

C. If the browser supports Basic authentication, the browser uses it. Otherwise, the browser uses NT Challenge/Response authentication.

Incorrect

The Web browser tries Anonymous, NT Challenge/Response, and then Basic authentication.

D. The Web browser tries to use Anonymous authentication, but if that fails, the user must provide a valid logon ID and password. Then, if the browser supports NT Challenge/Response authentication, that method is used. Otherwise, the browser uses Basic authentication.

Correct

If you have enabled all three authentication methods, the Web browser tries Anonymous authentication when a user requests a page. If that fails, the user must provide a valid logon ID and password. If the browser supports NT Challenge/Response authentication, the Web browser tries to use it. Otherwise, it tries to use Basic authentication.

For more information, see *Preventing Anonymous Logon*, page 218.

9. If you want to restrict access to the page private.asp on your Web site, but also enable all users to access other pages on your Web site, what should you do?

A. Configure the hard drive partition, where the Web site files are located, to use the FAT file system.

Incorrect

Only an NTFS partition has the required security settings to enable this type of restriction.

B. Enable Anonymous and Basic authentication for the Web server, and then remove the Internet Guest account from the access control list for the file Private.asp.

Correct

To allow all users to access your Web site, enable Anonymous logon. To restrict access to the file private.asp, remove the Anonymous logon account from the access control list for the file private.asp.

C. Enable the Guest account, and then remove the Guest account from the access control list for the file Private.asp.

Incorrect

To allow all users to access your Web site, enable Anonymous logon, not the Guest account.

D. Set the HIDDEN attribute of the file Private.asp.

Incorrect

If you set the HIDDEN attribute for a file, users can still access the file. To control access to a file, set NTFS file permissions for the file.

For more information, see *Setting NTFS Permissions*, page 219.

10. Which server-side script retrieves the name of the logon account that is used to access the Web site?

A. Request.Server("LOGON_USER")

Incorrect

There is no **Server** collection of the **Request** object. To retrieve the name of the logon account, use the **ServerVariables** collection of the **Request** object.

B. Request.ClientCertificates("LOGON_USER")

Incorrect

To retrieve the name of the logon account, use the **ServerVariables** collection of the **Request** object, and not the **ClientCertificates** collection.

C. Request.ServerVariables("LOGON_USER")

Correct

To retrieve the name of the logon account, use the **ServerVariables** collection of the **Request** object.

D. Session("LOGON_USER")

Incorrect

The logon account is not stored in the **Session** object.

For more information, see *Preventing Anonymous Logon*, page 218.

Chapter 5

1. When you add a data connection to a Visual InterDev project, how will your Web project be modified?

A. Script will be added to the global.asa file.

Correct

Script is added to the global.asa file to define the **Application_OnStart** event procedure and to store data connection information in application variables.

B. The **Data Command** control will be added to all of your existing ASP pages.

Incorrect

Controls are not added to pages. Script is added to the global.asa file.

C. Script will be added to all existing ASP pages.

Incorrect

Script is added only to the global.asa file.

D. Script will be added to the default ASP page.

Incorrect

Script is added to the global.asa file.

For more information, see *Using the Data Environment*, page 234.

2. What does a data environment hold?

A. The name of the database server to be accessed.

Correct

The name of the database server to be accessed is contained in the data connection.

For more information about data connections, see *Setting Data Connection Properties*, page 237.

B. The physical location of the database.

Incorrect

The physical location of the database is stored in the data source name.

For more information on data source names, see *Creating a Data Source Name*, page 234.

C. Information required to access data in a database.

Incorrect

The data environment is the focal point and repository for storing and reusing connection and command objects.

For more information, see *Using the Data Environment,* **page 234.**

D. The type of driver used for accessing the database.

Incorrect

The type of driver for the database is stored in the data source name.

For more information about data source names, see *Creating a Data Source Name,* **page 234.**

3. Where is a file DSN stored?

A. On the computer where the database is located.

Incorrect

A file DSN is stored on the developer's computer.

B. On the developer's computer.

Correct

A file DSN is stored on the developer's computer.

C. On the computer where the browser is located.

Incorrect

A file DSN is stored on the developer's machine.

D. On the end-user's computer.

Incorrect

A file DSN is stored on the developer's machine.

For more information, see *Creating a Data Source Name,* **page 234.**

4. When you create a data connection, Visual InterDev reads connection information from what source?

A. From the data environment.

Incorrect

Visual InterDev reads connection information from the DSN on your computer.

B. From the **Recordset** object.

Incorrect

Visual InterDev reads connection information from the DSN on your computer.

C. From the **Command** object.

Incorrect

Visual InterDev reads connection information from the DSN on your computer.

D. From the data source name stored on your computer.

Correct

Visual InterDev reads connection information from the DSN on your computer.

For more information, see *Setting Data Connection Properties*, page 237.

5. Where is the password for run-time authentication stored?

A. The run-time authentication password is stored with the project.

Correct

The run-time authorization password is encrypted and stored with the project.

B. The password for run-time authentication is stored in an SQL database.

Incorrect

The run-time authorization password is encrypted and stored with the project.

C. The password for run-time authentication is stored in a machine DSN.

Incorrect

The run-time authorization password is encrypted and stored with the project.

D. The password for run-time authentication is stored with a command object.

Incorrect

The run-time authorization password is encrypted and stored with the project.

For more information, see *Run-Time vs. Design-Time Authentication*, page 238.

6. What does a data command always refer to?

A. A data connection

Incorrect

A data command always refers to an SQL statement.

B. An SQL table

Incorrect

A data command always refers to an SQL statement.

C. A stored procedure

Incorrect

A data command always refers to an SQL statement.

D. An SQL statement

Correct

A data command always refers to an SQL statement.

For more information, see *Creating a Data Command*, page 241.

7. What mechanism handles the communication between a design-time control and a database when the contents of the control are changed?

A. The recordset

Incorrect

ActiveX handles the communication between a design-time control and a database.

B. DCOM

Incorrect

ActiveX handles the communication between a design-time control and a database.

C. PageNavbar

Incorrect

ActiveX handles the communication between a design-time control and a database.

D. ActiveX

Correct

ActiveX handles the communication between a design-time control and a database.

For more information, see *How Data-Bound Controls Work*, page 245.

8. How can you limit database access to users of your Web site?

A. Create a logon ID for your database that has limited rights, and use that ID to access the database.

Correct

To limit database access to users of your Web site, create an ID that has limited rights to your database, and use that logon ID to access the database.

B. Add records in a new SQL database for each user who needs access to the Windows NT Server and SQL Server.

Incorrect

Records in an SQL database do not have any effect on who has access to NT or SQL resources.

C. Hard code the SQL system administration account and password into the ActiveX Data Objects (ADO) connection string.

Incorrect

Hard coding an account and password is dangerous because it exposes the unrestricted administrative account for the SQL Server.

D. Disable the Internet Guest account and the Guest account.

Incorrect

Disabling these accounts guarantees only that users with valid NT accounts can access the NT computer. It does not change the database access rights.

For more information, see *Setting SQL Server Login Authentication*, page 236.

Chapter 6

1. Which ADO objects can you create with the CreateObject method?

  A. Only the **Connection** object

     Incorrect

     The **Command** and **Recordset** objects can also be created with the **CreateObject** method.

  B. Only the **Connection** and **Command** objects

     Incorrect

     The **Recordset** object can also be created with the **CreateObject** method.

  C. Only the **Command** and **Recordset** objects

     Incorrect

     The **Connection** object can also be created with the **CreateObject** method.

  D. The Connection, Command, and Recordset objects

     Correct

     The objects **Connection**, **Command**, and **Recordset** can all be created with the **CreateObject** method.

For more information, see *ADO Object Model*, page 281.

2. Assume that conn is a valid Connection object, and rsStudents is a valid Recordset object. Which statement will retrieve all of the records from the Students table?

  A. Set rsStudents = conn.OpenRecordset "select * from students"

     Incorrect

     There is not an **OpenRecordset** method for the **Connection** object.

  B. rsStudents.OpenRecordset "select * from students", conn

     Incorrect

     There is not an **OpenRecordset** method for the **Recordset** object.

  C. rsStudents.Open "select * from students", conn

     Correct

     To retrieve the records from the Students table, you can call the **Open** method on the **Recordset** object, and pass a query and the **Connection** object as arguments.

D. Set rsStudents = CreateObject ("ADODB.Recordset", "select * from students", conn)

Incorrect

You cannot pass an SQL string as an argument to the **CreateObject** method.

For more information, see *Retrieving Records*, page 286.

3. How is an ADO database error handled in an Active Server Page that does not have an error handler?

A. The error is ignored and processing continues. No message is returned to the user.

Incorrect

When an error occurs in an Active Server Page that does not have an error handler, processing stops and the error message from the database is included at the bottom of the Web page returned to the user.

B. An HTML document containing nothing but the error message from the database is returned to the user.

Incorrect

In addition to the error message, the Web page will include any HTML text that was generated before the error occurred.

C. The Web browser displays a dialog box with the message "Error processing Web page."

Incorrect

The Web browser is not aware of any processing errors that occur on the Web server. The server places the error in the HTML response, and returns it to the user.

D. The error message from the database is included at the bottom of the HTML document returned to the user.

Correct

When an error occurs in an Active Server Page that does not have an error handler, processing stops. The error description and any HTML text written before the error occurred is included in the Web page returned to the user.

For more information, see *Handling Errors*, page 296.

4. When you use RDS to retrieve records, where are the records cached?

A. On the Web client

Correct

By caching records on the client, the user can scroll through the records without requesting another page from the server.

B. In a business object on the Web server or Web client

Incorrect

Data is cached on the client, not in a business object.

In general, business objects do not cache data. This would not benefit the user because extra trips to the server would still be required to retrieve the cached data from the business object.

C. On the Web server

Incorrect

Data is cached on the client, not the server.

Caching data on a server would not benefit the user because extra trips to the server would still be required to retrieve the data. As more users were added to the system, server resources would be consumed by storing cached data.

D. On the database server

Incorrect

Data is cached on the client, not the database server.

Caching data on a database server would not benefit the user because extra trips to the server would still need to be made to retrieve the data. As more users were added to the system, server resources would be consumed by storing cached data.

For more information, see *RDS Component Overview*, page 307.

5. When you use the RDS.DataControl object, what properties do you set to specify the source of the data and the records to be retrieved?

A. Set the BINDINGS attribute of the **RDS.DataControl** object to the names of the data-bound controls in which the data will be displayed.

Incorrect

The BINDINGS attribute of the **AdvancedDataControl** object stores the names of all data-bound controls to bind to. Once set, these controls will be filled with data from the recordset in the **AdvancedDataControl** object.

B. Set the DATASOURCE attribute of the data-bound controls in which the data will be displayed to the name of the **RDS.DataControl** object.

Incorrect

You set the DATASOURCE attribute when working with the **Data** control in a Visual Basic application. The Advanced Data Connector (ADC) does not use this control for Web pages.

C. Set the BINDINGS attribute of the data-bound controls in which the data will be displayed to the name of the **RDS.DataControl** object.

Incorrect

Data-bound controls do not have a BINDINGS attribute.

D. Set the **Server, Connect,** and **SQL** properties.

Correct

Set the **Server, Connect,** and **SQL** properties to specify the source of the data and the records to be retrieved.

For more information, see *Inserting the RDS.DataControl Object,* page 311.

6. **What attributes of an HTML element do you set to bind it to a data source and fields within the data source?**

A. sqlsc and sqlfld

Incorrect

Set the datasrc and datafld attributes of an HTML element to bind it to a data source and fields within a data source.

B. datasrc and datafld

Correct

Set the datasrc and datafld attributes of an HTML element to bind it to a data source and fields within a data source.

C. datasql and sqlfld

Incorrect

Set the datasrc and datafld attributes of an HTML element to bind it to a data source and fields within a data source.

D. None of the above.

Incorrect

Set the datasrc and datafld attributes of an HTML element to bind it to a data source and fields within a data source.

For more information, see *Inserting the RDS.DataControl Object*, page 311.

Chapter 7

1. Which Visual Basic project template would you use to build an in-process COM component?

A. ActiveX Control

Incorrect

ActiveX controls are in-process, but they have a graphical interface and other features that are not necessary for a COM component.

B. ActiveX DLL

Correct

ActiveX DLLs are in-process, and can be used as COM components.

C. ActiveX EXE

Incorrect

The ActiveX EXE Visual Basic project template is an out-of-process COM component.

D. Standard EXE

Incorrect

A Visual Basic Standard EXE project template is a standard Windows application. It is not a COM component.

For more information, see *Choosing the Type of Component*, page 324.

2. **Assume that a business process is used to take customer orders. Before placing the order, the Inventory table must be checked to make sure the item is in stock. If it is, a new record must be added to the Shipping table to make sure the item gets shipped. Which of the following strategies should you use to implement this business process?**

A. Create a new ActiveX server component that implements the business process with an object named **Customer.Order,** and call it from an Active Server Page.

   Correct

   Building a COM component isolates the process from changes to user and data services.

B. Create a new Active Server Page that uses ActiveX Data Objects (ADO) to implement the business process.

   Incorrect

   This strategy will work only with Web browsers as clients. A better solution will work with multiple kinds of clients.

C. Create a stored procedure named customerorder that implements the business process, and call it from an Active Server Page.

   Incorrect

   Although this strategy will work, it is isolated to a specific type of database. If the business process is modified to include multiple databases, the process will need to be updated. If the single database is changed to a different type, it also requires the process to be updated.

D. Create an .exe file as a COM component on the server to hold this business process as well as other processes.

   Incorrect

   Although this strategy will work, it places all processes in a single .exe file. The file cannot be distributed across multiple computers, and does not scale well.

For more information, see *Business Objects and COM,* page 321.

3. **How do you export a method from a class module in Visual Basic 6?**

A. Mark the Visual Basic project for unattended execution.

   Incorrect

   In Visual Basic, unattended execution indicates that the project will not interact with the user, and makes the application apartment threaded.

B. Set the **Instancing** property to MultiUse.

Incorrect

The **Instancing** property determines if one or multiple clients can use the same instance of a component.

C. Add the **Public** keyword before the method.

Correct

The **Public** keyword causes a method to be available outside of the component.

D. Set the Visual Basic project type to ActiveX DLL.

Incorrect

Setting the project type does not enable methods to be exported.

The project type specifies whether the project is an ActiveX DLL, ActiveX EXE, or standard Windows program.

For more information, see *Setting Properties for Class Modules*, page 328.

4. What are all of the ways in which an in-process component can be registered?

A. During Setup, by using the file RegSvr32.exe, and when compiling the component with Visual Basic 6.

Correct

You can register an in-process component by compiling it in Visual Basic, running RegSvr32.exe, or by running a Setup program for the component.

B. During Setup, and when compiling the component with Visual Basic 6.

Incorrect

You can register an in-process component by compiling it in Visual Basic, or by running a Setup program for it. However, you can also use other registration methods.

C. By using the file RegSvr32.exe, and when compiling the component with Visual Basic 6.

Incorrect

You can register an in-process component by compiling it in Visual Basic or by running RegSvr32.exe. You can also use other registration methods.

D. During Setup, and by using the file RegSvr32.exe.

Incorrect

You can register an in-process component by running a Setup program for it or by running RegSvr32.exe. You can also use other registration methods.

For more information, see *Registering a Component*, page 334.

5. What is defined as an algorithm that determines how a piece of information should be processed?

A. A business rule

Correct

A business rule provides guidelines for how business activities should occur, and for how to ensure their integrity.

B. A business process

Incorrect

A business process is a sequence of related tasks that produce a specific response to a user's request.

C. A COM component

Incorrect

Formally known as Automation servers, COM components provide component functionality, such as a business rule.

D. A business object

Incorrect

A business object implements business processes and business rules.

For more information, see *Business Rules and Business Processes*, page 320.

Chapter 8

1. What is the ACID test?

A. Properties that a transaction should have so it does not fail.

Correct

The properties are atomicity, consistency, isolation and durability.

B. A test that you can perform to determine whether a transaction failed.

Incorrect

The ACID test is a set of properties that a transaction should have for it to succeed.

C. The change in the state of data.

Incorrect

Change of state refers to a transaction. A transaction changes a set of data from one state to another.

The ACID test is a set of properties that a transaction should have for it to succeed.

D. A test that can be performed on components before they are placed on a Web server.

Incorrect

The ACID test is a set of properties that a transaction should have for it to succeed.

For more information about the ACID test, see *Transaction Processing Concepts*, page 357.

2. How do you set a Microsoft Transaction Server component to require a transaction?

A. Set the transaction property of the component's package to require a transaction.

Incorrect

You set the transaction property of the component, not the package.

B. Set the transaction property of the component to support a transaction.

Incorrect

Setting the transaction property to "Supports Transactions" indicates only that a Microsoft Transaction Server component can participate in a transaction, but does not require that it does.

C. Set the transaction property of the component to require a transaction.

Correct

To set a transaction component to require a transaction, select the **Requires a Transaction** option on the **Transactions** tab of the **Properties** dialog box.

D. Write the component so that it calls the transaction functions **BeginTrans**, **EndTrans**, and **Rollback**.

Incorrect

When an object is created, Microsoft Transaction Server creates a corresponding **Context** object. A **Context** object eliminates the need to call any transaction functions, such as **BeginTrans** or **EndTrans**.

For more information, see *Adding Components to a Package.*, page 374

3. How do you enable a COM component to participate in transactions on Microsoft Transaction Server?

A. Call the transaction functions **BeginTrans**, **CommitTrans**, and **Rollback**.

Incorrect

A **Context** object eliminates the need to call any transaction functions, such as **BeginTrans** or **EndTrans**.

Instead, each public method of your business object calls **SetComplete** or **SetAbort** to indicate success or failure.

B. Modify the component to call the methods **SetComplete** and **SetAbort**.

Correct

Each public method of your business object calls the **SetComplete** or **SetAbort** method of the **Context** object to indicate success or failure.

C. Place the component in Microsoft Transaction Server Explorer.

Incorrect

Placing a component in the Microsoft Transaction Server Explorer will register it with Microsoft Transaction Server, but will not modify the component to support transactions.

D. Create the public methods **SetComplete** and **SetAbort** for the component.

Incorrect

The methods **SetComplete** and **SetAbort** are implemented by the **Context** object, so you do not need to implement them for the Transaction Server component.

For more information, see *Adding Transactional Support*, page 366.

4. What are the advantages of stateless objects?

A. They reduce the server load.

Incorrect

This answer is partially correct. The advantages of stateless objects include all of the answers to the question.

B. They ensure transaction isolation and database consistency.

Incorrect

This answer is partially correct. The advantages of stateless objects include all of the answers to the question.

C. They reduce the internal data dependencies of objects.

Incorrect

This answer is partially correct. The advantages of stateless objects include all of the answers to the question.

D. All of the above.

Correct

The advantages of stateless objects include all of the answers to the question.

For more information, see *Creating Efficient Objects*, page 371.

5. How do you get a reference to a context object created by Microsoft Transaction Server for a component?

A. Call the GetObjectContext API.

Correct

The **GetObjectContext** API function returns a reference to the **Context** object.

B. Call **CreateObject** ("object.context").

Incorrect

You cannot use the **CreateObject** function to retrieve a reference to the **Context** object.

The **Context** object is created by Microsoft Transaction Server. You use the **GetObjectContext** API function to set a reference to it.

C. Microsoft Transaction Server will automatically pass the parameter that gets the context object.

Incorrect

Microsoft Transaction Server creates a **Context** object but does not pass a reference to it back to your application.

D. Call **GetObject** ("object.context").

Incorrect

You cannot use the **GetObject** function to retrieve a reference to a **Context** object created by Microsoft Transaction Server.

For more information, see *Adding Transactional Support*, page 366.

6. Which of the following statements correctly describes package roles?

A. Roles are applied at the package level.

Correct

B. Roles allow bypassing of security checks for method calls that cross process boundaries.

Incorrect

An important consequence of roles is that security is automatically checked for method calls that cross process boundaries. MTS does this because it's possible for one client (that is authorized) to pass an interface pointer to another client (that may not be authorized.)

C. Roles can be created only when a component is deployed.

Incorrect

Roles are created at development time by the component programmer or Web developer. Roles are subsequently mapped onto actual NT users and user groups during package deployment, by the Web developer or administrator.

D. Roles can be configured dynamically using MTS Explorer.

Incorrect

Any dynamic configuration of security for MTS components can only be done programmatically.

For more information, see *Declarative Security: Roles and Identities*, page 384.

Chapter 9

1. Which of the following services is required for Internet users to send and receive e-mail?

A. An IMAP server.

Incorrect

Both an SMTP server and a POP3 server are required for sending and receiving e-mail over the Internet. Internet Mail Access Protocol (IMAP) is a specification for newer and more powerful Internet post office services, such as the manipulation of remote message folders.

B. An LDAP Directory Service.

Incorrect

Both an SMTP server and a POP3 server are required for sending and receiving e-mail over the Internet. The Lightweight Directory Access Protocol (LDAP) is a way for clients such as Internet Explorer to access the directory information held in a Microsoft Exchange Server.

C. An NNTP server.

Incorrect

Both an SMTP server and a POP3 server are required for sending and receiving e-mail over the Internet. Network News Transfer Protocol (NNTP) is the protocol used to send and receive news messages over the Internet.

D. An SMTP server (and a POP3 server).

Correct

Both an SMTP server and a POP3 server are required for sending and receiving e-mail over the Internet.

For more information, see *Mail Services for Windows NT*, page 409.

2. **Which of the following mail access technologies is appropriate for building simple e-mail functionality based on the SMTP protocol?**

A. CDO

Incorrect

The CDO 1.2 library, included with Microsoft Exchange 5.5, defines a set of objects that support advanced capabilities such as calendaring, collaboration, and workflow applications. Simple, scalable SMTP-based e-mail applications should use CDO for NT Server (CDONTS), a subset of CDO.

B. MAPI

Incorrect

MAPI is an industry-standard C-level mail and messaging interface that guarantees compatibility between different applications, messaging systems, and hardware platforms. However, SMTP-based e-mail applications should use CDO for NT Server (CDONTS), a subset of CDO 1.2. CDONTS is only available for IIS 4.0 and does not provide MAPI support.

C. CDONTS

Correct

SMTP-based e-mail applications, should use CDO for NT Server (CDONTS), a subset of CDO 1.2.

D. CDO Rendering Objects

Incorrect

CDO Rendering Objects is a component of CDO that can be used to display Exchange data in HTML format. SMTP-based e-mail applications should use CDO for NT Server (CDONTS), a subset of CDO 1.2.

For more information, see *Collaboration Data Objects for Windows NT Server (CDONTS)*, page 414.

3. **Which search engine does the FrontPage98 search WebBot use when it is installed with Visual InterDev 6 and IIS 4.0?**

A. The WAIS search engine.

Incorrect

It depends on whether the Index Server component of IIS 4.0 has been installed on the Web server. If it has, the search WebBot uses Index Server as the search engine. Otherwise, the WebBot uses the default WAIS search engine.

B. Index Server 2.0.

Incorrect

It depends on whether the Index Server component of IIS 4.0 has been installed on the Web server. If it has, the search WebBot uses Index Server as the search engine. Otherwise, the WebBot uses the default WAIS search engine.

C. FrontPage98 Server Extensions.

Incorrect

The FrontPage98 Server Extensions are required to run the search WebBot, but the particular search engine used depends on whether Index Server 2.0 has been installed on the Web server. If Index Server has not been installed, the WebBot uses the default WAIS search engine.

D. Dependent on whether Index Server is running on the Web server.

Correct

It depends on whether Index Server 2.0 has been installed on the Web server. If Index Server has not been installed, the WebBot uses the default WAIS search engine.

For more information, see *The FrontPage Search Bot*, page 427.

4. What mechanism does Index Server use to implement automatic index updates?

A. A change notification is provided through the file system (NTFS only).

Correct

Index Server uses the change notification mechanism provided by the Windows NT file system to implement automatic index updates.

B. An administrator must create an initial script for the update process to become automatic.

Incorrect

A script is not required. Index Server uses the change notification mechanism provided by the Windows NT file system to implement automatic index updates.

C. A change notification is provided through the file system (FAT or NTFS).

Incorrect

While Index Server does use a file change notification mechanism to implement automatic index updates, this is only provided by an NTFS file system.

D. This is controlled through the ForcedNetPathScanInterval registry parameter.

Incorrect

The ForcedNetPathScanInterval registry parameter controls the frequency of periodic scans of an index. However, Index Server uses the change notification mechanism provided by the Windows NT file system to implement automatic index updates.

For more information, see *Administering Index Server,* **page 437.**

Appendix B:
Lab Hints

Lab Hint 3.1

```
Function GetIEVersion
  Dim strName, strVersion

  strName = window.navigator.appName
  strVersion = Left(window.navigator.appVersion, 1)

  If strName = "Microsoft Internet Explorer" Then
      GetIEVersion = strVersion
  Else
      GetIEVersion = 0
  End If
End Function
```

Lab Hint 3.10

```
Sub Outline_OnScriptletEvent(strEventName, varEventData)
    window.parent.frames("main").location.href = varEventData
End Sub
```

Lab Hint 3.2

```
Sub Window_OnLoad()
    If GetIEVersion() >= 4 Then
        window.location.href = "ie4links.htm"
      Else
          window.location.href = "oldlinks.htm"
      End If
  End Sub
```

Lab Hint 3.3

```
Function AddParent(strName)
    Dim strID
    Dim strTemp

    strID = "ID" & intCount
    intCount = intCount + 1

    strTemp = "<DIV ID=""" & strID & """ CLASS=""parent""><IMG
CLASS=""image"" SRC=""images/blue.gif"" ALT=""*"" ALIGN=MIDDLE
BORDER=0 WIDTH=11 HEIGHT=11>" & strName & "<DIV CLASS=""child""></
DIV></DIV>"

    outlineDiv.insertAdjacentHTML "BeforeEnd", strTemp

    AddParent = strID
End Function
```

Lab Hint 3.4

```
Sub AddChild(strParentID, strName, strUrl)
    Dim strTemp
    Dim objTemp

    strTemp = "<A HREF=""" & strUrl & """ CLASS=""link"">" &
strName & "</A><BR>"

    Set objTemp = document.all.item(strParentID)
    objTemp.children(1).insertAdjacentHTML "BeforeEnd", strTemp
End Sub
```

Lab Hint 3.5

```
Sub DoClick()
    If (window.event.srcElement.className = "parent") Or
(window.event.srcElement.className = "image") Then
        ExpandCollapse
    End If
    window.event.cancelBubble = True
End Sub
```

Lab Hint 3.6

```
Sub DoMouseOver()
    If window.event.srcElement.tagName = "A" Then
        oldColor = window.event.srcElement.style.color
        window.event.srcElement.style.color = "red"
    End If
    window.event.cancelBubble = True
End Sub
```

Lab Hint 3.7

```
Sub DoMouseOut()
    If window.event.srcElement.tagName = "A" Then
        window.event.srcElement.style.color = oldColor
    End If
    window.event.cancelBubble = True
End Sub
```

Lab Hint 3.8

```
Sub Public_Put_StyleSheet(strUrl)
    document.stylesheets(0).addImport(strUrl)
End Sub
```

Lab Hint 3.9

```
Sub DoLinkEvent()
    Dim strUrl

    strUrl = window.event.srcElement.href
    'prevent default action for a link
    window.event.returnValue = False
    window.external.raiseEvent "linkClick", strUrl
End Sub
```

Lab Hint 4.1

```
<% If Not (IsEmpty(Request.Form("txtID"))) Then
  'request came from Submit button on form
  id = Request.Form("txtID")
  name = Request.Form("txtName")
  major = Request.Form("txtMajor")

  Response.Write "Welcome to State University, " _
      & name
  Response.Write "We see you are interested in " _
      & major
  Response.End
    End If %>
```

Lab Hint 4.2

```
Session("id") = id
Session("name") = name
Session("major") = major
```

Lab Hint 4.3

```
<H3>For student ID <%= Session("id")%></H3>
```

Lab Hint 4.4

```
'If user isn't requesting the profile page, redirect them there.
startPage = "/StateU/profile.asp"
currentPage = Request.ServerVariables("SCRIPT_NAME")

If strcomp(currentPage,startPage,1) Then
  Response.Redirect(startPage)
End If
```

Lab Hint 4.5

```
currentPage = Request.ServerVariables("SCRIPT_NAME")
Session("requestedPage") = currentPage
```

Lab Hint 4.6

```
'redirect to originally requested page
If InStr(Session("requestedPage"), "profile") = 0 Then
  Response.Redirect Session("requestedPage")
Else
  Response.Redirect "default.asp"
End If
```

Lab Hint 4.7

```
' Save form data in cookies.
Response.Cookies("id") = id
Response.Cookies("name") = name
Response.Cookies("major") = major

' Set path and expiration date for cookies.
For Each cookie In Response.Cookies
    Response.Cookies(cookie).Path = "/StateU"
    Response.Cookies(cookie).Expires = Date + 365
Next
```

Lab Hint 4.8

```
<SCRIPT LANGUAGE="VBScript" RUNAT="Server">
Sub Session_OnStart
    ' If user hasn't entered profile
    ' information redirect them to the profile page.

    If Request.Cookies("id") = "" Then
        profilePage = "/StateU/profile.asp"
        currentPage = Request.ServerVariables("SCRIPT_NAME")
        Session("requestedPage") = currentpage

        ' Do a case-insensitive compare, and if they
        ' don't match, send the user to the start page.
        If strcomp(currentPage,profilePage,1) Then
            Response.Redirect(profilePage)
        End If
    Else
        Session("id") = Request.Cookies("id")
        Session("name") = Request.Cookies("name")
        Session("major") = Request.Cookies("major")
    End If
End Sub
</SCRIPT>
```

Lab Hint 5.1

```
Sub Listbox1_onchange()
   ' Make the current record be the class the user selected.
   Recordset1.moveAbsolute(Listbox1.selectedIndex+1)
End Sub
```

Lab Hint 6.1

```
<%
Set conn = Server.CreateObject("ADODB.Connection")
conn.ConnectionTimeout = Application("StateU_ConnectionTimeout")
conn.CommandTimeout = Application("StateU_CommandTimeout")
conn.Open Application("StateU_ConnectionString"), _
    Application("StateU_RuntimeUserName"), _
    Application("StateU_RuntimePassword")
%>
```

Lab Hint 6.2

```
<%
'This code retrieves the student transcript
set rsTranscript = Server.CreateObject("ADODB.RecordSet")
rsTranscript.ActiveConnection = conn
rsTranscript.Open "select enrollment.classid" & _
    ",title,grade from enrollment,classes " & _
    "where classes.classid = enrollment.classid" & _
    " AND studentid=" & frmStudentID
%>
```

Lab Hint 6.3

```
<!- Transcript Table ->
<table BORDER="0" cellpadding="3">
<tr>
    <td><b>Class Number</b></td>
    <td><b>Title</b></td>
    <td><b>Grade</b></td>
</tr>
</table>
```

Lab Hint 6.4

```
<%
    '- Fill table with Transcript Records
    Do Until rsTranscript.EOF
        Response.Write "<TR>"
        Response.Write "<TD>" &
rsTranscript.fields("ClassID").value&"</TD>"
        Response.Write "<TD>" & rsTranscript.fields("Title").value&"</
TD>"

        'Convert grade to letter format
        Select Case rsTranscript.fields("Grade")
        Case 0
            grade = "F"
        Case 1
            grade = "D"
        Case 2
            grade = "C"
        Case 3
            grade = "B"
        Case 4
            grade = "A"
        Case Else
            grade = "In Progress"
        End Select
      Response.Write "<TD>" & grade & "</TD>"
      Response.Write "</TR>"
      rsTranscript.MoveNext
    Loop
%>
```

Lab Hint 6.5

```
<% ' Retrieves parameters from form
    frmRestime = Request.Form("restime")
    frmEase = Request.Form("ease")
    frmInteractive = Request.Form("interactive")
    frmUseful = Request.Form("useful") %>
```

Lab Hint 6.6

```
Set conn = Server.CreateObject("ADODB.Connection")
conn.ConnectionTimeout = Application("StateU_ConnectionTimeout")
conn.CommandTimeout = Application("StateU_CommandTimeout")
conn.Open Application("StateU_ConnectionString"), _
    Application("StateU_RuntimeUserName"), _
    Application("StateU_RuntimePassword")
```

Lab Hint 6.7

```
'- Add feedback from client as new record
    strSQL = "INSERT INTO feedback " & _
        "(Response, Useful, Interactive, Ease)" & _
        " VALUES (" & frmResponse & "," & frmUseful & _
        "," & frmInteractive & "," & frmEase & ")"
    conn.Execute strSQL

    Response.Write "Thank you! Your feedback has been recorded and
"
    Response.Write "will help us make improvements in the future."
    Response.End
```

Lab Hint 6.8

```
<%
'- Add feedback from client as new record
strSQL = "INSERT INTO feedback " & _
    "(Response, Useful, Interactive, Ease)" & _
    " VALUES (" & frmResponse & "," & frmUseful & _
    "," & frmInteractive & "," & frmEase & ")"
conn.execute strSQL

'- Check that record was added successfully
if err.number <> 0 then
    session("ErrorTitle") = "Feedback Form"
    session("ErrorText") = "The feedback could" & _
        " not be entered because of the following" & _
        " unexpected error:<p>"&err.description
    response.redirect "error.asp"
end if
%>
```

Lab Hint 7.1

```
Set EnrollObj = Server.CreateObject("Enroll.Enrollment")
errEnrollment = EnrollObj.Add(lngStudentID,strClassID)
DoAdd = errEnrollment    ' return True or False
```

Lab Hint 7.2

```
Public Function Drop(ByVal lngStudentID As Long, _
  ByVal strClassID As String) As Integer

  On Error GoTo ErrorHandler
  Dim conn As ADODB.Connection
  Dim strSQL As String

  Drop = 0
  Set conn = CreateObject("ADODB.connection")
  conn.Open "DRIVER=SQL
Server;SERVER=(local);UID=sa;DATABASE=StateU"

  'Make sure class isn't already completed
  If ClassCompleted(conn, lngStudentID, strClassID) Then
      Drop = 1
      Exit Function
  End If

  'Perform the work of dropping the student from the class
  strSQL = "DELETE FROM enrollment where ClassID ='" & _
      strClassID & "' AND Studentid =" & lngStudentID
  conn.BeginTrans
  conn.Execute strSQL
  conn.CommitTrans
  conn.Close
Exit Function

ErrorHandler:
  If Not IsEmpty(conn) Then conn.RollbackTrans
  Drop = 1
End Function
```

Lab Hint 7.3

```
Public Function Transfer(ByVal lngStudentID As Long, _
  ByVal strSrcClassID As String, _
  ByVal strDstClassID As String) As Integer

  On Error GoTo ErrorHandler
  Dim conn As ADODB.Connection
  Dim strDropSQL, strAddSQL As String

  Transfer = 0
  Set conn = CreateObject("ADODB.connection")
  conn.Open "DSN=StateU;UID=sa;PWD=;"

  'Create update strings
  strDropSQL = "DELETE FROM enrollment where classid = '" _
      & strSrcClassID & "' and studentid = " & lngStudentID
  strAddSQL = "INSERT INTO enrollment (ClassID, StudentID)" & _
      " VALUES ('" & strDstClassID & "'," & lngStudentID & ")"

  If ClassCompleted(conn, lngStudentID, strSrcClassID) Then
      Transfer = 1
      Exit Function
  End If

  'Perform work of transferring student
  conn.BeginTrans
  conn.Execute strDropSQL
  conn.Execute strAddSQL
  conn.CommitTrans
  conn.Close
Exit Function

ErrorHandler:
  If Not IsEmpty(conn) Then conn.RollbackTrans
  Transfer = 1
End Function
```

Lab Hint 8.1

```
Dim ctxObject As ObjectContext
'...
Set ctxObject = GetObjectContext()
```

Lab Hint 8.2

```
<%@ LANGUAGE=VBScript TRANSACTION = Required %>

<!- Main body of AddClass.asp here ->

' Display this page if the transaction fails.
Sub OnTransactionAbort()
Response.Clear()
Response.Write "<HTML> <BODY>"
Response.Write "The transaction failed because of internal" &_
    " inconsistencies. Please try again later.<P>"
Response.Write "If the problem persists, please contact" &_
    " webmaster@stateu.com."
Response.Write "</BODY> </HTML>"
Response.Flush()
End sub
```

Lab Hint 9.1

```
' Send a confirmation email if the transaction commits.
Sub OnTransactionCommit()
  Set objNewMail = Server.CreateObject("CDONTS.NewMail")
  objNewMail.Send _
      "registrar@stateu.edu", _
      lngStudentID + "@stateu.edu", _
      "Class Enrollment Confirmation", _
      "Congratulations, you have been registered for course " + _
      strClassID + " .", _
      1
Set objNewMail = Nothing ' cannot reuse it for another message
End sub
```

Lab Hint 9.2

```
<% else %>
<% REM then create the recordset object from querystring
    'Set the query object's properties
    SUQuery.Query = Request("qu")
    SUQuery.Columns = "filename, vpath, size, characterization"
    'Set maximum return set to 50
    SUQuery.MaxRecords = 50
    'Restrict the Search scope to StateU Web Site
    set SUUtil = Server.CreateObject("IXSSO.Util")
    SUUtil.AddScopeToQuery SUQuery, "/stateu", "deep"
    ' Submit the query and collect results
    set RS=SUQuery.CreateRecordSet("sequential")%>
<% end if %>
```

Glossary

activate

Also Activation. A programming process that loads an object into memory, putting the object into an executable or running state. Also, the process of binding an object so as to put the object into its running state.

active client

The client-side element of the active platform that enables cross-platform content and applications. It includes support for HTML, scripting (VBScript and JScript), Java applets, ActiveX Components, ActiveX Controls, and Active Documents.

active document

A Windows-based, non-HTML application embedded in a browser, providing a way for the functionality of these applications to be accessible from within the browser interface.

Active Group, The

A standards organization, under the auspices of The Open Group, an open, customer-driven steering committee responsible for the ongoing development and management of ActiveX technologies and licensing.

active platform

An integrated, comprehensive set of client, Active Client, and server, Active Server, component-based development technologies that make it easy for developers to integrate the connectivity of the Internet with the power of the personal computer.

active server

The server-side element of the Active Platform; specifically, a collection of server-side technologies that are delivered with Windows NT, and provide a consistent server-side component and scripting model and an integrated set of system services for component application management, database access, transactions, and messaging.

Active Server Page (ASP)

The server-side execution environment in Microsoft Internet Information Server 4.0 that executes ActiveX Scripts and ActiveX Components on a server.

ActiveX

A set of language-independent interoperability technologies that enable software components written in different languages to work together in networked environments. The core technology elements of ActiveX are COM and DCOM.

ActiveX automation

A language-neutral way to manipulate an ActiveX component's methods from outside an application. ActiveX automation is typically used to create components that expose methods to programming tools and macro languages.

ActiveX component

A compiled software component based on COM that encapsulates a set of business functionality. The functionality in an ActiveX component is accessed through ActiveX automation interfaces. The ActiveX component can execute either on a client computer or on a server computer, transparent to the calling application, through DCOM.

ActiveX controls

Small, reusable objects created using COM technology. Because ActiveX controls are intended to be used as visual programming components, they have additional requirements over standard COM components, such as self-registration, property sheet display, event generation, and so on.

ActiveX controls are implemented as in-process DLLs, usually having an .ocx extension. They can be used in ActiveX control containers, such as Visual Basic or Visual C++ programs, or used within a Web page in Microsoft Internet Explorer.

ActiveX Data Objects (ADO)

A set of object-based data access interfaces optimized for Internet-based, data-centric applications.

ActiveX scripting

The act of using a scripting language to drive ActiveX Components.

ActiveX Server Component

An ActiveX component designed to run on the server-side of a client/server application. See *ActiveX Component.*

aggregation

A programming composition technique for implementing component objects. Using this technique, developers can build a new object using one or more existing objects that support some or all of the new object's required interfaces.

anonymous FTP

Anonymous File Transfer Protocol. Used in the process of connecting to a remote computer as an anonymous or guest user in order to transfer public files to your local computer.

American National Standards Institute (ANSI)

ANSI serves as a quasi-national standards organization. It provides area charters for groups that establish standards in specific fields, such as the Institute of Electrical and Electronics Engineers (IEEE). Also, commonly used to refer to a low-level table of codes used by a computer.

apartment model multi-threading

COM supports a form of multi-threading in Windows 95 and Windows NT called the *apartment model*. Apartment is essentially a way of describing a thread with a message queue that supports COM objects.

apartment threaded

A model in which each object "lives in an apartment" (thread) for the life of the object. All calls to that object execute on the apartment thread.

Application Programming Interface (API)

Application Programming Interface. A set of routines that an application program uses to request and carry out lower-level services performed by a computer's operating system.

applet

An HTML-based program built with Java that a browser temporarily downloads to a user's hard disk, from which location it runs when the Web page is open.

asynchronous call

A function that enables processing to continue without waiting for the function to return a value.

Asynchronous Transfer Mode (ATM)

A communications protocol defined for high-speed data communications.

automation

See *ActiveX automation*.

bandwidth

The capacity of the transmission medium stated in bits per second (bps) or as a frequency (Hz). Generally, a higher bandwidth number indicates faster data-transfer capability.

bind

Also binding. To put an object into its running state, allowing the operations it supports to be invoked. Objects can be bound at run time, called *late binding* or *dynamic binding*, or at compile time, called *static binding*.

bytecode

The executable form of Java code that executes within the Java Virtual Machine. Also called interpreted code, pseudocode, or p-code.

cache

Usually a temporary local store for information, a special memory subsystem where frequently used data values are copied and stored for quick access.

call

To transfer program execution to some other section of code, usually a subroutine, while saving the necessary information to allow execution to resume at the calling point when the called section has completed execution.

Certificate Authority

Certificate Authorities are companies that distribute certificates to software developers. To guarantee a control's authenticity, a Certificate Authority, such as the Verisign Corporation, develops a digital certificate for each developer who uses Authenticode technologies from Microsoft.

class

A generalized category in object-oriented programming that describes a group of more specific items called objects. A class provides a template for defining the behavior of a particular type of object.

class factory

An object that implements the IClassFactory interface, which allows it to create objects of a specific class.

class identifier

Also CLASSID or CLSID. A unique identification tag (UUID) associated with a class object. A class object that is intended to create more than one object registers its CLSID in a task table in the system registration database to enable clients to locate and load the executable code associated with the object(s).

class library

A collection of one or more classes that programmers use to implement functionality.

class object

A member object within a class.

client

A program that facilitates a connection to server computers and manages and presents information retrieved from those sources. In a client/server environment, the workstation is usually the client computer. In referring to COM objects, an object that requests services from another object.

client/server

A model of computing whereby client applications running on a desktop or personal computer access information on remote servers or host computers.

COM component

A compiled software component based on COM that encapsulates a set of business functionality. The functionality in a COM component is accessed through Automation interfaces. The COM component can execute either on a client computer or on a server computer, transparent to the calling application.

Component Object Model (COM)

The object-oriented programming model that defines how objects interact within a single application or between applications.

Common Gateway Interface (CGI)

A server-side interface for initiating software services. A set of interfaces that describes how a Web server communicates with software on the same computer.

communications protocol

A set of rules or standards designed to enable computers to connect with one another and to exchange information with as few errors as possible.

component

See *ActiveX component.*

compound document

A document that contains data in different formats created by different applications.

Computer Aided Software Engineering (CASE)

Software that aids in application development including analysis, design, and code generation. CASE tools provide automated methods for designing and documenting traditional-structure programming techniques.

container application

A container application provides storage for the embedded object, a site for display, access to the display site, and an advisory sink for receiving notification of changes in the object.

context object

An object that tracks properties of an MTS server component as it runs within an activity, including its activation state, security information, transaction state (if any), and so on. This frees the component from tracking its own state.

control

In a graphical user interface, an object on the screen that can be manipulated by a user to perform an action.

cookies

A means by which, under the HTTP protocol, a server or a script can maintain state or *status* information on the client workstation.

CORBA

Common Object Request Broker Architecture. An Object Management Group specification for the interface definition between OMG-compliant objects.

cursor engine

A mechanism for managing data retrieved from a database, or a full transaction manager that optimizes the retrieval and update of server-based data.

Data Access Objects (DAO)

DAO includes the full functionality of the Microsoft Jet database engine for local data management.

data dictionary

A repository of information about data, such as its meaning, relationships to other data, origin, usage, and format.

dataspace

An object that creates instances of business objects that reside on a Web server.

deadlocks

A situation in which two or more threads of execution are permanently blocked (waiting), with each thread waiting for a resource exclusively held by one of the other threads that is blocked. For example, if thread A locks record 1 and waits to lock record 2, while thread B has locked record 2 and waits to lock record 1, the two threads are deadlocked.

debugger

A development environment that supports step-by-step execution of application code and viewing the content of code variables.

default catalog

A catalog is the directory in which Index Server data is stored. A catalog represents the highest level of organization, and contains information about one or more virtual directories. Catalogs along with other persistent data are stored in a special catalog directory, which by default is named Catalog.wci.

design-time ActiveX controls

Visual authoring components that help a developer construct dynamic Web applications by automatically generating standard HTML and/or scripting code. They are analogous to wizards.

Distributed Computing Environment (DCE)

An open set of services controlled by the OSF and designed to support performing distributed computing across heterogeneous platforms.

Distributed Component Object Model (DCOM)

Additions to COM that facilitate the transparent distribution of objects over networks and over the Internet.

distributed processing

The physical or logical distribution of software components, processing, data, and management of application software.

domain name

An entry in an Internet address, such as *microsoft.com* in the fictitious U.S. address www.example.microsoft.com/.

Domain Name Service (DNS)

A protocol that provides an Internet-wide database of host and domain names. For example, DNS is used to find the IP address of a host name written as *microsoft.com*.

e-commerce

Electronic commerce. The process of buying and selling over the Web, often based on software products such as the Microsoft Merchant Server.

event

Any action, often generated by a user or an ActiveX control, to which a program might respond.

event handlers

Functions that trap and process events such as keys being pressed, mouse buttons being clicked, menus being opened, and so on.

failfast

A policy of Microsoft Transaction Server (MTS) that facilitates fault containment. When MTS encounters an unexpected failure, it immediately terminates the process and logs a message to the Windows NT event log for details about the failure. MTS will also rollback any transactions affected by the failure.

FAQ

Frequently Asked Questions. Usually a document containing questions and answers that address the basics.

File Transfer Protocol (FTP)

The Internet standard high-speed protocol for downloading or transferring files from one computer to another.

firewall

A security mechanism, such as the Microsoft Proxy Server, that provides Internet access from desktops inside an organization, while at the same time preventing access to the corporate LAN by outside Internet users.

function

A general term used for a subroutine. In some programming languages, a subroutine or statement that returns values.

globally unique identifier (GUID)

Identifiers (IDs) assigned to COM objects that are generated through a sophisticated algorithm. The algorithm guarantees that all COM objects are assigned unique IDs, avoiding any possibility of a naming conflict.

Gopher

An early Internet protocol and software program designed to search for, retrieve, and display documents from remote computers or sites.

graphical user interface (GUI)

A user interface that displays graphics and characters and provides an event model for users to control the operating environment.

Graphics Interchange Format (GIF)

A computer graphics file format developed in the mid-1980s by CompuServe for use in photo-quality graphic image display on computer screens.

host

Any computer that provides services to remote computers or users.

hypertext

A hypertext document is a document that is structured in chunks of text, marked up (usually using HTML), and connected by links. Hence, the text in the document can properly be named hypertext because of its marked-up and navigable condition.

Hypertext Markup Language (HTML)

A tag-based notation language used to format documents that can then be interpreted and rendered by an Internet browser.

Hypertext Transfer Protocol (HTTP)

A basic communication protocol for Internet or Web server file input and output (I/O).

IMAP

Also IMAP4. A server standard that enables you to maintain e-mail on a server for easy access from different locations and desktops. IMAP4 also allows you to work with your messages on the server, including managing multiple folders on the server.

impersonate

Also impersonation. The process of allowing a thread to execute in a security context different from that of the process that owns the thread.

in-process

Also in-process component. A COM component that shares the same memory as the container application.

Indexed Sequential Access Method (ISAM)

An indexing mechanism for efficient access to rows of data in a file.

inheritance

A programming technique that duplicates the characteristics down a hierarchy from one class to another.

instance

An object for which memory is allocated or persistent.

instantiate

To create an instance of an object. The process of creating or activating an object based on its class.

Integrated Services Digital Network (ISDN)

An emerging technology that is beginning to be offered by most telephone service providers as a faster alternative to traditional modems.

interface

A group of related functions that provide access to COM objects.

International Standards Organization (ISO)

An organization involved in setting standards worldwide for all fields except electro-technical, which is the responsibility of IEC.

Internet Database Connector (IDC)

Provides database connectivity between IIS applications and any ODBC-compliant database.

Internet Engineering Task Force (IETF)

A protocol engineering and development organization focused on the Internet.

Internet Protocol (IP)

The packet-switching protocol for network communications between Internet host computers.

Internet Server Application Program Interface (ISAPI)

An application program interface that resides on a server computer for initiating software services tuned for Microsoft Windows NT operating system.

intranet

Use of Internet standards, technologies, and products within an enterprise to function as a collaborative processing infrastructure. The term intranet is generally used to describe the application of Internet technologies on internal corporate networks.

Java

A derivative of the C++ language, Java is the Sun Microsystems Corporation distributed programming language, offered as an open standard.

Java beans

An object model being developed by Sun Microsystems Corporation that is targeted to inter-operate with a variety of other object models, including COM and CORBA.

Java Database Connectivity (JDBC)

Data access interfaces based on ODBC for use with the Java language.

JavaScript

A scripting language that evolved from Netscape's LiveScript language and was made more compatible with Java. It uses an HTML page as its interface.

Jet

A Microsoft desktop database engine available in most of Microsoft's development tools and office products, including Microsoft Access, Microsoft Office, and Microsoft Visual Basic.

Joint Photographic Experts Group (JPEG)

A widely accepted international standard for compression of color image files, sometimes used on the Internet.

JScript

The Microsoft open implementation of JavaScript. JScript is fully compatible with JavaScript in Netscape Navigator version 2.0.

Just-in-Time (JIT) object activation

The ability for a MTS object to be activated only as needed for executing requests from its client. Objects can be deactivated even while clients hold references to them, allowing otherwise idle server resources to be used more productively.

Kerberos

The basis of most of the distributed computing environment (DCE) security services. Kerberos provides the secure use of distributed software components.

latency

The state of being latent, or to lie hidden; not currently showing signs of existence. Sometimes attributed to the time taken to retrieve pages from the World Wide Web.

Lightweight Directory Access Protocol (LDAP)

A standard for updating and searching directories using TCP/IP. LDAP allows you to easily find other Internet users by accessing any LDAP-based directory server, including Internet directories, such as Four11 and Bigfoot, or a company's intranet directory.

Local Area Network (LAN)

A connection among a set of computers. Computers connected to a LAN can generally share applications or files from a local file server and may be able to connect to other LANs or to the Internet using routers.

MAPI

Mail or Messaging Applications Programming Interface. An open and comprehensive messaging interface used by programmers to create messaging and workgroup applications, such as electronic mail, scheduling, calendaring, and document management. In a distributed client/server environment, MAPI provides enterprise messaging services within Windows Open Services Architecture (WOSA).

marshal

Also marshaling. The process of packaging and sending interface parameters across process boundaries in computer memory.

master index

A persistent on-disk index that contains the indexed data for a large number of documents.

message queuing

Server technology developers can use to build large-scale distributed systems with reliable communications between applications that can continue to operate reliably even when networked systems are unavailable.

method

Member functions of an exposed object that perform some action on an object, such as saving it to disk.

Microsoft Transaction Server (MTS)

Combines the features of a transaction-processing (TP) monitor and an object-request broker (ORB) in an easy-to-use product.

MIME

Multipurpose Internet Mail Extensions. An extension of the Internet mail protocol that enables users to send 8-bit based e-mail messages, which are used to support extended character sets, voice mail, facsimile images, and so on.

moniker

A name that uniquely identifies a COM object, similar to a directory path name.

multi-tasking

The ability to simultaneously execute multiple applications within an operating system.

multi-threading

Running several processes in rapid sequence within a single program, regardless of which logical method of multi-tasking is being used by the operating system.

multi-tier architecture

Also known as three-tier, multi-tier is a technique for building applications generally split into user, business, and data services tiers. These applications are built of component services that are based on an object model such as ActiveX.

Network News Transfer Protocol (NNTP)

The protocol used to send and receive news messages over the Internet.

node

A computer that is attached to a network; also called a host. Also, a junction of some kind. On a local area network, a device that is connected to the network and is capable of communicating with other network devices.

object

A combination of code and data that can be treated as a unit, for example a control, form, or application. Each object is defined by a class.

An object is an instance of a class that combines data with procedures.

Object Linking and Embedding (OLE)

A set of integration standards to transfer and share information among client applications.

Object Management Group (OMG)

A vendor alliance formed to define and promote CORBA object specifications.

Object Request Broker (ORB)

Manages interaction between clients and servers including the distributed computing responsibilities of location referencing as well as coordinating parameters and results.

ODBCDirect

Technology that makes the full functionality of RDO available from within DAO. Used to bypass the Microsoft Jet database engine for fast, small-memory-footprint access to remote data. See also *DAO*, *Jet*, and *RDO*.

OLE automation

See *ActiveX automation*.

OLE control

See *ActiveX control*.

OLE DB

Data-access interfaces providing consistent access to SQL and non-SQL data sources across the enterprise and the Internet.

Online Analytical Processing (OLAP)

A multi-dimensional database used for decision support analysis and data warehousing.

Open Database Connectivity (ODBC)

A developer can use ODBC to access data in a heterogeneous environment of relational and non-relational databases.

Open Group, The

Parent company of a number of standards organizations, including The Active Group, now managing the core ActiveX technology, X/Open, and OSF.

Open Software Foundation (OSF)

A vendor alliance that defines specifications, develops software, and makes available an open, portable environment. Now merged with The Open Group.

out-of-process

Also out-of-process component. A COM component that runs in its own separate memory space separate from a container application.

Point-to-Point Protocol (PPP)

The Internet standard for serial communications, PPP defines how data packets are exchanged with other Internet-based systems using a modem connection.

Point-to-Point Tunneling Protocol (PPTP)

The Internet can be used for low-cost, secure remote access to a corporate network with virtual private networking support on Windows NT.

pooling

A performance optimization based on using collections of pre-allocated resources, such as database connections.

Post Office Protocol version 3 (POP3)

Permits a workstation to dynamically access a mail drop on a server in a useful fashion. Usually, this means that a POP3 server is used to allow a workstation to retrieve mail that an SMTP server is holding for it. POP3 is specified in RFC 1725.

Private Communications Technology (PCT) 1.0

Designed to provide secure transactions over the Internet.

progID

A string expression that is the programmatic ID of the new object in a component.

property

A set of characteristics of an object.

protocol

A mutually determined set of formats and procedures for the exchange of information between computers.

proxy server

A proxy server acts as a go-between, converting information from Web servers into HTML to be delivered to a client computer. It also provides a way to deliver network services to computers on a secure subnet without those computers needing to have direct access to the World Wide Web.

Public Key Certificate Standard (PKCS)

Syntax standards covering a number of security functions, including a standard way of attaching signatures to a block of data, a form for requesting a certificate, and public key encryption algorithms.

race conditions

A situation where two or more threads of execution are attempting to perform the same action (for example, using the same resource or executing the same code), where the outcome for all the threads is dependent on the (unspecified) order in which they execute.

Remote Data Objects (RDO)

In version 2.0, RDO is a high-level object interface that directly calls ODBC for optimal speed, control, and ease of programming.

Remote Procedure Call (RPC)

A mechanism that extends the notion of a local procedure call, meaning contained in a single memory address space, to a distributed computing environment.

router

An intermediary device on a communications network responsible for deciding by which of several paths message traffic will flow over a network or the Internet.

RSA

A public key cryptography for Internet security. This acronym derives from the last names of the inventors of the technology: Rivest, Shamir, and Adleman.

RTP/RTCP

Real-time protocol and real-time control protocol, respectively. A packet format for sending real-time information across the Internet.

scalability

The capability to use the same software environment on many classes of computers and hardware configurations.

script

A kind of program that consists of a set of instructions for an application or utility program.

Secure Electronic Payment Process (SEPP)

A proposed specification that merged with STT, resulting in the SET standard for secure e-commerce transactions.

Secure Electronic Transaction (SET)

A standard that enables consumers, businesses, and banks and financial institutions to conduct secure, reliable transactions over the Internet. SET encrypts transaction pieces through a strong, exportable 128-bit encryption scheme that creates a three-way trust relationship between seller, buyer, and online bank.

Secure Sockets Layer (SSL) 3.0

Secure Sockets Layer. A standard for providing encrypted and authenticated service over the Internet. Uses RSA public-key encryption for specific TCP/IP ports.

Secure Transaction Technology (STT)

A proposed specification that merged with SEPP, resulting in the SET standard for secure e-commerce transactions.

server

A computer-running administrative software that controls access to all or part of a network and its resources.

server-side include

A server-side include (SSI) is a directive to include text, graphics, or application information into an HTML page just before sending the HTML page to a user. SSI can be used to include, for example, a time/date stamp, a copyright notice, or a form for a customer to fill out and return.

ServerName

A string that identifies the Web server where an instance of the server-side business object is created.

signature

The return value and parameter data types of a function or method. Also the return values and parameter data types for all methods in an interface.

Simple Mail Transfer Protocol (SMTP)

The Internet standard protocol for transferring electronic mail messages from one computer to another.

single-threaded

A model in which all objects are executed on a single thread.

SQL Access Group (SAG)

A consortium of vendors established in November 1989 to accelerate the Remote Data Access standard and to deliver protocols for interconnectivity among multiple SQL-based software products.

Standard Generalized Markup Language (SGML)

An original documentation markup standard promulgated by primary defense contractors as a standard for the development and display of documentation. HTML is a subset of SGML.

stored procedures

Pre-compiled software functions that are managed and that run within a remote database management system (RDBMS).

Structured Query Language (SQL)

The international standard language for defining and accessing relational databases.

Symmetric Multiprocessing (SMP)

A multiprocessor architecture in which all processors are identical, share memory, and execute both user code and operating system code.

synchronous

A function that does not allow further instructions in the process code to be executed until the function returns a value.

TCP/IP

Transmission Control Protocol/Internet Protocol. TCP/IP is a combined set of protocols that perform the transfer of data between two computers.

Telnet

A terminal emulation protocol users can employ to log on to other computers on the Internet. Alternatively, software that can be used to log on to another computer using the telnet protocol.

three-tier architecture

See *multi-tier architecture*.

transaction

A group of processing activities that are either entirely completed, or if not completed, that leave the database and processing system in the same state as before the transaction started.

Transaction Processing (TP)

The real-time handling of computerized business transactions as they are received by the system. Also called online transaction processing (OLTP) systems.

two-tier architecture

See *client/server*.

type library

A file that contains standard descriptions of data types, modules, and interfaces objects and types that can be used to fully expose objects such as COM components.

Virtual Machine

The mechanism the Java language uses to execute Java bytecode on any physical computer. The VM converts the bytecode to the native instruction for the target computer.

Virtual Reality Modeling Language (VRML)

A language for coding three-dimensional HTML applications.

Virtual Root

Also Vroot. A virtual tree of Web aliases that points to local, physical directories. This simplifies client URL addresses by presenting an entire set of content directories as a single directory tree.

Visual Basic Extension (VBX)

Custom controls originally designed for 16-bit applications created by Visual Basic.

Visual Basic for Applications (VBA)

The development environment and language found in Visual Basic that can be hosted by applications.

W3C

Acronym for the World Wide Web Consortium.

Web application

Also Web-based application. A software program that uses HTTP for its core communication protocol and delivers Web-based information to the user in the HTML language.

Windows sockets

Also Winsock. Winsock provides a single interface in Microsoft Windows to which multiple network software programs conform.

working copy

In a Visual InterDev project, a local, editable copy of a project file that is temporarily owned by the current developer.

Windows Open Services Architecture (WOSA)

An architecture and set of application programming interfaces for Windows that standardized the interfaces developers use in accessing underlying network services.

WYSIWYG

What You See Is What You Get. Authoring software programs that render a document on the computer screen the way it will appear in print, even as it is being edited.

X.500 (including DAP)

Directory Access Protocol is a standard for global directory services.

X.509 certificate

A protocol for a cryptographic certificate that contains a vendor's unique name and the vendor's public key.

XA

A transaction interoperability standard defined by X/Open. The Microsoft Transaction Server uses XA to connect with other transaction processing systems.

X/Open

An independent consortium of international computer vendors created to establish multi-vendor standards based on *de facto* and *de jure* standards.

Index

A

Here's the
key to building
dynamic
Web applications

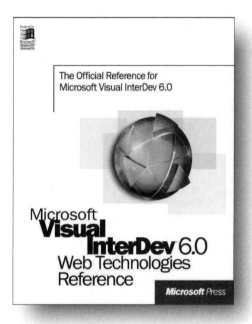

The Official Reference for
Microsoft Visual InterDev 6.0

Microsoft
Visual
InterDev 6.0
Web Technologies
Reference

Microsoft Press

U.S.A. **$39.99**
U.K. £36.99 [V.A.T. included]
Canada $57.99
ISBN 1-57231-871-6

An indispensable set of resources collected in a single volume, the MICROSOFT® VISUAL INTERDEV™ 6.0 WEB TECHNOLOGIES REFERENCE offers essential reference guides to scripting languages on both the client and server sides, including:

- *Dynamic HTML Reference* describes the set of innovative features in Microsoft® Internet Explorer 4.0 that enable you to easily add effects to your documents.

- *JScript® Reference* documents the fast, portable, lightweight interpreter for use in Web browsers and other applications that use ActiveX® controls, OLE Automation servers, and Java applets.

- *VBScript Reference* explains how you can bring Active Scripting to a wide variety of environments. The Visual InterDev development environment allows you to specify VBScript as your default scripting language for either client or server script.

- *Active Data Objects (ADO) Reference* shows you how to develop consistent, quick access to data, whether you're creating a front-end database client or middle-tier business object using an application, tool, language, or even a browser.

- *Visual InterDev Web Reference* lets you create the interface for your application using design-time controls and then write script to control the application using traditional object-oriented techniques.

Microsoft Press

Achieve
dynamic
new effects
on the Web

Microsoft® Mastering Series
Your *Complete* Training Solution

training skills solutions

Print Edition: Study at your own pace.

The Mastering Series Print Editions allow you to get up to speed on new technology whenever and wherever you need it. Print Editions provides in-depth, hands-on training in an affordable package. They are designed for the power user who wants to move to the next level.

▶ *More information:* **http://msdn.microsoft.com/mastering/books**

MSDN Training Online: Get in-depth coverage of the latest technology now.

Mastering Series online courses are offered by training centers around the world. They allow you to combine the best of self-study with the advantages of classroom training — without the hassles of travel and being away from work.

▶ *More information:* **http://msdn.microsoft.com/mastering/online**

Classroom Training: Learn from experienced developer/trainers.

Mastering Series instructor-led training classes are the premium way to get training. You learn in hands-on labs with detailed guidance from veteran developers, at thousands of Microsoft Certified Technical Education Centers around the world. The combination of in-depth training and experienced trainers gives you the clearest possible picture of how to use new technology in the real world.

▶ *More information:* **http://msdn.microsoft.com/mastering**

What's right for you?

If you need help sifting through the many training opportunities available for developers, the professionals at any Microsoft Certified Technical Education Center can recommend the most appropriate training program, tailored specifically for you and your needs! They'll help you decide which critical products and technologies are most important to you. And they will assist you in determining what training formats best suit your preferred learning style and resources. To find the Microsoft CTEC near you, visit the Microsoft Find Training web page at:

http://www.microsoft.com/isapi/referral/product_select.asp?train=84

Microsoft®
Mastering Series
Developer Training

Make the *Career You Deserve* with *Microsoft Training Programs*

Why get trained?

As a trained IT professional, you can:
- ▶ Take advantage of extensive opportunities in a growing industry
- ▶ Stay on top of changes in the industry
- ▶ Polish old technical skills and acquire new ones

As an IT manager, hiring trained IT professionals provides you with:
- ▶ Greater assurance of a job well done
- ▶ Improved service, increased productivity and greater technical self-sufficiency
- ▶ More satisfied employees and clients

What's right for you?

The professionals at any Microsoft Certified Technical Education Center can recommend the most appropriate training program, tailored specifically for you and your needs! They'll help you decide which critical products and technologies are most important to you. And they will assist you in determining what training formats best suit your preferred learning style and resources.

How do you get the best training?

With instructor-led, online, and self-paced training and instruction available at locations throughout the world and on the Web, you are sure to find what you need among our industry-renowned comprehensive solutions to give you the right method of training to produce the best results. And a combination of training formats sometimes called hybrid training may be more effective than a single methodology.

Where do you get the best training?

Choose from Microsoft Certified Technical Education Centers, Microsoft Authorized Academic Training Program institutions, Microsoft Press, and, Microsoft Seminar Online to get the job done right.

Microsoft®
Authorized Academic Training Program

Microsoft Press

Microsoft Authorized Academic Training Program (AATP) helps full-time and part-time students in participating high schools, colleges and universities prepare for jobs that demand proficiency with Microsoft products and technologies.
For more information, go to: http://www.microsoft.com/astp/

Microsoft Certified Technical Education Centers (Microsoft CTECs) are full-service training organizations that can deliver system support and developer instruction in a variety of flexible formats.
For more information, go to: http://www.microsoft.com/train_cert/

Microsoft Seminar Online delivers a virtual seminar experience right to your desktop, anytime, day or night.
For more information, go to: http://www.microsoft.com/seminar/

Microsoft Certified Professional Approved Study Guides (MCP Approved Study Guides), an excellent way to stay up to date on Microsoft products & technologies, are rigorously developed & reviewed to ensure adherence to certification objectives.
For more information, go to: http://www.microsoft.com/train_cert/train/mcpasg.htm/

Microsoft Press delivers "anytime, anywhere learning" via a full line of Microsoft Official Curriculum (MOC) self-paced training kits enhanced with print & multimedia that prepare you for the MCP exams.
For more information, go to: http://mspress.microsoft.com/

MICROSOFT LICENSE AGREEMENT

Book Companion CD

IMPORTANT—READ CAREFULLY: This Microsoft End-User License Agreement ("EULA") is a legal agreement between you (either an individual or an entity) and Microsoft Corporation for the Microsoft product identified above, which includes computer software and may include associated media, printed materials, and "online" or electronic documentation ("SOFTWARE PRODUCT"). Any component included within the SOFTWARE PRODUCT that is accompanied by a separate End-User License Agreement shall be governed by such agreement and not the terms set forth below. By installing, copying, or otherwise using the SOFTWARE PRODUCT, you agree to be bound by the terms of this EULA. If you do not agree to the terms of this EULA, you are not authorized to install, copy, or otherwise use the SOFTWARE PRODUCT; you may, however, return the SOFTWARE PRODUCT, along with all printed materials and other items that form a part of the Microsoft product that includes the SOFTWARE PRODUCT, to the place you obtained them for a full refund.

SOFTWARE PRODUCT LICENSE

The SOFTWARE PRODUCT is protected by United States copyright laws and international copyright treaties, as well as other intellectual property laws and treaties. The SOFTWARE PRODUCT is licensed, not sold.

1. **GRANT OF LICENSE.** This EULA grants you the following rights:

   a. **Software Product.** You may install and use one copy of the SOFTWARE PRODUCT on a single computer. The primary user of the computer on which the SOFTWARE PRODUCT is installed may make a second copy for his or her exclusive use on a portable computer.

   b. **Storage/Network Use.** You may also store or install a copy of the SOFTWARE PRODUCT on a storage device, such as a network server, used only to install or run the SOFTWARE PRODUCT on your other computers over an internal network; however, you must acquire and dedicate a license for each separate computer on which the SOFTWARE PRODUCT is installed or run from the storage device. A license for the SOFTWARE PRODUCT may not be shared or used concurrently on different computers.

   c. **License Pak.** If you have acquired this EULA in a Microsoft License Pak, you may make the number of additional copies of the computer software portion of the SOFTWARE PRODUCT authorized on the printed copy of this EULA, and you may use each copy in the manner specified above. You are also entitled to make a corresponding number of secondary copies for portable computer use as specified above.

   d. **Sample Code.** Solely with respect to portions, if any, of the SOFTWARE PRODUCT that are identified within the SOFTWARE PRODUCT as sample code (the "SAMPLE CODE"):

      i. **Use and Modification.** Microsoft grants you the right to use and modify the source code version of the SAMPLE CODE, *provided* you comply with subsection (d)(iii) below. You may not distribute the SAMPLE CODE, or any modified version of the SAMPLE CODE, in source code form.

      ii. **Redistributable Files.** Provided you comply with subsection (d)(iii) below, Microsoft grants you a nonexclusive, royalty-free right to reproduce and distribute the object code version of the SAMPLE CODE and of any modified SAMPLE CODE, other than SAMPLE CODE, or any modified version thereof, designated as not redistributable in the Readme file that forms a part of the SOFTWARE PRODUCT (the "Non-Redistributable Sample Code"). All SAMPLE CODE other than the Non-Redistributable Sample Code is collectively referred to as the "REDISTRIBUTABLES."

      iii. **Redistribution Requirements.** If you redistribute the REDISTRIBUTABLES, you agree to: (i) distribute the REDISTRIBUTABLES in object code form only in conjunction with and as a part of your software application product; (ii) not use Microsoft's name, logo, or trademarks to market your software application product; (iii) include a valid copyright notice on your software application product; (iv) indemnify, hold harmless, and defend Microsoft from and against any claims or lawsuits, including attorney's fees, that arise or result from the use or distribution of your software application product; and (v) not permit further distribution of the REDISTRIBUTABLES by your end user. Contact Microsoft for the applicable royalties due and other licensing terms for all other uses and/or distribution of the REDISTRIBUTABLES.

2. **DESCRIPTION OF OTHER RIGHTS AND LIMITATIONS.**

   - **Limitations on Reverse Engineering, Decompilation, and Disassembly.** You may not reverse engineer, decompile, or disassemble the SOFTWARE PRODUCT, except and only to the extent that such activity is expressly permitted by applicable law notwithstanding this limitation.

   - **Separation of Components.** The SOFTWARE PRODUCT is licensed as a single product. Its component parts may not be separated for use on more than one computer.

   - **Rental.** You may not rent, lease, or lend the SOFTWARE PRODUCT.

   - **Support Services.** Microsoft may, but is not obligated to, provide you with support services related to the SOFTWARE PRODUCT ("Support Services"). Use of Support Services is governed by the Microsoft policies and programs described in the user manual, in "online" documentation, and/or in other Microsoft-provided materials. Any supplemental software code provided to you as part of the Support Services shall be considered part of the SOFTWARE PRODUCT and subject to the terms and conditions of this EULA. With respect to technical information you provide to Microsoft as part of the Support Services, Microsoft may use such information for its business purposes, including for product support and development. Microsoft will not utilize such technical information in a form that personally identifies you.

- **Software Transfer.** You may permanently transfer all of your rights under this EULA, provided you retain no copies, you transfer all of the SOFTWARE PRODUCT (including all component parts, the media and printed materials, any upgrades, this EULA, and, if applicable, the Certificate of Authenticity), **and** the recipient agrees to the terms of this EULA.

- **Termination.** Without prejudice to any other rights, Microsoft may terminate this EULA if you fail to comply with the terms and conditions of this EULA. In such event, you must destroy all copies of the SOFTWARE PRODUCT and all of its component parts.

3. COPYRIGHT. All title and copyrights in and to the SOFTWARE PRODUCT (including but not limited to any images, photographs, animations, video, audio, music, text, SAMPLE CODE, REDISTRIBUTABLES, and "applets" incorporated into the SOFTWARE PRODUCT) and any copies of the SOFTWARE PRODUCT are owned by Microsoft or its suppliers. The SOFTWARE PRODUCT is protected by copyright laws and international treaty provisions. Therefore, you must treat the SOFTWARE PRODUCT like any other copyrighted material **except** that you may install the SOFTWARE PRODUCT on a single computer provided you keep the original solely for backup or archival purposes. You may not copy the printed materials accompanying the SOFTWARE PRODUCT.

4. U.S. GOVERNMENT RESTRICTED RIGHTS. The SOFTWARE PRODUCT and documentation are provided with RESTRICTED RIGHTS. Use, duplication, or disclosure by the Government is subject to restrictions as set forth in subparagraph (c)(1)(ii) of the Rights in Technical Data and Computer Software clause at DFARS 252.227-7013 or subparagraphs (c)(1) and (2) of the Commercial Computer Software—Restricted Rights at 48 CFR 52.227-19, as applicable. Manufacturer is Microsoft Corporation/One Microsoft Way/Redmond, WA 98052-6399.

5. EXPORT RESTRICTIONS. You agree that you will not export or re-export the SOFTWARE PRODUCT, any part thereof, or any process or service that is the direct product of the SOFTWARE PRODUCT (the foregoing collectively referred to as the "Restricted Components"), to any country, person, entity, or end user subject to U.S. export restrictions. You specifically agree not to export or re-export any of the Restricted Components (i) to any country to which the U.S. has embargoed or restricted the export of goods or services, which currently include, but are not necessarily limited to, Cuba, Iran, Iraq, Libya, North Korea, Sudan, and Syria, or to any national of any such country, wherever located, who intends to transmit or transport the Restricted Components back to such country; (ii) to any end user who you know or have reason to know will utilize the Restricted Components in the design, development, or production of nuclear, chemical, or biological weapons; or (iii) to any end user who has been prohibited from participating in U.S. export transactions by any federal agency of the U.S. government. You warrant and represent that neither the BXA nor any other U.S. federal agency has suspended, revoked, or denied your export privileges.

DISCLAIMER OF WARRANTY

NO WARRANTIES OR CONDITIONS. MICROSOFT EXPRESSLY DISCLAIMS ANY WARRANTY OR CONDITION FOR THE SOFTWARE PRODUCT. THE SOFTWARE PRODUCT AND ANY RELATED DOCUMENTATION ARE PROVIDED "AS IS" WITHOUT WARRANTY OR CONDITION OF ANY KIND, EITHER EXPRESS OR IMPLIED, INCLUDING, WITHOUT LIMITATION, THE IMPLIED WARRANTIES OF MERCHANTABILITY, FITNESS FOR A PARTICULAR PURPOSE, OR NONINFRINGEMENT. THE ENTIRE RISK ARISING OUT OF USE OR PERFORMANCE OF THE SOFTWARE PRODUCT REMAINS WITH YOU.

LIMITATION OF LIABILITY. TO THE MAXIMUM EXTENT PERMITTED BY APPLICABLE LAW, IN NO EVENT SHALL MICROSOFT OR ITS SUPPLIERS BE LIABLE FOR ANY SPECIAL, INCIDENTAL, INDIRECT, OR CONSEQUENTIAL DAMAGES WHATSOEVER (INCLUDING, WITHOUT LIMITATION, DAMAGES FOR LOSS OF BUSINESS PROFITS, BUSINESS INTERRUPTION, LOSS OF BUSINESS INFORMATION, OR ANY OTHER PECUNIARY LOSS) ARISING OUT OF THE USE OF OR INABILITY TO USE THE SOFTWARE PRODUCT OR THE PROVISION OF OR FAILURE TO PROVIDE SUPPORT SERVICES, EVEN IF MICROSOFT HAS BEEN ADVISED OF THE POSSIBILITY OF SUCH DAMAGES. IN ANY CASE, MICROSOFT'S ENTIRE LIABILITY UNDER ANY PROVISION OF THIS EULA SHALL BE LIMITED TO THE GREATER OF THE AMOUNT ACTUALLY PAID BY YOU FOR THE SOFTWARE PRODUCT OR US$5.00; PROVIDED, HOWEVER, IF YOU HAVE ENTERED INTO A MICROSOFT SUPPORT SERVICES AGREEMENT, MICROSOFT'S ENTIRE LIABILITY REGARDING SUPPORT SERVICES SHALL BE GOVERNED BY THE TERMS OF THAT AGREEMENT. BECAUSE SOME STATES AND JURISDICTIONS DO NOT ALLOW THE EXCLUSION OR LIMITATION OF LIABILITY, THE ABOVE LIMITATION MAY NOT APPLY TO YOU.

MISCELLANEOUS

This EULA is governed by the laws of the State of Washington USA, except and only to the extent that applicable law mandates governing law of a different jurisdiction.

Should you have any questions concerning this EULA, or if you desire to contact Microsoft for any reason, please contact the Microsoft subsidiary serving your country, or write: Microsoft Sales Information Center/One Microsoft Way/Redmond, WA 98052-6399.

Gear Up for Success

Register Today!

Return this
*Microsoft® Mastering: Web Application Development
Using Microsoft Visual InterDev® 6.0*
registration card today to receive advance notice about
the latest developer training titles and courseware!

For information about Mastering series products and training, visit our Web site at
http://msdn.microsoft.com/mastering

OWNER REGISTRATION CARD   0-7356-0902-0

Microsoft® Mastering: Web Application Development
Using Microsoft Visual InterDev® 6.0

_____   _____   _____
FIRST NAME   MIDDLE INITIAL   LAST NAME

_____
INSTITUTION OR COMPANY NAME

_____
ADDRESS

_____

_____   _____   _____
CITY   STATE   ZIP
                                              (   )
_____   _____
E-MAIL ADDRESS   PHONE NUMBER

U.S. and Canada addresses only. Fill in information above and mail postage-free.
Please mail only the bottom half of this page.

**For information about Microsoft Press®
products, visit our Web site at
mspress.microsoft.com**

Microsoft®Press